Connections

Empowering College and Career Success

• • •

Second Edition

Paul A. Gore
Xavier University

Wade Leuwerke
Drake University

A.J. Metz
The University of Utah

bedford/st.martin's
Macmillan Learning
Boston | New York

For Bedford/St. Martin's

Vice President, Editorial, Macmillan Learning Humanities: Edwin Hill
Senior Program Director for Communication and College Success: Erika Gutierrez
Program Manager for College Success: Allen Cooper
Marketing Manager: Amy Haines
Director of Content Development: Jane Knetzger
Senior Developmental Editor: Christina Lembo
Senior Content Project Manager: Gregory Erb
Senior Workflow Project Supervisor: Joe Ford
Production Supervisor: Robin Besofsky
Media Project Manager: Sarah O'Connor Kepes
Assistant Editor: Kathy McInerney
Copyeditor: Louise B. Ketz
Composition: Lumina Datamatics, Inc.
Text Permissions Manager: Kalina Ingham
Photo Permissions Editor: Angela Boehler
Photo Researcher: Richard Fox, Lumina Datamatics, Inc.
Director of Design, Content Management: Diana Blume
Text Design: Maureen McCutcheon
Cover Design: William Boardman
Cover Image: Volodimir Zozulinskyi/Shutterstock
Printing and Binding: King Printing Co., Inc.

Manufactured in the United States of America.

3   4   5   6   7   24   23   22   21

For information, write: Bedford/St. Martin's, 75 Arlington Street, Boston, MA 02116 (617-399-4000)

ISBN 978-1-319-10716-1 (Student Edition)
ISBN 978-1-319-10717-8 (Loose-leaf Edition)
ISBN 978-1-319-10721-5 (Instructor's Annotated Edition)

Connections

Empowering College and
Career Success

letter to students

Dear Student,

Congratulations and welcome to college! If this class marks the beginning of your college experience, welcome to a new chapter in your life. If you're returning to college, welcome back as you continue your educational adventure. We're excited for you to start this class, and we've written this book to help you develop the skills you'll need to succeed in school right now and in your career for years to come.

As educators we've spent many years focused on helping college students succeed. We've had the wonderful privilege of working closely with students as they learn inside and outside of class. It's always a tremendous thrill to help students explore their passions, nurture their talents, learn about themselves, overcome challenges, and ultimately discover their life path. Now, as authors, we're excited to join you on this journey.

You'll soon discover that *Connections* is different from your other textbooks. Rather than simply presenting information to you, we encourage you to engage with the material, act on it, and make it your own. Along with traditional textbook features — like facts, research, stories, and diagrams — the following pages are filled with ideas, activities, questions, tips, and exercises. With this book and in this class, you'll not only learn, you'll *use* what you learn to develop as a student and as a person. You'll have the chance to reflect, think critically, make connections, try new things, and set goals. At every stage, we'll help you figure out what works, change what doesn't, and celebrate your successes.

We wrote down the ideas and activities in *Connections* so that you might take them, shape them in a way that works for you, and use them to succeed. We promise that we put a ton of time, energy, brain power — and even some creativity! — into this book, and we ask that you put your own time, energy, brain power, and creativity into trying out the ideas in each chapter.

In our experience, the exact combination of strategies that helps each student succeed is unique to that student. We hope that the ideas in *Connections* will spark in *you* the creation of new skills and practices that help you accomplish your goals — both during your time in college and beyond.

Wishing you all the best,
Paul, Wade, and A.J.

about the authors

Courtesy of Christina Rodriguez

Paul A. Gore

Paul's efforts to promote college and career readiness, high school and college student persistence, and academic success are informed by more than 20 years of research, program development, implementation, evaluation, consulting, and teaching. Paul currently serves as the Dean of the College of Professional Sciences at Xavier University in Ohio. Paul earned his Ph.D. in Counseling Psychology, with an emphasis in student career development, academic success, and transition, from Loyola University–Chicago. He has held academic and administrative responsibilities at the University of Missouri–Kansas City, Southern Illinois University–Carbondale, ACT, Inc., and the University of Utah.

Paul's work focuses on noncognitive and motivational determinants of academic and career success. In particular, he is interested in how secondary and postsecondary institutions use data describing the noncognitive strengths and weaknesses of their students to promote transition, engagement, student success, and retention. He regularly consults with secondary and postsecondary institutions in the United States and abroad on developing and evaluating student academic and career success programs.

Paul has authored more than fifty peer-reviewed journal articles and book chapters. He is the past chair of the Society for Vocational Psychology and served as an advisory board member and journal editor for the National Resource Center for the First-Year Experience and Students in Transition. He is a fellow of the American Psychological Association and was the recipient of a 2013–2014 American Council on Education Emerging Leadership fellowship.

Courtesy of MRogalla Photography

Wade Leuwerke

Wade is an associate professor of Counseling at Drake University. He earned his Ph.D. in Counseling Psychology from Southern Illinois University–Carbondale. Wade has authored more than seventy journal articles and book chapters, as well as national and international conference presentations. One of his areas of research is the assessment and development of student and employee noncognitive skills. He has cocreated several noncognitive assessment tools, including the Academic and Career Excellence System (ACES), that help secondary and postsecondary students to identify and build their skills. He works with faculty and advisers at the college level and school counselors at the high school level to integrate noncognitive data into their work with students.

Wade has experience examining school counselors' roles and working with professional school counselors to positively impact students' academic development, career and college exploration, and the acquisition of personal and social skills that will prepare them for college and life beyond. He has worked with dozens of secondary and postsecondary institutions on a range of factors related to student success and persistence, including evaluation of institutional practices, use of data to drive student interventions, creating individualized student success plans, training, strategic planning, resource allocation, and collaboration to promote student success. He has also worked as a research project manager focusing on academic and career development research for Kuder, Inc.; ACT, Inc.; Career Cruising; and intoCareers. Wade provides executive and career coaching to corporations and the federal government.

A.J. Metz

A.J. is a tenured associate professor in the Department of Educational Psychology at the University of Utah. She directs the master's program in school counseling and the Positive Psychology Certificate Program. She also coordinates the Strategies for College Success courses in which ACES and the *Connections* textbook are used.

Courtesy of Andy Brimhall

A.J. earned an M.Ed. in Vocational Rehabilitation Counseling and a Ph.D. in Urban Education (specialization in Counseling Psychology) from the University of Wisconsin–Milwaukee. Her research examining factors related to academic and career success in underrepresented and underserved student populations has led to numerous journal articles, book chapters, conference presentations, workshops, and faculty in-service training sessions.

A.J. has extensive teaching, counseling, and career advising experience in high schools, community colleges, and four-year public and private institutions of higher education. Her passion for teaching motivates her to experiment with innovative teaching methods and to develop new and engaging activities and instructional materials. In 2015 she received the University of Utah's Early Career Teaching Award, and in 2017 she received the College of Education Teaching Award. She is the past president of the Utah Psychological Association and serves on multiple state-level task forces and advisory councils promoting school counseling, college access, and career readiness.

brief contents

contents

1 Building a Foundation for Success *1*

mimagephotography/Shutterstock

mapodile/Getty Images

2 Thinking Critically and Setting Goals *21*

3 Motivation, Decision Making, and Personal Responsibility 47

Don Mason/Getty Images

Rudy Sulgan/Getty Images

4 Organization and Time Management *71*

5 Understanding Learning 95

© Hiya Images/Corbis/Getty Images

Helena Schaeder Söderberg/Getty Images

6 Reading for College Success 121

7 Taking Effective Notes *147*

AJ_Watt/Getty Images

Jacob Lund/Shutterstock

9 Performing Well on Exams 195

Paul Thomas/Getty Images

cristovao/Shutterstock

10 Information Literacy and Communication 219

Hector Mandel/Getty Images

Maria Sbytova/Shutterstock

13 Academic and Career Planning *299*

Hero Images/Getty Images

Reggie Casagrande/Getty Images

preface

Throughout our careers, we've had the great privilege of interacting with students as instructors at two- and four-year schools, as advisers and mentors, as student success administrators, and as researchers in the area of student transition and success. It's because of our fascinating and fulfilling experiences with students from all walks of life that we wrote *Connections*, giving us the opportunity to put in one place the combined knowledge, experience, and expertise we've garnered over many years of working with college students and studying the factors that impact their success. To help increase student satisfaction, retention, and completion, we built this book from the ground up and integrated an exciting student self-assessment tool called the Academic and Career Excellence System (ACES). Available to be packaged with the text, ACES focuses on noncognitive as well as cognitive factors.

As counseling psychologists, we strongly believe that there's more to student success than academic achievement alone. That's why we use a holistic, strengths-based approach in *Connections* that integrates a balance of motivational skills, study skills, and life skills. Our goal is to help students understand themselves, appreciate their own strengths, acknowledge where their challenges lie, and work to strengthen current skills and build new ones. Our experience has shown us that one of the best ways to accomplish this is through an emphasis on personal reflection, self-assessment, and action—an emphasis that has its **foundation in positive psychology**, concepts from which are woven throughout this text. While research has shown us that past academic performance is a good predictor of future academic performance, recent and compelling research also clearly establishes the role of motivational—*noncognitive*—factors in promoting college and career success.[1] These noncognitive factors include attitudes, behaviors, and skills such as critical thinking, self-efficacy, resilience, and working with others, and they form the scaffolding for achievement. Colleges and universities across the country are increasingly using noncognitive measures to better understand their students so they can provide them with the support they need to succeed.

Because research strongly supports the idea that noncognitive skills, in concert with cognitive skills, are crucial to student success, we jumped at the chance to create a student self-assessment platform that can be packaged with *Connections*. The **Academic and Career Excellence System (ACES)** is a powerful, norm-referenced self-assessment that helps students pinpoint their strengths and challenges and use that information to build skills throughout the term. Here's how it works:

- Students can take ACES at the start of this course to better understand their own abilities and attitudes in twelve critical areas, both cognitive and noncognitive, that correspond to specific chapters in the book.

---

[1] S. B. Robbins, K. Lauver, K., H. Le, D. Davis, R. Langley, and A. Carlstrom. "Do Psychosocial and Study Skill Factors Predict College Out-comes? A Meta-analysis." *Psychological Bulletin*, 130, no. 2 (2004): 261–288. W. J. Camara. "Broadening Predictors of College Success," in W. J. Camara and E. W. Kimmel (Eds.), *Choosing Students: Higher Education Admissions Tools for the 21st Century* (Mahwah, NJ: Erlbaum, 2005). N. Schmitt, J. Keeney, F. L. Oswald, T. J. Pleskac, A. Q. Billington, R. Sinha, and M. Zorzie, "Prediction of Four-Year College Student Performance Using Cognitive and Noncognitive Predictors and the Impact on Demographic Status of Admitted Students." *Journal of Applied Psychology*, 94, no. 6, 1479–1497.

- Students can then use the information in *Connections* to help them develop and strengthen their skills in each area. Callouts throughout the book prompt students to reflect on their ACES results and plan how to use what they've learned about themselves to effect change in their lives.

- New to the Second Edition, **students can also take ACES a second time** at the end of the term. By comparing their later results—available in a new ACES Progress Report—with their earlier ACES scores, they're able to celebrate areas of improvement and identify areas for future growth. A new section in Chapter 14 helps students reflect on their scores, process the change that has occurred during the term, and think metacognitively about how different factors in their lives—including their decisions, actions, and experiences—have influenced their outcomes. A new capstone activity on LaunchPad further encourages this reflection and metacognition.

The idea to pair *Connections* and ACES comes from our shared experience in counseling and assessment. Rather than a self-assessment that serves as an "add on," we wanted to develop one that was woven into the fabric of the book, thereby providing two valuable resources that are even more beneficial when used together. Our goal was to ensure that information would lead to action, because it has been our experience that the act of responding to questions has zero value in and of itself. What *does* have value is what you *do* with or how you *act* upon that information. We achieved this goal by creating a powerful and easy-to-use assessment, along with tools and guidance that students can use to act on their results.

To further emphasize the importance of taking action to effect change, in *Connections*, Second Edition, we've added the new ACES + ACTION feature, which appears at the beginning of Chapters 2–13 immediately after the ACES Reflection prompt. ACES + ACTION spotlights three chapter-related active learning strategies that students can try right away to strengthen their skills and apply their learning.

The idea of translating information into action also prompted us to develop another key feature of this book: the **Personal Success Plan (PSP) goal-setting tool.** Students learn about themselves through ACES and then can apply that knowledge in each chapter using the PSP to create SMART goals and purposeful, personalized action plans to achieve those goals. Students can track their PSPs throughout the term, helping them document the action steps and goals they've achieved, and demonstrate the specific ways they're building important skills for college, career, and life. In this Second Edition, we've tweaked the steps of the PSP to provide even more guidance: Suggested goals are included in Step 1 to serve as inspiration and scaffolding for students, who tend to struggle with generating goals of their own; students then transform the general goal they've selected into a personally meaningful SMART goal in Step 2.

As crucial as self-reflection and self-assessment are to the identity of *Connections*, Second Edition, there is another driving force behind the text that is just as crucial: making **the connection between college and career success** meaningful to today's students. Throughout the book we emphasize specific ways that the attitudes, habits, and skills needed to succeed in college—such as persistence, communication, critical thinking—are the exact same attitudes, habits, and skills needed to succeed in the workplace. Our goal is to help students see how the material they are learning now can be applied directly in any work environment.

In the Second Edition, we've added a new category of Voices of Experience stories to further strengthen this college/work connection: first-person profiles from *employers* who are directly responsible for making hiring decisions and helping employees build successful careers (see Chapters 1, 6, and 11). In a concrete and applied way, these profiles illustrate how students can use the skills spotlighted in the chapter to get a job and excel in a work environment.

Our work on this Second Edition of *Connections* and ACES has been rewarding and invigorating, and we've been gratified by very positive feedback and reviews from instructors around the country. We hope that *Connections*, Second Edition, and ACES prove as meaningful and effective for you and your students as they have been for us and for our reviewers. We hope that you, too, find this program a powerful mix of engaging content, practical strategies, effective activities, thought-provoking research, and useful self-assessment data that will help students build the skills they need to succeed in college, in their careers, and in life.

Using ACES with *Connections*, Second Edition

ACES gives students, instructors, and administrators the data they need to succeed. Available to be packaged with *Connections*, Second Edition, the ACES online self-assessment helps students develop a thoughtful, strengths-based understanding of themselves. ACES measures student strengths in twelve critical areas, both cognitive and noncognitive. Norm-referenced reports indicate whether students are at a high, moderate, or low skill level in these areas, as compared to students in other schools across the country.

- **Students** take ACES at the start of the term to get a snapshot of their own attitudes, skills, habits, and opportunities for improvement. Throughout the book, students reflect on their results, which they can use to set and achieve goals with the Personal Success Plan. In addition, at the end of the term, students now have the opportunity to take ACES for a second time. By comparing these new results with their earlier ACES scores, they're able to celebrate areas of improvement and identify areas for future growth.

- **Instructors** can use ACES data to start conversations with students—individually and as a class—about how to achieve excellence in college and in their careers. ACES data can also help instructors prioritize the topics they teach, highlight relevant programs or events outside of class to provide additional support for addressing students' weaknesses, and identify strong students who might be willing to report on the ways they practice a skill.

- **Administrators** can use aggregate information about student performance on ACES to track progress within the program and individual classes, and to determine the type and level of resources needed to help students succeed.

ACES has been designed with ease-of-use in mind. It takes students about 20 minutes to complete and offers intriguing questions in a clean, appealing interface, helping ensure high student satisfaction and participation rates.

ACES works in concert with *Connections*. Students answer questions about twelve areas, or scales, that match the chapter topics in *Connections*, Second Edition. They reflect on their results throughout the book, and use what they've learned to strengthen their strengths and use challenges as opportunities for growth.

Students respond to 80+ empirically reliable statements. Questions have been thoroughly tested in a national pilot study and are organized to obtain the clearest possible picture of students' attitudes and skills. Reverse scoring on select questions helps ensure that students are honest with their responses.

Targeted, thorough feedback helps each student take his or her own next steps. Students get feedback on their responses in each of the twelve skill areas. Each area is correlated as higher, moderate, or lower compared with the national sample. Feedback offers students an assessment of their current skills, encouragement to improve, and concrete suggestions for activities and resources to help them achieve their goals.

Individualized and class-level reports give students and instructors the information they need to understand student strengths and weaknesses, and to formulate realistic plans for improvement. Data can be organized in several ways and output for use in standard quantitative programs like Excel and Qualtrix.

Students can take ACES a second time at the end of the term. ACES now provides an end-of-term Progress Report that helps instructors and students quantify student growth over the term and reset goals for continued success. In addition, a new section in Chapter 14 of the text helps students reflect on these results and think metacognitively about how different factors in their lives have influenced their outcomes, and a new capstone activity on LaunchPad further encourages this reflection and metacognition.

ACES is available in the LaunchPad for *Connections*, Second Edition. To give your students access to ACES, assign the text with LaunchPad for *Connections*, Second Edition—which includes ACES. LaunchPad brings together all the media content for the textbook, curated and organized for easy assignability and assessment, and presented in a powerful, yet easy-to-use interface.

- LaunchPad is available at a significant discount when packaged with the book. To package the paper text with LaunchPad, use ISBN 978-1-319-21277-3. To package the loose-leaf edition with LaunchPad, use ISBN 978-1-319-21272-8.
- LaunchPad is also available as a stand-alone resource purchased separately. To order LaunchPad stand-alone, use ISBN 978-1-319-10720-8.

Key Features in *Connections,* Second Edition

Firmly rooted in the concepts of positive psychology. The text encourages all students to develop their strengths, celebrate progress, and use setbacks as opportunities for growth. Positive psychology concepts are introduced in Chapter 1 and referenced continuously throughout.

Balanced and holistic coverage of important college success topics. *Connections,* Second Edition, begins with a look at the foundational skills and mindsets necessary for college success (critical thinking, goal setting, decision making, motivation, personal responsibility, learning, and time management), before providing comprehensive, balanced coverage of both academic and life skills. This holistic approach emphasizes the importance of both cognitive and noncognitive skills.

Designed for a broad range of students and institutions. With coverage and examples drawn from a diverse group of students and institutions, the text is designed for an audience with a wide range of experiences—including recent high school graduates, returning adult learners, commuters, and students living on campus.

Integrates ACES prompts throughout the text. References to ACES are integrated throughout *Connections,* Second Edition, which enables these resources to work together as a unified system. Students reflect on their ACES results (ACES Reflection) and try out active learning strategies related to chapter skills (ACES + ACTION) at the beginning of Chapters 2–13. In addition, a new section in Chapter 14 helps students analyze how their ACES scores have changed from the beginning to the end of the term and think metacognitively about how different factors in their lives—including their decisions, actions, and experiences—have influenced these outcomes.

Prominent and practical coverage of critical thinking and goal setting.

- Chapter 2, Thinking Critically and Setting Goals, presents these essential skills up front in one cohesive chapter to illustrate how critical thinking concepts are applied during the goal-setting process.

- Self-assessments and activities throughout the text encourage students to think critically about their work and themselves.

- Included at the end of Chapters 2–14, the **Personal Success Plan** (PSP) goal-setting tool provides students with a structured platform for SMART goal setting and action planning. It encourages students to think metacognitively about the skills they develop as they set and achieve goals, and to consider how those skills might be useful in a future career. Instructors can assign as many or as few PSPs as desired based on the structure and needs of the class.

A strong emphasis on college and career connections. A discrete section at the end of each chapter illustrates how chapter topics apply to the world of work; Chapter 13 on academic and career planning helps students begin creating their own personal roadmaps to success; College Success = Career Success activities at the end of each chapter emphasize the college/career connection; and an in-depth appendix focuses on conducting a job search.

Clear connections to students' academic and life plans. Students often wonder how the material they learn in this class connects to what they're doing in their other classes — and their careers. *Connections*, Second Edition, addresses this question head on:

- **Connect exercises integrated throughout each chapter.** These prompts encourage students to think about how the chapter's ideas connect to their personal experiences, current coursework, career goals, and available resources.

- **Voices of Experience narratives included in each chapter.** These first-person stories show the real-world effects of chapter concepts in the lives of college students and graduates. Eight Voices are new to the Second Edition, and three of these Voices come from employers who are directly responsible for making hiring decisions and helping employees build strong careers. Their stories concretely illustrate how students can use the skills in the chapter to get a job and excel in a work environment.

A strong foundation in research. Research backs the authors' guidance to students throughout the book, and the Spotlight on Research feature introduces original research to students in an accessible way. New and updated Spotlight topics in the Second Edition include "Behaviors and Attitudes Drive Your Success" (Chapter 1), "Grit Leads to Success!" (Chapter 3), "Time Management: It Works!" (Chapter 4), "Longer Course? More Time for Distributed Learning!" (Chapter 5), "Money Matters: Get Informed about Finances" (Chapter 12), and "Understand Yourself through Campus Engagement" (Chapter 13).

Chapter Activities reinforce key themes, prompt self-reflection, and strengthen skills. Each chapter concludes with four activities that instructors can assign as homework or use to prompt class discussion and student engagement.

- The **Journal Entry** encourages written reflection on a wide array of topics.
- **Adopting a Success Attitude** focuses on positive psychology concepts.
- **Applying Your Skills** helps students apply the skills they've learned in the chapter.
- **College Success = Career Success** helps students connect what they're learning in college with skills they'll need in their careers.

Key Chapter-by-Chapter Content

Chapter 1, Building a Foundation for Success, makes a strong case for the benefits of a college education to students in our society and lays the foundation for the book's holistic coverage of motivational, academic, and life skills. Topics include the benefits of personal reflection, the power of positive psychology, the importance of recognizing one's own strengths and weaknesses, and the strong connection between skills needed to succeed in college and in one's career. A newly expanded section on purpose underscores the importance of understanding one's own personal motivators, and an expanded section on meeting college expectations sets students up for success early in the term.

Chapter 2, Thinking Critically and Setting Goals, examines what it means to be a critical thinker and covers higher-level thinking skills, critical thinking processes, and Bloom's taxonomy. The chapter then shows how critical thinking connects to goal setting, gives step-by-step goal-setting guidance, and introduces the powerful Personal Success Plan (PSP) goal-setting tool, which students can use to map out their goals and build a plan for achieving them. The steps of the PSP have been tweaked in this Second Edition to provide even more guidance: Suggested goals are included in Step 1 to serve as inspiration and scaffolding for students, who tend to struggle with generating goals of their own; students then transform the general goal they've selected into a personally meaningful SMART goal in Step 2.

Chapter 3, Motivation, Decision Making, and Personal Responsibility, offers a strong emphasis on noncognitive skills, ensuring that students read about key motivational topics early in the term. Students learn concrete ways to stay driven and focused; make effective decisions; adopt active learning and metacognitive principles to take responsibility for their success; and develop a growth mindset. There is also a new section on attribution theory ("Understand Why Outcomes Occur") and a new Spotlight on Research on the power of grit. In this chapter, as in all chapters, the discussion concludes by examining how the major topics apply in the working world.

Chapter 4, Organization and Time Management (formerly Chapter 5), helps students take ownership of their time and use this valuable resource in a way that fits their priorities and helps them meet their very personal goals. It also includes a unique section on strategies for getting organized and examines ways to beat procrastination and deal with distractions. This chapter has been moved up in the Second Edition, since many instructors prefer to teach these foundational concepts early in the term, and it includes expanded coverage of online organizational tools and tips students can use to get back on track if they have trouble following their schedules.

In **Chapter 5, Understanding Learning** (formerly Chapter 4), students assess their own approaches to learning and use what they read to become stronger learners, work more effectively with others, and excel in a wide variety of environments. A brand new section introduces the concept of learning science and presents five evidence-based learning strategies that are useful for all learners. Students then think metacognitively about their own preferences for learning via an introduction to the Myers-Briggs Type Indicator and VARK models, and discover techniques for excelling as multimodal learners in all environments—even those that don't match their preferences.

Chapter 6, Reading for College Success, introduces a three-step process for getting the most out of college reading—preparing to read, reading with focus, and reviewing what's been read. Unlike many competing texts, which fail to make the connections among different academic skills clear to students, this chapter illustrates the relationship between reading and other key study skills. And because students are hungry for suggestions they can use to excel in math, science, and online classes, this content is also included.

Chapter 7, Taking Effective Notes, introduces note taking not as a mechanical activity, but as a method of working with—and mastering—information. In addition to presenting a clear, four-step strategy for participating in class and recording information effectively, the chapter spotlights methods and strategies students can use to take notes in a variety of settings. And to emphasize that note taking is a lifelong skill, the chapter focuses on the importance of taking notes in the workplace.

Chapter 8, Memory and Studying, spotlights strategies students can use to study effectively and remember what they've learned. Based on current research, the chapter discusses memory basics, including the processes of encoding, storage, and retrieval. Students are introduced to a wide variety of study strategies they can use to stay focused and productive and retain the information they've learned. A new discussion of studying as a metacognitive process has been added in this edition.

Chapter 9, Performing Well on Exams, provides students with the information they need to know to take tests of all kinds—and to do so successfully. In addition to specific test-taking strategies, other key topics include managing test anxiety and taking tests with integrity. And unlike other texts, the chapter illustrates how good test-taking skills—a seemingly academic topic—come in handy in the working world. The section on after-test reflection has been updated to give students a framework they can use to think metacognitively about their test results and, if needed, adjust their strategies for next time.

Chapter 10, Information Literacy and Communication, connects these key academic skills to broader approaches to critical thinking and explores three essential components of information literacy—locating information, evaluating its quality, and communicating that information through writing and speaking. The chapter also discusses how to navigate the writing process, avoid plagiarism, and give strong class presentations. An expanded section on evaluating Web sites and online materials has been added, and a revised end-of-chapter activity on this topic prompts students to apply these concepts firsthand.

Chapter 11, Connecting with Others, focuses on key skills that students need to build and sustain relationships, with special emphasis on active listening and effective speaking. The chapter explores how to strengthen emotional intelligence and manage conflict, and examines how connecting with others can enhance existing relationships, help students build new ones, and strengthen their relationships with people from different backgrounds. The diversity section has been expanded significantly to include coverage of multicultural competence and ways students can work to support issues of social justice that are meaningful to them.

Chapter 12, Personal and Financial Health, draws important connections between the discrete but closely related topics of stress, personal health, and financial health. Through a self-management lens, the chapter introduces a variety of strategies that students can use to promote physical well-being and mental health, maintain sexual health, and take control of their finances—all of which can help them manage stress and live happier, more fulfilled lives. New content includes an added section on self-care, an expanded discussion on understanding and repaying student loans, and a new Spotlight on Research about the value of financial counseling.

Chapter 13, Academic and Career Planning, helps students personalize academic and career planning by considering their own interests, values, skills, and goals. Topics include conducting career research; making an academic plan; and managing important milestones in the academic and career development processes. In response to reviewer requests, career planning is now presented before academic planning to better reflect the sequencing in which the material is presented in many classrooms, and content is now included on Guided Pathways.

Chapter 14, Celebrating Your Success and Connecting to Your Future, serves as a capstone chapter for the course. Both active and metacognitive, this chapter encourages students to revisit and reassess their ACES results, complete activities designed to solidify what they've learned over the term, and identify strategies they can use to sustain their success in the years to come. A new section helps students process their results after taking ACES for a second time at the end of the term.

Instructor Resources

 ### LaunchPad for *Connections,* Second Edition, with ACES and LearningCurve

LaunchPad combines an interactive e-book with high-quality multimedia content and ready-made assessment options, including the ACES student self-assessment and LearningCurve adaptive quizzing. Prebuilt units are easy to assign or adapt to your material, such as readings, videos, quizzes, discussion groups, and more. LaunchPad also provides access to a gradebook that provides a clear window on performance for your whole class, for individual students, and for individual assignments.

- **Unique to LaunchPad: ACES student self-assessment.** See the earlier discussion of ACES for more detail.

- **Unique to LaunchPad: LearningCurve for *Connections,* Second Edition.** LearningCurve is an online self-quizzing program that quickly learns what students already know and helps them practice what they haven't yet mastered. LearningCurve motivates students to read and engage with key concepts before they come to class so that they are ready to participate, and it offers reporting tools to help you discern your students' needs. LearningCurve has been fully updated for the Second Edition.

- **Ordering information.** Please note that *Connections,* Second Edition, is not automatically packaged with LaunchPad. To package the paper text with LaunchPad, use ISBN 978-1-319-21277-3. To package the loose-leaf edition with LaunchPad, use ISBN 978-1-319-21272-8. To order LaunchPad stand-alone, use ISBN 978-1-319-10720-8.

Instructor's Annotated Edition

A valuable tool for new and experienced instructors alike, the Instructor's Annotated Edition includes the full text of the student edition along with abundant marginal annotations that include activity suggestions, writing prompts, topics for discussion, resources for further reading, and notes about using the book's key features.

Instructor's Manual

The Instructor's Manual, available online, is packed full of activities and resources. Content includes sample syllabi; chapter objectives and summaries; class activities, topics for discussion, and writing assignments for each chapter; and a guide to using the ACES self-assessment in class.

Computerized Test Bank

The Computerized Test Bank contains more than 700 multiple-choice, true/false, short-answer, and essay questions designed to assess students' understanding of key concepts. A midterm and final exam are also included, and all questions are accompanied by an answer key.

Lecture Slides

Available online for download, lecture slides accompany each chapter of the book and include key concepts and art from the text. Use the slides as provided to structure your lectures, or customize them as desired to fit your course's needs.

iClicker Questions

If you use iClicker in your classroom, don't miss the brand-new suite of iClicker questions for *Connections*, Second Edition. These questions test students' knowledge of foundational concepts in each chapter, making it easy for you to assess your students' understanding and progress. The questions come pre-loaded into LaunchPad.

Custom Solutions Program

Our new Curriculum Solutions group brings together the quality and reputation of Bedford/St. Martin's content with Hayden-McNeil's expertise in publishing original custom print and digital products. With our new capabilities, we are excited to deliver customized course solutions at an affordable price. Make *Connections*, Second Edition, fit your course and goals by integrating your own institutional materials, including only the parts of the text you intend to use in your course, or both. Please contact your local Macmillan Learning sales representative for more information and to see samples.

Bedford Select for College Success Custom Database

The Bedford Select for College Success database allows you to create a textbook for your college success course that reflects your course's objectives and uses just the content you need. Start with one of our core texts; then rearrange chapters, delete chapters, and insert additional content—including your own original content—to create the book you're looking for. Get started by visiting **macmillanlearning.com/csSelect**.

TradeUp

Bring more value and choice to your students' first-year experience by packaging *Connections*, Second Edition, with one of a thousand titles from Macmillan publishers at a 50 percent discount off the regular price. Contact your local Macmillan Learning sales representative for more information.

The Macmillan Learning College Success Community

The College Success Community is our online space for instructor development and engagement. Find resources to support your teaching like class activities, video assignments, and invitations to conferences and webinars. Connect with our team, our authors, and other instructors through online discussions and blog posts at **https://community.macmillan.com/community/the-college-success-community**.

Student Resources

LaunchPad for *Connections,* Second Edition, with ACES and LearningCurve

LaunchPad is an online course solution that offers our acclaimed content, including an e-book, the ACES self-assessment, LearningCurve adaptive quizzes, videos, and more. For more information, see the Instructor Resources section.

- **Unique to LaunchPad: ACES student self-assessment.** See the earlier discussion of ACES for more detail.

- **Unique to LaunchPad: LearningCurve for *Connections,* Second Edition.** LearningCurve is an online, adaptive, self-quizzing program that quickly learns what students already know and helps them practice what they haven't yet mastered. LearningCurve has been fully updated for the Second Edition.

- **Ordering information:** Please note that *Connections,* Second Edition, is not automatically packaged with LaunchPad. To package the paper text with LaunchPad, use ISBN 978-1-319-21277-3. To package the loose-leaf edition with LaunchPad, use ISBN 978-1-319-21272-8. To order LaunchPad stand-alone, use ISBN 978-1-319-10720-8.

E-book Options

E-books offer an affordable alternative for students. You can find e-book versions of our books when you shop online at our publishing partners' sites. Learn more at **macmillanlearning.com/ebooks**.

Macmillan Learning Student Store

You want to give your students affordable rental, packaging, and e-book options. So do we. Learn more at **store.macmillanlearning.com**.

Bedford/St. Martin's Insider's Guides

These concise and student friendly booklets on topics that are critical to college success are a perfect complement to your textbook and course. One Insider's Guide can be packaged with *any* Bedford/St. Martin's textbook at no additional cost. Additional Insider's Guides can also be packaged for additional cost. Titles include: *Insider's Guide for Adult Learners; Insider's Guide to Academic Planning; Insider's Guide to Beating Test Anxiety; Insider's Guide to Career Services; Insider's Guide to Getting Involved on Campus; Insider's Guide to Time Management,* Second Edition; and many more. For more information on ordering one of these guides with the text, go to **macmillanlearning.com/ collegesuccess**.

Acknowledgments

We wish to express our gratitude to all the people who have helped to make this book a reality. Paul would like to thank his parents, who taught him balance between critical reflection and creativity; his mentors Waded Cruzado, Steve D. Brown, Virginia Rinella, and Michael Anch, who have supported his personal and professional development for almost thirty years; and the staff of the National Resource Center for the First-Year Experience and Students in Transition for embracing his passion for promoting student success. Wade thanks his mother, who was steadfast in her support and expectation that he earn a college degree, as well as his wonderful partner Lesley and his three great yahoos at home. They put up with a lot over the past few years and he couldn't have done this without their support. A.J. wishes to thank her parents (Kay and Jerry), brothers (Mike and Dave), and academic colleagues for their continuous interest, support, and encouragement through the course of writing this book. Together, we'd like to thank our students—especially Ali Pappas, Natalie Noel, Keith Gunnerson, Alex Kelly, Laken Shirey, Jenna Leishman, Derek Smith, Qin Hu, and Summer Hickam—who helped nuture our thinking and gave thoughtful feedback. We'd also like to thank all of the students and professionals who shared their stories with us and made the Voices of Experience feature possible. The richness and variety of their stories helped bring the book content alive, and we hope that you find their wisdom and advice as helpful as we do.

At Bedford/St. Martin's, thanks to Edwin Hill, Vice President, Editorial, for taking a chance on new authors; we wouldn't have gotten this project off the ground without your support. To Allen Cooper, Program Manager, thank you for providing insight and encouragement along the way. To Christina Lembo, Senior Editor, thank you for steering us through this process. The book is a testament to your guidance, patience, and skill at helping us make our vision a reality. Our appreciation also goes out to Greg Erb, Senior Content Project Manager, for his invaluable attention to detail; Erika Gutierrez, Senior Program Director, for her ideas and leadership; Tom Kane, Senior Media Editor, for his work on ACES; Kathy McInerney, Assistant Editor, for managing the accompanying ancillaries; and Amy Haines, Marketing Manager, for her enthusiasm in sharing our work with instructors across the country.

Finally, we would like to thank the reviewers who took the time to provide detailed, thoughtful feedback through all stages of the development process for this Second Edition. Your comments and suggestions were instrumental in creating exciting new revisions of both *Connections* and ACES:

Josie Adamo, Buffalo State College; Rhonda Black, West Virginia University; Cecelia Brewer, University of Central Missouri; John Cichowski, Bergen Community College; Anna D'Andrea, Georgia State University; Christine Deacons, Eastern Michigan University; Jaime Duran, Fresno City College; Melissa Filkowski, Columbia Basin College; Cathy Gann, Missouri Western State University; Kei Graves, Lorain County Community College; Elizabeth Harris, Georgia State University Perimeter College–Dunwoody; Amy Hassenpflug, Liberty University; Lyndsay Isham-Morton, Berkshire Community College; Charlene Latimer, Daytona State College; Gail Malone, South Plains College; Rachelle Powell, North Lake College; Mary Treuting, Louisiana State University Alexandria; and Brent Via, Virginia Western Community College.

In addition, we offer our continued thanks to the reviewers, survey participants, and focus group attendees who provided valuable feedback on the first edition of *Connections* and the initial release of ACES:

Sandra Albers, Leeward Community College; Fred Amador, Phoenix College; Holly Andress-Martin, Culver-Stockton College; Bonnie Bailey, Central New Mexico Community College; Christopher Barker, Miami Dade College; Wesley Beal, Lyon College; Jennifer Beattie, Tri-County Technical College; Ashley Becker, Florida

Institute of Technology; Sheila Bedworth, Long Beach City College; Kristine Benard, Bryant & Stratton College, Eastlake Campus; Edie Blakley, Clark College; Dustyn Bork, Lyon College; Jennifer Boyle, Davidson County Community College; Beverly Brucks, Illinois Central College; Alim Chandani, Gallaudet University; Rebecca Coco, Massasoit Community College; Colleen Coughlin, University of Massachusetts; Melanie Deffendall, Delgado Community College; Erika Deiters, Moraine Valley Community College; Susan Delker, Community College of Baltimore County; Bob DuBois, Waukesha County Technical College; Denise Dufek, Bay de Noc Community College; Kim Dunnavant, Martin Methodist College; Darin Eckton, Utah Valley University; Carly Edwards, Campbell University; Shawna Elsberry, Central Oregon Community College; Annette Fields, University of Arkansas at Pine Bluff; Stephanie M. Foote, Kennesaw State University; Karen Frost, University of Arkansas at Little Rock; Kate Frost, Arizona State University; Susan Gaer, Santa Ana College; Cathy Gann, Missouri Western State University; Linda Gannon, College of Southern Nevada; Margaret Garroway, Howard Community College; Nicole Gilbertson, Mt. Hood Community College; Carlen Gilseth, Minot State University; Tracey Glaessgen, Missouri State University; Joselyn Gonzalez, El Centro College; Tymon Graham, Coker College; Barbara Granger, Holyoke Community College; Laurie Grimes, Lorain County Community College; Betsy Hall, Illinois College; Timothy Hare, Morehead State University; Angie Hatlestad, Ridgewater College; Robin Hayhurst, Western Nebraska Community College; Teresa Hays, DeVry University; Lorraine M. Daniels Howland, NHTI, Concord's Community College; Cedric Jackson, University of Arkansas at Pine Bluff; Barbara Jaffe, El Camino College; Jody Kamens, Jacksonville University; Kim Keffer, Ohio University Southern; Alice Kimara, Baltimore City Community College; Stacy Kirch, Orange Coast College; Ray Korpi, Clark College; Fatina LaMar-Taylor, Prince George's Community College; Teresa Landers, Lee College; Christopher Lau, Hutchinson Community College; Kristina Leonard, Daytona State College; Andrew Logemann, Gordon College; Judith Lynch, Kansas State University; Malinda Mansfield, Ivy Tech Community College; Melanie Marine, University of Wisconsin Oshkosh; Lisa Marks, Ozarks Technical Community College; Mickey Marsee, University of New Mexico–Los Alamos; Patrick McConnell, Rio Hondo College; MaryAnn McGuirk, North Lake College; Maureen McMahon, Paul Smith's College; Ryan Messatzzia, Wor-Wic Community College; Pat Missad, Grand Rapids Community College; Pamela Moss, Midwestern State University; Jodi Murrow, Fort Scott Community College; Tami Mysliwiec, Pennsylvania State University Berks; Nicole Nagy, Madonna University; Chaelle Norman, Cedar Valley College; Scott O'Leary, University of Saint Mary; Ellen Oppenberg, Glendale Community College; Taunya Paul, York Technical College; Elizabeth Price, Ranger College; Cynthia Puckett, Eastern Florida State College; Linda Refsland, William Paterson University; Leigh-Ann Routh, Ivy Tech Community College; Danielle Rowland, University of Washington Bothell and Cascadia College; James Rubin, Paradise Valley Community College; Carolyn Sanders, University of Alabama in Huntsville; Sarah Sell, Wichita State University; Mark Shea, Buena Vista University; Barbara Sherry, Northeastern Illinois University; Sarah Shutt, J. Sargeant Reynolds Community College; Cheryl Spector, California State University Northridge; Charlene Stephens, Wesley College; Pamela Stephens, Fairmont State University; Chris Strouthopoulos, San Juan College; Brenda Sudan, Georgia Perimeter College; Susan Sullivan, Louisiana State University Alexandria; Ricardo Teixeira, University of Houston–Victoria; Kim Thomas, Polk State University; Virginia Thompson, Grayson County College; Althea Truesdale, Bennett College; Adanta Ugo, San Jacinto College; Dominick Usher, University of Massachusetts Amherst; Sherri VandenAkker, Springfield College; Jodie Vangrov, Chattahoochee Technical College; Angela Vaughan, University of Northern Colorado; Melanie Wadsworth, Western Nevada College; Jacob Widdekind, Miami Dade College; Cheryl Wieseler, Luther College; Margaret Williamson, Dillard University; Cornelia Wills, Middle Tennessee State University; Leslie Wilson, Chestnut Hill College; and Marguerite Yawin, Tunxis Community College.

1 Building a Foundation for Success

Find Your Purpose

Understand College Expectations

Feel the Power of Positive Psychology

Embrace Your Strengths — and Learn from Your Weaknesses

College Success Leads to Career Success

Welcome to college! Are you a recent high school graduate? Did you put your education on hold to raise a family, and now you're returning to school? Are you a veteran beginning college after a tour of duty in the military? Did you take a gap year after high school to travel or work, and now you're ready for college? Regardless of your personal situation, congratulations! Starting college is a huge accomplishment that you can be proud of, and it's a major step toward your future success — not only academically, but also in your personal and professional life.

This book is designed to help you take that step. As educators we've worked with thousands of college students, and we've found that almost all of them want to succeed. We've met students who struggled to define their goals or didn't feel confident that they could achieve them. We've also met students who had a hard time translating their goals into action or finding help when they needed it. But no matter what their challenges, these students were all in school with one objective in mind: to improve their lives. We assume that you have this same objective, and we're committed to helping you meet it.

But wanting to improve your life is only the beginning. Getting through college requires effort and persistence, and colleges and universities understand that. That's why so many schools have developed courses like this one to equip you with the attitudes, skills, and resources you need to achieve your goals. Research from hundreds of experts over the past thirty years shows that students who complete these courses achieve higher grades, are more likely to stay in school, graduate faster, and make better decisions than students who don't.[1] So the good news is, you're in the right place! With the help of your instructor, this book, and other resources available on your campus, you'll develop the tools you'll need to excel in college and embark on a satisfying career.

As you go through this course and this book, keep in mind that successful people don't succeed on their own. Rather, they draw on connections to achieve their goals — connections with other people, with new knowledge they encounter along the way, and with their own strengths and intentions. Now that you're in college, a great way to set the stage for your success is to make similar connections. By doing so, you'll gain a new understanding of yourself and help to maintain your motivation in school. For example, when you connect the skills you learn in college with those you'll use in your career, every course you take will have more meaning and value for you. That means you'll be more motivated to do well in these courses. And by making connections with the people around you—instructors, classmates, college staff—you'll build a network of supporters who can help you through tough times and join you in celebrating your successes.

Connections are a big theme in this book—and in this course. As you'll discover, *nothing* you do or learn is isolated: The information you read about in one chapter relates to topics in other chapters; what you learn in this class will be useful in your other classes; and the skills you build here will be the same ones that will help you excel at work.

In this chapter you'll learn about critical components of your success: why you're attending college, what it means to be here, the power of positivity, understanding your strengths and weaknesses, and how college success is connected to career success. In fact, this chapter introduces many of the big ideas you'll learn more about as you go through this class. We'll expand on these big ideas later in the book, and you'll have plenty of time to get your head around the details. For now, as you read, ask yourself: How does the material in this chapter apply to my other classes? How does it relate to my current or future career? How can I use what I'm learning now to create my own success?

Find Your Purpose

Life is full of choices, and you've already made an important one: to attend college and further your education. Now that you've made this choice, ask yourself a basic question: Why are you here? Ultimately, all students have their own reasons for going to school, whether it's training for a specific occupation, pursuing a love of learning, or generally trying to give themselves a chance for a better life. It's figuring out your own reasons for being here—what drives *you* to succeed, even when you're up against challenges—that makes college meaningful. That's why, in this opening section, we'll focus on two key ideas: why education is important for society in general, and why education is important for you personally.

Education: Good for Society, Good for You

As you start your college journey, it's crucial to understand one thing: By pursuing your education, you're making a smart investment in your future. Just over half a century ago, fewer than 50 percent of adults in the United States had a high school diploma.[2] Today, that number has risen to 89 percent, and 44 percent of all adults have an associate's degree or higher.[3] What prompted the change? Think of everything that's happened in the past fifty years: We've landed on the moon, sent scientific equipment to Mars, invented the Internet and smartphone, advanced civil rights, and made countless gains in medicine, communications, agriculture, and energy. Improving any society in these ways requires education, and the more sophisticated our society becomes, the higher the demand will be for educated people—people like you.

Education not only strengthens societies but it also pays off for individuals—and in more ways than you might realize. For example, a recent report by the College Board suggests that compared to high school graduates, college graduates

- are more engaged in their communities
- lead healthier lifestyles
- participate more actively in their children's education
- earn higher salaries (thousands of dollars more per year—see Figure 1.1)
- are more likely to have jobs[4]

In fact, by the time you graduate, more than 60 percent of all jobs will require some form of college education.[5] As you can see, when it comes to preparing yourself for the future, you're in the right place at the right time.

Learn about Yourself

As the data above shows us, education is valuable for individuals and for society. But in order for this information to really mean something, we need to get personal. Why, exactly, is education important for *you*? If someone asks, "Why are you in school?" what would you tell them? Understanding why you're pursuing your education—your purpose for being in college—can be an important motivator when the alarm clock goes off for your 8:00 a.m. class, when you get a poor

FIGURE 1.1

Average Annual Salary in the U.S. by Level of Education (2016)

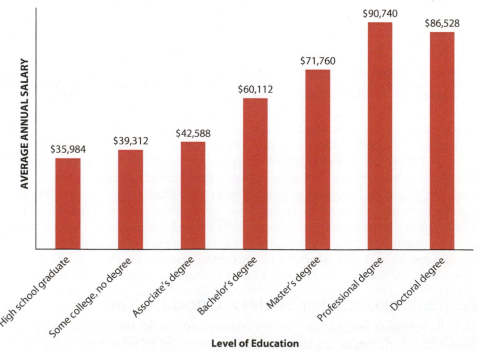

Information from U.S. Bureau of Labor Statistics, Current Population Survey, https://www.bls.gov/emp/ep_chart_001.htm

grade on your first quiz, or when life gets complicated and you're wondering whether you should take a break from school.

Identifying your sense of purpose starts with *personal reflection*, which is a time for you to think about your hopes, wishes, and what you're looking for from college and from life. Reflection helps you better understand your goals and come up with specific plans to achieve those goals. Doing this gives classes more meaning, makes it easier to stay focused, and helps you feel more confident when you make important decisions, such as what major to declare or certificate to pursue.

Throughout this book you'll have many opportunities to learn more about yourself, your goals, and what drives you to succeed. To get started, think carefully about three personal attributes that influence your purpose: your motivations, your values, and your interests.

In the Driver's Seat. What drives you to get up and go each day? What keeps you focused on learning new things and getting your degree? Understanding your own personal motivators is a great way to stay energized to meet your goals—from the start of the race all the way to the finish line. ssuaphotos/Shutterstock

Learn What Motivates You.

People take many actions every day—we're on the move, going places, and doing things—and our behaviors are driven by our motivations or desires. For example, when you're tired, you're motivated to sleep; when you're hungry, you're motivated to eat. You can think of motivation as the engine that powers your effort, and the gas that keeps the engine running. It directs your goal-seeking behaviors and prompts you to push forward in the face of any challenges or setbacks. Right now, for example, you're motivated to enroll in college, register for classes, and pursue your education—likely because each of these actions will help you achieve something that's important to you.

To get a better sense of your own motivations, reflect on a time in your life when you accomplished a goal—maybe you won an award, performed well in a competition, or worked up the nerve to introduce yourself to a classmate who became a good friend. Now think about what prompted you to pursue this accomplishment. Were you driven by a desire for achievement? The desire to make new friends? The need to learn something new? What specific forces moved you forward to achieve your goal?

You'll learn much more about motivation in later chapters, but in the meantime, start thinking about what drives you to take action (both in school and outside of school) each and every day. Take a look at the following list of reasons that students just like you are pursuing higher education.[6] Are any of these suggestions similar to your own reasons for being here now?

- To prepare for a specific job or career path
- To increase earning potential
- To learn more about topics that I find interesting
- To continue my education in graduate school

Discover Your Values.

Your values are what you consider important—really important. They stem from your experiences with your family, your community, or your faith. For example, your values may include getting a good job, taking care of your family, or making a difference in your community. Values are essential because they can influence your behavior and your choices. You're more likely to pursue goals and activities that are consistent with what you care about most.

⚡ CONNECT TO MY EXPERIENCE

Write down two reasons why you're motivated to attend college. Then, list specific actions you can take *right now* to help you achieve what's important to you. Who might you connect with (either on or off campus) to assist you in meeting these goals?

Consider Tasha, a first-year student who is picking courses to fulfill her general-education requirements. Her values include treating people fairly and helping those in need—values she learned from growing up with parents who behaved in these ways with others. Tasha's adviser suggests that she take political science and U.S. history courses. In these classes Tasha will learn how the United States has, over time, developed legal systems and political and social support structures aimed at treating people fairly and helping those in need. Because the subject matter in these courses connects to ideas that mean a lot to Tasha—it connects to her values—she'll likely find the classes interesting and be motivated to master the material.

What are your values? For starters, the fact that you're in college means you value education. Perhaps you and your family make sacrifices so that you can attend school. Maybe you juggle commitments, taking out loans and cutting back on your work hours to free up time and energy for class. You're making these sacrifices because you appreciate what a college education has to offer.

Take a moment to think about what other values you hold dear. All of these values affect the decisions you make. For example, if you want to build a meaningful career after you graduate, reflecting on your values can help you pick a major that will help prepare you for such a career. If taking care of others is one of your values, majoring in nursing, teaching, or social work might be rewarding. If you value financial independence, majors that lay the foundation for lucrative careers, such as finance, could work well. The more you know about yourself, the more meaningful your chosen goals will be—and the more motivated you'll be to keep working toward those goals.

Follow Your Interests. Like your values, your interests powerfully influence your goals and motivations. Interests are your preferences for activities, things, people, and places—everything from exercise to animals to cars to music. Why are interests so important? When you define goals that connect with your interests, you're more likely to feel motivated to achieve those goals. For instance, if you're

More than Just Hobbies. Your interests matter. If you connect them to your coursework, you'll be more likely to stay motivated even when you encounter challenges. And who knows where your interests could lead you? You might find yourself gravitating toward a career that's not only stimulating but also financially rewarding and personally meaningful. *Left:* Hannamariah/ Shutterstock; *Right:* Jaromir Chalabala/ Shutterstock

> ## My life is bright and fulfilling, simply because I finally found my purpose.

NAME
Russell Jackson

SCHOOL
Iowa State University

MAJOR
Psychology

CAREER GOALS
Professor, Counselor

Courtesy of Megan Jackson

LEARNING ABOUT YOURSELF

I've struggled to find my purpose in life. I've worried that I don't know myself well enough to make the right decision, and I don't want to travel down a road, taking my family with me, if it's not the right path. I used to go to someone I trusted, listen to *his* suggestion about my future, and run with it.

Recently, I ended a career that just didn't fit me. My situation was frustrating and stressful, and I was running out of steam with no idea where to go or what to do. I needed to create some happiness. I realized then that I had never sat down and considered what *I* wanted, what *I* loved, and where *I* wanted to go. I knew I couldn't simply follow everyone else's desires for me anymore. I had to take charge of my destiny and mold it to meet my needs. I had to make changes that would help me prepare for a different career.

For the next year, I worked on finding my purpose in life. I put aside what others thought I should do and focused on my own thoughts, desires, talents, and goals. I thought critically about myself and found my calling. It didn't come all at once, but it did finally develop into a recognizable goal: I want to be a counseling psychologist.

Once my goal was set, everything else fell into place. I enrolled in school, registered for classes, spoke with professors, and found opportunities like volunteering, working in research labs, and helping at the Student Counseling Service. Granted, it's still difficult; sometimes I have to fight off doubts that I made the right decision. However, I'm able to overcome those fears and doubts by remembering that *I know what I want from my life*. My life is bright and fulfilling, simply because I finally found my purpose.

> **YOUR TURN** Do you have a sense of what your purpose might be? If so, what is it? Does it influence the goals you define for yourself? If you don't yet know your purpose, how might learning more about your motivations, values, and interests help you find clarity?

interested in the outdoors, physical activity, and nature, you'll be motivated to complete assignments in courses that incorporate these elements, such as wilderness management and forestry. Finding ways to connect your coursework with your interests—even when the connection isn't obvious—is a great way to stay motivated.

Consider what you like and don't like as you evaluate the courses you're taking, interact with your fellow students, and reflect on your past academic and work experiences. The more you're interested in the work you're doing in school, the more energized you'll feel as you pursue your goals.

Understand College Expectations

Learning about yourself and finding your purpose is hugely important, but it won't be your only area of focus as you settle into academic life. As a new college student, you'll need to get to know and understand the expectations of your instructors and your institution. So now that you're in college, what should you expect? And what will be expected of you?

What It Means To Be in College

First and foremost, it's important to recognize that college is a whole new world, and you'll encounter new challenges. More so than in high school, you'll have to take personal responsibility for your time, participate more actively in your learning, and make important decisions that will influence your future. Instructors will expect you to figure out *how* and *what* to study, to determine how to apply what you've learned to new situations, and to think carefully about concepts you might have just accepted as fact in high school. They'll also assume you'll ask for help when you need it, schedule your own study time, and keep up with your assignments. For more on the differences between college and high school, see Table 1.1.

TABLE 1.1

Common Differences between High School and College

In high school	In college
Your time and schedule was structured by others.	You must manage your time and choose how to spend it.
You were told what to learn and often how to learn it. Learning was teacher-focused.	You must figure out what to learn and how to learn it. Learning is student-focused.
You needed your parents' permission to participate in extracurricular activities.	You must choose whether to participate in co-curricular activities, and which fit best with your academic, personal, and other goals.
You could count on parents and teachers to remind you of your responsibilities and to give regular guidance in setting priorities.	You must set your own priorities and take responsibility for achieving them.
You attended classes five days a week and proceeded from one class directly to another.	You often have hours between classes and may not attend classes every day. Much of your work will happen outside of class time.
Most of your classes were determined by school counselors.	You must choose which classes to take in consultation with faculty and academic advisers. Your schedule may look easier than it actually is.
Students are not responsible for knowing what is required to graduate or for tracking their own progress.	Students are expected to select their own majors and/or minors and are expected to learn the graduation requirements for their programs of study.
Summary: Students are told what to do and corrected if their behavior is not in line with expectations.	**Summary: Students are expected to take responsibility for their path and academic success, as well as the consequences and rewards of their actions.**

"Common Differences between High School and College." Used by permission of the Altshuler Learning Enhancement Center at Southern Methodist University.

Starting Off on the Right Foot

If the responsibilities of being a college student feel difficult at times, that's okay. College is designed to push you out of your comfort zone. It's about growing intellectually and personally so that when you graduate, you're ready to launch a career that meets your needs. Fortunately, this book is packed with information that can help you become an active, successful learner. To get you started, here's a quick list of five high-value tips that you can use right away—here and now—to take charge of your education, exceed expectations, and kick your first term off right.

1. **Schedule study time.** Carefully map out what, when, and where you're going to study, so you don't get distracted by other opportunities—socializing, work, hobbies—and fall behind. As a general rule, plan to set aside two hours of studying for every hour of class time. (More about this in the time management chapter.)

2. **Go to class.** It sounds simple, right? After all, that's why you're in school: to go to class and learn new things. But students sometimes find themselves sleeping through alarms and getting distracted by nonacademic opportunities, which causes them to veer off track. The classroom isn't the only place you can learn, but it forms the foundation for learning and can help support and direct your reading, study time, and interactions with other students; do your best to attend each scheduled class session.

3. **Be realistic about online learning.** "Going to class" may look a little different if you're studying online—you probably won't meet in a classroom—but you'll still need to schedule time each day to complete your work. Online classes often require as much (or more) of a time commitment than do in-person classes, so do everything in your power to get ahead and stay ahead.

4. **Always ask questions.** If you don't understand something being presented in class, raise your hand and ask your instructor to explain the concept again, or in a different way. You're in charge of your education, so it's up to you to get the most of it—be an active participant!

5. **Get involved.** Learning can be a team sport, so make an effort to meet people in your classes and on campus. For example, join a study group or seek out a club or organization related to your major or career goals. Not only will you meet people, you'll also get to practice professional networking, build leadership skills, and get engaged with the community. Trust us: It's a win-win.

Feel the Power of Positive Psychology

Have you ever heard the saying "Attitude is everything"? It's a popular phrase that resonates with many people, likely because it touches on an important concept: the power of positivity. If you maintain a positive attitude, you're more likely to achieve your goals and lead a fulfilling life.

The idea that positivity can lead to success forms the foundation of **positive psychology**, a branch of psychology that focuses on people's strengths rather than on their weaknesses and that views weaknesses as growth opportunities.[7] Positive psychology has become a major influence in educational and workplace settings, and it plays an important part in this book.

positive psychology: A branch of psychology that focuses on people's strengths rather than on their weaknesses and that views weaknesses as growth opportunities.

FIGURE 1.2
**Four Key Concepts in
Positive Psychology**

FIGURE 1.2
**Four Key Concepts in
Positive Psychology**

The positive psychology movement emphasizes four central concepts: self-efficacy, resilience, hope, and personal responsibility (see Figure 1.2). All four will play a large role in your academic and professional success.

Build Self-Efficacy

Self-efficacy is your belief in your ability to do the things required to achieve your goals. Students with a stronger sense of self-efficacy perform better on tasks and persist in those tasks even when things get rough. But not all self-efficacy is created equal. Self-efficacy works best when it's based on a *realistic* assessment of your skills and abilities—and on evidence from your past performance, such as grades and instructor feedback. If your sense of self-efficacy is based more on self-deception than on evidence from your actual experiences, it can be overinflated. That can be dangerous: If you don't live up to your own expectations of yourself, you could experience a painful "reality check." But you also don't want to underestimate your skills and judgment. If you lack confidence in your ability to do something you're actually good at, you probably won't perform your best.

Many students arrive at college with a strong sense of self-efficacy, only to have it shaken by poor grades or unexpected setbacks. For instance, Kathleen went to a small high school, where she easily got straight A's and graduated near the top of her class. She enrolled in a large college and quickly discovered that the courses were much more challenging than in high school. She got some B's and even a C in her first-term and started asking herself, Can I really succeed in college?

If you have similar experiences, understand that they can present you with valuable learning opportunities. Use those opportunities to turn setbacks into success. For example, if you do poorly on your first accounting test, don't think of it as a failure; think of it as a starting point for improving your performance. How did you study for the exam? Did you complete all the practice problems at the end of each chapter or find a tutor? If not, would it be worth taking those steps for your next exam? Use learning opportunities like this to develop realistic self-efficacy beliefs and to improve your future performance.

Be Resilient

Have you ever known someone who went through a rough patch in life but came out of the experience stronger and more driven to succeed? Perhaps you have a friend who was devastated when she lost her job but turned things around by getting support from her family, obtaining financial aid, and going back to school to train for a new career. Or maybe you know someone who suffered from workload "shock" during his first college term but got help from his adviser and instructors and ended the term with strong grades and a better approach to time management. Both of these people displayed **resilience**, the ability to cope with stress and setbacks.[8]

resilience: The ability to cope with stress and setbacks.

Resilience in Action. Resilience helps you cope with the stresses you'll experience in college, at work, and in your personal life. Although Hurricane Harvey was devastating for Houston and southeast Texas in 2017, many residents developed potent strategies for helping their neighbors, rebuilding their homes, and resuming their lives. For some, their resilient response made them stronger than ever.
Joe Raedle/Getty Images

College students often face challenges such as balancing academic work and personal responsibilities. At times these challenges may cause you to feel stressed out or overwhelmed. During these times, you can demonstrate resilience by getting support and making positive changes. If you receive a low grade on a paper, for example, you can work to improve your writing and research skills so you'll do better on future assignments. Resilience helps you manage challenges, big and small, and stay motivated to achieve your goals.

Keep Hope Alive

Hope is the feeling that you can achieve your goals and that events will turn out for the best. Hope is strong when you have realistic self-confidence and a goal that you're motivated to achieve—one that's personally relevant to you. Charles Snyder, a specialist in positive psychology, suggests that there are two components to hope: the emotional energy that supports a feeling of optimism (*willpower*) and the resources, plans, and skills to achieve your desired outcomes (*waypower*).[9]

For example, suppose you've always wanted to be a veterinarian. Getting into a school that awards a doctorate of veterinary medicine is tough, so your willpower might inspire you to research colleges that offer a pre-veterinary curriculum, apply to several schools, and get accepted at one of your top choices. Your waypower, on the other hand, might include critical resources like the time and energy you expend to research colleges, as well as the plans you make to apply for financial support to help pay your tuition.

According to Snyder, it's not enough to believe that good fortune awaits us. We also need a plan and the skills to make that good fortune become real. In other words, we have to transform our thoughts and intentions into actions, a process that you'll have many opportunities to practice throughout this book.

"Really, only you can tell yourself to giddyup."

Horse Sense. Why is it so important to take personal responsibility for your success? Because it puts *you* in charge. You don't have to wait for someone else to define your goals, tell you how to reach them, and explain what you can learn from setbacks. You can do it yourself. Personal responsibility: It just makes sense. Bruce Eric Kaplan/ The New Yorker/The Cartoon Bank

Accept Personal Responsibility

Positive psychology is also about personal responsibility—taking charge of defining your goals, creating plans for accomplishing them, and seeking out resources that can help you achieve them. Personal responsibility gives you control: *You* have the power to turn negative results into positive ones by treating disappointments as learning opportunities. After all, most of your instructors aren't going to approach you and say, "I see you got a bad grade on the exam; here's what I think you should do about it." It's up to you to come up with strategies for doing better on the next exam. You'll get a chance to think about this topic more fully later in the book, but for now, just remember: When it comes to your success, *you're* the boss.

Embrace Your Strengths— and Learn from Your Weaknesses

If someone asked you to describe your strengths, what would you say? Maybe you'd point out that you can negotiate a subway system like a pro, give great advice, or play guitar. What about your weaknesses? Would you find it harder to acknowledge that you have poorly developed writing skills or that you're shy around people you don't know?

Everyone has strengths and weaknesses, and a key to success and happiness is knowing what these are. Armed with this understanding, you can *use* your strengths, while also improving areas you find challenging.[10] Using your strengths and working on your weaknesses takes effort, and you'll need the four key ingredients of positive psychology to make it happen: self-efficacy, resilience, a sense of hope, and a willingness to take personal responsibility.

As you think about building your strengths, consider basketball. Every team has players with different specialties. For example, the point guard has long-range shooting skills and the best ball-handling skills, while the center is typically the tallest player on the court and can secure rebounds. The coach makes sure each player uses his or her best skills while also addressing weak areas. Everyone has to practice ball handling, free throws, rebounding, and distance shooting—regardless of whether it comes naturally—because these skills are necessary for the team to succeed.

When it comes to the game of college, you're your own coach. You need to take advantage of your strengths and play to them regularly, but you also need to work on your weak areas. This book, your instructors, and the resources available on campus will help you build winning attitudes and skills, but ultimately, it's your responsibility to put those attitudes and skills into action. By focusing on using your strengths *and* addressing your weaknesses, you'll become as versatile in the classroom as professional athletes are on the court.

Identify Your Strengths and Your Weaknesses: ACES and Other Tools

Before you can use your strengths and address your weaknesses, you need to know what they are. Figuring this out isn't always easy. It requires a healthy dose of self-reflection (and a reality check) to acknowledge what you do well and where you struggle. It also involves collecting concrete information about yourself, which can come from the following sources:

- **The Academic and Career Excellence System (ACES).** Did you know that with this book you likely got access to an online self-assessment that will help you understand yourself better? It's called ACES (which stands for Academic and Career Excellence System). Have you taken ACES already? If not, you probably will soon. ACES helps you identify your strengths and weaknesses and use that information to establish goals. You'll revisit different ACES scores at the beginning of each chapter in the rest of this book and reflect on how you might better use a strength or improve a weak area. By engaging in such reflection, you can read each chapter with a better understanding of what you want to accomplish.

- **Past successes and failures.** Reflecting on your past successes and failures can provide a wealth of useful information. For example, can you recall a time when you were well prepared for an exam and another time when you weren't? How did your grades reflect your preparedness? What lessons can you gain from these contrasting experiences? How can you apply those lessons so that you do better on future exams?

- **Class experiences.** Think about your current classes. Are some more difficult for you than others? What do you think makes them harder for you? Reflecting on where you struggle can help you identify which skills you need to strengthen.

- **End-of-chapter activities.** The activities at the end of each chapter often require you to consider how the chapter material relates to your strengths and weaknesses. You'll also have further opportunities to practice developing your skills.

Once you've consulted these sources, then what? Learning about your strengths and weaknesses is great, but this information is useless if you don't use it to create positive change. That's what this book and this class are for: to help you achieve the necessary changes. In each chapter, you'll work on developing a new skill, such as setting goals, managing your time, reading a wide range of course materials, taking notes, and studying for exams. As you build these skills in this class, you can use them to succeed in your other classes, too. Why? Because, as you discovered earlier, all your learning is connected!

Recruit Help

There are many ways to build skills on your own, but you don't have to "fly solo" in this effort: You can recruit a team of supporters to help you when you struggle. According to a growing body of research, seeking help can *increase* your level of success.[11] Also, getting help is a form of taking personal responsibility: When you identify what challenges you face, what resources exist, and how to use them, you take charge of your own success.

Help is everywhere, once you know what's available and where to look for it (see Figure 1.3). Off campus, you can find help from family members,

FIGURE 1.3
Examples of Supports

friends, and community resources. On campus, you can find help from instructors, classmates, advisers, and support services like the math lab, writing center, and career center. To take advantage of the support resources around you, follow these three steps:

1. **Know what resources exist.** You can choose from countless resources, so find out which ones are available to you. If you're not sure which resources exist at your school or in the surrounding community, seek help from your instructor, an adviser or a counselor, or the campus Web site.

2. **Know which resources you need.** Think about which resources you need in a particular situation. If you're struggling in English class, for example, you won't get much help from the financial aid office. If you don't know which resources to seek out, ask your instructor or an academic adviser. They're skilled student-success specialists and will point you in the right direction.

3. **Use available resources.** Once you know which resource is appropriate for a particular need, take action. For example, find out how best to contact the tutoring center (do you need to make an appointment or can you just walk in?); then do it. If you don't know how to approach campus resources, ask your instructor or adviser for advice, or search your school's Web site for information. Table 1.2 provides examples of questions you can ask to get help from several key sources.

TABLE 1.2

Sample Questions You Might Ask When Visiting Support Services on Campus

Advising center	May I please meet with an adviser? I have some questions about scheduling my classes for next term.
	I'd like to find classes that will help me decide on my major. Can you help with that?
	I want to declare a major in psychology, but my adviser is in the English department. Can she still be my adviser?
	I'm having difficulty in my algebra class. Can you suggest where I can get some help?
Financial aid office	I missed the deadline for applying for aid this year. What are my options for paying for classes this term?
	I need to work while I'm in school. Are there any opportunities to work on campus?
	I don't want to take on too much debt. Can you help me create a plan for managing my finances?
	What scholarships are available in my field of study?
Instructors	I'm really struggling in this class. Can you recommend some additional reading materials or support services that can help me?
	Do you know of an advanced student who might be interested in helping me understand this material?
	I'm very interested in what we're covering in this class, and I'm thinking about majoring in this area. Can you give me the name of someone I can discuss this with?

Behaviors and Attitudes
Drive Your Success

When it comes to success in college, your past academic performance is only part of the equation. In fact, according to research, while your high school grade point average and college admissions tests scores are important predictors of college success, a host of other factors are also important predictors of college grades — many of which are related to behaviors and attitudes.

When researchers analyzed data from more than 200 past studies, they found significant relationships between grades and characteristics such as self-efficacy, hope, conscientiousness (being careful and efficient), organizational skills, critical thinking, learning goals, and help-seeking behavior. Many of these are characteristics that you've been reading about in this chapter, and *all* of them are areas you can further develop in this course.

The relative size of the relationship between these characteristics and positive academic outcomes is portrayed in the figure shown below. In other words, the larger the circle, the larger a role that particular characteristic plays in influencing student success.

THE BOTTOM LINE

Your success is largely dependent on your own attitudes and behaviors. By maintaining a positive attitude, reflecting on your strengths and weaknesses, and establishing concrete goals for improvement, *you* can help to control your own future.

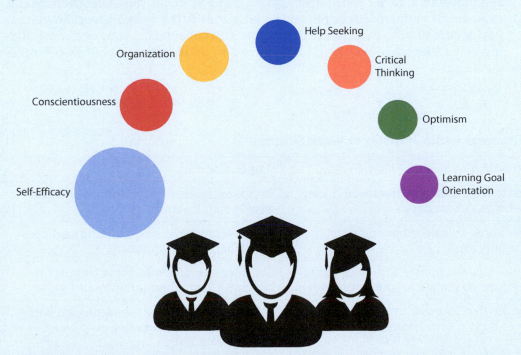

Help Seeking

Organization

Critical Thinking

Conscientiousness

Optimism

Self-Efficacy

Learning Goal Orientation

The larger the circle, the more that particular characteristic influences student success.

Information from M. Richardson, C. Abraham, and R. Bond, "Psychological Correlates of University Students' Academic Performance: A Systematic Review and Meta-analysis," *Psychological Bulletin* 138 (2012): 353–87. Image: Tuk Tuk Design/Shutterstock.

College Success Leads to Career Success

In this chapter we've talked a lot about connections—connections between self-knowledge and your success, between a positive attitude and meeting your goals, and between embracing your strengths and weaknesses and growing as a learner. But another type of connection is equally important to your future: the connection between college and career. The skills, attitudes, and behaviors you're developing in class will be just as valuable to you in the working world. It's the ultimate two-for-one deal: When you invest in your education, you also succeed at work.

Take the ability to communicate. Not only is it important to your academic success, but it's also something employers look for in potential hires.[12] Communicating is known as a **transferable skill** because it's useful in many different settings, not just in school. Attitudes and behaviors—including motivation, resilience, personal responsibility, and self-efficacy beliefs—can also be transferable. And according to surveys, many of the skills you're building in college and in this class are valued by employers—for example, processing information, working in teams, making decisions, and staying organized.[13]

We'll discuss transferable skills in more detail throughout this book, and you'll see how the skills you develop in school will serve you well in your chosen profession. To get you started, Table 1.3 shows how a series of specific skills can benefit a student in college and an employee in the working world. Whether you're sure of your career path now or are still considering your options, building skills like these will help you succeed in your career—whatever it turns out to be.

transferable skills: Skills that can be applied in many different settings, such as work, home, and school.

TABLE 1.3

Examples of How College Success Skills Transfer to Work Settings

Skill	Application at school	Application at work
Goal setting	Decide to meet with your instructor during office hours at least once a week.	Decide to improve your on-time arrival at weekly staff meetings.
Communication	Deliver a well-researched presentation to your history class.	Deliver a presentation explaining employee health benefits to your team.
Self-reflection	Consider how the transferable skills you're learning in class relate to your future career.	Consider how your efforts are helping or hindering your organization's sales goals.
Personal responsibility	Recognize that your low test score may have resulted from not studying enough.	Take responsibility for submitting a report too late, and develop strategies to better manage your time.
Teamwork	Complete a small-group experiment in your biology lab.	Work with representatives from other branch offices to prepare a regional sales report.
Listening	Pay attention to your instructor's comments and classmates' questions.	Consider the concerns expressed by a high school student's parents about courses you've recommended for her senior year.

> # Successfully navigating the challenges of college is excellent preparation for a career.

THE QUALITIES OF A GREAT JOB CANDIDATE

NAME
Shelly Sherman

PROFESSION
Executive Director of Human Resources

DEGREE
Master's Degree in Human Resource Development

I've been working in human resources (HR) for over 25 years. In that time I've worked in the financial services, consumer packaged goods, industrial apparel, and health care industries, and now I secure and promote talent at a large university. I've gained experience in just about every aspect of HR, but hiring the best qualified employees is one of the most important things I do in my job.

We recently established a Talent Acquisition and Retention Center for Expertise in our organization. Part of the pre-employment process includes using behavioral-based interviewing. In a behavioral-based interview, candidates are asked how they've handled situations in the past that are similar to those they might face in the job to which they are applying. For example, we might ask a job candidate to tell us about a time she set a goal and how she was able to achieve that goal or to describe a stressful situation she's experienced and how she handled it.

Candidates' responses to these questions give us great insight. We get a good idea of their self-awareness, whether they tend to assume responsibility for their actions, how they deal with failure or setbacks, and whether they're able to make adjustments in response to the outcomes of their actions. Even if a candidate doesn't have a long work history, he or she likely has many life and educational experiences that will enable him or her to respond to these questions.

We are looking for employees who can engage in personal reflection and provide thoughtful and authentic responses based on the experiences they've had. In many ways, successfully navigating the challenges of college is excellent preparation for a career.

As a candidate preparing for a behavioral-based interview, it's important to think about your previous experiences and how you want to position and convey your skills and accomplishments. It's also important to think about setbacks, because we all experience them. You'll be successful to the extent that you are confident, self-aware, and have the ability to self-correct!

Courtesy of Shelly Sherman

> **YOUR TURN** Have you had any experiences so far this term that you could share during an interview to demonstrate your skills and self-awareness? How can you document these and future experiences so that you can talk about them when it's time to look for a job? Does learning that these experiences interest future employers change how you think about your current classes and assignments? If so, how?

CHAPTER SUMMARY

In this chapter you've learned about a number of this book's key themes: the importance of college, self-awareness, understanding expectations, thinking positively, and recognizing your own strengths and weaknesses. You also saw how these themes connect to one other and to your college and career success. Revisit the following points and reflect on how this information can support your success now and in the future.

- College is important. You're at the right place at the right time. By getting your degree or certificate, you'll have more career options, earn more money, and be more likely to get involved in your community.

- By reflecting on why you're in college, you can start to identify sources of motivation that will help drive your success and sustain you when you experience setbacks. Understanding your values and interests can also motivate you to achieve meaningful goals.

- Your long-term success depends on understanding what's expected of you in college and getting off to a good start by attending class, asking questions, studying, and engaging with those around you.

- According to positive psychology, when things don't go your way, you can maintain a positive attitude by reframing negative results as opportunities for improvement. Four key ingredients of positive psychology are self-efficacy, resilience, a sense of hope, and a willingness to take personal responsibility.

- You're your own success coach — it's up to you to identify the skills you have and those you need to develop. Use every opportunity to play to your strengths while also addressing your weaknesses.

- Many resources are available to help you meet your goals. You can seek help from family, friends, instructors, and support services on campus and in your community.

- There's more to college than learning class material. You'll also develop transferable skills and attitudes that you can apply in whatever career you choose. Succeeding at school is directly connected to succeeding in your work life.

CHAPTER ACTIVITIES

Journal Entry

FINDING YOUR PURPOSE

The perfect way to begin your college journey is to reflect on why you're here — your purpose in attending college. Having a purpose will help you set meaningful goals, overcome obstacles, stay motivated, and make changes if needed. To begin identifying your own reasons for being here, write a journal entry in which you respond to the following questions:

1. How do you feel about being in college?
2. What does a college degree mean to you?
3. Who or what influenced your decision to attend college at this time?
4. What obstacles or barriers made it difficult to get here?
5. What strengths or personal characteristics did you develop working through those obstacles? How can these help you succeed in college?

Adopting a Success Attitude

COACHING YOURSELF TO MOTIVATION

One aspect of personal responsibility is self-motivation. How can you motivate yourself to keep working toward your goals if you're discouraged or overwhelmed? This chapter has a great suggestion: Be your own success coach. A coach is a source of moral support and inspiration when the going gets tough. To be your own success coach, identify a *mantra*: a quotation, saying, or poem that you find meaningful and that can inspire you when you encounter challenges this year. Why did you select this particular mantra? Where will you place it so it's easily visible or accessible? How will you use it to stay motivated?

Applying Your Skills

ENGAGING PERSONAL SUPPORTS AND RESOURCES

Successful people know when to ask for help or use resources to accomplish their goals, and they're not ashamed to seek support. In college, people across campus — advisers, career counselors, tutors — are employed specifically to help you. Find out who they are and what forms of support they can offer. Resist any temptation to think that asking for help reflects negatively on you. Remind yourself that successful students and employees surround themselves with personal supports to keep them motivated and to help them improve and succeed. In this exercise you'll learn more about available resources — both in your personal life and on campus.

Personal Supports

1. On a separate sheet of paper, list three people in your life you interact with regularly. (They can be friends, roommates, parents, siblings, a significant other, children, bosses, coworkers, and so forth.)
2. Next to each name, identify three to five ways this person could support you in your quest to be a successful student. For instance, "My roommate could allow me quiet time to study," "My mom could call me once a day, not three or four times a day, to see how I'm doing," or "My older sister could share the study strategies that she used during her time in college."
3. After you graduate, will any of these people remain personal supports for you as you launch a new or different career? If so, how might they support you in the future? If not, who else could support you, and how?

Campus Resources

1. Visit your college's Web site.
2. Search the Web site and identify five available resources that could help you succeed in school or plan your career.
3. Write down the name of each resource. Describe how you think it could help you, where it's located, and contact information.

College Success = Career Success

HIRE ME, PLEASE

If you're currently working, you're probably familiar with a *job description,* which is a document that outlines the duties, tasks, and qualifications of a specific job. Reviewing the job description before you apply to a job will help you prepare to meet the employer's expectations. You'll better understand the strengths you bring to the position, as well as any possible opportunities for growth that are relevant. This activity helps you think about your strengths and opportunities for growth as a college student.

Part 1: Pretend you are a human resource manager and want to hire someone for the job of "college student." Complete the job description template provided below. *Hint:* This chapter includes many ideas that can help you!

Part 2: Now pretend you are applying for this job. On a separate sheet of paper, answer the following questions:

▶ In what ways are you a good applicant? What strengths do you bring to this position?

▶ In what ways do you not meet some of the criteria? What are your opportunities for growth as a college student?

JOB DESCRIPTION TEMPLATE

Job Title: College Student

Principal purpose of this position:

_____

_____

_____

Essential job functions of this role:

- _____

- _____

- _____

Skills, abilities, and general qualifications required for this role:

- _____

- _____

- _____

Attitude and demeanor helpful for this role:

- _____

- _____

- _____

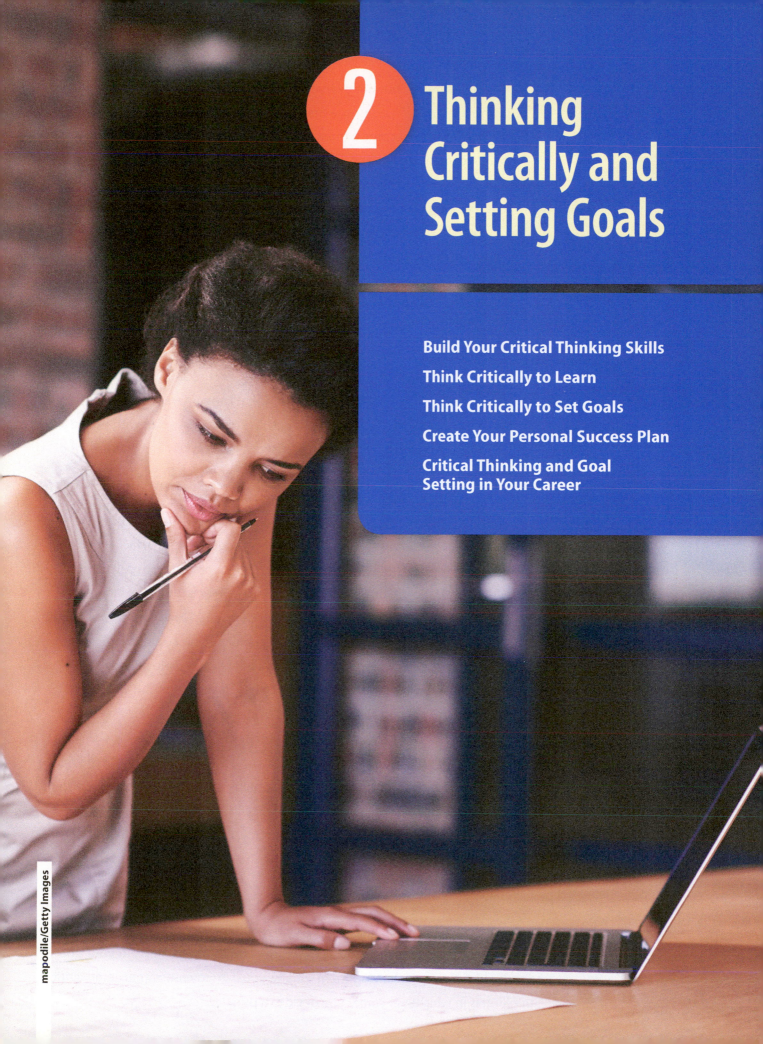

2 Thinking Critically and Setting Goals

Build Your Critical Thinking Skills

Think Critically to Learn

Think Critically to Set Goals

Create Your Personal Success Plan

Critical Thinking and Goal Setting in Your Career

Everyone thinks, but not everyone thinks critically — that is, in a careful, unbiased way. Take Jason, a first-year student majoring in criminology who wants to become a forensic crime-scene investigator. He's watched a lot of crime shows and visited several Web sites related to crime-scene investigation, so he's sure he's found the perfect path for him. He believes that majoring in criminology will prepare him for his dream job. He also expects that he'll work in exciting locations, interact regularly with police and witnesses, and make lots of money.

But if Jason thought critically about his choices, he would realize that his assumptions were misinformed. For one thing, many forensic specialists start out as forensic science technicians and major in chemistry or biology — not in criminology. Moreover, technicians often work in laboratory environments and interact mostly with other scientists and technicians — not with police and witnesses. Starting salaries for technicians are modest, sometimes coming in at less than $40,000 a year.

These facts don't mean that Jason shouldn't pursue his interests — he may do so and have a successful, rewarding career. In fact, the U.S. Department of Labor projects job growth for forensic specialists to be higher than the national average.[1] But Jason *does* need to think critically about his goals and expectations using accurate information — not TV shows. Critical thinking will help him make informed decisions based on solid facts and analysis.

In fact, critical thinking is a fundamental element of success in college and the workplace, and that's why we highlight it in this chapter and address it throughout the rest of this book. Critical thinking helps you learn new course content so that you can succeed academically. It also helps you learn about yourself so that you can set meaningful personal goals. In addition, it helps you keep learning and growing as an employee and sets you up for workplace success: Most employers highly value strong critical thinking skills.

In this chapter you'll explore how critical thinking influences your learning (spoiler alert: it helps you learn more deeply) and how it helps you set goals. You'll also try out the Personal Success Plan, a tool you can use to map out your goals and build a plan for achieving them. Finally, you'll discover how necessary critical thinking is in whichever career you decide to pursue.

ACES Reflection:
Critical Thinking and Goal Setting

Self-knowledge gives you the power to make positive change. That's why you're using the Academic and Career Excellence System (ACES): to learn more about your strengths and areas where you could improve. By knowing what you're good at, you can use those skills to master course content and build other skills. By acknowledging your weaknesses, you can target areas for improvement.

My ACES Score ....
☐ **High**
☐ **Moderate**
☐ **Low**

At the beginning of most chapters in this book, you'll review your score on the related section of ACES. Then you can use that information to focus on the chapter content that will best help you become a stronger student.

To find your **Critical Thinking and Goal Setting score**, go to the LaunchPad for *Connections*, Second Edition.

LaunchPad
macmillan learning

Let's start: Retrieve your Critical Thinking and Goal Setting score and add it in the box to the right. This score measures your beliefs about how well you think critically and set goals. How do you feel about your score? Do you think it accurately reflects your skills? Let's explore how you can use these results to become a more effective critical thinker and goal setter.

■ **IF YOU SCORED IN THE HIGH RANGE** on ACES, strengthen your strengths. Take pride in your results, but remember that even if you're good at something, you can always build up that skill even more. A swimmer might win first place at a swim meet, but she'll be back at practice the next morning to improve her time and refine her stroke. That way, she can work toward her goal of competing against more advanced swimmers.

■ **IF YOU SCORED IN THE MODERATE OR LOW RANGE** on ACES, don't worry; instead, target ways to improve. You'll have many opportunities to build your skills throughout the term, and the ideas in this chapter can help you get started.

ACES + ACTION

ACES paired with action is what leads to positive change. Now that you've reflected on your ACES results, how will you *use* what you learned about yourself to build your critical thinking and goal-setting skills? Try these concrete suggestions, or get inspired and create your own!

▶ **Make it personal.** Create your own critical thinking journal, and record one or more ways that you use critical thinking skills each day — in college, at home, or on the job. Use examples from your own life to make this concept come alive.

▶ **Explore sources.** Find an article through Google, Facebook, or Twitter and investigate whether it comes from a reliable source. Make a list of reasons you do (or don't) trust the information you've found.

▶ **Put it in writing.** To get comfortable setting goals, it helps to practice. Use the Personal Success Plan tool at the end of the chapter to record your first concrete goal of the term. What do you plan to achieve?

Build Your Critical Thinking Skills

critical thinking: The ability to consider information in a thoughtful way, adopt logical and rational thinking skills, and apply these skills in your classes and your life.

Critical thinking is the ability to consider information in a thoughtful way, adopt logical and rational thinking skills, and apply these skills in your classes and your life.[2] You use critical thinking in all kinds of situations: For instance, when you make the tough decision of figuring out how many college loans you should apply for. You also use it to assess whether information—such as a candidate's political position, an article you've read online, or claims made in a product advertisement—makes sense or is trustworthy.

In this section we'll look at key elements of critical thinking, including the skills involved and tips you can use to master those skills.

The Ingredients of Critical Thinking

Critical thinking is like a hearty soup—it's good for you, and it's made up of a number of ingredients that work well together. These "ingredients" are higher-level thinking skills that help you do things like assess information, answer questions, and make decisions. They require you to think in sophisticated ways, yet all higher-level thinking is based on lower-level thinking skills that we use every day, such as remembering facts, dates, and definitions or describing objects or ideas.

One way to understand the relationship between lower- and higher-level thinking is to consider the six questions journalists typically ask when tracking a story: *Who?, What?, Where?, When?, How?, and Why?* These first four are lower-level questions because they focus on basic facts and information, while *How?* and *Why?* are higher-level questions because they require you to connect and work with those basic facts. While both levels are important and useful, the higher-level questions require you to think more deeply and reason more carefully to reach your conclusions—in other words, they require you to think critically.

Truth or Myth? When you think critically, you assess whether information is trustworthy: Does it make sense? Does it come from a credible, unbiased source? Critical thinking helps you avoid the mistake of blindly accepting whatever you see, hear, or read. So it saves you from reacting to information in a knee-jerk way—like driving for days to see a supposed UFO landing site.
AP Photo/Eric Draper

TABLE 2.1

Examples of Higher-Level Thinking Skills

Skill	Definition	Example
Comparing and contrasting	Identifying similarities and differences between two or more concepts	• You're thinking of changing smartphone carriers, so you **compare and contrast** data plans and other terms offered by several providers to see which offers the best deal.
Deducing	Arriving at a conclusion using reason and logic	• You notice that all your friends who take time to study for exams get better grades than those who don't study. You **deduce** that you can improve your grades if you study more.
Synthesizing	Combining facts into a larger understanding of a concept	• As a marketing assistant, you review and **synthesize** comments from a focus group that has been assembled to examine a new product. Participants' comments suggest that the product name is intriguing but that it doesn't communicate the product's key benefits clearly.
Evaluating	Judging the authenticity or soundness of an argument	• For a journalism class assignment, you read an article arguing against vaccinating children and adults against influenza (the flu) because the vaccine can have side effects and doesn't guarantee immunity. You **evaluate** the argument as weak because the author doesn't address the fact that vaccination significantly lowers hospitalization rates for the flu.[3]
Prioritizing	Determining the order of importance of tasks	• Your manager has just given you several new responsibilities. You **prioritize** those that directly support an important goal your manager has set for the team: increasing sales.

Table 2.1 shows several examples of higher-level thinking skills, from comparing and contrasting to evaluating and prioritizing. As you read through the rest of this chapter and this book, consider how you'll use these and other critical thinking skills to make smart decisions about your coursework, life, and career.

How to Use Your Higher-Level Thinking Skills

Now that you have a sense of the higher-level thinking skills involved in critical thinking, let's explore how to use these skills. The next time you have a decision to make, a question to answer, or an argument to consider, follow these guidelines to reach careful conclusions.

Gather and Evaluate Information. To think critically, you need information. The kind of information you need depends on what you're trying to accomplish. For example, if you want to choose a major, you'll need information about your interests, values, strengths, and possible career goals. If you're writing a term paper, you'll need information found in books, your class notes, or readings on reserve in the library.

Having good information can steer you in the right direction and help you avoid mistakes. Imagine you're a supervisor trying to decide which candidate to hire for a new position. If you hire a person based on inaccurate or incomplete information, you might end up stuck with an employee who underperforms or doesn't work well with others. That's why you have to *evaluate* how reliable your information is. If a source is questionable or hard to assess, you'll need another source to back up the claims before you can trust the information. Remember Jason? His sources—TV shows and Web sites—left out important facts and even distorted information, so they weren't very reliable. Better sources lead to better choices.

Keep an Open Mind. Critical thinking involves keeping an open mind. This means being open to new possibilities presented by information you gather, thinking about old information in new ways, and considering information from different angles. When you do this, you demonstrate characteristics of creative thinking in addition to criticial thinking—and that's a good thing! **Creative thinking** is a way of approaching information or problems from a fresh perspective, and it involves processes like imagination, innovation, playfulness, and curiosity—all of which can help you maintain an open mind as you weigh evidence and decide on your next move. In fact, experts agree that both critical and creative thinking have value and that, when combined, they can help you achieve greater success than either can alone.[4]

Practice your critical *and* creative thinking skills by embracing new ideas, asking yourself what would happen if you rejected the standard format for problem solving, and taking multiple perspectives on a problem. If Jason had approached his career decision this way, he might have identified possibilities other than crime-scene investigation that interest him and provide the benefits he's looking for.

creative thinking: The ability to consider information or problems from a fresh perspective using processes like imagination, innovation, playfulness, and curiosity.

Strange Idea? Or Strangely Brilliant? Critical thinkers see new possibilities in the information they gather. For instance, who'd ever get the strange idea that old shipping containers could serve as student housing? Architects in France did. They created this student-housing complex by stacking one hundred recycled containers, with each one serving as a different student's room. Not so strange after all.
© Andia/Alamy

Apply What You've Learned. To be an expert critical thinker, you need to *do* something with the information you have—either disregard it because it didn't pass your evaluation, or apply it in your life and work. For instance, you might use what you've learned about your strengths to set a personal goal, or use information from a class to complete an assignment correctly.

Another way to apply information is to connect something you learned in the past to what you're learning now. What do you already know about mathematics that you can use to learn college algebra? If you've worked on a construction crew, how can you apply knowledge gained from that experience in your architectural design class?

Review Your Outcomes. Reflection is an important part of critical thinking, so set aside time to review the outcomes of your decisions and actions. Ask yourself whether your choices are built on solid critical thinking, or whether you need to improve your thinking process. For example, if your instructors have been skeptical about arguments you've made in several writing assignments, consider whether you need to do a better job of evaluating your sources' reliability. Experiences like these are great opportunities for positive change, and you can always reach out for help if you need to strengthen your critical thinking skills.

Critically Cool Creations.
Critical thinking can spark critically cool inventions. Take Nao, the robot that can stand in for a sick child in the classroom during the child's hospital stays. From the hospital the child uses a tablet computer to control the robot and follow along with the lessons. Here a boy tests this use of the Nao robot, drawing on his own critical thinking skills to evaluate the robot's abilities. Amelie-Benoist/ Science Source

Think Critically to Learn

Now that you've read about the basics of critical thinking, let's explore how you can apply these skills to learning—which is, after all, your primary reason for being in college. Just as there are lower and higher levels of thinking, there are also different levels of learning, and some of them require more critical thinking skills than others.

Levels of Learning

To get a sense of how the different learning levels work together, consider your experiences in school over the years. When you were in elementary school, you focused mostly on the fundamentals, such as how to spell, do simple arithmetic, and remember facts (like names and dates for historical events). But you may not have thought deeply about what you were learning. For example, you probably knew that Christopher Columbus sailed the ocean blue from Europe to the Americas in 1492, but you may not have pondered why he made the trip or what impact his arrival had on the peoples already living in the Americas.

As you've progressed in your education, though, you've come to use higher-level thinking skills more and more. You've likely learned that some questions have more than one right answer and that there can be multiple opinions on a topic. For instance, you and your classmates may have had different ideas about what Columbus's arrival in the Americas meant for the people already living there. To deal with such ambiguities, you used critical thinking skills (maybe without even knowing it) to compare, contrast, and evaluate information. Now that you're in college, these sophisticated, higher-level thinking skills are more important than ever.[5]

Using Bloom's Taxonomy

To better understand how learning moves from a simple to a more complex form, consider the work of educational psychologist Benjamin Bloom.[6] Bloom's taxonomy (Figure 2.1) shows how critical thinking relates to different levels of learning. The lowest level represents learning in its simplest form. At the higher levels, learning becomes more complex—and that's when you really start needing critical thinking skills. Not everything you learn in college will involve these higher levels of learning, but much of it will. Let's explore each level in more detail.

- **Remember.** Remembering is the most basic level of learning. When you learn a set of facts and recall them on a test, you demonstrate remembering. Perhaps you know that the American Revolution ended in 1783 or that the Cuban missile crisis happened in 1962. As the bottom level of Bloom's pyramid, these facts form a foundation that you can build on to better understand a topic.

- **Understand.** At this level, you can restate facts in your own words, compare them to each other, organize them into meaningful groups, and state main ideas. For example, in your communications class, you may learn two facts: Facebook was launched in 2004, and the current CEO is Mark Zuckerberg. You might categorize Facebook as a type of social media platform, a group that also includes Twitter, Snapchat, Instagram, and LinkedIn. You might further organize these social media platforms according to whether they focus on personal or professional networks.

- **Apply.** At this level, you use your knowledge and understanding of a concept to solve problems. For example, as a supervisor or manager at work, you'll be expected to juggle multiple projects and employees. You can use what you know about time management to successfully coordinate all of your responsibilities. In this way, you apply what you know to a real-life challenge.

  In some college majors, including business, economics, the sciences, health care, and engineering, you're expected to understand a topic and

FIGURE 2.1

Bloom's Taxonomy

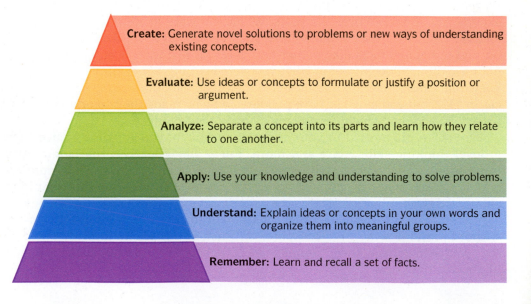

Create: Generate novel solutions to problems or new ways of understanding existing concepts.

Evaluate: Use ideas or concepts to formulate or justify a position or argument.

Analyze: Separate a concept into its parts and learn how they relate to one another.

Apply: Use your knowledge and understanding to solve problems.

Understand: Explain ideas or concepts in your own words and organize them into meaningful groups.

Remember: Learn and recall a set of facts.

apply that understanding to real problems. In a science class, for example, you may learn how various metals react when subjected to high heat. Later, when asked to identify a mystery metal in science lab, you might heat the metal to test whether it behaves more like magnesium, aluminum, or nickel.

- **Analyze.** At this level of learning, you approach a topic by breaking it down into meaningful parts and learning how those parts relate to one another. You may identify stated and unstated assumptions and distinguish between facts and educated guesses or opinions.

  You'll be expected to use this level of learning frequently in college. For essay exams, group projects, debates, and term papers, you'll formulate arguments based on your undertanding of different pieces of information and how those pieces relate to each other. In a modern history course, for example, you may analyze how conflict in the Middle East influenced the foreign and domestic policies of President George W. Bush.

- **Evaluate.** When you evaluate information, you examine evidence critically. You assess the relevance of information you're gathering, judge its quality, and identify any inconsistencies in the information that's available to you. Then, you reach conclusions or make arguments based on the evidence you collect. You can think of evaluation as advanced analysis, because you're not just analyzing information, you're making judgments or taking actions based on that analysis.

  Here's an example: To develop a research question for a psychology class, you review recent findings on *altruism* (doing good things for others). After analyzing your sources and confirming their quality, you're confident in the accuracy of what you've learned: that people are less likely to help when they don't feel personally responsible for the situation, or when there are

CONNECT TO MY CLASSES

Select two questions from a textbook reading or homework assignment you completed in another class this term. If possible, choose questions for which you've received feedback. Carefully examine each question and identify which level of learning in Bloom's taxonomy it falls under.

others around who could also lend a hand. You use this information to propose a new study on the likelihood that diners in the college cafeteria would help a fellow student who slips and spills her tray.

■ **Create.** At this highest level of learning, you combine different pieces of information together to form new patterns, identify new relationships not previously observed, or generate new solutions to problems. For instance, an essay question might ask you to create a new U.S. strategy to combat global terrorism based on your knowledge of successful and failed policies in years past. Creating is the "expert" level of learning—a level you'll want to achieve in college, especially in your chosen major.

Your college instructors want you to remember facts and understand concepts, but beyond that, they'll also encourage you to apply, analyze, evaluate, and create as you take tests, write papers, and complete projects. This book will help you practice learning at each of the six levels. For instance, later chapters provide tips on how to remember information, read textbooks strategically, take good notes, and study for exams, among other things. For now, review Table 2.2 to see examples of test questions associated with each level of learning.

TABLE 2.2

Sample Test Questions at Different Levels of Bloom's Taxonomy

Level in Bloom's taxonomy	Sample key words in test questions for this level	Sample test question
Remember	define describe list name	**List** the two dominant models of nursing care.
Understand	compare contrast classify summarize	**Classify** the following molecules based on their state (gas, liquid, or solid) at room temperature.
Apply	solve organize plan develop	Use your knowledge of education principles to **develop** a health curriculum for middle school students.
Analyze	explain categorize examine investigate	Drawing on your understanding of *Beowulf* and *King Lear*, **examine** how the theme of heroism is treated in these two works.
Evaluate	synthesize conclude criticize predict	**Predict** how U.S. fiscal policy might change if unemployment rose above 5 percent.
Create	compose generate design improve	Based on your review of the specific evidence presented during the mock trial and your understanding of U.S. law, **design** an argument for the defense.

Think Critically to Set Goals

A **goal** is an outcome you hope to achieve that guides and sustains your effort over time. When you set goals, you use many of the critical thinking skills you've just read about, but this time it's for a more personal reason: to better understand yourself. For instance, to set a goal, you *evaluate* your options. And as you work toward a goal, you *analyze* your progress and any obstacles facing you so that you can develop strategies for overcoming the obstacles. In this way, goal setting represents critical thinking in action.

Goals have different timeframes. *Short-term* goals are those you can achieve in a week or two (like studying for an upcoming exam) whereas *long-term* goals are those you work toward for months or years (like earning a degree). Goals also support and build on one another. For instance, before you can achieve a long-term goal to enter a particular profession, you need to set and achieve another long-term goal: graduating from college. And in order to graduate, you need to achieve short-term goals like completing assignments and class projects so you can pass required courses. Because using critical thinking to set and achieve your goals is vital, you'll have the opportunity to set a number of goals in this book—many of them short-term goals that will support your long-term endeavors.

Setting any goal involves a five-step process (see Figure 2.2), and each step requires you to apply critical thinking skills. Let's take a closer look at how the process works.

goal: An outcome you hope to achieve that guides and sustains your effort over time.

Step 1: Identify a Goal

The first step of goal setting is identifying a goal that you'd like to achieve. How do you decide on a goal that's right for you? One option is to think about your strengths and weaknesses: You can review your ACES results and reflect on the classes you find challenging, the grades you've received, and past experiences you've had. You can also consider whether you want to address a weakness, or focus instead on strengthening what you're already good at. For instance, if you're a chronic procrastinator, you may want to improve your time-management skills. If you're a masterful note-taker, you might want to become a tutor, since teaching a skill to others often makes you even better at it yourself.

There is no right or wrong way to identify a goal—what's most important is that it is something you'd like to achieve. That being said, for the purposes of this class, we suggest starting with a short-term goal—that way, you can experience for yourself how great it feels to accomplish what you've set out to do!

SMART goal: A goal that is specific, measurable, achievable, relevant to you personally, and time-limited.

FIGURE 2.2
The Steps of Goal Setting

Step 2: Make Your Goal SMART

Once you've identified a goal you'd like to work on, the next step is to make it SMART. A **SMART goal** is **s**pecific, **m**easurable, **a**chievable, **r**elevant to you personally, and **t**ime-limited. It can be tempting to state goals in general terms, such as "I'm going to study more" or "I want to get good grades," but it's hard to know whether you've actually achieved vague goals like this. (For instance, what does "to study more" actually mean?) By contrast, the SMART approach helps you

TABLE 2.3
Weak Goals versus SMART Goals

Weak goal	SMART goal
Get good grades in class	Get a B or better in my algebra class this term
Spend more time studying for biology	Study my biology class notes and textbook at least five hours each week this term
Make some new friends	Attend a meeting of at least two on-campus clubs or organizations in the next month
Organize my work, school, and social time more effectively	Create a schedule this weekend that accomodates my work hours, study hours, and social activities for the next two weeks
Learn about study-support resources on campus	Make appointments to visit the learning assistance center and math lab next week to learn about their services

CONNECT
TO MY EXPERIENCE

Think about a personal, professional, or academic goal you set but never achieved. Write down elements from the SMART goal system that might have helped you achieve your goal, and explain why those elements would have been useful.

think critically about your goal, which empowers you to create strong, realistically achievable goals and take concrete steps to accomplish them (see Table 2.3). Let's look at each step in the SMART process more closely.

Specific. When you express a goal in specific terms, you know exactly what you're trying to achieve. Contrast the vague goal "Get good grades" with the specific goal "Get a GPA of 3.0 or higher this term." The vague goal doesn't say what qualifies as a good grade (an A? a B+?), so you don't have a clear idea of what you're working toward.

Measurable. When a goal is measurable, you know when you've reached it. For instance, it's easy to determine if you've earned a GPA of 3.0 or higher by the end of the term. Your school calculates your GPA, so one quick look at your grades for the term tells you if you've met your goal.

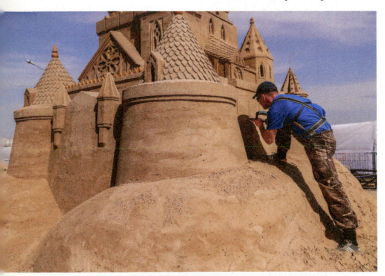

The Achievability Advantage. Defining a goal? Make sure it's achievable — for you. When this sculptor first started building sand castles, he probably didn't set out to create a structure of this size and complexity. Instead, he first aimed to master the basics of working with sand. So, as you're defining goals, take it one tower at a time: Start with an achieveable goal that inspires you, then gradually challenge yourself to try more complicated projects.
Sergei Savostyanov/Getty Images

Achievable. Nothing is more frustrating than establishing a goal that's beyond your reach. What is and isn't achievable differs from person to person. For example, if you're working full time and raising two kids while attending college, setting a goal to take five classes and study four hours a day probably isn't achievable. On the other hand, taking one or two classes and studying 1.5 hours a day on weekdays and two hours a day on weekends may be a more reasonable goal.

If you have doubts about whether a goal is achievable, consider revising your goal to increase the chances you'll reach it. Then, once you succeed, you can set the bar higher for yourself. The key is to set goals that are challenging enough to inspire you but not so challenging that you'll never reach them.

Relevant to You. When you set goals that matter to you personally (for example, they reflect your values, interests, and career plans), you'll be more motivated to achieve them. If you enjoy learning about science and want to become a pharmacist, it will be easier for you to reach a goal of studying chemistry three additional hours a week. And if you plan on a career in the food services industry and believe that hunger is a pressing social problem, volunteering once a week at a food pantry would be relevant to you.

Time-Limited. SMART goals include deadlines by which you aim to achieve the goals (such as earning a GPA of 3.0 or higher by the end of the term). Take care in setting deadlines. If the deadline is too far in the future, you may procrastinate on working toward the goal. But if you set a deadline that's too soon, the goal may start to seem unachievable, and you might feel too overwhelmed and discouraged to tackle it. Setting a time limit for achieving a goal helps you assess whether you've actually accomplished what you intended.

Step 3: Create an Action Plan

To achieve your goals, you need an **action plan**, a list of the steps you'll take to accomplish a goal and the order in which you'll take them. Think of your action plan as a to-do list for achieving your goal.

Write Down Your Actions. The first step in developing a good action plan is to write down the actions you'll take to achieve your goal. You might be tempted to make a mental list of these actions, but writing them down is a *much* better idea. In a recent study at Dominican University, participants who didn't write down their goals and plans achieved only 43 percent of their goals, whereas those who wrote them down achieved more than 76 percent of their goals.[7] Don't worry about making the list perfect or recording the steps in a particular order—just write them down as they pop into your mind. For example, if your SMART goal is to submit your English term paper on the day it's due, you might brainstorm a list of action steps like this:

Action Steps
• *Submit final term paper by due date*
• *Prepare rough draft of term paper*
• *Submit rough draft to writing tutor*
• *Buy a dictionary*
• *Schedule appointment with writing tutor*
• *Incorporate feedback from writing tutor into final version*

Prioritize Your Action Steps. Once you've brainstormed action steps and written them down, determine which steps are critical and which aren't. (Noncritical steps are those that, if ignored, wouldn't jeopardize your goal.) In this example, you might decide that buying a dictionary isn't a top priority—after all, there's one built into your computer—so you cross that off the list. The items that remain should be those that are most important.

Put Your Steps in Order and Set Deadlines for Them. Once you've eliminated noncritical steps from your list, arrange the remaining steps in the order in which you'll complete them. For example, if you need feedback from the writing center before editing your paper, put a visit to the writing center higher on your list. Also, add a deadline for each step so you can track your progress.

⚑ **CONNECT**
TO MY CAREER
Think about a career you've decided to pursue or, if you're undecided, a career you're considering. What short-term goal could you set today that would help you reach your long-term goal of succeeding in that career? Write your short-term goal in the form of a SMART goal now.

action plan: A list of steps you'll take to accomplish a goal and the order in which you'll take them.

Here's how your action plan might look now:

Action Plan Steps (in order)	Deadlines
1. Schedule appointment with writing tutor	This Friday
2. Prepare rough draft of term paper	Three weeks before due date
3. Submit rough draft to writing tutor	Same day as above
4. Incorporate feedback from writing tutor into final version	Within one week of due date
5. Submit final term paper	On due date

Step 4: List Barriers and Solutions

Even when you have an action plan for achieving a goal, you can still encounter barriers. A **barrier** is something that prevents you from making progress toward your goal. It might be a personal characteristic (like a tendency to procrastinate) or something in your environment (like too many family commitments). Some barriers, such as poor time management, are under your control. With others, like family or work demands, you might have less control.

As you set your goals, write down the types of barriers you may face. By acknowledging potential barriers, you won't get blindsided if you actually encounter them. Also, you can brainstorm in advance how to overcome them. For example, suppose you're worried that your job will get very busy during midterms and interfere with your study time. By anticipating this barrier, you can figure out ways to avoid it—such as trading hours with a coworker.

And remember that you don't have to face barriers alone. Many helpful resources are available to provide support and encouragement—for example, faculty members, tutors, and academic and career advisers can work with you to overcome common barriers. To get help, you just have to ask.

barrier: A personal characteristic or something in your environment that prevents you from making progress toward a goal.

⚲ CONNECT TO MY RESOURCES

Write down two barriers that might prevent you from achieving your goals this term. Then identify and write down two resources on campus or in your community that could help you overcome these barriers.

Oops! Even if you've built an action plan for achieving a goal, you can still encounter barriers: You get stuck in a traffic jam, so you're late for a group-project meeting. A family member is ill and requires your attention, so you have less time to study than you had hoped. By anticipating possible barriers, you can craft strategies for overcoming them if they do arise. Berkomaster/Shutterstock

> # Making mistakes doesn't mean failure, unless you fail to learn from your mistakes.

Courtesy of Kerry Maxime

NAME
Thamara Jean

SCHOOL
Broward College

MAJOR
Pre-Nursing

CAREER GOAL
Nursing

FOCUSING ON SOLUTIONS

Since I was seven years old, I've wanted to be a doctor — I think my goal was influenced by my parents and from watching lots of doctor shows on TV. With that goal in mind, I arrived at college and really struggled with courses like organic chemistry and pre-calculus. It wasn't until I attended a required advising meeting that I realized I wasn't thinking very critically about my goal. I didn't know what was required to get through pre-med and medical school. I realized that choosing medicine was probably a mistake but that making mistakes doesn't mean failure, unless you fail to learn from your mistakes. My adviser and I discussed a backup plan that included switching to pre-nursing, getting experience in health care settings, and continuing to gather information about medical school.

That same semester I attended a leadership and goal-setting workshop where I learned about SMART goals and was encouraged to get more involved in campus leadership activities. I learned to question, assess, analyze, and even research everything, because my future depends on me!

I immediately set a number of specific goals, like joining the campus Honors Committee, passing my classes the next semester, and researching information about how to get into nursing school. To support my goal of passing classes, I set additional goals like getting tutoring in math and science and getting feedback on my papers before submitting them in literature classes. I feel back on track. I recently transferred to Florida Atlantic University, where I'm applying for acceptance into the nursing program, and I'm looking forward to a successful career in nursing.

> **YOUR TURN** Have you ever set a goal and then discovered significant barriers blocking your way? If so, what did you do to overcome those barriers or adjust your goal to make it more realistic?

Step 5: Act and Evaluate Outcomes

Evaulation is a key part of critical thinking, so regularly evaluate your progress as you work to set and achieve your goals. Are the steps you're taking effective? Are you completing them on time? Are they getting you closer to meeting your goal? If you're not making the progress you'd hoped for, evaluating your outcomes helps you recognize this immediately so you can change your action plan or find resources to get you back on track. Also, evaluation can help you stay motivated: By recording and celebrating your accomplishments on short-term goals that support your long-term goals, you build up proof that you're making progress on what's meaningful to you.

If your evaluation shows that you've experienced a setback, stay positive. The point of evaluating your progress is to identify and deal with setbacks. Each time you do so, you'll get even better at achieving your goals, and you can seek out help if you need it. Remember: Setting and achieving goals takes practice. You didn't learn how to ride a bike on the first try either!

spotlight on research

The Academic Benefits of
Goal Setting

Recently, a group of researchers conducted a study to answer an important question: Does goal setting actually promote college success? To investigate, they divided eighty-five undergraduate students into two groups:

▶ **Group 1:** Students completed surveys measuring their career interests, curiosity, and initiative. They also listed past accomplishments that they were proud of. They received no training on setting and achieving goals.

▶ **Group 2:** Students participated in a Web-based program introducing them to a process for setting and achieving personal goals. They wrote down seven or eight goals, prioritized them, and described how meeting those goals would improve their lives.

On average, students in group 1 (no goal-setting training) achieved GPAs of 2.46, whereas those in group 2 (goal-setting training) achieved GPAs of almost 3.0. Compared to group 1, students in group 2 also completed more academic credits, stayed in school at a higher rate, and said they felt less anxious, less stressed, and more satisfied with life.

THE BOTTOM LINE
Goal setting can lead to good things: When you learn how to set goals, you'll likely improve your grades, feel more satisfied with your life, and achieve more of what's important to you.

Research suggests that setting goals helps you earn higher grades.

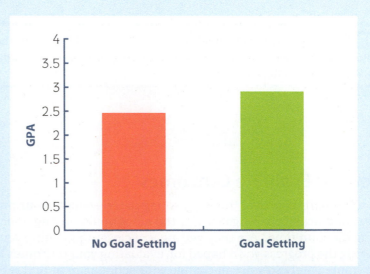

Information from D. Morisano et al., "Setting, Elaborating, and Reflecting on Personal Goals Improves Academic Performance," *Journal of Applied Psychology* 95 (2010): 255–64.

Create Your Personal Success Plan

Now that you've explored how to set and achieve goals using critical thinking skills, put your learning into action with the **Personal Success Plan (PSP)**. This tool guides you through the five steps of the goal-setting process. You can use it to establish SMART goals, build action plans, evaluate your outcomes, and revise your plans as needed as you go through this course. You can also use the PSP to set and achieve goals in other courses, on the job, or in your personal life.

The PSP's major sections mirror the five goal-setting steps you just learned:

1. Identify a Goal
2. Make Your Goal SMART
3. Create an Action Plan
4. List Barriers and Solutions
5. Act and Evaluate Outcomes

An additional section—Connect to Career—helps you consider how a goal you've defined using the PSP can help prepare you for success in your chosen career or a career you're considering.

As you start using the PSP, you'll become a stronger critical thinker and a more independent learner. You'll use critical thinking to gather information, make decisions, and evaluate what you've learned about yourself so that you can get better and better at setting and achieving goals. In short, you'll discover that *you're* in the driver's seat when it comes to defining and meeting your goals—and you'll gain practice taking personal responsibility for your own learning.

Personal Success Plan (PSP): A tool that helps you establish SMART goals, build action plans, evaluate your outcomes, and revise your plans as needed.

The PSP in Action

In this section, you'll get a firsthand look at how the PSP functions. You'll read about the experience of one student, Samantha, as she sets up her PSP, and you'll see the steps she takes to create and accomplish her goal. This is goal setting in action!

Identify a Goal. Samantha has enrolled in a first-year seminar course, and one of her assignments is to establish a specific goal and action plan. As a first step, Samantha identifies a goal that's important to her by reflecting on her strengths and weaknesses. She knows that she's a very motivated student but that she also struggles to manage her time. Therefore, she decides that setting a regular study schedule will help her stay on track.

Make Your Goal SMART. Samantha works to rewrite her goal so that it's SMART: "I'll study for my first-year seminar at least one hour each weekday." This is a *specific* and *measurable* goal. Based on her existing schedule, Samantha believes that this goal is *achievable*. She's motivated to get good grades this term, so it's also personally *relevant* to her success. Finally, the goal has a clearly established *time limit*, which will help her check her progress within a day or two.

Create an Action Plan. To identify the steps she'll take to meet her goal, Samantha considers her class and work schedules and upcoming personal commitments. She knows that she is more motivated to study in the afternoons, so setting aside time after lunch is best. She also knows that she prefers to work in quiet, out-of-the-way places. With this information in mind, she makes a plan.

- By Friday, she'll meet with her roommate to plan quiet, afternoon study time in their apartment.
- By Sunday, she'll enter her study schedule into her smartphone.
- By Sunday night, she'll develop a log to record how much she studies.

List Barriers and Solutions. On her PSP, Samantha lists several barriers that might prevent her from achieving her goal and brainstorms solutions for overcoming those barriers. For example, her roommate may need to use the apartment when Samantha wants to study. (Perhaps her roommate is a music major and needs to practice her tuba.) As a backup plan, Samantha decides to look for alternative study areas in the school library. Also, Samantha might not always be able to follow her set schedule—for example, she could get called into work or feel pressure to socialize when she's supposed to be studying. If these things happen, she develops strategies she can use to stay on track.

Act and Evaluate Outcomes. For the next two weeks, Samantha implements her action plan and records her results in the PSP. She works with her roommate to set aside quiet study time at their apartment and identifies a backup study location just in case the apartment becomes noisy. She also enters her study schedule into her smartphone and creates a log to record how much she studies.

Samantha experiences a setback in week 2, when she misses two study periods due to work obligations. But she doesn't give up; instead, she makes up her study time over the weekend and revises her schedule to make it more realistic. And she's so pleased with how useful this study strategy has been that she decides to build a study schedule for her other courses, too.

Connect to Career. On her PSP, Samantha identifies three skills she's learning as she works toward her goal: managing her time, prioritizing her action steps, and mastering her new smartphone calendar app. These are transferable skills she can use in any current job or any future employment. By recording these skills on her PSP, she can refer to them when she prepares a résumé, writes cover letters, and describes her qualifications during job interviews.

Turn It Down! Building flexibility into your action plan helps you keep barriers from standing between you and your goal. For instance, if your neighbor is an aspiring deejay, take that into account when designing your study plan: Identify a quiet location where you can study in case your neighbor decides to crank up the volume just as you crack open your textbook. Maxim Blinkov/Shutterstock

my personal success plan

Samantha Gonzales

1 my general goal

Sometimes it's hard for me to manage my time.

I need a regular study schedule to stay on track.

2 my SMART goal

I'll study for my first-year seminar at least one hour each weekday.

 ✓**S**PECIFIC ✓**M**EASURABLE ✓**A**CHIEVABLE ✓**R**ELEVANT ✓**T**IME-LIMITED

3 my action plan

1. I'll discuss apartment quiet time with my roommate (by Friday).
2. I'll enter study times into my smartphone calendar (by Sunday).
3. I'll make a log to record how much I study (by Sunday night).

4 my barriers/ solutions

1. If my roommate has a conflicting schedule, I'll find a place to study in the library.
2. If I miss a scheduled study session, I'll find a makeup time.
3. If family and friends want to get together during study time, I'll find a different time for us to meet.

5 my actions/ outcomes

1. My roommate and I set quiet hours for the apartment. I also found a good place to study in the library, just in case.
2. I entered my study schedule into my smartphone and created a study log.
3. In week 2, I missed two study periods. I'll make up this study time over the weekend and revise my schedule to be more realistic!

6 my career connection

1. I'm learning to manage my time, which will help me meet deadlines on the job.
2. I'm setting priorities, and I can use this skill to focus on the most important tasks at work.
3. I've mastered my new smartphone app, which I can use to schedule appointments during the workday.

Create Your First Personal Success Plan

Samantha is off to a great start this term, and now it's time for you to create your first Personal Success Plan. To begin, follow the steps below and sketch out your ideas on the following page. Or visit the LaunchPad for *Connections*, Second Edition, to access the PSP online.

1. **Identify a goal.** What goal do you want to achieve in the short-term? Try reflecting on your strengths and weaknesses and reviewing your ACES results. Is there a strength (high score) you want to develop further or a low score suggesting an area in which you could improve? Is there a goal you're interested in pursuing that relates in some way to the content of this chapter?

2. **Make your goal SMART.** Rewrite your short-term goal so that it meets the SMART criteria. You can always revise your goal later, so don't worry about making it perfect.

3. **Make an action plan.** List steps you'll need to take to achieve this goal, and arrange them in the order that makes the most sense to you. Give each step a deadline.

4. **List barriers and solutions.** Identify possible barriers to your action steps and brainstorm solutions for overcoming each barrier. If these barriers occur, you'll be ready.

5. **Act and evaluate outcomes.** It's up to you to put your plan into action and to record the completion of each action step and any problems you encounter. Do this to track your progress.

6. **Connect to career.** List the skills you'll develop as you progress toward your goal. Then identify how those skills will help you succeed on the job.

Once you've filled out your Personal Success Plan, you'll have set your first academic success goal of the term. Congratulations—this is a great first step! Remember, though, that goal setting is an ongoing process that takes practice, and that's why you'll get the chance to set multiple goals over the course of the term. How many goals should you plan to set? Your instructor may provide guidance on the number required for your particular class. Some instructors may ask you to set one goal for each chapter, while others may require only a few goals over the course of the term. Either way, we have included a sample PSP at the end of each chapter to inspire you and to walk you through the goal-setting process. If you aren't setting a goal in a particular chapter, the PSP will still be there to offer suggestions and serve as a model.

You might need some time to get used to the PSP, but as you progress through this course, you'll become an expert goal setter. By the end of the term, you'll have set and achieved a number of goals, and you'll be well on your way to academic and career success.

my personal success plan

_____

1 my general goal

_____
_____
_____
_____

2 my SMART goal

_____
_____
_____
_____

☐ **S**PECIFIC ☐ **M**EASURABLE ☐ **A**CHIEVABLE ☐ **R**ELEVANT ☐ **T**IME-LIMITED

3 my action plan

_____
_____
_____
_____

4 my barriers/ solutions

_____
_____
_____
_____

5 my actions/ outcomes

_____
_____
_____
_____

6 my career connection

_____
_____
_____

Critical Thinking and Goal Setting in Your Career

Using critical thinking to learn and set goals helps you not only to succeed academically but also to launch and maintain a successful, satisfying career. In the workplace you'll stand out if you use reliable information to make decisions, consider all points of view, set meaningful personal and professional goals, and brainstorm innovative solutions to problems. You can do all of these things by *applying* the information you've learned in this chapter to your current or future job.

Never Stop Learning. You'll want — and need — to keep learning on the job so that you can excel at your work and advance in your career. For instance, teachers often need continuing education credits to maintain their teaching certification. No matter where you work, critical thinking can help you keep building your skills and knowledge. michaeljung/ Shutterstock

Learn on the Job

When you graduate from college, you don't stop learning. In fact, to advance in your career, you'll be expected to learn new skills and acquire new knowledge all the time. Some professions even require you to take continuing education credits each year to maintain your credentials or license, while in other professions you'll need to stay current on the latest technologies to remain productive and competitive. For example, after only two weeks of working for a transportation consulting firm, Abigail's boss asks her to review three transportation dispatch software platforms and recommend one for the company to adopt. Abigail will need to rely on critical thinking skills like synthesis and evaluation to weigh the options, assess strengths and weaknesses, and make a thoughtful recommendation.

Think Outside the Box

In the workplace, employers are searching for new team members who can think both critically *and* creatively. Why? Because work environments are less structured today than they've ever been, which means that as an employee, you'll be expected to problem solve, innovate, and develop strong social relationships to succeed. By applying your critical and creative thinking skills, you'll be open to new ideas, question existing problem-solving methods, and take multiple perspectives. These qualities will serve you well in almost any position and will make you better prepared to tackle the workplace challenges you're likely to face.

Set Goals on the Job

The goal-setting strategy you're learning in this course can also help you set career goals. Let's say you want to take on more responsibility at your job, communicate more effectively with colleagues, or complete tasks more efficiently. You can reframe these general statements as SMART goals and use the PSP to achieve them.

As you develop your own work-related goals, be sure to consider how they support your organization's goals. For example, as a licensed practical nurse, you might decide to increase the number of patient charts you review each hour by

> Having a very clear, concrete goal helps me focus on what I need to do each day.

NAME
Chris Funderburk

PROFESSION
Branch Manager, Car Rental Office

SCHOOL
Indiana University

DEGREE
Bachelor of Science

MAJOR
Biology

SETTING GOALS FOR WORKPLACE SUCCESS

Back in college, I had some difficulty — in fact, I was asked to leave my university due to low grades. It took me some time, but I went back to school and improved my GPA. Failing in college gave me a new perspective. It gave me purpose and made me stronger, and goal setting helped. I refocused on my ultimate goal of graduating and used a lot of short-term goals to stay motivated. Having specific, achievable goals was critical to this success.

Now that I'm working, I use the goal-setting skills I developed in college all the time. We have monthly sales and customer service targets to meet each month. Having a very clear, concrete goal helps me focus on what I need to do each day to achieve my goals for the month. Not every month is perfect, and it's easy to get down when I don't meet a personal goal or my team doesn't meet its goal. However, that's when I take a minute to reflect on what was happening during that month.

Sometimes I reach out to successful colleagues and ask them for input. Other times I return to strategies that worked in the past. I get back to the basics of making sure I put both customers and my employees first. When I combine reflection with perseverance and a strong work ethic, I can ramp up to make my goals the next month.

I've faced huge challenges in the past, but I'm able to build upon everything I learned to keep pushing forward.

> **YOUR TURN** Have you ever experienced difficulty achieving work-related goals? If so, what did you do about it? What results did you get? How can you use what you've learned from this experience to set work-related goals in the future?

Courtesy of Chris Funderburk

10 percent in the next month. This goal demonstrates enthusiasm and a desire for self-improvement. However, you'll want to consult with your supervisor about which goals would best support both the organization's success and your own professional development. If your employer prefers that you focus on learning how to use a new piece of equipment instead, you might have to modify your original goal to support your employer's top priorities. Developing goals in consultation with your supervisor is a win-win situation and a great way to show your ability to take the initiative.

CHAPTER SUMMARY

This chapter introduced you to one of the most fundamental factors in your college and career success: critical thinking. You can use critical thinking to learn and to set goals — in school and at work. Revisit the following key points and reflect on how you can use this information to support your success now and in the future.

- Critical thinking is the process of approaching information in a thoughtful way, adopting logical and rational thinking skills, and applying these skills in your classes and your life. It involves using higher-level thinking skills such as synthesis and evaluation.

- You can use critical thinking to learn in every course you're taking. Bloom's taxonomy helps you identify the level at which you're learning and think about how that learning will be assessed on exams or assignments.

- You can use critical thinking to set and achieve goals through this five-step process: (1) identify a goal you'd like to achieve, (2) make that goal SMART, (3) create an action plan, (4) list possible barriers and solutions, and (5) act and evaluate your outcomes.

- The Personal Success Plan can help you set and achieve goals. The steps in the PSP mirror the five goal-setting steps, with one additional step, connecting to career. You can use the PSP to list your goals and action steps, document which steps you've completed, evaluate your progress, and revise your plan if needed.

- Thinking critically helps you launch and maintain a successful career. You can use the techniques you read about in this chapter to continually acquire new knowledge and skills, to be a creative and flexible worker, and to set goals on the job.

CHAPTER ACTIVITIES

Journal Entry

SETTING SHORT- AND LONG-TERM GOALS

Both long- and short-term goals play a role in helping you achieve what you care about. Having a clear and specific long-term goal can keep you headed in the right direction while you're in school, and it can provide you with a sense of purpose and meaning. Short-term goals are the stepping stones to long-term goals: They help us organize our actions and provide us with day-to-day momentum as we work toward our long-term objectives. In this journal entry, you'll have the chance to reflect on a long-term goal that's important to you, as well as the short-term goals that support it.

1. What is your long-term goal when it comes to your college education? What do you hope to accomplish with a college degree? Be as specific as you can.

2. Break your long-term goal into smaller objectives. Reflect on what you'll need to do each term to be ready to achieve your long-term goal when graduation comes. In addition to coursework, think about additional knowledge, skills, training, and experiences you could develop along the way.

3. Describe how achieving each of these short-term goals will help you meet your long-term goal. Why are these smaller goals important to your overall objective?

Adopting a Success Attitude

USING CRITICAL THINKING TO OVERCOME SETBACKS

Regardless of how realistic your goals are and how many barriers you anticipate, at some point you won't accomplish something you want to. Dealing effectively with your emotions when you experience setbacks and maintaining a positive attitude separates successful students from unsuccessful ones. Let's use critical thinking and reflection to turn a goal-setting setback into a learning opportunity.

1. Describe a goal you set (something that was important to you) but never achieved. Using your critical thinking skills, evaluate this goal using the SMART criteria described in this chapter. Was the goal specific, measurable, achievable, relevant to you, and time-limited? If not, how could you have redefined the goal so that it met all of those criteria?

2. Analyze how you felt when you didn't achieve this goal. Did you experience negative feelings? Did these feelings affect your motivation to continue pursuing your goal?

3. Reflect on what made it difficult to achieve your goal. Try not to place blame, but do consider the ways in which you may have been responsible for the setback.

4. Identify what you could do differently to achieve this goal now and how you could maintain your motivation and stay positive. Also, who could help you reach this goal? List the names and contact information for personal or campus resources who could provide support if you experience this setback again.

Applying Your Skills

CONSTRUCTING SMART GOALS

This activity gives you practice turning broad, general goals into specific, measurable, and time-limited goals. We aren't focusing on the *A* (achievable) and the *R* (relevant to you) of the SMART acronym, because only you can determine if a goal is achievable or relevant.

First, review the Make Your Goal SMART section of this chapter. Then rewrite the following goals to make them specific, measurable, and time-limited.

1. Goal: *Look for a job soon.*

   SMarT Goal: _____

2. Goal: *Figure out my major.*

   SMarT Goal: _____

3. Goal: *Make some networking contacts before I graduate.*

   SMarT Goal: _____

4. Goal: *Lead a healthier life.*

   SMarT Goal: _____

5. Goal: *Do well in class.*

   SMarT Goal: _____

College Success = Career Success

APPLYING CRITICAL THINKING ON THE JOB

In the workplace, you'll need to think critically and innovatively about procedures, customers, solutions, and new products. Consider the following four scenarios, which require critical thinking. Explain in writing how you'd respond to each scenario.

1. You're hiring a new employee. You've reviewed résumés for two applicants and conducted interviews with them. Both seem friendly and competent. Applicant A has a college degree but very little work experience related to the open position. Applicant B has no degree but a lot of relevant work experience. A college degree is not required for the job. Whom would you select? Why?

2. You're marketing a new breakfast cereal. Do you package and market your product to appeal to children or to parents? Explain your answer and how you would put your marketing strategy into action.

3. You're a customer service agent for a major utility. A customer calls and asks if you can extend the due date of his bill, for which his payment is overdue. (You have the authority to do this.) How would you respond to him, and why? Would any additional information or something about this customer's attitude cause you to be more or less likely to extend the due date? If so, explain your answer. Is it okay to treat one customer differently from another? Why or why not?

4. You own a manufacturing company, and you're considering moving your operations to a country where wages are lower so that you can cut your costs. Describe the factors you'd need to consider before deciding whether to outsource operations to that country. Who would be affected if you did outsource, and how? Who would be affected if you kept the operations in your home country, and how?

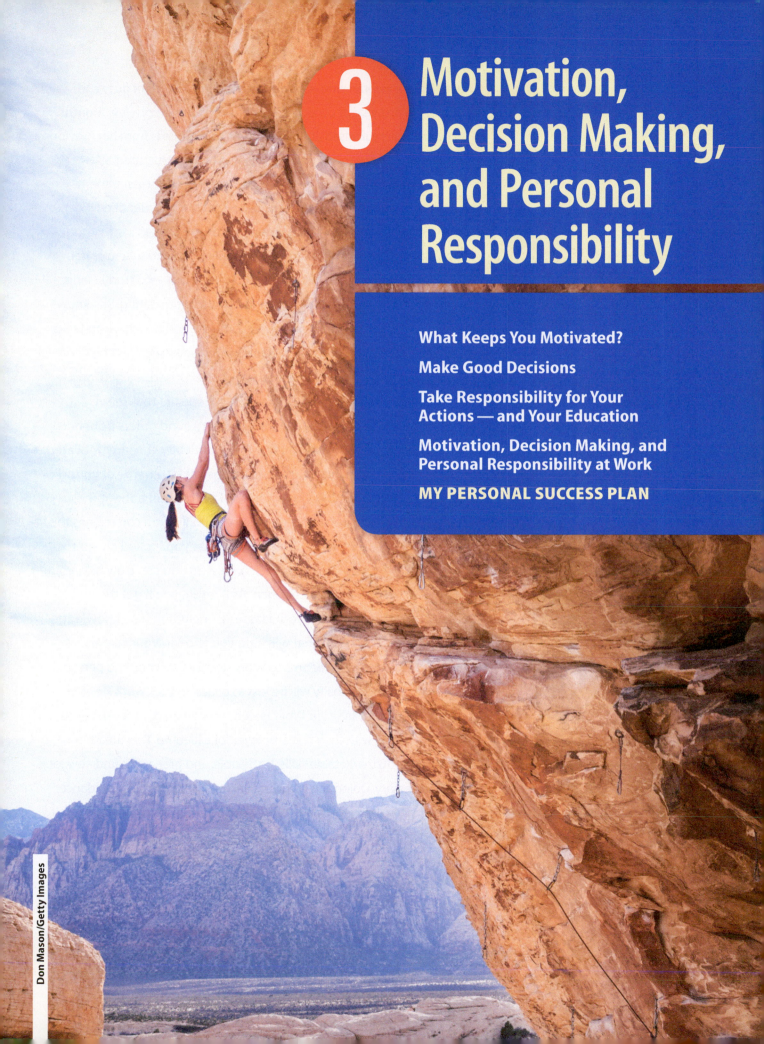

3 Motivation, Decision Making, and Personal Responsibility

What Keeps You Motivated?

Make Good Decisions

Take Responsibility for Your Actions — and Your Education

Motivation, Decision Making, and Personal Responsibility at Work

MY PERSONAL SUCCESS PLAN

Meet Nadia, a veteran who recently returned from a tour of duty and began her first year of college. Nadia has been in school a few months now, and she's surprised at how different college life is from her previous experiences. In the military Nadia's life was highly structured; she maintained a constant schedule and received her duty assignments from her commanding officer and other superiors that clearly identified what she needed to do, when, and with whom. In college, Nadia's instructors don't provide as much structure. They expect Nadia to schedule her own time and figure out how—and how much—to study. Nadia finds this new freedom exciting but also intimidating. She knows it's up to her to stay motivated, make good decisions, and take responsibility for achieving her own goals.

Like Nadia, you may be surprised, excited, and intimidated by aspects of college life that seem unfamiliar, even if your background differs from hers. As a result, you may have difficulty staying motivated, making smart choices, and taking charge of your learning. But by understanding more about these important college survival skills, you can restore the initial enthusiasm you felt as you looked ahead to your first term at school. And you can truly *own* your college experience. As a result, you'll get the most value from your classes — including new knowledge and skills that will help you excel in your career.

In fact, motivation, decision making, and personal responsibility will be just as critical in your work life as in your college life. Why? Recent college graduates can't expect to stay with their first employer for a lifetime. They need to develop marketable skills, be flexible, and prepare to find new jobs if necessary. Doing this involves seeking out mentors for guidance, regularly assessing your abilities and needs, and creating action plans to build new skills and strengthen others. In short, to be competitive in today's work world, you need to assume responsibility for your own success.

In this chapter you'll learn how to activate three forces that will keep you motivated in school: believing you can succeed, viewing your coursework as relevant to your goals, and cultivating a positive attitude. In addition, you'll learn strategies you can use to make careful decisions and take personal responsibility for your education. Finally, you'll see how each of these skills can help you excel in your professional life.

Don Mason/Getty Images

ACES Reflection:
Motivation, Decision Making, and Personal Responsibility

ACES
Academic & Career Excellence System

Take a moment to reflect on your Motivation, Decision Making, and Personal Responsibility score on ACES. Find your score and add it in the box to the right.

This score measures your beliefs about how well you stay motivated, make decisions, and take responsibility for your learning. Do you think it's an accurate snapshot of your current skills in these areas? Why or why not?

- **IF YOU SCORED IN THE HIGH RANGE** and you think this score is accurate, you may be very good at staying motivated, making careful decisions, and taking responsibility for your education. This is great news! Now, though, look for new ways to improve. As you read this chapter, focus on developing even better ways to stay motivated, make decisions, and actively drive your own learning. The more strategies you build up, the better prepared you'll be when you run into those inevitable moments of feeling overwhelmed.

- **IF YOU SCORED IN THE MODERATE OR LOW RANGE**, don't be discouraged. You *can* strengthen your motivation, learn how to make good decisions, and take more responsibility for your learning. This chapter is filled with tips you can begin using now — and you can start with the ideas below!

My ACES Score ....
- ☐ **High**
- ☐ **Moderate**
- ☐ **Low**

To find your **Motivation, Decision Making, and Personal Responsibility score**, go to the LaunchPad for *Connections*, Second Edition.

LaunchPad
macmillan learning

ACES + ACTION

ACES paired with action is what leads to positive change. Now that you've reflected on your ACES results, how will you *use* what you learned about yourself to stay motivated, make better decisions, and take personal responsibility? Try these concrete suggestions, or get inspired and create your own!

▶ **Make a list.** Write down the top three reasons that you're in college, and use that list to get inspired when you grow tired of studying. Remind yourself why you're here each and every day.

▶ **Stay focused.** You're getting ready to read one of the most important chapters of this book. Set a goal to stay focused as you read: plan to take a 5-minute break every hour to refresh yourself.

▶ **Talk to an instructor.** Take responsibility for getting the most out of your education: Identify a course that you find challenging and make an appointment with the instructor to discuss difficult concepts or assignments.

What Keeps You Motivated?

Imagine it's Friday night, and you have five chapters to read in your nutrition textbook to prepare for a test on Monday morning. Let's say that you're not very confident in your reading abilities; you don't think you'll spend much time reading in your career; and you often feel frustrated when you have to read long passages about topics that don't really interest you. Given these feelings and thoughts, you probably won't feel motivated to work through the chapters this weekend.

FIGURE 3.1

Three Key Components of Motivation

self-efficacy: Your belief in your ability to carry out the actions needed to reach a particular goal.

Now imagine a different scenario. Once again, it's Friday night, but this time you have an investigative story due Monday for your journalism class. You believe you're a good writer, and you think you have a meaningful and important story to tell—plus, you love this class. Given these thoughts and emotions, you'll probably feel motivated to work hard on the story over the weekend. Why? You believe you can do a good job, meaning you have strong *self-efficacy* in your journalism skills. You see this writing task as *relevant* to what matters most to you. And you have a positive *attitude* about the task facing you. These are three key components of motivation (see Figure 3.1).

Let's begin by taking a closer look at each component. Then we'll compare two types of motivation—and explore which is more powerful.

Self-Efficacy

Self-efficacy refers to your belief in your ability to carry out the actions needed to reach a particular goal. In other words, you *believe* you can be effective. The stronger your sense of self-efficacy, the more likely you'll do what's needed to achieve your goals and to keep trying even when you encounter setbacks.

Take Moira, who always struggled in her high school Spanish classes. She didn't believe she could improve, so she gave up easily on projects and her grades suffered as a result. If Moira had believed that she could do what was needed to master Spanish, she would have taken action to make it happen—for example, by finding a tutor or joining a study group. Her grades would have ultimately improved. Her sense of hope that she could succeed in school would have been restored. And she would have built new knowledge that would have equipped her for jobs that require Spanish speaking and writing skills.

If you find yourself in a situation like Moira, how can you strengthen your sense of self-efficacy? Try the following tactics, suggested by psychologist Albert Bandura.[1]

- **Experience success.** One important component of a SMART goal is that it's achievable. Achieving a desired goal enhances your self-efficacy beliefs ("I did it once, so I can do it again!") and spurs you to take on your next challenge. In that way, success builds on success. By proving to yourself that you're making progress, as you do when you use the Personal Success Plan, you strengthen your sense of self-efficacy and are more likely to succeed at your next goal.

- **Observe others who are successful.** You can strengthen your self-efficacy beliefs by watching other people complete a task successfully. Psychologists call this process *modeling*. For instance, join a study group and see how students who get the best grades take notes during lectures. Or ask tutors at the math and writing centers to show you which strategies they've used in the past to master the subject matter. Doing so will help motivate you to try these activities yourself in the future.

- **Seek support and encouragement.** Being supported and encouraged in your pursuits helps you believe more strongly in your ability to achieve goals. So surround yourself with people who want you to succeed. Let them know not only when you're struggling but also when you're making progress toward your goals. Their encouragement will help you feel even more confident in your abilities.

Self-Efficacy Secrets. These dance students are building self-efficacy by experiencing successes gained through practice. They can strengthen their self-efficacy even more by observing each other's best techniques and sharing suggestions.

PeopleImages/Getty Images

- **Turn stress into a motivator.** Stress is natural—everyone feels it—and it isn't *always* a bad thing. In fact, a little bit of stress can energize you to tackle a challenge. Too much stress, however, can sap your motivation. The key is to find a middle ground—just enough stress to inspire you, but not so much that it paralyzes you.

Relevance

If you think that a goal has relevance for you—that achieving it will make a positive difference in some way—you'll feel more motivated to work toward that goal. (Remember the R in SMART?) Relevance can even motivate you to achieve a goal that seems boring or unpleasant in the short term, because you know that by meeting this challenge now, you'll get something that's important to you in the long term. For instance, maybe you dread your English composition class. Still, you force yourself to work at the class assignments because you understand that knowing how to write well will help you in your professional life, no matter what career you choose to pursue.

If a subject or an assignment seems irrelevant to your life at first, connect it to something that is relevant. If your motivation for a particular task starts to wane, try out these strategies.

- **Find something interesting in every class.** Almost all academic topics relate to one another in some way. For example, if you're a psychology major taking a history class, you might be able to write a paper on the history of psychoanalytic thought. Even though the paper is for your history class, the topic connects with something that interests you. If you remind yourself of such connections, seemingly irrelevant projects will become more relevant than you thought at first—and you'll be more motivated to do a good job on them.

- **Connect coursework to your long-term goals.** Doing well in college can give you the knowledge and skills needed to achieve your long-term goals—such as going to graduate school, getting into a highly competitive program like nursing, or effectively managing family or community responsibilities. Always try to keep the big picture in mind.

- **Focus on practical benefits.** Remind yourself of the practical benefits of achieving a goal—for instance, "If I can maintain a 3.5 GPA, I can keep my scholarship" or "If I pass this class, I'll avoid the cost of retaking it."

❧ CONNECT
TO MY EXPERIENCE

Write down two goals you have for yourself right now—one that you're highly motivated to achieve and one that you're less motivated to achieve. What is the difference between these two goals? How could you link the latter goal to something that's highly relevant to your life, in order to improve your motivation to succeed?

The Power of Relevance. When your goals have relevance to you, you'll stay motivated to achieve them—even in the face of serious setbacks. Take Malala Yousafzai, the Pakistani activist for female education and the youngest person to ever receive the Nobel Peace Prize. After a gunman shot and nearly killed her and the Taliban threatened her life and her father's, her commitment to education only grew stronger—so strong that she's now attending college. ODD ANDERSEN/AFP/Getty Images

- **Build transferable skills.** Use general-education courses to develop transferable skills like note taking, writing, time management, and critical thinking.
- **Focus on a love of learning.** The feeling of accomplishment you get from mastering new material—even if that material isn't your favorite—can give a task meaning.

Attitude

A positive attitude is a beautiful thing: It makes you more resilient in the face of difficulties, helps you learn from your mistakes, and increases your enjoyment when you succeed. It's also a powerful motivator that can keep you energized and focused on your goals. Use the following strategies to stay positive, even when a project, an assignment, or a class leaves you feeling uninspired.

- **Identify something positive resulting from the work you're doing.** Even little rewards can make difficult tasks more pleasant. Look for those small moments of enjoyment or positivity, and take time to appreciate them. For instance, if you're reading your ecology textbook, you might unexpectedly find a photo of the natural world that takes your breath away. Or if you're working with a classmate on a calculus assignment, you might realize that you have a lot in common and that this person could become a good friend.
- **If possible, take at least one course in your intended major each term.** That way, you can spend some time each week focused on the content you most enjoy.
- **Think and speak positively.** Monitor your *self-talk*: what you tell yourself about the courses you're taking, the assignments you're working on, and your goals. Positive self-talk—thinking positive thoughts and making positive statements—protects you from stress, promotes creative thinking, aids in problem solving, and can help you stay motivated.[2] Interestingly, *how* you

Fake It 'til You Make It.
Maintaining a positive attitude can help you remain motivated to work toward your most challenging goals. So practice thinking positive thoughts and making positive statements about yourself and your studies. Does positive self-talk feel awkward or contrived to you? If so, remind yourself that sometimes you have to "fake it 'til you make it." marekuliasz/Shutterstock

TABLE 3.1

How Key Components of Motivation Help You Achieve Goals

Goal	Strong self-efficacy	High relevance	Positive attitude
Conduct research in the library for an English composition paper	I used the online catalog successfully last week, so I should be able to find the materials I need this week.	This isn't my favorite class, but I'll need to conduct research in other classes, too. If I build my skills now, I can apply them in my other classes.	Instead of telling myself that this project will be boring, I'll think about how good it will feel to check this task off my to-do list.
Read three chapters in my textbook for Foundations of Education	I've worked with a tutor to create a reading schedule, so I know what I have to do to finish the chapters on time.	I want to become a teacher, so this reading is relevant to my long-term goal.	I feel too tired to complete all my reading this weekend, but I do like the boxes in the chapter where real people share their stories. I'll read those first to energize myself.
Do a group marketing campaign project for my business class	Last spring I worked with some neighbors to design a fund-raising campaign for our local after-school program. I can apply what I learned about working in a group to this assignment.	I want to do creative work and eventually manage a team. This project will let me create something I can show employers as part of my portfolio.	One of my classmates on this project seems especially creative. I think it'll be fun to work with her on this assignment.

refer to yourself when engaging in self-talk makes a difference. According to one recent study, addressing yourself as "you" rather than "I" tends to be more effective.[3] So, the next time you're studying for an upcoming biology exam, you may be tempted to mutter something like "There's no way I'll ever remember this stuff on the test." Instead, try telling yourself, "You can understand the concept of photosynthesis; you just need to stay focused and spend time mastering this topic."

When your self-efficacy is strong, your task is relevant, and you have a positive attitude, you'll feel especially motivated to work toward a goal. See Table 3.1 for examples of how these components fit together to help you achieve what is important to you.

Tap into Your Internal Motivation

In your school, work, and personal life, multiple motivations underlie the choices you make. Maybe you decided to go to college because you enjoy learning new things, but also because you need to build skills that will get you a good job. Perhaps you've joined a study group because you'll meet friendly people, but also because it will help you get better grades. Each of these decisions reflects the two kinds of motivation identified by psychologists: intrinsic and extrinsic motivation. **Intrinsic motivation** stems from your inner desire to achieve a specific outcome. **Extrinsic motivation** derives from forces external to you, such as an expected reward or a negative outcome that you want to avoid. If you study hard because you enjoy the feeling of success, then you're motivated for intrinsic reasons. If you study hard because you need to maintain a 3.0 GPA to keep your scholarship, then you're motivated for extrinsic reasons. Sometimes you'll be

intrinsic motivation:
Motivation that stems from your inner desire to achieve a specific outcome.

extrinsic motivation:
Motivation that derives from forces external to you, such as an expected reward or a negative outcome that you want to avoid.

influenced by both intrinsic and extrinsic motivation. For example, you may genuinely enjoy the subject you're studying, but also work hard to keep up your GPA.

Both types of motivators can prompt you to meet your goals, but intrinsic motivation has some special benefits over extrinsic motivation. First, intrinsic motivation is usually more reliable because you control it. How? You stay focused on the positive feelings you'll experience when you achieve the goal, and that keeps you motivated. Also, intrinsic motivation is especially helpful in unfamiliar or confusing situations — both of which can occur during your first year in college. For example, your professors will assign course material, but they may not tell you *how* to learn it. You have to figure that out, and intrinsic motivation can spur you on.

But how can you find an approach to building intrinsic motivation that works for you? Many techniques are covered in this chapter: using positive self-talk, identifying positive aspects, and finding something interesting in challenging situations. In addition, leaders of industry, professional athletes, psychologists, salespeople, Navy SEALs, and others often use another powerful technique — visualization.[4] In visualization you imagine the outcome you'd like to see happen and the steps it takes to get there using your senses, including sight, sound, smell, and feel. Visualizing a desirable outcome can stir up positive emotions and motivate you to work hard. It prompts you to think about your values, the relationship between your short-term and long-term goals, and the steps needed to reach these goals.

To visualize effectively, relax and clear your mind. Imagine your future self accomplishing the goal you set out to achieve. Where are you? Who are you with? What are you doing? How do you feel? Use these images and feelings to maintain motivation. You'll have a chance to try a visualization activity at the end of the chapter.

Make Good Decisions

In your school, work, and personal life, you might make hundreds of decisions every day. Some choices are straightforward and quick, like selecting tuna over turkey for lunch. Others are more complex, with higher stakes. For example, should you stay in school even if your spouse isn't supportive? Should you buy a car to get to class even though you're already carrying heavy credit card debt? What major

> ## "Breaking things down helps me stay motivated even when I don't enjoy the work as much.

NAME
Patricia Perez

SCHOOL
Georgia State University

MAJOR
Nutrition

CAREER GOAL
Registered Dietitian

Courtesy of Patricia Perez

STAYING MOTIVATED IN COLLEGE

Many factors keep me motivated in school. As an international student, it's very important for me to be successful in college, not just for my own fulfilment but also to keep my scholarships. My family members, who still live in Venezuela, are working extremely hard to support me and give me an opportunity for a bright and successful future. I feel it is my responsibility to be successful not just for myself, but also for them.

I'm also motivated to earn my degree so I can become a well-prepared registered dietitian, and when the time comes, I can go back to my country to help rebuild its health care system. I want to help others with my knowledge and change people's lives through the benefits of eating well.

When I'm in class for my favorite subjects, staying motivated isn't a problem — I can sit down and enjoy listening to the lecture. However, right now, I'm taking a chemistry class that I'm struggling in, which makes it very difficult for me to stay motivated and get good grades. For this reason, I spend a little bit of time each day studying. Breaking things down helps me stay motivated even when I don't enjoy the work as much. I usually have a to-do list for that day's assignments and crossing out one thing per day for my chemistry class makes me feel I've accomplished something really, really good. It's just a rewarding feeling that encourages me to continue!

Additionally, I attend supplemental instruction (SI) sessions at least once per week. SI sessions are classes taught by students who previously took the same class and aced it. A great part about those sessions is that I can invest time in studying while also meeting other people. For my chemistry class, I met another student, and we set up times during the week to study the material together. We're now great friends, and we encourage each other to excel in this class, even though it's not our favorite!

> **YOUR TURN** Like Patricia, do you have particular strategies that you use to stay motivated in courses that you find challenging or less interesting? If so, what are those strategies? How well do they work for you?

will you declare? The outcomes of the choices you make, along with the complexity or difficulty of such choices, can affect your motivation. And your level of motivation can ultimately influence whether you achieve the goals that have personal meaning for you.

With tough choices, you need to weigh your options carefully, but you also have to make reasonable decisions that help you move forward. If you obsess

⟩ CONNECT
TO MY EXPERIENCE

Select one choice you've made recently—personal, academic, or professional—and reflect on the decision-making process you used. In a brief paragraph, answer these questions: What decision-making steps did you take? Which steps *didn't* you take? How could the steps you didn't take have been helpful to you?

about making a perfect decision, you can fall victim to "analysis paralysis," which can sap your motivation and leave you feeling hopeless about selecting a course of action.

How do you make a reasonable decision even if you're feeling overwhelmed or frightened by a choice you're facing? Try the following steps, which have a lot in common with the steps in the Personal Success Plan.

1. **Identify the decision to be made.** Articulating the decision sets the stage for the rest of the process.

2. **Know yourself.** Identify your strengths, weaknesses, interests, and values. This self-knowledge helps you think broadly about your options.

3. **Identify your options.** With a friend, colleague, or family member, brainstorm options available to you and write them down on a sheet of paper.

4. **Gather information about each option.** Research the details of each option you've listed, such as what actions you'd need to take if you chose that option and who could help you take those actions.

5. **Evaluate your options.** List the pros and cons of each option. Rate each option based on how attractive it is to you and how it will affect the people who are important to you.

6. **Select the best option.** The option with the highest rating is often your most reasonable choice. If you feel nervous about committing to this choice, remind yourself that you can always change your mind later if the decision doesn't work out as well as you had hoped.

7. **Develop and implement an action plan.** List the actions you'll take to follow through on your decision. Then take those actions.

8. **Evaluate the outcomes of your decision.** Determine whether your decision has worked out. If not, follow this eight-step process again to arrive at a new decision.

Making complex, high-stakes decisions will always be challenging, but this process can help you take a systematic approach (see Figure 3.2 and Table 3.2). Also, the more you practice using it, the easier it gets.

FIGURE 3.2
The Decision-Making Process

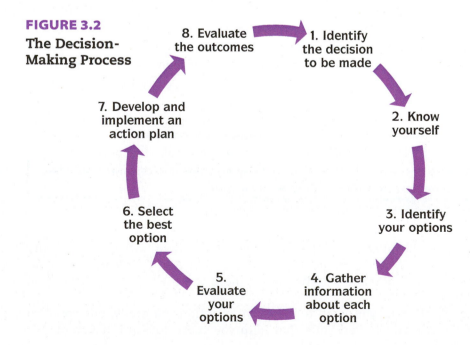

TABLE 3.2
Examples of the Decision-Making Process

Step	Example 1	Example 2
Identify the decision to be made	I need to select a major.	My mom is sick in another country. Should I leave school to take care of her, or should I continue my studies?
Know yourself	I love history, art, music, and literature, but I'm not an artist or a musician. I enjoy interacting with people. I value family, so I don't want to work sixty hours a week. I may want to work in a museum or in arts management.	I value my family and my education. I'm the oldest of three, so my mom relies on me a lot. I'm also the first in my family to go to college, which is a point of pride for my loved ones.
Identify your options	I'm considering a major in art history, finance, business, or psychology. Taking various electives is also an option.	I called my brother back home and discussed options: Take a year off from school to help mom, or stay in school and my brother will care for mom.
Gather information about each option	I'll learn more by meeting with my academic adviser, visiting the career center library, and interviewing recent graduates who are working in museums and the entertainment industry.	I'll research the answers to some key questions: If I take time off from school, can I keep all my credits? Is my brother in a better position to help? Can we arrange for someone else to visit during the day?
Evaluate your options	The information I gathered suggests that art history and business could prepare me for jobs in the arts.	Taking a year off from school would make things tough for me. My brother works days and could be with mom every evening. Hiring a visiting nurse to check on mom at lunch would ensure regular care for mom during the day.
Select the best option	I'll major in art history but take electives in business and management.	We'll have a nurse visit mom once a day and my brother will be there each night.
Develop and implement an action plan	I'll declare my major and meet with my new art history academic adviser to create a course plan.	My brother lives near mom, so he'll interview nurse candidates. My brother and I will split the costs. We'll also ask several of mom's friends to check in on her when they're able.
Evaluate the outcomes of your decision	I've taken courses in my major for one term and I like them, but my gut tells me that declaring a business major will give me the most options after graduation. I'll need to do more career research before I'm comfortable with my decision.	This arrangement has worked out well. Mom's nurse and friends check in on her during the day, and my brother comes by after work. I'm doing well in school, but I really miss mom—I'll visit her during the next school break.

Take Responsibility for Your Actions— and Your Education

We're all accustomed to some degree of personal responsibility in our lives, but in college, personal responsibility is a whole new ball game. For one thing, if you just graduated from high school, you'll likely notice that in college you have more independence *and* more responsibility than you had in high school. And if you entered college a number of years after graduating from high school, you're probably used to personal responsibility, but you'll also find yourself accountable

Cross That Finish Line. No matter what your goals are, only you can cross the finish line and reach them. By taking personal responsibility in college, you drive your own learning and growth, rather than look to others to lead you. That's real power — but you have to embrace it. Cultura/Getty Images

✎ CONNECT TO MY RESOURCES

List your *most* important responsibilities this term. Identify two resources, either on campus or in your community, that can help you build a plan for managing these high-priority responsibilities.

for new kinds of decisions. For example, you may be accustomed to balancing child care and work, but now you'll have another area to look out for: staying focused on your studies.

Only you can decide how to balance your various responsibilities as you pursue your degree and that's okay: Ownership is a good thing. In fact, taking personal responsibility for your education is empowering. It puts *you* in control of maintaining your motivation and making smart choices. For instance, if you don't see why a particular assignment is important, *you* can find reasons to care. If you keep missing class, *you* can set two alarms so you'll wake up on time.

By taking responsibility in these ways, you drive your learning and your personal growth. You also prove to yourself that you value your education and show respect for your instructors and the classmates who depend on you to complete group projects and assignments. Taking responsibility for our actions isn't always easy, but every college student—and every professional in the workplace—needs to do it.

In the next section, we'll explore four ways to take ownership of your success: two that involve putting yourself in the right frame of mind to take responsibility for your actions, and two that involve taking concrete steps to get the most out of your education.

Develop a Growth Mindset

growth mindset: The belief that one can further develop or improve one's talents, skills, and abilities.

Stanford University psychologist Carol Dweck proposes that there are two types of students. Those with a **growth mindset** believe they can change aspects of their lives and further develop or improve their talents, skills, and abilities.[5] They assume personal responsibility for their success and learn as much as they can from their failures. Maintaining a growth mindset and believing that they can improve is motivational for these students.

fixed mindset: The belief that one cannot improve one's talents, skills, and abilities.

By contrast, students with a **fixed mindset** believe they can't improve their talents, skills, and abilities, and tend to see themselves as victims of circumstance, which saps their motivation completely. Take Justin, who turned in a project late

Keep a Growth Mindset. When you have a growth mindset, you're willing to see setbacks and disappointments from a whole new angle. Instead of coming up with excuses or blaming others for failures, you look for the lessons hidden in these experiences — such as what you can do differently in the future to get a better result.
serg_dibrova/Shutterstock

and was penalized one letter grade. He blamed work and family demands for missing the deadline, and he didn't reflect on his behaviors or learn how to manage his time more effectively; as a result, he struggled to turn in his work on time when the next project came around.

When you have a growth mindset, you take responsibility for setbacks. You examine the behaviors that led to the failure, identify what you could have done differently, and apply those lessons to the next situation. For example, if Justin had adopted a growth mindset after losing a letter grade, he might have identified behavior changes to make in the future, such as exchanging work shifts as a deadline approaches or working on assignments when his kids are in school.

If you feel that your abilities are fixed and you blame others for setbacks, you miss an opportunity to learn how you can improve in the future. Adopting a growth mindset is a win-win situation: When you fail, you take steps to improve, and when you succeed, you get the credit for making a positive change. Either way, you become a better student and get more value from your education.

Understand Why Outcomes Occur

In addition to growth mindset, another related factor influences our sense of personal responsibility: Whether we believe that *we* control what happens to us or that outcomes occur as a result of someone (or something) outside of ourselves.

Psychologists have studied how people explain outcomes for almost a century, and in doing so, they've developed a concept called **attribution theory**. According to this theory, we tend to attribute what happens in our lives to either *internal* or *external* causes (those within ourselves or outside ourselves), and we tend to believe that those causes are either *stable* or *transient* (meaning that they stay the same or they can change). Generally speaking, when we can attribute causes to factors that are both internal and transient, we're in a better position to take responsibility for our choices and the outcomes we face: We believe that *we* are in control and that things can change for the better next time around.

attribution theory: Theory about how people use information to explain the events that occur in their lives.

TABLE 3.3

Possible Explanations for Poor Test Performance

	Stable	Transient
Internal	• I'm not smart. • I'm bad at math. • I'm a procrastinator.	• I didn't study. • I was sick that day. • I crammed the night before the exam.
External	• I had a bad instructor. • This college is too hard. • My life is too hectic for me to succeed in school.	• It was a hard exam. • The course material was difficult. • Other obligations prevented me from preparing for this exam.

To get a better sense of how attribution theory works, let's take a look at Raisa, who received a poor grade on her first math test. If Raisa attributes her grade to the fact that she's not a good learner and never has been, she's attributing her failure to internal and stable causes—causes within herself that she doesn't think will change (see Table 3.3). But if Raisa credits her grade to the fact that she didn't study enough for this one exam, she's attributing her performance to internal and transient causes—causes within herself that she can change next time. This may keep her motivated to work toward a different, more positive result on an upcoming test.

And what about external causes? Attributing outcomes to external causes can be problematic because it allows us to dodge responsibility. For example, say Raisa blames her poor test grade on the quality of her instructor ("My professor doesn't explain concepts well"), which is a stable, external cause. Or say she blames it on the specific test itself ("This exam had too many essay questions"), which is a transient, external cause. In either case, if Raisa doesn't think she played a role in the outcome, why would she be motivated to pursue a different result next time?

Of course, there may be times when external causes really are to blame for outcomes. For example, if Raisa performed poorly on her test because she had to attend to a sick relative unexpectedly rather than study, she could appropriately attribute the outcome to an external and transient cause. But even in this situation, Raisa has the opportunity to create change: She can schedule an appointment with her instructor, explain the reasons for her performance, and request an opportunity to earn extra credit toward a future exam.

How you explain the outcomes of your efforts in this class and others can have a profound impact on your motivation and future success. If you're realistic about why certain outcomes occur *and* you have a growth mindset about your own abilities ("I can change and get better"), you're well on the way to improving your performance, taking responsibility, and putting yourself in a positive frame of mind.

Take an Active Approach to Your Learning

In addition to developing a growth mindset and realistically explaining outcomes, you can take personal responsibility for yourself and your education by becoming an *active learner*. Many high schools have passive learning environments, where teachers are considered experts who impart knowledge and students memorize the information that is presented. By contrast, college instructors expect students to participate fully in the learning experience and make it their own—for example, by thinking critically, engaging in discussion and debate, and applying their knowledge to real-world settings. Instead of simply attending class and listening to your instructor, in college you identify and use your own *learning strategies*, which are methods for mastering course material.

Consider Cody, who is studying to become a certified medical assistant and is taking a course in medical terminology. While reading one evening, he encounters an unfamiliar term: *neuropathy*. Deciding to puzzle out the meaning instead of Googling the word's definition, Cody recalls information he learned in his biology and anatomy courses: *Neurology* is the study of the nervous system, and *pathology* means "disease." He combines these two pieces of information and determines that *neuropathy* means "a disease of the nerves." By coming up with his own strategy to learn this material, he has adopted an active learning approach: connecting past learning to a new term to figure out its meaning.

As you read this book, you'll find dozens of active learning strategies — from the best ways to schedule your time and preview your textbooks to tactics for effective note taking and paper writing. (The ACES + Action suggestions at the beginning of the chapter are active learning strategies, too!) Not all strategies work in all situations, but if you experiment, you'll figure out which ones work best for you with each course and assignment. In the meantime, get a head start by giving these strategies a try.

"What Do *You* Think This Term Means?" Joining a study group can help you take an active approach to your learning in college. You can discuss assignments with other group members, brainstorm which questions you might see on an upcoming test, or debate concepts from class. Hybrid Images/AGE Fotostock

1. **Get involved.** Asking questions in class can help clarify content you find confusing. Briefly summarize what you do understand about the topic, and then ask about the parts that are unclear. In addition, form or join study groups to discuss assignments, brainstorm possible test questions, or debate ideas you're learning about in class.

2. **Look for connections.** What you learn in one class often relates to something you're learning in another class or to an experience you've had in the past. As Cody discovered, connecting new, unfamiliar material to other material is a powerful active learning strategy. When you make such connections, you're more likely to remember what you've learned, which means you can use your new knowledge long after the class ends.

3. **Seek applications for your new knowledge.** Look for ways you can apply what you're learning to your personal life, your current job, or your future career. Applying what you've learned is an important critical thinking skill and makes the concepts you're learning more concrete.

❧ CONNECT TO MY CLASSES
Pick an active-learning strategy described in this section and explain how you'll apply it in a class this week or next.

Think about Thinking and Learning

If you're an active learner who takes responsibility for your education, you monitor your learning and adjust your strategies based on your results. You're also aware of how you think and learn. Scholars call this awareness **metacognition**, which means "thinking about thinking" or "thinking about learning." For instance, you're engaging in metacognition if you notice that you have an easier time learning biology than learning European history, if you discover that one

metacognition: Thinking about how you think and learn.

study strategy works better for you than another, and every time you reflect on your ACES results. You're also using metacognition when you consider why outcomes occur (attribution theory), and determine whether you have a fixed or a growth mindset. And when you think metacognitively in any of these ways, you can use what you learn about yourself to take targeted action.

To get a better sense of how metacognition works, consider Cholena's experience. Cholena got a C– on her first writing assignment in Freshman Composition, but she didn't lose hope; instead, she turned into a metacognitive detective, asking herself questions about what could have gone wrong, and focused on getting help. She reflected on her instructor's comments and how she had approached the assignment by asking herself: Did I spend enough time creating an outline? Did I revise my first draft and proofread the final version for errors? Did I ask anyone else to give me feedback before handing it in? She also took the paper to a tutor in the writing center. Together, they discussed her writing strategies, the instructor's comments, and approaches she might take to get better grades in the future.

Research shows that metacognition promotes learning.[6] Students who reflect on their approach to coursework remember more information, apply that information to new situations more effectively, and get higher grades. To make use of metacognition to improve your performance in school, try these strategies.

- **Plan and organize.** Set learning goals and preview assignments so you can decide how best to approach them.

- **Monitor your progress.** Check your progress against time lines you set for yourself. Troubleshoot problems. Ask yourself whether you're doing your best work or whether you could improve your effort.

- **Evaluate your results and make adjustments.** Consider how well your learning strategies helped you achieve a goal. If you weren't as successful as you had hoped, plan how to change your strategy the next time.

These metacognitive strategies may seem familiar because you've seen many of them before. Critical thinking, goal setting, and decision making also call for you to evaluate your learning, apply new knowledge, reflect on your results, and make changes as needed to get better results. Since these skills are all connected, you can use them over and over again, in any setting.

Take a moment now to assess your metacognitive skills. What are you thinking about as you read this section of the chapter? Are you daydreaming, contemplating all the assignments that are due in your other classes, or pondering what to make for dinner? Or are you considering how these concepts can benefit you, be useful in other courses and assignments, and help your future career? If you reflect on both the *content* you're studying and the *processes* you're using to understand and apply material, you're well on your way to becoming an active, metacognitive learner.

Think Your Thoughts. How do you usually think through class assignments? What study strategies work best for you? When you explore these kinds of questions, you're using metacognition — thinking about how you think and learn. And the more you use it, the greater the chance you'll improve your performance in school.

PeopleImages/Getty Images

spotlight on research

In this chapter we've suggested that your success depends on a number of different factors, including motivation, mindset, and a willingness to take personal responsibility for your actions. According to a recent study, there's one more item to add to this list of important success factors: a related concept called *grit*.[7] You can think of grit as your level of perseverance and passion for achieving long-term goals: Students with higher levels of grit would be more persistent in working toward their goals than students with lower levels of grit. "Gritty" students are also more likely to persist when faced with setbacks, distractions, or boredom.

In this study, researchers set out to explore the relationship between grit and metacognition; did students with higher levels of grit also use more metacognitive learning strategies than other students? To investigate, they administered a measure of grit to more than 200 college-aged students, as well as a measure of planning and learning strategy skills (metacognitive skills). When they analyzed these two variables to determine their relationship to each other, here's what they discovered:

▶ Grit was strongly and positively related to metacognitive skills: Students with high levels of grit tended to use more metacognitive strategies than students who reported lower levels of grit.

▶ In addition, grit was an even better predictor of metacognitive learning strategies than prior academic achievement. In other words, your success in school is more a function of your persistence and drive than how well you've performed in the past.

THE BOTTOM LINE

It's time to get gritty. By working hard to go after your goals, you may also become a more metacognitive, thoughtful learner. Your future success is in your hands!

Grit Leads to Success!

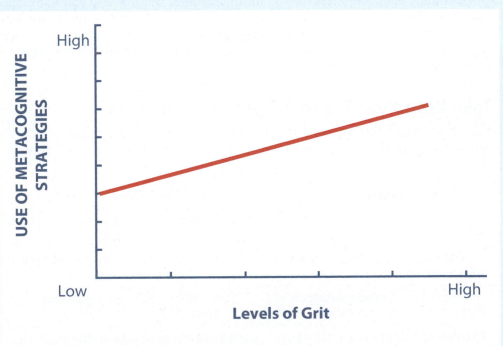

Students with high levels of grit tended to use more metacognitive strategies.

Information from C. A. Wolters and M. Hussain, "Investigating Grit and Its Relations with College Students' Self-Regulated Learning and Academic Achievement," *Metacognition Learning* 10 (2015): 293–311.

Motivation, Decision Making, and Personal Responsibility at Work

Imagine that you're a manager who needs to fill an open position. What qualities would you look for in a job candidate? You'd likely look for someone who can stay motivated, make good choices, and take responsibility for his or her actions—all characteristics you'll develop by taking this course and applying what you learn in this textbook. So keep up the good work! If you do, you'll be more likely to get a rewarding job, perform well in that job, and advance quickly in your career.

Apply Motivational Strategies on the Job

Staying motivated is just as important in your professional life as it is in college. In fact, psychologists who focus on workplace success study the role of motivation closely,[8] since you have to stay motivated in order to be a productive employee who does your best work. Look at Table 3.4 to see how staying motivated in school relates to staying motivated in the workplace.

Make Good Choices at Work

On the job, you make choices every day that can impact your career and your organization. Sometimes choices are tough. If a salesperson on your team gives a friend an unauthorized discount, what do you do? If you own a restaurant and revenues decrease, do you lay off employees or raise prices? In cases like these, the decision-making process outlined in this chapter can help you make sensible choices.

Of course, not every decision you make will work out the way you had hoped it would. When that happens, stay positive, rethink strategies that aren't working, and consider how best to make a change. By doing so, you'll demonstrate meta-cognition and a growth mindset. *Choose* to own your successes and take steps to bounce back from your mistakes.

Take Responsibility to Boost Career Success

Taking responsibility on the job can enhance your career prospects. In fact, research shows that employees who have more independence—and therefore

TABLE 3.4

Staying Motivated in School and at Work

Staying motivated in school	Staying motivated at work
Take a variety of courses so that at least a few each term motivate you.	With your boss, design your job so that you can use a variety of skills.
Establish goals in each class that feel relevant to you.	Find aspects of your job that relate to your passions.
Develop active-learning strategies and participate in your education.	Take responsibility for your workplace choices.
Evaluate the results of your learning strategies, and if needed, adjust your strategies to get better results.	Reflect on the results of your work efforts, and if needed, change your strategies to get better results.
Identify your strengths and take advantage of them. Find ways to address your weaknesses. Graduate!	Seek out opportunities for growth and advancement at work.

> "Knowing the facts and the options available can help you make the best decision."

NAME
Tiona Blyden

PROFESSION
Entrepreneur

SCHOOL
Morgan State University

DEGREE
Bachelor of Science

MAJORS
Communications and Broadcast Journalism

MAKING DECISIONS ON THE JOB

As an entrepreneur and small-business owner, decision making is critical for my success as well as my family's livelihood. While I make lots of small decisions every day, major decisions about my business can make a difference in success or failure. I recently had a critical decision to make regarding staffing in my business. I was spending a lot of time working and wasn't seeing much income for all of my efforts. I knew it was time to make a decision about how to move the business forward.

I started with a self-evaluation. Through this process of introspection and gathering information about myself, I laid out the fact that I've always had lots of ideas and tons of passion to give back to the world. I also discovered that I'm sometimes short on execution, or seeing my ideas through to the end. I was also spending three to four hours a day conducting administrative tasks for the business—not a good use of my time and creative energy. Using this information, I evaluated my options and made the major decision to hire a personal assistant to free up time. This was a significant expense for my small business, but I believed that it was the best choice.

Looking back on the past few months, this has turned out to be a wonderful choice. I'm working fewer hours and my income has increased. To be an effective leader and catapult your business to success, you have to make tough decisions. Knowing the facts and the options available can help you make the best decision. Often the best option requires a leap of faith.

YOUR TURN Have you had to make a tough decision in a work situation? If so, how did it turn out? What did you learn from the outcome of your decision?

more responsibility—experience greater job satisfaction, better performance evaluations, and more success.[9]

Taking responsibility can also help you deal with work challenges. Psychologist Marla Gottschalk describes one common challenge in today's workplace: Feeling as though you don't have enough time to complete all the tasks facing you.[10] When this happens, people sometimes point to others as the source of the problem: "My coworkers are always interrupting me" or "We have too many meetings." (In attribution theory, these are external attributions, since other people are getting the blame.) Gottschalk suggests another response: acknowledging your role in the problem. Ask yourself: Do I value my own time and communicate that to my coworkers? Or: What am I going to do to remedy this situation? With this approach, you make yourself part of the solution to your problem. And that means *you* can control your own effectiveness at work.

my personal success plan

MOTIVATION, DECISION MAKING, AND PERSONAL RESPONSIBILITY

Based on your ACES results and what you learned in this chapter, are you inspired to set a new goal aimed at improving your motivation, decision-making skills, or ability to take personal responsibility? If so, the Personal Success Plan can walk you through the goal-setting process. Read the advice and examples; then sketch out your ideas in the space provided.

To access the Personal Success Plan online, go to the LaunchPad for *Connections*, Second Edition.

1 IDENTIFY A GOAL

Choose a motivation, decision making, or personal responsibility goal to work toward this term. Here are some general ideas you might draw from; you can also create a goal of your own.

- ▶ Identify something that motivates me in every class.
- ▶ Practice using positive self-talk.
- ▶ Use the decision-making process to make choices.
- ▶ Develop a growth mindset.
- ▶ Become an active learner.

2 MAKE YOUR GOAL SMART

Rewrite your specific goal so that it's SMART, and make sure to use the SMART goal checklist.

SAMPLE: I'm struggling to stay motivated in my sociology class. By the end of the week, I'll figure out how to make the course content more relevant to my interests and goals.

3 CREATE AN ACTION PLAN

Outline the specific steps you'll take to achieve your SMART goal, and note when you'll complete each step.

SAMPLE: Tomorrow, I'll ask my instructor if I can write my term paper on a topic I'm passionate about: factors that cause economic inequality.

4 LIST BARRIERS AND SOLUTIONS

Think about possible barriers to your action steps; then brainstorm solutions for overcoming them.

SAMPLE: My instructor might reject my term paper idea. If she does, I'll explain my areas of interest to see if there's another topic that I'm just as passionate about that would meet the course requirements.

5 ACT AND EVALUATE OUTCOMES

Now that your plan is in place, take action. Record each action step as you take it. Then evaluate whether you achieved your SMART goal, and make any adjustments needed to get better results in the future.

SAMPLE: My instructor and I were able to identify several alternative topics that interest me and would meet the course requirements.

6 CONNECT TO CAREER

List the skills you're building as you progress toward your SMART goal. How will you use these skills to land a job and succeed at work?

SAMPLE: I'm learning more about my interests and how to incorporate them into my coursework. These skills could help me work with a supervisor to design job responsibilities that appeal to these interests.

my personal success plan

1 my general goal

2 my SMART goal

☐ Specific ☐ Measurable ☐ Achievable ☐ Relevant ☐ Time-limited

3 my action plan

4 my barriers/solutions

5 my actions/outcomes

6 my career connection

CHAPTER SUMMARY

In this chapter you learned how motivation, decision making, and personal responsibility affect college and career success. Revisit the following key points, and reflect on how you can use this information to support your success now and in the future.

- Three key components of motivation are *self-efficacy*, or your belief in your ability to carry out the actions needed to reach a particular goal; the *relevance* of a goal to you; and your *attitude* toward the goal. The stronger these components are, the more motivated you'll feel to work toward the goal.

- You can be motivated by either intrinsic rewards (for example, a feeling of accomplishment) or extrinsic rewards (such as praise from others). But intrinsic motivators are more powerful than extrinsic motivators.

- The eight-step decision-making process can help you transform your motivation into action by making carefully considered choices.

- To take personal responsibility for your learning in college, you can develop a growth mindset, consider why different outcomes occur, take an active approach to learning, and reflect on how you think and learn and make the changes needed to improve (metacognition).

- Motivation, decision making, and personal responsibility set the stage for career success as well as college success. By acquiring or strengthening these skills now, you'll make an attractive candidate for jobs that interest you, and you'll perform better in those roles.

CHAPTER ACTIVITIES

Journal Entry

TURNING A FIXED MINDSET INTO A GROWTH MINDSET

In this chapter you read about the difference between a fixed mindset and a growth mindset. People who adopt a growth mindset believe that intelligence and talent aren't fixed; rather, they believe that these qualities can be developed. They're also more likely to embrace challenges and persist in the face of obstacles.

In this journal entry, describe an activity or an academic subject area in which you don't feel confident or don't believe you would do well. With respect to this activity or subject area, have you ever felt you just weren't smart enough or talented enough to succeed? Explain. Now, challenge yourself to think differently: Take on a growth mindset for the activity or academic subject area you just described, and outline at least three concrete steps you could take to develop skills and abilities that you don't have now. To structure your discussion, you may wish to respond to the following questions:

1. What skills and abilities would you work to build?

2. How would you build them?

3. What would you do or tell yourself to keep going and stay motivated if things got difficult?

Adopting a Success Attitude

VISUALIZING SUCCESS

Visualization is a powerful success strategy that can instill positive emotions, help you assess the relevance of your goals, and motivate you to follow through on your intentions. Try a short visualization activity designed to help you reflect on your motivation for being in college.

1. Find a quiet, peaceful place where you can be alone. Close your eyes and breathe in deeply through your nose. Hold for a count of three, and then breathe out through your mouth. Repeat this process until you feel your body relaxing and your mind clearing.

2. Imagine yourself in a graduation gown walking across the stage to receive your diploma. You shake hands with the college president, and as you walk off the stage you notice a video camera pointed at you. A reporter asks if she can interview you for a "graduation success story." You agree. Think about how you would respond to her questions: "How are you feeling right now? What does this accomplishment mean to you? What explains your success? How did you stay motivated when the going got tough? How will your life change now that you have this degree?" The reporter thanks you for your time, and you walk back to your seat.

3. Translate your thoughts and feelings about getting your degree into action steps. What three actions could you take this week to ensure that you're on the right path and to make this graduation scenario come true?

Applying Your Skills

GETTING THE GRADE YOU WANT

In this chapter you read about ways to be an active, metacognitive learner. By monitoring your attitude and effort, evaluating your results, and adjusting your strategies as necessary, you can get the outcome you want. This activity will help you practice these skills.

Monitoring Your Progress

Pretend that you're the instructor of this course and that you have to assign yourself a letter grade as a student. Give yourself a grade that honestly reflects three class-performance criteria: your attitude, effort, and results up to this point in the term. You may use + or − designations such as A− or C+.

Evaluating Results

Explain why you gave yourself this grade by responding to the following questions:

1. How would you describe your attitude toward this class? How might you consciously or unconsciously convey this attitude toward your actual instructor?

2. What kind of effort have you put into this course so far? Such effort might include reading, taking notes, completing assignments, participating in classroom discussions, reflecting on course material, and applying your new knowledge.

3. What results have you achieved in this class up to this point? Results can include quiz grades, written feedback on a journal entry, points for completing an assignment, and your instructor's verbal acknowledgment of a thoughtful response you provided, as well as class attendance, participation in discussions, and assignments turned in on time.

Making Adjustments

Give yourself both positive and constructive feedback on your attitude, effort, and results:

1. What are you doing well?

2. What could you improve?

3. What adjustments will you make in the next week to improve your performance (or maintain outstanding performance) in this class?

College Success = Career Success

LEVERAGING INTRINSIC MOTIVATION IN YOUR CAREER

In this chapter you've learned about intrinsic motivation, which in some cases can be more powerful than extrinsic motivation. To explore how intrinsic motivation can affect your career success, respond to the following scenarios.

1. You've won the lottery, but one condition of receiving the money is that you have to work forty hours a week. What three occupations would you consider pursuing? Why? (Don't worry if they require more education — you'll have the money to pay for it.)

2. A company offers you a job with an annual salary of $2 million. You're asked to create a unique job title for yourself and outline five job responsibilities based on activities you most enjoy doing. What title and responsibilities would you select?

3. Identify the worst job you've ever had (or could imagine having). Besides an inadequate salary, what made (or would make) it the worst job?

Based on your responses to these three scenarios, create a list of intrinsic rewards that motivate you. How might you use this list to make career-related decisions, such as choosing a major, identifying a career path, applying for a job, accepting a job, or leaving a job?

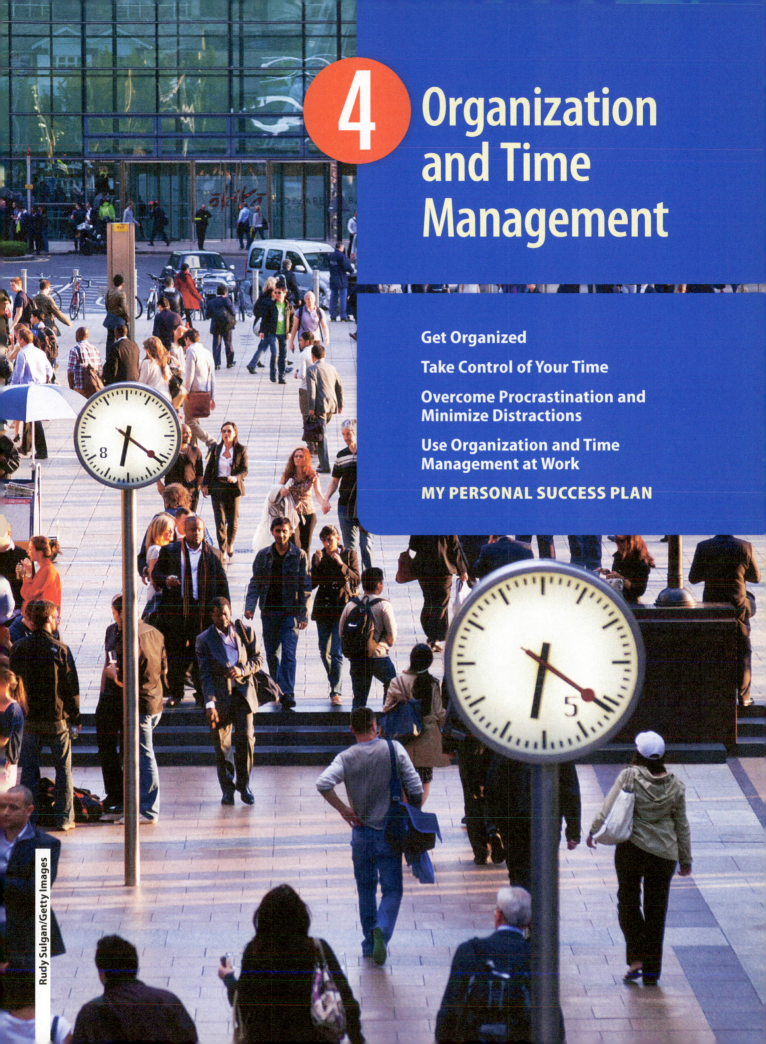

4 Organization and Time Management

Get Organized

Take Control of Your Time

Overcome Procrastination and Minimize Distractions

Use Organization and Time Management at Work

MY PERSONAL SUCCESS PLAN

Do you know people who are *very* organized — people who label every drawer in their house, arrange their socks by color, or schedule each week down to the minute? If so, you may be tempted to dismiss those behaviors as excessive or over the top. After all, taken to extremes, any behavior can be unhealthy. But to a degree, the skills of being organized and managing your time are not only healthy, they're essential for succeeding in college. These skills help you take control of your environment by clarifying what you have to do, when you have to do it, and what resources you'll need. When you're in control, it's easier to stay focused on your goals and minimize distractions that threaten to derail your plans.

Take Marcus and Ethan. Marcus puts all of his classes and study times, his work schedule, and even his regular pickup basketball game into the calendar on his smartphone. When he and Ethan meet to study chemistry, Marcus has a neatly organized binder full of notes, practice problems, and the assignment due each week. Ethan is always a few minutes late to their study sessions and sometimes even forgets to show up. He often leaves his notes at home and asks to share Marcus's notes.

In this scenario Marcus is more likely than Ethan to succeed in college and in the workplace. By staying organized and managing his time, Marcus keeps his academic life on track. And he'll make an attractive job candidate because managers want employees who arrive at work on time, show up for meetings, and keep track of important documents.

With these realities in mind, this chapter examines how you can take control of your environment and manage your life effectively. We start with organization — how you can get a handle on your course materials. Then we explore strategies for improving your time management and dealing with procrastination and distractions. Finally, we look at how organization and time-management skills translate into a successful career.

ACES Reflection:
Organization and Time Management

ACES

Academic & Career Excellence System

Take a moment to reflect on your Organization and Time Management score on ACES. Find your score and add it in the box to the right.

This score measures your beliefs about how organized you are and how well you manage your time. Do you think it's an accurate snapshot of your current skills in this area? Why or why not?

My ACES Score ....
- ☐ **High**
- ☐ **Moderate**
- ☐ **Low**

- ■ **IF YOU SCORED IN THE HIGH RANGE** and you feel this score accurately reflects your skills, you're probably quite organized and manage your time well. That's great news! As with all skills, however, you can improve on your strengths. For instance, if you already use a weekly schedule to organize your time, you might add a to-do list for each day so that you can track your progress and stay on target. Trying new organization and time-management strategies will keep you at the top of your game.

- ■ **IF YOU SCORED IN THE MODERATE OR LOW RANGE**, don't be discouraged. You *can* get more organized and manage your time more effectively. This chapter is filled with ideas for getting a better handle on your class materials and your commitments.

To find your **Organization and Time Management score**, go to the LaunchPad for *Connections*, Second Edition.

LaunchPad
macmillan learning

ACES + ACTION

ACES paired with action is what leads to positive change. Now that you've reflected on your ACES results, how will you *use* what you learned about yourself to build your time management and organization skills? Try these concrete suggestions, or get inspired and create your own!

▶ **Go for the goal.** Create an organization or time-management goal using the Personal Success Plan at the end of the chapter.

▶ **Compare and contrast.** Find a classmate and ask that person to share two tips for managing time and staying organized. Share two of your own in return, and then give each other's tips a try.

▶ **There's an app for that.** Explore new time-management apps that can help you take control of your schedule. Select a highly rated option from the Apple or Android app store and try it out for a week. Was this a useful tool? Will you use it again?

Get Organized

Think about your life: Does it sound more like Marcus's or like Ethan's? If you have to fish through piles of papers to find a syllabus, a class assignment, or a project file, you may identify more with Ethan. If that's the case, consider how you feel when you can't find a book when it's time to study, or when you show up at a meeting without the documents you were supposed to bring. Do you feel out of control? Embarrassed? Incompetent? If so, you can make positive changes. Getting organized can be challenging, particularly if you're juggling competing demands of school, work, and family. But with practice and commitment, you can learn to manage your many priorities.

Everything in Its Place. As a student, you have many tools that help you get your work done—from books and notepads to pens and paperclips. Find creative ways to keep your items organized and easy to access: A clean, orderly space can help you stay focused when you study. DwaFotografy/Shutterstock

cloud: A place on the Internet where you can store your files.

Create a Clean Study Space

The first step in getting organized is to find a clean space where you can study. When your study space is clutter-free, you can concentrate better on what you're doing and quickly find documents and other items that you need. There's no one "right" way to create a clean work area—pick what works best for you based on how and where you study.

- **Office space.** If you have a dedicated office space at home or a quiet room in a residence hall, fix it up to make it inviting. Find a place to stash your books and papers, and give yourself plenty of room for your computer. Set aside a drawer or some cups for pens and pencils, and pick an area to spread out books and notes.

- **Multipurpose space.** Does your study space serve as the kitchen table during the day and then become your desk when the kids go to bed? If so, make your study materials mobile: Use totes or a rolling cabinet to organize everything you need. When the dishes are done and the table is clear, you can pull out your materials and get to work.

- **At work or on the go.** Do you study in the break room at work? In the coffee shop between work and school? In the library because things are too chaotic at home? If you're often on the move, a well-organized backpack is key; that way, you can easily find your pens, highlighters, notebooks, and other tools and still have room for your laptop, books, and class assignments.

Organize Your Documents

To keep your study space clean, you'll need to keep track of all the documents you collect and generate for your classes—both in hard copy and online. If you set up a system for organizing and storing your documents, you'll be able to find what you need when you need it, instead of wasting your time hunting for things and getting stressed out.

Digital Systems.   You'll produce most of your school papers and projects electronically, and you'll need a way to organize them. Give these options a try.

- **Use your computer.** If you're using word-processing tools that come already loaded on your computer—for example, Microsoft Word, Excel, and PowerPoint—you may wish to organize all of your materials directly on your hard drive. The benefit of this approach is that you can use the robust tools of the Microsoft system to create your documents, and when you're done, everything is stored in one place. The downside is that you can't access your materials if your physical computer isn't nearby.

- **Use the cloud.** If you need to access your documents from multiple devices or share them with others, try a **cloud**-based system. Available on the Internet, cloud systems let you store files online and access them from your laptop, tablet, or smartphone or even from an on-campus computer lab. Google Drive is one popular Internet storage system, which you can use in conjunction with Google Docs for writing papers, Google Sheets for creating spreadsheets, and Google Slides for presentations. Because the system stores your files online, you can access them from any electronic device, and interactive editing features allow multiple people to work on the same document at the same time—which can come in especially handy when you have a group project to complete. Other popular cloud-based systems include Dropbox and Box.com, which offer large storage capabilities and the ability to work on documents offline (meaning your materials will update when your device returns to wi-fi access).

Paper Systems. Depending on your preferences or those of your instructors, you might also want a system for organizing documents in paper form. For example, some instructors hand out hard copy syllabi on the first day of class, and a paper-based system can help you store these syllabi so you can find them easily. Also, people often feel secure using a paper-based system because they don't have to worry about computer problems. (Paper files can't get viruses.) To store paper documents, use an alphabetized filing cabinet or tote, or binders and folders that you can carry with you. Pick something that works with how you've arranged your study space and how mobile your materials need to be.

File and Folder Labels. Whether your system is electronic, paper, or a combination, develop a labeling system for your documents and your folders. That way, you can find whatever you need quickly and easily.

- **Use names that are consistent and easy to decode.** For example, for each class, create folders with the names "Syllabus," "Notes," "Exams," "Papers," and "Projects," and then name your files based on the folder in which they belong: "Notes from Sept 5," "Project—Voting Rights," and so on.
- **Create "In Progress" and "Complete" folders.** In the In Progress folder, store documents for projects you're actively working on. As you finish an exam or a paper, move it to the Complete folder so you can focus on documents that need your active attention.

File Backup. If you've ever spilled coffee on a document or crashed your computer, you know how crucial it is to back up your files. To keep paper files safe, scan your documents and save them in an electronic format you can access if the originals get lost or destroyed. For electronic files, use an external hard drive or a thumb drive to store backup files separately from your computer. Or, use the cloud: You can arrange to back up your entire hard drive online, which gives you added security if something happens to your machine.

Whatever system you create to get organized, take time each day to keep it working smoothly. For instance, spend just five minutes every night putting papers into folders or organizing your electronic files. Keep clutter and confusion from creeping back into your life!

How Organized Are You?
Whether it's with a folder in the cloud (like this one) or a binder on your bookshelf, here's how to stay on top of your schoolwork: Organize all your materials, then store and label them in a logical way so you can find what you need, when you need it.

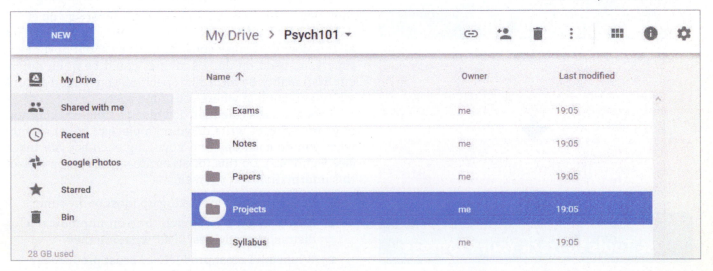

Take Control of Your Time

Organizing your class materials is a great first step, but to really set the stage for success in college and work, you also have to take control of your time. To see why these two skills make a powerful combination, picture yourself in the following two scenarios.

Scenario 1: You check your calendar and see that you've planned to spend two hours tonight working on a paper that's due in a week. You walk into your study space, pull the exact course materials you need from a shelf, and sit down to begin working.

Scenario 2: You never scheduled time to work on an assigned paper. The night before it's due, you suddenly remember that you haven't even started it. You paw through a mound of papers on your desk, searching for the syllabus to see what the assignment is. When you finally find it and read the instructions, you realize that you're unprepared and have little hope of turning it in on time. You're so stressed out that you try to distract yourself by playing a game on your smartphone. An hour slips by before you force yourself to start working on the paper.

What can you do to avoid scenario 2? Get organized using the strategies in this chapter, and master the art of time management using the four-step process shown in Figure 4.1: First, track your time, by documenting how you spend your time during the course of a week. Second, identify your priorities—the activities that matter most to you—based on your values and goals. Third, build a schedule that focuses on your priorities. And fourth, use tools to track your progress on all of your assignments.

Let's explore each of these steps in detail.

Step 1: Track Your Time

If you're like most college students, you sometimes (maybe even often) feel as though you have too much to do and not enough time to do it. That's not surprising: You're probably juggling lots of different demands, such as going to class, caring for kids or elderly parents, or holding down a job. If you're just out of high school, you might also be setting your own schedule for the first time, a responsibility that can feel overwhelming. Whatever your situation, before you can take control of your time, you have to figure out where your time is currently going. What do you actually do as the hours tick by every day?

To get a complete picture of how you're spending your time, you need to record—in writing—what you do every day and how long each activity takes. Why bother writing all this down? Because your perceptions about how much time you spend on daily activities could be quite different from reality. By recording specifics, you'll build a more accurate picture of where your time goes.

To begin, use a calendar, download a time-tracking app of your choice, or write down on a piece of paper exactly what you do each day and how long each activity takes (see Figure 4.2). Do this for an entire week. As you collect this information, ask yourself:

- What activities are taking up most of my time?
- Am I spending too much time on unproductive or distracting activities? If so, what are they?
- When am I most productive? Least productive?

FIGURE 4.1

Four Steps to Effective Time Management

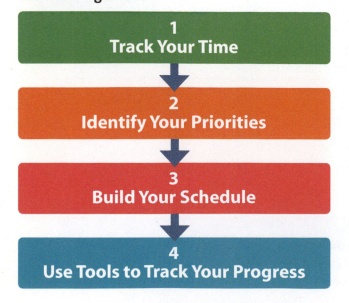

1 Track Your Time

2 Identify Your Priorities

3 Build Your Schedule

4 Use Tools to Track Your Progress

FIGURE 4.2

Sample Time Tracker

Look at this excerpt from one student's time tracker. On Monday, the student had some down-time — just the right amount. But on Tuesday, she streamed a long TV show, had a leisurely lunch, and texted *a lot*, even while she was reading. When it finally came time to study that night, she fell asleep. Had she made different choices earlier in the day, she could have finished studying and still made it to bed at a reasonable hour. Now she has the information she needs to make a change.

September		
Time	**Mon** **25**	**Tues** **26**
7:00 am		
	7:30a – Woke up	7:30a – Woke up
8:00 am	8a – 9a Drove to campus/breakfast	8a – 9:30a Breakfast/streamed TV show
9:00 am	9a – 10a Biology 101	9:30a – Drove to campus
10:00 am	10a – Coffee, texting	10a –11:30a Algebra 115
	10:30a– Read for Algebra class	
11:00 am	11a – 12p First-Year Experience 100	11:30a – 12:30p Biology study group
12:00 pm	12p – Surfed online	
	12:30p – Lunch	12:30p – 2p Lunch with friends
1:00 pm	1p – 2p Economics 125	
2:00 pm	2p – Drove to work	2p – Went to library to study
	2:30p – 5p Work	2:30p – Texting/social media
3:00 pm		3p – Read for Econ (10 mins)/texting
		3:30p – Texting/social media
4:00 pm		4p – 5p Biology lab
5:00 pm	5p – Drove home	5p – 6p Read for Algebra/did problems
	5:30p – Dinner	
6:00 pm	6p – TV	5p – 7p Texting
	6:30p – 8p Read for Biology	
7:00 pm		7p – Dinner/drove to work
		7:30p – 10p Work
8:00 pm	8p – 9:30p Did problems for Algebra	
9:00 pm		
	9:30p – 10:30p Read for First-Year Exp.	
10:00 pm		10p – Drove home
	10:30p – 11:30p Down-time/texting	Studied for Econ quiz (10 min) Crashed – fell asleep on couch
11:00 pm		
	11:30p – Went to bed	

Then give your critical thinking skills a workout: Examine the patterns you see in your time tracker, and analyze your responses to the questions. Use all this information to draw conclusions about how you're spending your time and how you might manage it more effectively. For example, let's say that before you started this exercise, you believed that your many obligations left you little time to study. As you evaluate the information you've gathered, you realize that you spent twenty-five hours gaming this week alone. Because you're studying English literature, not video-game design, you conclude that you can free up time to study by cutting back on your gaming. You've uncovered a wealth of time that you didn't realize was available.

Once you understand where your time is going, you can start thinking about better ways to allocate it. After all, there are only so many hours in a day (and a night). It's up to you to spend this precious resource wisely.

Step 2: Identify Your Priorities

Once you've tracked your time for a week and analyzed the results, consider whether you're allocating enough time to the things that matter to you most. Are trivial tasks eating up too many hours? Does your current use of time reflect how important your education is to you? With numerous obligations and activities competing for your attention, you have to make choices about where to focus your energies. In other words, you have to **prioritize** your commitments and use these priorities to decide how much of your time an activity deserves.

Prioritizing commitments is a deeply personal process that depends on your values and goals. For one person, earning a degree while also spending time with family may be top priorities. For another person, completing college and getting a promotion at work may be most important. When you're clear about your priorities, you make smarter choices about how to use your time. For instance, if doing well in your classes is a top priority, you'll probably choose to study for an exam the night before, instead of going out with friends who don't have a test tomorrow.

To practice prioritizing, review your one-week time tracker, and write down the activities that currently take up most of your time (see Figure 4.3). Describe these activities in broad terms, such as "attending class," "studying," and "working." Determine how important each activity is to you personally, and indicate that importance using the following four-point scale:

- 4 = critically important
- 3 = highly important
- 2 = moderately important
- 1 = of little or no importance

Critically important activities (those you've rated 4) are those that you've decided you must do because they relate directly to your values and responsibilities. For instance, each week you may need to go to work, attend all of your classes, and be home by 3:00 p.m. when your children get off the school bus. Highly important activities (rank = 3) will also have an impact on your success—such as doing five extra problems for math each evening.

prioritize: To give an activity or a goal a higher value relative to another activity or goal.

FIGURE 4.3

Prioritizing Your Commitments

When you prioritize, you identify what's most important to you, a process that helps you allocate more time to your top priorities. For this student, attending class, working, studying, and spending time with family are critically important.

Activity	Importance
Attending class	4
Working	4
Studying	4
Spending time with family	4
Coaching daughter's softball team	3
Exercising	3
Meeting with study group for biology class	3
Regular Saturday lunch with friends	2
Watching TV	1

4 = critically important
3 = highly important
2 = moderately important
1 = of little or no importance

Activities you've rated 4 and 3 may not always be fun or exciting, but you consider them crucial for achieving your goals or living your values. Activities you view as moderately important (rank = 2) or of little or no importance (rank = 1) are less essential to your values or goals.

To define your priorities, you need to think critically about what's most important to you. And to honor your priorities, you sometimes have to make tough decisions, such as giving up activities that you enjoy or disappointing someone who wants some of your time. For example, what if your niece's school play is the same day as your statistics exam? What if your boss needs you to work Tuesday night, but you're supposed to meet with classmates from your history course to start a group project? These kinds of choices are never easy, but we all face them and have to learn how to manage them. If you know what your priorities are, you can make the tough calls and be at peace with your decisions.

spotlight on research

Time Management: It Works!

What variables impact academic success in college? A group of researchers set out to investigate the answer to this question by conducting a study of 230 college students. In the study, the researchers explored the impact that time-management skills and other factors have on students' grade point averages. They also asked students to track their time for a week to see how they actually spent the hours in the day. When they analyzed all of the data, here's what they found:

▶ Time management had the strongest connection to students' grades of all the factors they studied.

▶ Abstract thinking (which is used to measure intelligence) was the second most important factor related to grades.

▶ The amount of time students spend studying, as determined by their week-long time-tracking journal, was the third most important variable.

▶ Getting up earlier in the morning also had a positive influence on grades.

THE BOTTOM LINE

Time-management skills can have a big impact on your success, and using these skills to budget more time for studying is a wise move. Time management can also help you stay focused and productive, so you're able to go to bed at a reasonable hour and wake up early each morning.

Time Management

Abstract Thinking

Study Time

Getting Up Early

SIZE OF INFLUENCE ON GRADE POINT AVERAGE ◀

The larger the circle, the larger the influence that factor had on student grades.

Information from D. George, S. Dixon, E. Stansal, S. L. Gelb, and T. Pheri, "Time Diary and Questionnaire Assessment of Factors Associated with Academic and Personal Success among University Undergraduates," *Journal of American College Health* 56 (2008): 706–15.
Photos (left to right): kenex/Getty Images; RENGraphic/Getty Images; RENGraphic/Getty Images; Pakkad Sah/Shutterstock.

Step 3: Build Your Schedule

Once you've tracked your time and clarified your priorities, you can build a schedule that reflects the most important commitments in your life. To find a scheduling method and tools that work for you, try out a paper planner, an app on your phone, a calendar tied to your e-mail system, a calendar hanging in your kitchen, or a mix of these. You can also create schedules that cover different time frames — terms, months, weeks, and days. (For an example of a five-day schedule, see Figure 4.4.)

In this section, we'll look at how to create a comprehensive schedule of any type and time frame, as well as how to stick to that schedule once you have it.

Schedule Your Activities. When building a schedule, your main task will be to record your activities. The activities you put on your schedule will depend on your priorities, but because you're in college, we assume that one of your top priorities is graduating. So you'll need to think about and plan for the following responsibilities:

- **Classes.** Include class time in your schedule. If your class is on campus rather than online, plan to arrive a few minutes early so that you can get settled and prepare to learn.

- **Study time.** Set aside two hours of study time for each hour of class time. The most common college class format is about three hours of class time a week, which involves six hours of studying outside of class. If you're taking four three-hour classes this term, you should budget twelve hours of class time and twenty-four hours of study time each week.

  Research shows that full-time students spend an average of a little less than fifteen hours per week studying.[1] That's not nearly enough time. If you can find two hours to study for each hour of class time and if you use that study time wisely, you'll likely get much better grades than students who invest less time in studying.

  Also, arrange your study time in a way that maximizes your learning. Spacing out your study time across multiple days and studying in small blocks of time is the most productive way to learn new material.[2]

- **Exams and assignments.** In your schedule, include the time needed to take exams, to complete regular assignments and major projects, and to develop presentations for class.

- **Work.** Add your work hours to your schedule. If you commute between home, work, and school, factor in travel time.

- **Family.** Include high-priority family time in your schedule, such as having dinner together each evening or blocking off an afternoon to celebrate a loved one's birthday. These relationships can be a source of support as you manage the many demands of being a college student.

- **School events.** Schedule time for high-priority events at school, such as attending tutoring sessions and study groups for difficult classes, going to important cultural events, or participating in student organizations. While it can be difficult for busy students to make time for these activities, it's worth it: Active involvement on campus can strengthen your commitment to college and help you develop teamwork and communication skills.

- **Exercise and leisure.** To do well in college, you have to be healthy — both physically and mentally. So be sure to schedule time for regular exercise and leisure activities to balance out the great amount of time and effort you'll be devoting to your coursework.

CONNECT TO MY CLASSES

Time for some quick math: How many hours should you study for each class this term? To get your target number, multiply the number of hours you're in class each week by two. Now, consider how much you *actually* study; are you on the right track, or do you need to put in more time to meet this goal? Record your findings.

FIGURE 4.4

Sample Schedule

Building a complete schedule — including time for classes and studying, as well as for exercise, work, and relaxation — helps you take control of your time. Hold yourself accountable for sticking to your schedule, and celebrate when you accomplish everything you planned each day.

October					
Time	**Mon 2**	**Tues 3**	**Wed 4**	**Thur 5**	**Fri 6**
7:00 am	7a – Breakfast	7a – Drive to Campus	7a – Breakfast	7a – Drive to Campus	7a – Breakfast
	7:30a – Drive to Campus	7:30a – 8:30a Yoga	7:30a – Drive to Campus	7:30a – 8:30a Yoga	7:30a – Drive to Campus
8:00 am	8a – 9a Chemistry 101	8:30a – Coffee/Breakfast	8a – 9a Chemistry 101	8:30a – Coffee/Breakfast	8a – 10a Chem Lab
9:00 am	9a – 11a Study Chem and English	9a – 10:30a Algebra II (QUIZ!!)	9a – 11a Study Chem and FYE (First-Year Experience)	9a – 10:30a Algebra II	
10:00 am					10a – Drive to Work
11:00 am	11a – 12:30p English 124		11a – 12:30p English 124	10:30a – 12:30p Study Algebra and Sociology	10:30a – 6p Work
12:00 pm					
	12:30p – Lunch	12:30p – Lunch	12:30p – Lunch	12:30p – Lunch	
1:00 pm	1p – 2:30p First-Year Experience (FYE) 102	1p – 2p Sociology Club Meeting	1p – 2:30p First-Year Experience (FYE) 102	1p – 4p Study Chem, English, FYE	
2:00 pm		2p – 5p Study FYE and Sociology			
3:00 pm	2:30p – 4p Chem Study Group		2:30p – 5p Study Algebra and Sociology		
4:00 pm	4p – Drive Home				
5:00 pm		5p – Drive Home	5p – Drive to Work		
		5:30p – Dinner		5:30p – Dinner	
6:00 pm	6p – 7p Dinner With Cousins! Fresh Grill	6p – 7:30p Study Algebra and Chem	5:30p – 8:30p Work		6p – Dinner
7:00 pm	7p – 8:30p Study Algebra and Chem			6p – 9p Sociology 105	6:30p – 11p Time with Friends Lila's House
8:00 pm		7:30p – 9p Edit English Paper			
			8:30p – Drive Home		
9:00 pm			9p – Dinner	9p – Drive Home	
10:00 pm					
11:00 pm	10:30p – Go to Bed	10p – Go to Bed	10p – Go to Bed	11p – Go to Bed	11p – Drive Home
					11:30p – Go to Bed

- **Rewards.** Schedule time to reward yourself for your successes in college. For instance, schedule a movie with friends or family members the night after an exam. These rewards don't have to consume a lot of time, but they can help recharge your batteries so you can stay motivated for another round of hard work at school.

As you create your schedule, try to build some flexibility into it, in case something goes wrong. For instance, suppose you commute to school, and one of your classes starts at 8:30 a.m. on Tuesdays and Thursdays. You know traffic can be heavy at that time, so when you schedule time for commuting on those days, you add a "cushion" in case you get stuck in traffic. Or let's say you're scheduling time to study for a final exam. You pencil in a few hours of study on an alternative night, in case an emergency comes up and you can't study on the original night you planned for. When you build flexibility into your schedule, you can shift gears more easily if surprises come up.

Reflect and Adjust. When we start out using a schedule, most of us have the best of intentions; we tell ourselves, "I'm going to stick to this schedule, no matter what!" But as great as that sounds at the beginning of the term, and as much as you may mean it, time management can be quite challenging—especially if you've never really done it before. These best practices can help you follow your schedule from the get-go, or help you get back into a routine if something ends up going wrong.

- **Plan ahead.** Long before you run into problems, plan out several steps you can take if you do get off track. As with the "barriers and solutions" step of the Personal Success Plan, having this plan ready to go will make things a lot easier when (or if) it comes time to use it.

- **Find a partner.** Ask a classmate, friend, or family member to help you monitor your time management. Arrange a time once a week when the two of you can talk about how your schedule is going, give each other tips, and support one another.

- **Create a time check.** Add a five-minute time check to your schedule every other week. Use this time to consider whether your current schedule is realistic, whether you're sticking to it, and whether there's anything you need to do to adjust your approach. If you're using a calendar on your smartphone or computer, try setting a reminder so you remember to reflect.

- **Be honest with yourself.** If you do notice that you've stopped using your schedule, it's okay to tell yourself "I haven't been using this tool consistently, but I'll get back to using it right now." The sooner you resume following your schedule, the easier it will be to stay in the habit.

- **Ask for help.** Talk with your adviser, mentor, or instructors, and ask these trusted individuals for help with managing your time. These are all people who support your success, and they'll likely be happy to suggest strategies and make recommendations.

Step 4: Use Tools to Track Progress on Your Projects

Building a schedule is a crucial part of managing your time, but it's not the only tool you can use to stay productive. To-do lists and project plans can help you track your progress on various tasks. They allow you to hold yourself **accountable**, or responsible, for meeting the obligations that are connected to your priorities.

accountable: Responsible for completing tasks and meeting obligations.

To-Do List. A to-do list helps you manage time and activities on a daily basis by reminding you of key tasks (see Figure 4.5). Try creating a to-do list for the next day each night before you go to bed or for the current day when you get up in the morning. It takes only a couple of minutes. You can make your list using an e-mail

To-Dos
Date: Wednesday
1. ~~Read for history class.~~
2. ~~Complete biology lab write-up.~~
3. Read book on reserve in the library for literature class.
4. Go running.
5. Go to dinner with the kids.

FIGURE 4.5
Sample To-Do List

CONNECT TO MY EXPERIENCE

Think about everything you have to accomplish tomorrow, and create a to-do list—either just before you go to bed tonight or just after you get up tomorrow morning. What are your main tasks for the day?

program, the calendar on your smartphone, apps on your tablet, or a piece of paper. Experiment with color-coding or numbering the tasks on your to-do list by priority. Try different methods to discover which strategies work best for you.

Project Plan. Your schedule will include time to work on major school projects, and when you create a project plan, you can track your progress on each of these projects. A project plan helps you break down an assignment into smaller, more manageable steps and budget time to complete each step. This tool builds on key concepts in the chapter on thinking critically and setting goals, such as identifying action steps, prioritizing them, and giving each step a deadline. To create a project plan, you estimate how much time will be required to complete each step in the project. That way, you can build enough time into your schedule to complete all the steps by the assignment's due date.

Consider Mia, who has six weeks to write a major paper on Greek architecture. Figure 4.6 shows how Mia has broken down the tasks involved in completing this paper. She starts with the due date and adds a goal statement for this assignment. She lists the steps needed to complete her paper. Since Mia is a new college student, she isn't sure how much time each task will take, but she wrote papers in high school and often pulls together documents for her boss. She draws on these experiences to estimate how much time she'll need for each task.

Project:	Greek architecture paper		
Due date:	October 31		
Goal:	Demonstrate new knowledge of Greek architecture through written work		
Action steps	**Estimated time**	**Deadline**	**Done**
Read assigned textbook chapters	5 hours	September 20	X
Find and read three additional resources	18 hours	October 3	X
Find six images of architecture	4 hours	October 5	
Write an outline for the paper	3 hours	October 10	
Write first draft	12 hours	October 20	
Revise to create second draft	6 hours	October 24	
Revise to create third draft and polish the paper	4 hours	October 28	
Hand in the paper and celebrate!		October 31	

FIGURE 4.6
Project Plan

CONNECT TO MY CAREER

In many careers, people have to manage projects, write reports, or complete major assignments. Explain how you might use a project plan to manage a project in your current job or, if you're not currently working, a project that you may have to do in a career you're considering.

One advantage of creating a project plan is that you can use the deadlines in your plan to hold yourself accountable. Also, crossing off tasks as you complete them gives you a feeling of accomplishment, which can be crucial for maintaining momentum throughout the project.

Manage Time in Your Online Classes

If your schedule includes online classes, keep in mind that they often present unique time-management challenges. Your traditional courses are scheduled on particular days and times, and you can block off this class time in your schedule. With many online classes, though, the time you spend participating in class is less structured. Most online courses don't require you to attend at any specific time, so deciding when you'll create and respond to online posts and complete other course requirements is up to you. In addition, while some students expect online classes to be easier or less intensive than face-to-face courses, most online classes take as much time as in-person classes (and sometimes even *more* time). So, be sure to schedule enough time to complete your assignments. Try these tips for staying on top of your online coursework.

- **Get comfortable with this class format.** If you're new to online classes, block out time in your schedule to learn how to navigate the online class system. Your instructor and institution can help.

- **Devote time *each week* to work on your assignments.** Be sure that your weekly schedule includes time for studying, reading, and posting work online for your class. Creating a consistent schedule is particularly critical to mastering course material for online classes.

- **Log in to your online class each day.** Even if it's just for five minutes, log in to check for updates from your instructor or posts from other students. That way, you can make sure you're keeping up with assignments and monitoring class discussions.

- **Know your deadlines.** If your instructor gives specific due dates for class assignments, enter them into your schedule for each week of the term.

- **Schedule time for live meetings hosted by your instructor.** Sometimes hosted via tools like Skype or a text chat, live meetings give you opportunities to interact with classmates and instructors in real time.

- **Take personal responsibility.** Online classes require a great deal of discipline, particularly with respect to managing your time. You'll likely have to make sacrifices in order to get your work done well and on time. Make a commitment at the start of the class to hold yourself accountable, keep to your schedule, and make your education a priority.

- **Build in a buffer.** Build some extra time into your schedule to read, study, and complete assignments when you're first adjusting to online learning. If you don't end up needing it, you can squeeze in a break or a quick nap instead.

Consistency Is Key. Online classes are often less structured than face-to-face courses, which means it's up to you to create your own schedule. Your best bet? Keep it consistent: Devote regular time each week to working on your assignments and log in to your courses every day.
Jacob Lund/Shutterstock

> A paper planner works best for me—I don't go anywhere without it—and sometimes I create reminders on my phone.

voices of experience
student

NAME
Talia Edgar

SCHOOL
Eastern Michigan University

MAJOR
Secondary Education with focus on English Literature and Writing

CAREER GOAL
English Teacher

TOOLS FOR TIME MANAGEMENT

As a first generation college student and the oldest of six siblings, I didn't know the basics of being a successful student—sometimes I had to learn through trial and error. But when I came to Eastern Michigan, two things really helped: I got a four-year planner that helped me manage my time and stay organized, and I took a college success class. Early in the class we had a whole lecture on time management, and I started using the scheduling tool from the *Connections* book to organize my week. I put my classes on the schedule and then added study times and other things I needed to do.

I still find that a paper planner works best for me—I don't go anywhere without it—and sometimes I create reminders on my phone. I also have a white board in my room where I write things down, and I use sticky notes to remind myself of things I need to do.

This year I'm working as a tutor and a mentor on campus, which means I attend the college success class with the first-year students. I assist the instructor by participating in discussions, grading reading logs, and planning activities. I also meet with students every other week to see how they're managing their time and doing in their classes. So, my schedule has gotten even more complicated this term, to say the least. To manage it all, I fill out my schedule in my planner each week, and I make sure to use all my other time-management tricks. My system continues to work and I haven't missed a thing!

> **YOUR TURN** Do you have strategies you use to stay focused on your top priorities, particularly when you're juggling many commitments? If so, what's an example of a strategy you've found helpful? If not, which of Talia's strategies might be useful to you?

Courtesy of Talia Edgar

Overcome Procrastination and Minimize Distractions

If you're like most people, you sometimes put off getting started on your work. You check Twitter one more time, send another text—do anything except what you're supposed to be doing. In short, you **procrastinate**. When you procrastinate, you open yourself up to distractions—events or objects in your environment that take your attention away from the task you need to complete.

procrastinate: To delay or put off an action that needs to be completed.

Procrastination and distractions can undo all the effort you've put into getting organized and taking control of your time. So the next time you find yourself procrastinating or getting distracted, use your critical thinking skills. Ask yourself: Why am I putting off this task? or Why am I not focusing on what I should focus on? The more you know about what's causing you to veer off track, the more you can work to change your behavior and accomplish your goals.

Beat Procrastination

People procrastinate for various reasons. By understanding the most common root causes, which we'll explore in the section that follows, you can identify when you're falling victim to these causes—and apply the right antidotes.

Low Motivation. If you don't feel motivated to complete a task, you might be tempted to procrastinate. Fight low motivation with these tactics.

- **Engage in self-reflection.** You may feel unmotivated because you lack a sense of self-efficacy regarding the task at hand, you don't see it as relevant to you, or you have a negative attitude about your studies in general. (See the chapter on motivation, decision making, and personal responsibility.) Try to identify which of these three key ingredients of motivation you're missing. Sometimes simply understanding why you're unmotivated can spur you to take action.

- **Just get started.** If you have reading to do, pick up your textbook and begin. If you have to do research for a paper, log on to the library's Web site and start searching for articles. In some cases, just telling yourself it's time to work will revive your motivation.

- **Move.** Grab your materials, go somewhere new, and clear your head. Physical motion may be enough to motivate you to focus on the work you need to do.

- **Give it twenty minutes.** Make a commitment to study for just twenty minutes. Set a timer on your phone, pick up a book, and read. When the timer goes off, move onto another task, but be sure to give yourself credit for what you've accomplished.

Not-So-Good Housekeeping. Let's say you have a test tomorrow, but instead of studying, you've suddenly decided it's time to do laundry. Guess what: You're likely procrastinating—and you'll have less time to prepare for the test. The lesson? If a task isn't crucial, do it after finishing your *real* priorities. Don't worry—that laundry isn't going anywhere. Robyn Breen Shinn/ Getty Images

Perfectionism. Some people avoid starting projects because they want to achieve a perfect result and worry that they won't be able to. If this happens to you, try these strategies to combat perfectionism.

- **Reframe your expectations.** Give yourself permission to let go of perfectionistic thinking. Instead of telling yourself that everything you work on must be perfect, tell yourself that you'll put your best effort into each project or task.

- **Start small.** Complete some small tasks related to the work you're procrastinating on; then use your success to gain momentum for finishing another set of tasks. Eventually, you'll complete the whole project.

Feeling Overwhelmed. If you feel overwhelmed by the amount of work facing you, it may be daunting just to get started. Try these tactics to keep moving forward.

- **Be realistic.** Remind yourself that you can't do everything at once and that every journey—however long or short—starts with a single step. Then pick a place to start.

- **Trick yourself.** Tell yourself that you're going to read or write for only ten minutes or that you'll read or write only three pages. Once you get involved in the work, you may look up forty-five minutes later and discover that you're almost finished—and that's a good reason to keep going.

- **Use a project plan.** Create a project plan to break down one large task into smaller, more manageable parts (see earlier in this chapter). This way you can tackle each element of the project individually, rather than pressuring yourself to finish everything at once.

Minimize Distractions

Distractions can be a big challenge for some students, causing them to veer off track. If you intend to study chemistry for two hours but then spend an hour watching YouTube videos, you'll lose time you can't get back. To protect yourself against distractions, consider these tips.

- **Find strength in numbers.** With your roommates or family members, agree on a time when everyone focuses on coursework (or schoolwork for your kids) or other quiet tasks. Doing so creates an environment of support and accountability: When everyone around you is studying or working quietly, you'll find it easier to stay focused.

- **Use the "off" switch.** Turn off the television, your phone, and any other devices that create visual or auditory distractions. Log out of Facebook, Twitter, and other social networking sites. Click the setting that turns off that annoying little chime that lets you know you've just received an e-mail or an instant message. As you plan your study time, allow five minutes each hour to check these devices and respond to messages. That way, you won't feel tempted to do so while you work.

- **Block out other sources of distraction.** For example, close the curtains or pull down the shades in your room so you can't see what's happening outside. If your neighbor is playing loud music, invest in a set of earplugs to block out the noise.

Be a Productivity Pro. Take a lesson from these unfocused felines: Distractions can gobble up your time. Before you know it, you fall behind in your work. To avoid watching your productivity plummet, resist any urge to give into distractions — as irresistible as they may seem. Stick to the schedule you've created, and reward yourself once your work is done. Eric Hodecker/ CartoonStock.com

Use Organization and Time Management at Work

The strategies you use to get organized and take control of your time at school are just as essential in your work life. If you manage projects and meet with clients and coworkers every day, you know that things fall apart when you're disorganized and that deadlines are missed when you don't stick to a schedule. Let's consider how you can apply the ideas from this chapter in the workplace.

Get a Job

When you apply for a job, the skills of organization and time management make all the difference. First, you can use these skills to prepare a stellar résumé. Describing your accomplishments will be easier if you've kept track of all the papers and presentations you created in college. For example, if you designed a social media campaign during an internship, keep a copy of the campaign so you can explain in detail what you did.

Second, you'll arrive for interviews on time, and you will have prepared questions for the interviewers and information about your qualifications. Arriving prepared shows that you understand the importance of organization and timeliness—all before you've even said a word. And that can make you stand out in a crowd of job applicants.

Show That You're Dependable

Once you get a job, being organized and effectively managing your time can help you excel in that job—no matter what it is. Let's say you're in auto repair and you tell a customer that her car will be ready by a certain date. You'll be more likely to build customer loyalty if you deliver as promised, which you can do only if you have the necessary tools at your fingertips and if you've scheduled enough time to do the work right. In any job, your boss, customers, and colleagues will appreciate that you're organized and in control of your time. As a result, you'll gain a reputation for getting work done—and done right. Such a reputation could lead to huge opportunities for career advancement.

Make Time for Your Personal Life

When you're organized at work and you control your time, you can boost your productivity on the job, without necessarily having to put in longer hours. In short, you'll work smarter, not harder. As a result, you'll free up more time for your personal life, enabling you to maintain a healthy *work/life balance*. Your job matters, but you also need time for your education, family, friends, health, and fun. Without that balance, you might get so burned out on the job that you have little energy to fulfill your nonwork obligations and goals.

Prioritizing tasks at work helps you complete crucial tasks first. That way, you generate the business results that matter most to your

Organization: The Best Tool. Carpenters who keep their workspaces organized can quickly find the tools they need to complete jobs for their customers. That makes them more efficient and productive, helping them deliver high-quality work on schedule. John Lund/Drew Kelly/Getty Images

> # "Staying organized and on top of things is critical for me to do my job well."

voices of experience
employee

NAME
William Hatchet

PROFESSION
New College Student Academic Facilitator

SCHOOL
Augustana College

DEGREE
Bachelor of Arts

MAJORS
Sociology and Africana Studies

Photo by Erin L. Maltby

MANAGING A BUSY WORK SCHEDULE

After graduation I moved into my first job as a New College Student Academic Facilitator — I help students navigate college and support programs designed to help them stay in school. I wear several hats in this job and continually balance large projects, meetings across campus, and regular meetings with students. Staying organized and on top of things is critical for me to do my job well.

I figured out quickly that I needed to create a structure to stay organized and manage my busy schedule. I have two main strategies to keep everything straight. First, I use a projects list to keep track of everything I need to get done. As soon as I get a project, I write it down on a list that I carry with me, or I type it into a Word document if I'm at my computer. I add a few details to help me remember everything I need to do for each project. I also use calendars to schedule my time. I have separate work and personal calendars, and I sync them electronically so I always know what I have going on during the week at work and on evenings and weekends away from campus.

The combination of my projects list and my calendars has been working great. Using these tools has really helped relieve my stress. I know that everything I need to do is written down in one of two places. I often carry my iPad with me so I can look things up anytime I need to. These systems also allow me to look ahead, so I can keep track of what I need to work on during any given day and into the future.

> **YOUR TURN** If you currently have a job, which of the strategies that William describes might help you stay organized at work and manage your time? Have you developed other strategies that work well for you? If so, what are they? If you don't currently have a job, which of William's strategies sound useful for staying organized and managing your time in a job you'd like to get?

boss and your organization, but work doesn't take over your life. You can also find ways to "unplug" from work outside your normal job hours. For example, resist the urge to respond to work-related e-mails and phone calls at 11:00 p.m., when you should be sleeping. And take advice from Tony Schwartz, a well-known author who writes about balance and work satisfaction: Assess your contribution at work in terms of the *value* you create rather than the amount of time you log in. In other words, focus on doing good work (quality) versus simply measuring the number of hours you work (quantity).[3]

my personal success plan

ORGANIZATION AND TIME MANAGEMENT

Based on your ACES results and what you learned in this chapter, are you inspired to set a new goal aimed at improving your organization and time-management skills? If so, the Personal Success Plan can walk you through the goal-setting process. Read the advice and examples; then sketch out your ideas in the space provided.

To access the Personal Success Plan online, go to the LaunchPad for *Connections*, Second Edition.

1 IDENTIFY A GOAL

Choose an organization or time management goal to work toward this term. Here are some general ideas you might draw from; you can also create a goal of your own.

- ▶ Use a calendar to schedule my time.
- ▶ Organize my work space.
- ▶ Use the cloud to store documents.
- ▶ Make a to-do list each day.
- ▶ Remove distractions.

2 MAKE YOUR GOAL SMART

Rewrite your specific goal so that it's SMART, and make sure to use the SMART goal checklist.

SAMPLE: I'll use the calendar on my phone to schedule my time for the next two weeks.

3 CREATE AN ACTION PLAN

Outline the specific steps you'll take to achieve your SMART goal, and note when you'll complete each step.

SAMPLE: Tomorrow night, I'll enter my class, study, work, and activity schedules for the next two weeks into my calendar.

4 LIST BARRIERS AND SOLUTIONS

Think about possible barriers to your action steps; then brainstorm solutions for overcoming them.

SAMPLE: Sometimes I forget to check my calendar, so I'll set up reminders on my phone that alert me before each scheduled event. When the alerts go off, I'll remember where I'm supposed to be.

5 ACT AND EVALUATE OUTCOMES

Now that your plan is in place, take action. Record each action step as you take it. Then evaluate whether you achieved your SMART goal, and make any adjustments needed to get better results in the future.

SAMPLE: I entered my schedules into my calendar as planned and created alerts for each event. I'm doing a good job of staying on top of my commitments.

6 CONNECT TO CAREER

List the skills you're building as you progress toward your SMART goal. How will you use these skills to land a job and succeed at work?

SAMPLE: I work part-time as a Web designer, and using a calendar will help me meet deadlines and remember client meetings.

my personal success plan

1 my general goal

____

____

____

____

____

____

____

2 my SMART goal

____

____

____

____

☐ SPECIFIC ☐ MEASURABLE ☐ ACHIEVABLE ☐ RELEVANT ☐ TIME-LIMITED

3 my action plan

____

____

____

____

____

4 my barriers/ solutions

____

____

____

____

____

5 my actions/ outcomes

____

____

____

____

____

6 my career connection

____

____

____

____

____

CHAPTER SUMMARY

In this chapter you learned about many important aspects of organization and time management. Revisit the following key points, and reflect on how you can use this information to support your success now and in the future.

- Getting organized helps you quickly and easily find the materials and information you need to carry out the activities required to achieve your goals.

- To get organized, you need a clean, quiet study space and a system for managing and backing up course documents.

- Applying a four-step process can help you manage your time: (1) Track how you're using your time now, (2) identify your priorities, (3) build a schedule that allocates enough time to your top priorities, and (4) use tools to track your progress on your projects so you can hold yourself accountable for meeting your obligations.

- If you get off track with your time-management strategies, acknowledge the problem, apply a plan for getting back on track, and consider getting help from a classmate, adviser, or mentor.

- Procrastinating can prevent you from reaching your goals and make you vulnerable to distractions. When you figure out why you're procrastinating, you can address the cause, which may range from low motivation to perfectionism.

- Eliminating distractions (for example, by turning off electronic devices) can help you focus on the work at hand and use your time wisely.

- Getting organized and taking control of your time can help you get a job, excel in that job, and free up time for your personal life so that you maintain a work/life balance.

CHAPTER ACTIVITIES

Journal Entry

WHERE DOES THE TIME GO?

In this chapter we asked you to track your time for one week as a way to think critically about your time-management skills (see Figure 4.2). Complete this activity and respond to the following questions:

1. How would you rate your ability to manage your time?

2. What do you do well regarding time management? What isn't working so well?

3. What positive changes could you make in the next week to better manage your time?

4. What challenges might you encounter trying to implement these changes? How will you deal with these challenges?

5. Who could offer support, and in what forms?

Adopting a Success Attitude

UNDERSTANDING MY PRIORITIES

Your priorities represent the things you value that are meaningful to you. As described in this chapter, knowing your priorities can help you make decisions about how to spend your time.

Part 1: On a separate sheet of paper, draw a large circle. This represents your life for a one-week period (168 hours). Thinking through the last week (and referencing your time tracker from earlier in this chapter), draw a "slice" that represents how much time you spent on *each* activity you engaged in. For example, think about how much time you spent working, attending class, studying, sleeping, exercising, cooking, cleaning, taking care of others, volunteering, engaging in spiritual pursuits, watching television, surfing the Internet, playing video games, spending time with friends and family, and so on. Be honest!

Part 2: Once you've drawn a pie chart that represents how you actually spent your time, reflect on this exercise by responding to the following questions:

- ▶ Are you spending time on things that are important to you?
- ▶ Are these things helping you be a successful student? How?
- ▶ Are these things helping you develop skills for career readiness? How?
- ▶ Is there something you would like to spend more/less time doing? Explain.
- ▶ How can you make that happen?
- ▶ What did you learn about yourself?

Part 3: As a concluding step to this activity, draw an aspirational pie chart that represents how you would *prefer* to be spending your time next week. How does this aspirational pie chart differ from the actual pie chart you just drew? What specific steps can you take to turn these aspirations into a reality?

Applying Your Skills

PLANNING FOR LARGE CLASS ASSIGNMENTS

If you break down large, complex class assignments into smaller chunks and distribute the workload over the course of a term, they'll seem much more manageable. Review Figure 4.6 and create your own project plan for a big, complicated assignment you'll need to complete this term.

Be sure to record the name of the project, the date that it's due, and a goal statement for the assignment. Then list your action steps, the estimated time required for each, and the deadlines that you've set for yourself. Once you've started using the project plan, reflect on the following: How is this tool working for you? Has it helped you track your progress and complete your assignment on time? Why or why not?

Project:	
Due date:	
Goal:	

Action steps (List all steps)	Estimated time	Deadline	Done

College Success = Career Success

IDENTIFYING PROCRASTINATION TRIGGERS

Procrastination can impact your ability to succeed in school and work. When you procrastinate in school, you may end up cramming for an exam or staying up all night to finish a project. This may cause you anxiety, guilt, frustration, and exhaustion, and it may even result in a low grade. When you procrastinate at work, the consequences might be even greater: You could receive a poor performance review, and if this behavior continues over time, it could even get you fired. The following activity will help you identify procrastination triggers and brainstorm strategies you can use to overcome them.

1. Identify an activity at school or at work that you've been putting off.

2. Check off the reasons you are procrastinating on this activity:

   _____ Boring   _____ Frustrating

   _____ Difficult   _____ Ambiguous

   _____ Unstructured   _____ Not intrinsically rewarding

   _____ Lacking in personal meaning   _____ Other: _____

3. Reframe your attitude about this activity by brainstorming concrete ways to make completing it more appealing. For example, if the task is boring, can you turn it into a game, or reward yourself for completing it? If it's unstructured, can you give it structure by breaking it into smaller tasks? Can you focus on the task for short increments of time at the beginning, and work your way up to spending more time on the activity? Can you enlist the help or support of someone else in completing this activity?

4. Once you have a list of ideas, select three actions that you'll take to make this particular activity more appealing. Be specific about what you'll do, how you'll do it, when you'll do it, and who will help you (if anyone).

5. Finally, list the personal costs of procrastination in this instance ("I'll receive a low grade on this assignment, which will affect my grade in this course") and identify the benefits that will likely come your way if you complete this activity ("I'll receive a better grade on the assignment, which will affect my course grade and GPA and make me a more competitive job applicant").

5 Understanding Learning

Learning that Works: What the Research Tells Us

Make Learning Personal

Succeed in Different Learning Environments

Apply Your Knowledge of Learning at Work

MY PERSONAL SUCCESS PLAN

t's difficult to succeed in college without understanding how to learn, and that's why this chapter is all about learning: what science tells us about learning, what we know about our own learning preferences, and how we can use what we know to excel in different environments.

But what is learning, exactly? That's a broad question, but it's also an important one! Learning is the process of acquiring knowledge or skills through practice, study, or being taught. You're learning all the time, both inside and outside of class. When you work on a goal for this chapter's PSP, you're learning. When your coworker shows you how to add a column of expenses in a spreadsheet, you're learning. You're even learning when you brainstorm new ways to vanquish the bad guy in your favorite video game.

Learning happens all the time, but we don't always think about *how* or *why* it happens — in other words, we don't always think metacognitively about the learning process. But doing so is important, and it gives you several advantages in college. For one thing, it makes you more self-aware and self-directed; as a result, you'll make better decisions about how to study. It also helps you identify and overcome your blind spots. For example, if you study a single subject for a long block of time, only to discover that spacing out your studying is more effective, you might alter your behavior.

Learning on the job is just as important as learning in the classroom, so embracing learning basics will also prove useful in your career. Your preferences and the learning strategies you use affect how you approach work tasks and projects. And understanding how you learn (and how your coworkers learn) will enable you to fine-tune your interactions with them, especially when you're working in teams.

To kick off this chapter, we'll look first at what research tells us about learning, including which strategies are useful for everyone. We'll then investigate the latest information about learning preferences, along with two ways to classify your own personal preferences: the Myers-Briggs Type Indicator and the VARK model. Finally, we'll consider best practices for succeeding in a variety of learning environments — including those that go outside your comfort zone.

ACES Reflection:
Your Learning Preferences

ACES
Academic & Career Excellence System

Take a moment to reflect on your Learning Preferences score on ACES. Find your score and add it in the box to the right.

This score measures your beliefs about how well you understand your learning preferences. Do you think it's an accurate snapshot of your understanding? Why or why not?

■ **IF YOU SCORED IN THE HIGH RANGE** and you feel that this score is accurate, you may have a solid understanding of how you learn. Put that information to good use in your classes and when you study. As you read this chapter, be on the lookout for new techniques you can use to learn information. Seize the opportunity to hone your existing learning strategies *and* develop new strategies.

■ **IF YOU SCORED IN THE MODERATE OR LOW RANGE**, now is the perfect time to discover more about how you learn: Use this chapter to develop a better understanding of yourself, your options, and which strategies can work for you.

My ACES Score ....
- ☐ High
- ☐ Moderate
- ☐ Low

To find your **Learning Preferences score**, go to the LaunchPad for *Connections,* Second Edition.

LaunchPad
macmillan learning

ACES + ACTION

ACES paired with action is what leads to positive change. Now that you've reflected on your ACES results, how will you *use* what you learned about yourself to develop more effective learning strategies? Try these concrete suggestions, or get inspired and create your own!

▶ **List your favorites.** Make a list of three strategies you like using to learn. As you read this chapter, note when one of your preferred strategies is discussed. Then, write down if there's anything you can do to improve on this strategy based on the tips presented in the chapter.

▶ **Ask the experts.** Meet with an instructor in another class and ask what learning strategies work best for students in that academic subject. Compare the response you get with the strategies you listed above: Do they match? If not, identify one new strategy you'll develop for that class.

▶ **Reach out.** Make an appointment with an office on campus that offers tutoring. Share the preferred strategies you listed above, and ask if there are additional materials available to help you develop different or more effective study strategies.

Learning that Works: What the Research Tells Us

Scientists have been studying how we learn for over one hundred years, and they've discovered that not all learning strategies are created equal. For example, which of the following strategies do you think is more effective in helping you learn new material: recopying your notes in the evening when you get home from class, or creating your own practice tests that cover the material you're expected to learn? In this section, you'll find out the answer. (Hint: Your instructors aren't the only ones who should be creating tests!)

We'll begin with an introductory look at what we know about learning and the brain. Then we'll review *learning science,* which is the study of how we learn and which learning strategies are effective, and we'll focus on specific techniques that research shows are useful.[1] These techniques will empower you to learn and remember important material—both in the classroom and beyond.

Your Brain Is Required for Learning!

The title of this section may seem self-evident: Of course your brain is required for learning. But what, exactly, do we mean by that? What happens in our brains when we learn, and why do some learning strategies work better than others? Let's look at key findings that decades of cognitive neuroscience research have revealed about the brain, how it functions, and how it helps you master information.

- **Your brain cells (called *neurons*) are organized in interconnected systems and pathways.** These interconnected cells enable you to do all kinds of things, from riding a bike to talking, listening, and learning. Learning occurs when new connections are established between these neurons.[2] In college, for example, you can build connections by listening to a lecture, talking with other students, taking notes, reading your textbooks, and using the learning strategies described in this section of the book. The more you use proven learning techniques to master material, the stronger these connections between neurons will become.

- **Your brain is a dynamic organ.[3]** People used to believe that the number of brain cells you'd have for your whole life was set by the time you were a teenager. Now, science suggests that the brain can grow new neurons and make connections between neurons across your entire life span. That means your capacity to learn isn't fixed: Learning depends more on your level of effort than your age.

- **Learning can be fun but it can also be stressful** — like when you're studying for a big exam. That's because emotions influence your ability to learn.[4] If you're too stressed out, your brain won't be as effective at learning new material. Interestingly, though, a small to moderate amount of stress may facilitate learning new information. The key is to keep an eye on how stressed you are and look for ways to alleviate stress that's too severe.

- **More information doesn't necessarily result in more learning.[5]** The term *cognitive overload* describes the point at which more information is detrimental to learning: when your brain just can't divide its attention between all the different elements presented to it. To overcome this, you can minimize distractions while you learn and practice recognizing the point at which "a lot" becomes "too much"—and if you reach that point, you can take a break and come back later.

With this quick introduction to brain basics, you're getting a general sense of how the brain operates. Now, let's build on this understanding by exploring specific strategies that you can use to learn effectively. Which of the strategies in this section will you try out today?

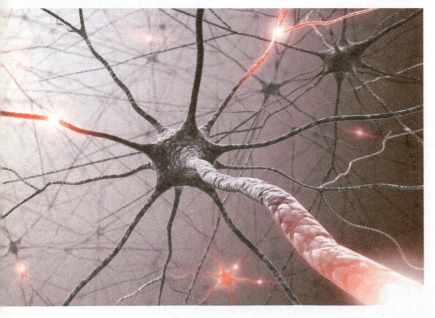

The Power of Neurons. Learning occurs when connections among neurons (like those shown in this illustration) are activated by new stimulation—for example, when you learn to ride a bike, solve a chemistry problem, or comprehend new words in Spanish class. The learning strategies in this chapter can help you strengthen these neural connections and maximize your understanding. Brand X Pictures/Getty Images

Test Yourself

As a student you've taken countless tests—primarily those that are written by instructors to evaluate how much class material you've learned. But there's also another type of testing that every student should use on a regular basis: self-testing. Self-testing is the process of creating practice tests for yourself as a study tool, and research shows that you can use this method to create long-lasting learning in a wide variety of subject areas.

Luckily, creating your own tests doesn't have to be complicated. One method of self-testing that's both easy and effective is making flash cards (see Figure 5.1). For example, if you're studying a foreign language and trying to learn vocabulary, create a set of flash cards with the foreign word on the front and the English translation on the back. Prompt yourself to provide either the English translation or the foreign word, and get immediate feedback by flipping the card over to see if you're correct. Then be sure to review the cards periodically to make sure the learning sticks.

Self-tests can be used in other classes as well, and you can use different methods to create them. If you're trying to learn human anatomy, make a photocopy of a picture in your book and white out the correct labels to create an effective self-test. You can also try your hand at creating your own multiple-choice, short-answer, or essay tests to assess your learning in other subjects. And don't hesitate to make this a team effort: If you pair up with another student, you can each create your own tests and then exchange them with one another to assess your knowledge of the concepts. (See more self-testing suggestions in the Memory and Studying chapter.)

Why is self-testing so effective? First off, this method helps you learn the correct answers to test items, which is clearly a good thing. In addition, it forces you to think more deeply about the material, helping you strengthen the connections that you're establishing between neurons in your brain. It also prompts you to consider what information your instructor has identified as most important—that is, which concepts should be tested in the first place—and how to understand similarities and differences between closely related content.

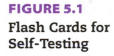

**CONNECT
TO MY EXPERIENCE**

Earlier, we asked which strategy you thought was more effective: self-testing or recopying your notes. Now you know: Self-testing is the way to go. Identify a chapter you're struggling with in a current class and create a short self-test to help you study. Reflect on the process of creating the self-test as you build it. How might this process require you to think about the material more deeply than another type of study tool?

FIGURE 5.1

**Flash Cards for
Self-Testing**

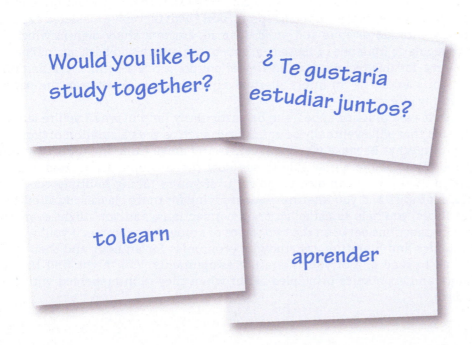

Space Out Your Studying

You've probably heard the term *all-nighter*, which refers to a frantic, last-ditch effort to cram for an exam or prepare a paper the night before it's due. All-nighters deprive you of sleep at a time when your brain needs to rest and process the learning that occurred that day. Further, any illusion that you've found your second wind when the sun comes up is just that—an illusion. You're exhausted and probably very anxious. Needless to say, this isn't the best way to approach learning, and it won't get you the best results.

Research strongly supports the idea that *distributed studying* is the best method to promote long-term learning. Distributed studying involves spacing your studying out over multiple days or weeks. For example, you'd be better off studying for your American History midterm two hours a week for six weeks (a total of twelve hours) than you would be staying up all night studying the evening before your exam. Both require you to invest the same amount of time, but spacing out studying is likely to get the best results.

When researchers investigated why distributed studying works, they came up with a couple of possible explanations. One explanation suggests that when you study over multiple days or weeks, each study session occurs in a different context—in a different place or during a different time of the day—and this is beneficial because the more you vary the contexts in which you learn, the more likely it is that the learning will stick. A second compelling explanation suggests that when you study on multiple occasions, you're able to retrieve what you learned in previous sessions and use it to facilitate and provide structure for the learning in your current study session. To put this simply, the learning sessions are interdependent (they inform one another) and thus they're more effective.[6]

Change Up Your Material

Research shows that if you switch between different topics rather than focusing on one topic at a time, you may learn more effectively.[7] For example, if you're studying for an accounting exam that will cover principles of expense, revenue, and gross and net profit, don't wait till you've mastered expenses before you tackle revenue and profit. Instead, create a study plan in which you move regularly from one of these concepts to the others and back again. The official name for this technique is *interleaved practice*, since a common definition of the term *interleave* is "to insert alternatively and regularly between the parts of something else."[8]

Interleaved practice appears to be particularly helpful when you're learning concepts that will eventually be connected, such as the calculation of gross and net profit. Why? Because when you constantly move from one topic to another related topic, you're better able to see how the concepts are related. But this method of studying can also be powerful if you're taking multiple classes on different topics and you intermix your studying for these classes. By alternating your focus, you help to establish brain connections, and you might even reinforce connections between the two topics of study. For example, if you're taking economics and literature, try studying economics for an hour and then taking a break to read one of your literature assignments. You might find that you understand economics principles better when they're interspersed with some *Macbeth*.

Room to Breathe. "Cramming" right before a test is like trying to pack a lot of items into a small suitcase: Chances are, not everything you need is going to fit. Instead, give yourself some breathing room: Space your studying out over multiple days and weeks and you'll find that you're a lot less anxious — and a lot better at remembering what you've learned. Hill Street Studios/Getty Images

spotlight on research

As you saw in this section, spreading out your learning over time promotes deeper understanding of course material. But what happens if you decide to take shorter, more condensed courses in college, which many students have the option to do? Does condensing your learning leave you at a disadvantage? A group of researchers decided to investigate.

The researchers compared two groups of students who were taking a statistics class. Students in Group 1 took a section that lasted only eight weeks, whereas students in Group 2 completed the class over six months. Both groups completed a measure of learning at roughly the same point during the course, and then again after the end of the term. The results offer important insights into distributed learning:

▶ During the term, students who were taking the longer course demonstrated learning at a level that was 65 *percent higher* than students who were taking the condensed course.

▶ That learning advantage persisted over time. After the end of the term, students who took the longer course demonstrated learning at a level that was 50 *percent higher* than students who completed the condensed course.

▶ The advantages of taking the longer course, the authors of the study concluded, were the result of distributed practice.

Longer Course?

More Time for Distributed Learning!

THE BOTTOM LINE

What do these results mean for you? First, spreading out your learning will promote a deeper and longer-lasting understanding of class material. Second, if given the choice, think twice about taking a condensed course—especially if that course is conceptually difficult. And third, if you do decide to take a condensed course, be extra vigilant about studying every day to maximize your distributed practice.

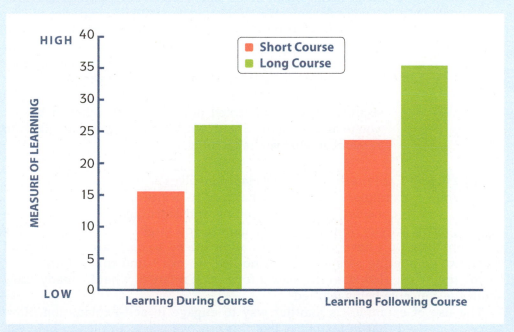

Spread out your studying over a longer period of time to promote deeper and more long-lasting learning.

Information from L. Bude, T. Imbos, M. W. van de Wiel, and M. P. Berger, "The Effects of Distributed Practice on Students' Conceptual Understanding of Statistics," *Higher Education* 62, no. 1 (2011): 69–79.

"How do 'Do not walk on the grass' signs, get there?"

Keep Those Questions Coming. As you learn, ask yourself probing questions: Why are you studying this material? Why do these facts make sense? Keep the deep thoughts coming, and don't be afraid to ask "Why?" (and "When?", and "How?", and "Where?", and "What?") as a way to get your brain in gear.

Graham Waters/CartoonStock.com

Make Connections So Learning Lasts

To make learning last, try linking new material to memories you already have, to your own experiences, or to information you already know. Connecting new learning to something familiar accelerates the learning process because it forms new connections in brain circuits that have already been established by your existing knowledge. To use a car metaphor, it's much quicker to drive down an already existing highway than it is to build a new road of your own. According to research, a number of learning techniques can help you connect current learning with prior learning. We'll explore two of them below.

Ask: Why? *Elaborative interrogation* is a learning strategy that involves asking yourself an important question: Why?[9] This method of self-questioning appears to be particularly useful for learning factual information, and it's more effective when you already have a basic familiarity with the content you're trying to learn (as opposed to brand-new facts) because it helps you make connections between old and new information.

Let's say that you're in a physiology class and you need to remember a key fact: Arteries are thicker and more elastic than veins. Let's also suppose that you already know a bit about circulation: Arteries carry recently oxygenated blood from the heart to the organs of the body and the heart pumps in spurts. If you ask yourself a "why" question ("Why are arteries thicker and more elastic than veins?"), your basic knowledge about arteries might prompt you to reach a well-reasoned conclusion: "We need larger and more elastic arteries to accommodate the varying rhythms of our heart—for example, how our heart beats at rest versus during a 5k running race." In this example, you've connected new facts with other facts that you're already familiar with, which makes you more likely to remember what you're learning.

Engage in Self-Explanation. *Self-explanation* involves asking yourself questions or generating examples related to what you're learning.[10] Self-explanation prompts you to consider your own thinking and learning, which makes it a metacognitive activity. To use self-explanation, you might find yourself asking questions like, Do I have all the information I need to compare and contrast these two competing perspectives? If not, where can I find that information? Or you might ask, How does this new information relate to what I already know about the concepts being learned?

The use of examples is another way to engage in self-explanation. Have you ever noticed that in textbooks like this one, we use examples to help you learn new concepts? That's because examples help you put learning in context and promote the generalization of what you're learning to different situations. Creating your *own* examples can also be a powerful method for learning new material.

> # The more connections you have, the easier it will be for you to remember the information.

Courtesy of Lisa Tacherra

NAME
Dara Tacherra

SCHOOL
Fresno City College

MAJOR
Administration of Justice

CAREER GOAL
Forensic Specialist

USING LEARNING STRATEGIES IN COLLEGE

I've tried a couple of different things in college that have helped me learn. One thing is that when I study, I think of personal examples to help me remember material. When I needed to learn that John F. Kennedy was assassinated in 1963, I thought about the fact that my sister is nineteen, there are six people in my family, and I have three siblings. Using this method helps me a lot when I need to remember important things for tests.

Sometimes I connect ideas from other classes together, too. For example, I use new words that I learned in my English class in my other classes. This is a good way to learn, because the more connections you have, the easier it will be for you to remember the information.

I've also learned to spread out my studying. I take 30 minutes out of my day, or whatever spare time I have, and go over my notes for upcoming tests. I didn't always do this — I used to study two days before my test was due. But I finally decided to try something new instead of cramming, and I feel like this has impacted my test-taking skills for the better. I no longer feel so stressed out about trying to learn information in a short amount of time.

These learning strategies work for me, but see what works best for you. If you aren't happy with your studying routine, then find a new one that you are happy with!

YOUR TURN Have you ever used any of the learning strategies that Dara describes? If so, which ones? If not, will you try any of these in your classes this term?

The simple act of engaging in self-explanation can be helpful because, as with asking why, it encourages you to connect new material to your existing knowledge. It also causes you to slow down your learning process, which prompts you to become more reflective (metacognitive) about your learning, to think critically, and to ask questions about what comes next. Better yet, these activities also strengthen the brain networks that you'll use to recall this information and apply it later.

Use Verbal *and* Visual Information

Later in this chapter, we'll describe how some people prefer processing information using language (e.g., verbally or through reading and writing) while others prefer learning visually (by looking at diagrams or creating mental images of what they're learning). As it turns out, no matter what your preferences happen to be, doing both might help you learn even better.[11] Verbal information and visual information are processed differently by the brain—to some extent, they're even processed in different parts of the brain. According to one theory, called *dual coding*, learning is strengthened by making connections between the visual and the language portions of our brains.

Consider the example from the last section—learning about the elasticity of arteries. When you read that example, did you also create a mental image of a rapidly beating heart and envision how the arteries coming from the heart could expand and contract to accommodate blood flow? If you did, you were using both language and visual imagery to learn simultaneously, and, as a result, you'll probably remember this fact better. In a later section we'll provide other examples of how it's beneficial to develop *multimodal*, or flexible, learning strategies like this.

Make Learning Personal

Now that you're familiar with what science says about effective learning, it's time to think more deeply about your own preferences for learning and the preferences of others around you—including your classmates, your colleagues at work, and even your instructors. A *learning preference* is the way a person prefers to acquire and work with different types of information. Most students can identify ways that they prefer to learn, if given the choice. For example, you might love attending lectures and taking notes but feel less enthusiastic about a group discussion or group project. Alternatively, you might prefer focusing on big-picture concepts before tackling the details, or vice versa.

While these preferences exist, it's important to note that our ability to learn isn't limited by these preferences. In fact, there is little evidence for the idea that you actually learn better using your preferred styles of learning, or even that you learn better when someone teaches according to your preferences.[12] Preferences aren't a specific prescription for learning, and we shouldn't treat them as such; rather, they're important because of what they teach us about ourselves, about people we interact with, and about the learning environments in which we find ourselves.

Different classes will require different types of learning, different teachers will structure their classes different ways, and different classmates and group members will bring different preferences to the table. When you understand what preferences involve, and how they work, you'll be prepared to learn as effectively as possible in many different kinds of environments. In other words, by thinking metacognitively about your own (and others') preferences for learning, you'll stay flexible, self-aware, and responsive in different learning situations.

In the section that follows, we'll look at two different models you can use to better understand yourself as a learner: the Myers-Briggs Type Indicator (MBTI) and the VARK (Visual, Aural, Read-Write, and Kinesthetic) model. You can use each of these instruments independently, or both in combination, to identify your learning preferences and get a better sense of how you tackle course material.

Use the Myers-Briggs Model

Katharine Briggs and her daughter Isabel Myers created the Myers-Briggs Type Indicator (MBTI) based on the work of psychologist Carl Jung. In Jung's theory, four dimensions of our personalities guide our behavior, influencing where we focus our energy, the kinds of information we prefer working with, how we make decisions, and how we organize our time. Each of the four dimensions can be thought of as a continuum, with some students preferring one end or the other, and some students falling closer to the middle.[13]

Extravert/Introvert. The Extravert/Introvert dimension describes where you tend to focus your energy. Extraverts are action oriented and like spending time with others. Being with people energizes them, and they often enjoy interacting and discussing their learning with others or applying their learning to real-life problems.

By contrast, Introverts are more thought oriented and are energized by spending time alone. Introverts often prefer to learn through reflection and feel most comfortable discussing ideas once they've had a chance to think about them. They can still work effectively in groups, but they may want time to process new information before they feel prepared to discuss it with others.

Sensing/Intuitive. The Sensing/Intuitive dimension relates to the kind of information you prefer working with: details and facts or the big picture. Sensing learners prefer working with information as it comes to them through their senses. They love details and facts and have an easy time remembering and organizing such information. Sensing learners use the facts to build an understanding of the big picture.

By contrast, Intuitive learners prefer to pay attention to facts and details only long enough to understand the big picture—the theory behind the concept or how the concept connects to other material. They like to get an overview of a topic before digging into the specifics and want to know answers to broad questions, such as, How does this topic relate to the last topic presented in class?

⸮ CONNECT
TO MY EXPERIENCE
When you're learning something new, do you focus on details and facts or on the big picture? Think about the advantages and disadvantages of each preference. Then, in writing, describe a time when focusing on details caused you to miss out on the big picture, or when focusing on the big picture caused you to overlook important details.

What's Your Sense of Snow? Suppose you've never seen snow before. If you're a Sensing learner, you'd probably look at the snowflakes (the details) first as a way to understand the concept of a snowstorm (the big picture). If you're an Intuitive learner, you'd pay attention to the snowstorm and then use your understanding of it to grasp the concept of individual snowflakes. Left: Kichigin/Shutterstock; Right: Creative Travel Projects/Shutterstock

Thinking/Feeling. The Thinking/Feeling dimension relates to how you make decisions. Thinking decision makers prefer to use analysis and logic to arrive at a decision. By contrast, Feeling decision makers tend to make choices that maintain harmony or that demonstrate concern about human values and needs.

Being a Thinking learner or a Feeling learner can influence how you react during the various steps in the decision-making process (see the chapter on motivation, decision making, and personal responsibility). When evaluating the available options and weighing the pros and cons of each alternative, Thinkers may focus on the option that has more pros, whereas Feelers may concentrate on how the decision will affect the important people in their lives.

Judging/Perceiving. The Judging/Perceiving dimension describes how you organize your time. Judging learners plan the details of their actions before proceeding, focus on actions that directly contribute to achievement of a goal or task, and generally have structured routines. They prefer making decisions and sticking with them and like to complete one project before starting another.

Perceiving learners are more comfortable taking action without first developing a plan. They multitask and juggle different projects at once and prefer keeping their options open rather than committing to a decision.

You may have developed a good sense of where your organizational preferences lie on this dimension when you read the organization and time management chapter. If you're a Judger, you'll likely appreciate that chapter's material on scheduling. If you're a Perceiver, you may have cringed at the thought of organizing your life so systematically.

Your Preferences. Now that you're familiar with the four dimensions of the MBTI, take a moment to record where you think you fall on each dimension. Using Figure 5.2, place an X on each line to designate your preference and how

FIGURE 5.2
Myers-Briggs Self-Rating Chart

	Strong Preference	Moderate Preference	Neutral	Moderate Preference	Strong Preference	
Spend time with people Learn through discussion	Extravert				Introvert	Prefer time alone Learn through reflection
Focus on details Prefer facts	Sensing				Intuitive	Focus on big picture Prefer concepts
Consider facts when making decisions Make decisions based on logic	Thinking			Feeling		Consider people when making decisions Make decisions based on values
Like coming to decisions Like planning and structure	Judging			Perceiving		Avoid decisions in favor of exploring options Go with the flow

strong you think it is. For example, an X far to the right on the Extravert/Introvert line would indicate that you have a strong Introvert preference, whereas an X far to the left would show a strong Extravert preference. An X somewhere in the middle would suggest a more moderate or a neutral preference.

Learning Strategies. Once you've recorded your self-rating, ask yourself: How can I use this information to become a better learner in all my classes? Knowing more about your preferences isn't meant to define how you must learn, but it can prompt you to try out new strategies that you haven't considered previously. In Table 5.1 you'll find a list of learning strategies paired up with each MBTI type; try some of the suggestions that are in your comfort zone, as well as others that are totally new to you.

TABLE 5.1

Learning Strategies for Myers-Briggs Dimensions

Extravert	• Ask a family member, friend, or classmate to listen as you explain concepts from class. • Find a study group and meet regularly to share your ideas. • Meet with your instructor or a tutor to discuss key course concepts.
Introvert	• Set aside quiet study time. • If you join a study group, learn topics in advance so you're prepared to discuss them. • After class, write a summary of what you've learned. Refer to your summary when sharing your thoughts in the next class.
Sensing	• Outline the details of your study goals and study strategy. • Combine facts in ways that help you tell a story about the big picture.
Intuitive	• Rather than feeling frustrated by the repetitive tasks associated with some classes, consider how these tasks help you better understand the big picture. • Look for the connections: Focus on how your big picture understanding of concepts relates to concepts in other courses you're taking.
Thinking	• If class material seems unorganized and illogical, reorganize it so it makes sense to you. • Identify principles in material you're learning, and apply them systematically to new situations.
Feeling	• You're most comfortable in study groups in which students agree with one another, but disagreement and debate are a natural part of learning. Step out of your comfort zone, and learn from different perspectives. • To feel personally connected to course material, find ways to make it relevant to your life.
Judging	• Create binders for each of your classes so you can stay organized. • Create structured study schedules based on deadlines. • When you finish a task, reward yourself by doing something enjoyable.
Perceiving	• Instead of saving studying until the last minute, use spare moments to review class notes. • Break down large assignments into smaller, more manageable chunks. • If you start many projects, prioritize them, and deal with the most important ones when deadlines are approaching.

Use the VARK Model

VARK is another model that can help you understand how you prefer to learn. Proposed by Neil Fleming, a high school and university teacher, VARK describes what types of information people prefer to work with while learning—**V**isual, **A**ural (auditory), **R**ead-Write, and **K**inesthetic (hands on, action based).[14] Many people feel comfortable working with more than one of these types of information. As you read the descriptions of each preference, consider which one(s) fits you best.

- **Visual (V).** Visual learners prefer working with information that comes in forms such as charts, diagrams, maps, and graphs. They might translate material presented in class into concept maps, flowcharts, or other graphic forms to better understand course concepts and see how they relate to each other.

- **Aural (A).** Aural learners prefer working with information that comes in auditory forms, such as lectures, podcasts, and discussions with others. In class, for example, Aural learners might ask to record their instructors' lectures, so they have the opportunity to listen again later.

- **Read-Write (R).** Read-Write learners prefer learning from the written word. They may read a lot, use text-heavy slide presentations, and seek out books and journal articles using popular online sources such as Google Scholar. They may prefer to study by reading through important material, revising and reorganizing class notes, or preparing brief written responses to anticipated essay questions.

- **Kinesthetic (K).** Kinesthetic learners prefer experience and practice as a means of learning. They learn by doing or by watching others, and they enjoy watching demonstrations, trying their hand at simulations, analyzing case studies, and conducting lab experiments.

Learning by Doing. The people hanging from these poles are taking a climbing course offered by a utility company. They're students at a workforce institute affiliated with a nearby community college. The three-week course supports kinesthetic learning—learning by doing. Students master skills that will prepare them to compete for jobs in the utility industry, such as pre-apprentice lineworker.
Justin Sullivan/Getty Images

The VARK Questionnaire. Now that you understand the VARK model, you can assess your preferences using the VARK dimensions. Take a few minutes to respond to the items on the following pages and score your assessment. Place a check mark next to all the answers that apply to you; you can choose more than one response per question, or you can leave the question blank if none of the responses apply to you.

Keep in mind that your score in each category (V, A, R, and K) represents the strength of your preference for that type of information. Some students have clear preferences (e.g., **V = 11**, A = 3, R = 1, K = 1), while other students' preferences are more evenly distributed (for instance, V = 2, A = 1, **R = 6, K = 7**).

Once you have your results, reflect on them. What is your highest score? Does that learning preference make sense to you based on your understanding of yourself? Do you have two or three scores that are relatively close together? If so, what are they? How might this new understanding of yourself help you learn and study for different types of classes?

Learning Strategies. According to VARK, do you have a strong Visual, Aural, Read-Write, or Kinesthetic preference? A combination of several types? How can you use this information to become a better learner? As you saw in the MBTI section, knowing more about your preferences isn't meant to define how you must learn, but it can help you identify some interesting new strategies that might appeal to you. Check out the suggestions in Table 5.2, which are paired up with different VARK types. Which of these will you try? For which classes?

TABLE 5.2
Learning Strategies for VARK Dimensions

Visual (V)	<ul><li>Underline, highlight, or use other tactics to mark up printed course materials.</li><li>Draw pictures or diagrams in your notes to illustrate examples. Reference these images when you study.</li><li>Ask your instructor for copies of visually complex materials presented in class.</li></ul>
Aural (A)	<ul><li>Study in groups, and discuss concepts with others.</li><li>Record lectures (with your instructor's permission), and listen to them later.</li><li>Use word associations to learn terms, and repeat newly learned terms out loud.</li></ul>
Read-Write (R)	<ul><li>After reading your assigned textbook, write a short self-test to help you strengthen your understanding of the material.</li><li>Find alternative written resources on a topic to supplement class-assigned reading.</li><li>Write out questions that you have for your instructor about material presented in class. Then write a short summary of the response your instructor provides to those questions.</li></ul>
Kinesthetic (K)	<ul><li>Find hands-on ways to learn course content (such as computer simulations or lab experiments).</li><li>Incorporate movement into your note taking by drawing charts or diagrams of important relationships covered in class.</li><li>Take breaks from studying and move around. Use the exercise to review or rehearse material that you've already learned.</li></ul>

VARK Questionnaire

1. You are helping someone who wants to go to your airport, the center of town, or a railway station. You would:
   - ☐ **A.** go with her.
   - ☐ **B.** tell her the directions.
   - ☐ **C.** write down the directions.
   - ☐ **D.** draw, or show her a map, or give her a map.

2. A Web site has a video showing how to make a special graph. There is a person speaking, some lists and words describing what to do, and some diagrams. You would learn most from:
   - ☐ **A.** seeing the diagrams.
   - ☐ **B.** listening.
   - ☐ **C.** reading the words.
   - ☐ **D.** watching the actions.

3. You are planning a vacation for a group. You want some feedback from them about the plan. You would:
   - ☐ **A.** describe some of the highlights they will experience.
   - ☐ **B.** use a map to show them the places.
   - ☐ **C.** give them a copy of the printed itinerary.
   - ☐ **D.** phone, text, or e-mail them.

4. You are going to cook something as a special treat. You would:
   - ☐ **A.** cook something you know without the need for instructions.
   - ☐ **B.** ask friends for suggestions.
   - ☐ **C.** look on the Internet or in some cookbooks for ideas from the pictures.
   - ☐ **D.** use a cookbook where you know there is a good recipe.

5. A group of tourists wants to learn about the parks or wildlife reserves in your area. You would:
   - ☐ **A.** talk about, or arrange a talk for them about, parks or wildlife reserves.
   - ☐ **B.** show them maps and Internet pictures.
   - ☐ **C.** take them to a park or wildlife reserve and walk with them.
   - ☐ **D.** give them a book or pamphlets about the parks or wildlife reserves.

6. You are about to purchase a digital camera or mobile phone. Other than price, what would most influence your decision?
   - ☐ **A.** Trying or testing it.
   - ☐ **B.** Reading the details or checking its features online.
   - ☐ **C.** It is a modern design and looks good.
   - ☐ **D.** The salesperson telling me about its features.

7. Remember a time when you learned how to do something new. Avoid choosing a physical skill, e.g., riding a bike. You learned best by:
   - ☐ **A.** watching a demonstration.
   - ☐ **B.** listening to somebody explaining it and asking questions.
   - ☐ **C.** diagrams, maps, and charts — visual clues.
   - ☐ **D.** written instructions — e.g., a manual or book.

8. You have a problem with your heart. You would prefer that the doctor:
   - ☐ **A.** gave you something to read to explain what was wrong.
   - ☐ **B.** used a plastic model to show what was wrong.
   - ☐ **C.** described what was wrong.
   - ☐ **D.** showed you a diagram of what was wrong.

9. You want to learn a new program, skill, or game on a computer. You would:
   - ☐ **A.** read the written instructions that came with the program.
   - ☐ **B.** talk with people who know about the program.
   - ☐ **C.** use the controls or keyboard.
   - ☐ **D.** follow the diagrams in the book that came with it.

10. I like Web sites that have:
   - ☐ **A.** things I can click on, shift, or try.
   - ☐ **B.** interesting design and visual features.
   - ☐ **C.** interesting written descriptions, lists, and explanations.
   - ☐ **D.** audio channels where I can hear music, radio programs, or interviews.

11. Other than price, what would most influence your decision to buy a new nonfiction book?
   - ☐ **A.** The way it looks is appealing.
   - ☐ **B.** Quickly reading parts of it.
   - ☐ **C.** A friend talks about it and recommends it.
   - ☐ **D.** It has real-life stories, experiences, and examples.

12. You are using a book, CD, or Web site to learn how to take photos with your new digital camera. You would like to have:
   - ☐ **A.** a chance to ask questions and talk about the camera and its features.
   - ☐ **B.** clear written instructions with lists and bullet points about what to do.
   - ☐ **C.** diagrams showing the camera and what each part does.
   - ☐ **D.** many examples of good and poor photos and how to improve them.

(continued)

13. Do you prefer a teacher or a presenter who uses:
    - ☐ **A.** demonstrations, models, or practical sessions.
    - ☐ **B.** question and answer, talk, group discussion, or guest speakers.
    - ☐ **C.** handouts, books, or readings.
    - ☐ **D.** diagrams, charts, or graphs.

14. You have finished a competition or test and would like some feedback. You would like to have feedback:
    - ☐ **A.** using examples from what you have done.
    - ☐ **B.** using a written description of your results.
    - ☐ **C.** from somebody who talks it through with you.
    - ☐ **D.** using graphs showing what you had achieved.

15. You are going to choose food at a restaurant or cafe. You would:
    - ☐ **A.** choose something that you have had there before.
    - ☐ **B.** listen to the waiter or ask friends to recommend choices.
    - ☐ **C.** choose from the descriptions in the menu.
    - ☐ **D.** look at what others are eating or look at pictures of each dish.

16. You have to make an important speech at a conference or special occasion. You would:
    - ☐ **A.** make diagrams or get graphs to help explain things.
    - ☐ **B.** write a few key words and practice saying your speech over and over.
    - ☐ **C.** write out your speech and learn from reading it over several times.
    - ☐ **D.** gather many examples and stories to make the talk real and practical.

The VARK Questionnaire, Version 7.8. Copyright © held by Neil D. Fleming, Christchurch, New Zealand. Used by permission.

Your VARK Score

Use the following scoring chart to find the VARK category that each of your answers corresponds to. Circle the letters that correspond to your answers. For example, if you answered B and C for question 3, circle V and R in the question 3 row.

Responses to Question 3:	A	B	C	D
VARK letter	K	(V)	(R)	A

Question	A category	B category	C category	D category
1.	K	A	R	V
2.	V	A	R	K
3.	K	V	R	A
4.	K	A	V	R
5.	A	V	K	R
6.	K	R	V	A
7.	K	A	V	R
8.	R	K	A	V
9.	R	A	K	V
10.	K	V	R	A
11.	V	R	A	K
12.	A	R	V	K
13.	K	A	R	V
14.	K	R	A	V
15.	K	A	R	V
16.	V	A	R	K

MY HIGHEST SCORES

Total number of Vs circled =

Total number of As circled =

Total number of Rs circled =

Total number of Ks circled =

Succeed in Different Learning Environments

Preferences are fun to learn about, and they can be useful when it comes to identifying interesting study strategies. But regardless of your VARK or MBTI results, and even regardless of your academic major, you'll need to learn in a number of different environments in college: Instructors across campus will expect you to work both independently and in groups; in classrooms, online, and in labs; and possibly in simulated or real work environments. As you learn in these different settings—both in and outside your comfort zone—it's important to anticipate possible challenges and brainstorm strategies you can use to stay successful. Here we'll focus on three specific scenarios: how to work effectively in a group, how to become a multimodal learner, and how to seek help if you have a learning disability.

Work in a Group

Many instructors are fans of group projects and with good reason: Research has shown that group work contributes to learning and success in college,[15] and many jobs require you to work effectively in groups. As beneficial as it can be, though, group work can also be challenging—you'll be collaborating with other students, and many of them will have preferred strategies for processing and remembering information that differ from your own. The good news? The more you understand how learning works, the more you'll all be able to leverage each person's strengths. For instance, suppose your group includes Fadi, a Visual, Intuitive, and Judging learner who loves big ideas and staying organized. Fadi takes responsibility for creating a project plan during the group's first meeting. This "big picture" plan takes the form of a chart outlining which tasks have to be done when, and by whom, so that the group can submit a high-quality project on time. Fadi would likely do a great job with this responsibility, and your group would benefit as well.

When the inevitable difficulties arise, group members can also use their understanding of learning to resolve issues. For example, suppose you notice that group member Anatole seems to get overwhelmed during marathon work sessions where everyone focuses on one task for several hours. With your knowledge of distributed learning and interleaved practice, you can suggest alternating between different tasks instead, as well as meeting more frequently but for shorter amounts of time. Or suppose you realize that Irene is having a difficult time grasping the structural relationships that exist in a new database. You might suggest that she draw a diagram of these relationships so she can use dual coding to better understand how the database works.

Make Sure You're Multimodal

No matter what your preferred mode(s) of learning are, as a student you'll be expected to excel in a variety of learning environments: After all, most students have to attend lectures, participate in hands-on learning activities in labs, read lots of books, and write lots of papers—whether they're Read-Write or Visual learners, Introverts or Extraverts, or big-picture thinkers or detail people. As a college student, it's your job to get comfortable

Team Effort. In every group project you're involved in during your college and professional career, group members will have different learning preferences and go-to strategies. When all group members understand how learning works, they can take advantage of diverse strategies and work more effectively as a team. Klaus Vedfelt/Getty Images

using the learning strategies that are called for in the classes you take. In other words, you'll need to become a **multimodal learner**—someone who can use different learning strategies based on the situation at hand.

By developing the ability to use different learning strategies, you boost your chances of doing well in *all* your classes—not just the ones you like best. You also demonstrate personal responsibility: Instead of passively expecting instructors to change their approaches to suit your preferences (which they won't do!), you take charge of your own education.

To increase your pool of learning strategies, try the following tactics.

Flex Your Learning Muscles. Not every course you take will be a perfect fit — perhaps your instructor loves to lecture, while you prefer hands-on projects. But succeeding in a variety of environments means having different learning strategies at your fingertips and making sure you're multimodal. This takes practice — but it also makes you a flexible learner who gets the most from your courses. © DisabilityImages.com

- **Review the strategies that are included in this chapter,** and try out several that differ from those you typically use. Cut yourself some slack as you try out these new techniques; applying new strategies can take time and practice.

- **Talk with students in your classes** whose preferences match how your instructor likes to teach. Use these students as models. Ask them to share what works for them; then try the strategies they recommend.

- **Visit a tutor** associated with a course you find difficult. Ask for advice on how to develop learning strategies that work for that course.

- **Talk to your instructors.** Visit them during office hours and have a conversation. Instructors may be able to suggest specific ways to master the course content, even if that content challenges you to go outside your comfort zone.

multimodal learner:
Someone who uses multiple learning strategies and methods to learn.

Seek Help for Learning Challenges

As you've seen in this chapter, people have different ways they prefer to learn. Beyond differences related to learning preferences, however, some people experience differences in how their brain receives or processes information—differences that can cause significant difficulty in listening, speaking, reading, writing, spelling, and interacting socially. In such cases, these people may be diagnosed with what's called a *learning disability*. Don't let this term fool you: People with a learning disability still learn—just not in the same way as people without one. A learning disability is really a learning *difference*.

Because learning disabilities can affect how people work with course material, students with diagnosed learning disabilities may be eligible to have their learning environment adapted (or *accommodated*) to suit their learning needs. For example, a student might be able to record lectures or receive extended time in which to complete an exam. The purpose of these adaptations is not to provide an advantage but rather to "level the playing field." That way, all students have an equal chance to learn the material and demonstrate their new knowledge and skills.

If you have a learning disability and need academic accommodations, visit your school's disability services office. The staff will review documentation of your disability and determine your eligibility for services. You can also visit the disability services office if you suspect you have an undiagnosed learning disability. The staff will help you seek appropriate testing, which will determine if you meet specific criteria to be diagnosed with a learning disability. The disability services office is a valuable resource you can use to better understand learning disabilities—and to get any help you might need.

**⟡ CONNECT
TO MY RESOURCES**

Do you need to register for accommodations in the classroom? Do you know a friend who does? On your college Web site, find the name and location of the campus office that provides these services. Write it down. Then record the steps a student would need to follow to set up accommodations.

Apply Your Knowledge of Learning at Work

When you understand the basics of learning, as well as your own learning preferences, you're at a professional advantage: Most companies want employees who can think metacognitively, adjust to different work environments as needed, and use proven strategies to perform new responsibilities. Here's how you can use your learning skills to excel on the job—and exceed expectations.

Work in a Team

To succeed in many careers today, you need to work in teams.[16] As in college, members of a work team will likely have different learning preferences and different go-to strategies that they use to work with information. When team members understand the learning process, they can use these differences as an advantage and play to each person's strengths.

Take Roger and Katarina, who are developing a training program for hospital nurses. Roger is a Sensing and Perceiving learner who likes to work on several projects at once and focus on details. Sometimes he misses the big picture, and he juggles so many projects that none move forward as fast as his supervisor wants.

Katarina, on the other hand, is an Intuitive and Judging learner who prefers to move one project forward at a time and readily grasps the big picture associated with each (but is less effective at tracking details). Roger and Katarina understand each other's learning preferences and use that understanding to accomplish their work. For instance, Katarina uses her grasp of the big picture to help Roger understand the project's overall goals, while Roger uses his grasp of the details to suggest steps they can take to execute the project. By thinking metacognitively and working as a team, Roger and Katarina take advantage of their learning differences; this makes them more successful together than either would have been alone.

This flexibility is equally important for cultivating a good working relationship with your boss. The more you understand how your supervisor operates, the more you can customize how you work together. For instance, you learn that your boss prefers to receive status updates by e-mail every Monday, rather than by informal chats in the hallway, so you adapt your communication to her preference. One of your weekly reports alerts her to the possibility of a missed deadline on a project. She meets with you to discuss solutions, such as finding someone to help you meet the deadline. Both you and she benefit.

Working in Sync. Good teamwork matters in every work setting—whether you're a member of a competitive rowing team, a carpenter helping to build a house, or a data analyst in a team charged with identifying new customer segments. When teammates understand how learning works, they can leverage one another's strengths and support one another. Result? Team performance that's totally in sync. Ingram Publishing/Getty Images

Expand Your Understanding

New technologies, new markets, and the globalization of work will challenge you to continue to learn once you're in your career. Further, if you hope to advance, you'll be expected to develop new skills and become familiar with new aspects of the work.

Take Leah, who is looking to get promoted to regional account manager at the insurance company she works for. In order to be successful in that new role, Leah needs to study up on principles of management and human resource issues. Relying on her understanding of how learning works, she identifies training materials on these topics and establishes a six-month study plan for herself. She alternates among topics (interleaved practice), spends time each week studying (distributed practice), connects new material to material she learned in school, and creates self-tests to strengthen her understanding. In this way, Leah will take her career to the next level.

> "Using different learning strategies and adapting to the styles of others has been critical to my success."

NAME
Grace Ku

PROFESSION
Social Media Manager

SCHOOL
University of Utah

DEGREE
Bachelor of Science

MAJOR
Business Marketing

Courtesy of J. Doucette

USING LEARNING STRATEGIES ON THE JOB

While I was in college, I developed learning strategies that worked great for me. Once I got into the working world, I discovered that I needed to rely on a range of learning strategies to interact effectively with my boss and the people I supervise.

When I started as a Social Media Intern, one of my first tasks was to create reports for my boss. I used the skills I built in college to organize and write reports. Then I'd e-mail them to my boss, and when she had questions I'd refer her to the report that I wrote. I discovered very quickly that this wasn't working for her. She wanted me to boil down the information in the report so it fit onto a sticky note, and to give her answers myself when she had questions. I basically had to adapt to her learning preferences and get out of my comfort zone. Instead of writing and submitting reports like I had been, I needed to summarize information and be prepared to provide verbal answers on the spot.

After ten months on the job, I was promoted to Social Media Manager. When this happened, I had to find ways to communicate effectively with the whole team I supervise. I regularly send out information to my team members about what we need to get done that week. I quickly discovered that one of my team members is an Aural learner — I need to tell him what I expect face-to-face. If I send it in an e-mail, it won't get done, but if I take a moment to discuss things verbally, he does great work. Using different learning strategies and adapting to the styles of others has been critical to my success.

> **YOUR TURN** Have you ever had to adopt an unfamiliar learning strategy to work more effectively with a boss, a coworker, or an employee? If so, which strategy? What was the outcome?

Supervise and Train Others

As you advance in your career, your job may include supervising or training less experienced employees. Understanding how people learn can help you tailor your approach to each employee to support their learning and development.

Consider Juanita, who has asked her assistant Derek to learn a new inventory-tracking system. She has given him the printed instruction manual, but he's struggling to make sense of it. By observing Derek at work, Juanita realizes that he's a strongly Visual and Kinesthetic learner, and she remembers reading about the value of dual coding. She enrolls Derek in a workshop where he can practice using the new system and gives him access to an online tutorial with diagrams and process flowcharts. Juanita also teaches Derek about how to create self-tests to learn the material more effectively. Derek soon masters the new system — demonstrating the benefits that come when supervisors understand learning basics, as well as their employees' preferences.

my personal success plan

Based on your ACES results and what you read about in this chapter, are you inspired to set a new goal related to understanding learning? If so, the Personal Success Plan can walk you through the goal-setting process. Read the advice and examples; then sketch out your ideas in the space provided.

To access the Personal Success Plan online, go to the LaunchPad for *Connections,* Second Edition.

1 **IDENTIFY A GOAL**

Choose a learning-related goal to work toward this term. Here are some general ideas you might draw from; you can also create a goal of your own.

- ▶ Create a distributed learning schedule.
- ▶ Try out self-testing.
- ▶ Combine verbal and visual learning strategies.
- ▶ Try two new strategies that fit with my MBTI preferences.
- ▶ Join a study group of students with diverse learning preferences.

2 **MAKE YOUR GOAL SMART**

Rewrite your specific goal so that it's SMART, and make sure to use the SMART goal checklist.

SAMPLE: By Friday, I'll create a distributed learning schedule to prepare for my history exam.

3 **CREATE AN ACTION PLAN**

Outline the specific steps you'll take to achieve your SMART goal, and note when you'll complete each step.

SAMPLE: Tomorrow I'll study history for an hour between classes and one hour after dinner.

4 **LIST BARRIERS AND SOLUTIONS**

Think about possible barriers to your action steps; then brainstorm solutions for overcoming them.

SAMPLE: If I get distracted by other opportunities during my break between classes, I'll refocus myself by remembering how important distributed practice is for optimal learning.

5 **ACT AND EVALUATE OUTCOMES**

Now that your plan is in place, take action. Record each action step as you take it. Then evaluate whether you achieved your SMART goal, and make any adjustments needed to get better results in the future.

SAMPLE: An unexpected math assignment prevented me from studying for history last night, so I've revised my schedule for the rest of the week to make up for that lost hour.

6 **CONNECT TO CAREER**

List the skills you're building as you progress toward your SMART goal. How will you use these skills to land a job and succeed at work?

SAMPLE: By following a pattern of distributed studying, I'm developing a habit that will help me learn new and complex material at work.

my personal success plan

1 my general goal

____

____

____

____

____

____

2 my SMART goal

____

____

____

____

☐ SPECIFIC ☐ MEASURABLE ☐ ACHIEVABLE ☐ RELEVANT ☐ TIME-LIMITED

3 my action plan

____

____

____

____

____

4 my barriers/ solutions

____

____

____

____

____

5 my actions/ outcomes

____

____

____

____

____

6 my career connection

____

____

____

____

____

CHAPTER SUMMARY

As you saw in this chapter, understanding how you learn can help you succeed in college and your career. Revisit the following key points, and consider how you can use this information to support your success now and in the future.

- Learning-science research can help you understand and apply proven strategies to promote learning. These strategies include self-testing, spacing out and alternating studying, making connections between new information and prior learning, and using dual coding.

- A learning preference is the way a person prefers to acquire and work with information. Using your preferences doesn't guarantee success, but it can help you better understand your learning challenges or successes when combined with research-based learning strategies. Considering preferences is also a way of practicing metacognition.

- The MBTI and the VARK models represent two ways of thinking about learning preferences. According to the MBTI, four dimensions affect our behavior: Extravert/Introvert, Sensing/Intuitive, Thinking/Feeling, and Judging/Perceiving. The VARK (Visual, Aural, Read-Write, Kinesthetic) provides another way to understand how people prefer to take in and process new information.

- To succeed in the diverse learning environments of college, you'll need to learn to work in a group successfully and become a multimodal learner.

- If you're challenged by a learning disability, reach out to someone at your school's disability services office.

- Learning doesn't end at graduation. Your employer will expect you to learn new information, master new processes, and work effectively with team members who have different ways of building new skills and knowledge. Using your understanding of how people learn, you can improve your relationship with your supervisor, build your own skill set, and teach and supervise others more effectively.

CHAPTER ACTIVITIES

Journal Entry

LEARNING HOW TO LEARN EFFECTIVELY

Now that you've read this chapter and developed a better sense of how the learning process works, write a journal entry in which you reflect on this process and the strategies that can help you learn new information most effectively. Respond to these questions:

1. How would you define learning in your own words?

2. What happens in your brain when you learn something new?

3. Describe one of the learning strategies outlined in this chapter and explain how this particular strategy promotes learning.

4. Provide an example of a time when you learned something new and employed one of the strategies outlined in this chapter. How was this strategy helpful? Were there any other strategies you could have used? Explain.

5. Which learning strategy or strategies described in this chapter will you "test out" in this class or in another class this term?

Adopting a Success Attitude

ENSURING A POSITIVE GROUP WORK EXPERIENCE

As you think about working with your classmates on a group project, what's your initial reaction? If it's worry, dread, or annoyance, you may have had a negative experience working with others in the past, or you may be anticipating conflict over differences in group members' learning preferences. You can use your knowledge of the MBTI to make your future group-work experiences positive and productive.

Imagine you've been assigned to work in a group, and your task is to determine whether college athletes should be paid for playing their sport. The group has to research each position in the debate and put together a presentation in which you argue for one side or the other. Respond to the following scenarios:

1. You don't know anyone in the group. What could you do to get to know your group members and feel more comfortable working with them?

2. The group has four Extraverts and four Introverts. How could you ensure that everyone has a voice in the group process?

3. The group has four Sensing and four Intuitive people. How could you best use everyone's strengths in doing the research and writing the presentation?

4. The four Thinkers in the group disagree with the four Feelers as to whether college athletes should be paid. The group needs to choose one position. What do you say to your fellow group members? How do you make a decision that will make the greatest number of people happy?

5. The four Judgers want the group to create a plan for meeting, distributing tasks, and setting deadlines. Three of the Perceivers aren't comfortable with so much structure. Although you're a Perceiver, you see the benefits of creating a plan. What can you say to the other Perceivers to help them understand these benefits?

6. The group creates a plan for managing the tasks involved in this assignment. At the next meeting, two students arrive without having completed their assigned tasks. Those who completed their tasks are angry. How do you bring the group together and refocus everyone's attention on the goal?

Applying Your Skills

TESTING YOURSELF

In this chapter you learned that self-testing is an effective way to learn. For this activity, you'll create a brief quiz and a set of flash cards based on important material in this chapter. To do so, follow these steps:

1. First, review the chapter and write down seven to ten key concepts. How do you know which concepts are important? If you see these concepts in the introduction, referenced in a photo or heading, or in the end-of-chapter summary, that's a good clue. (These are all good places to look for important concepts and terms.)

2. Next, create one test question for each concept. The question can be multiple choice, short-answer, or an essay question. You may want to share your test questions with other students in the class or review them together.

3. Lastly, to test yourself further, create a set of flash cards with a word or concept on one side and the definition or explanation on the other side. Use these flash cards to review key concepts on a regular basis.

College Success = Career Success

APPRECIATING DIFFERENCES IN THE WORKPLACE

The Myers-Briggs Type Indicator (MBTI) is commonly used in the workplace to promote employee success. Think about how you could use your knowledge of the four MBTI dimensions to address the following situations:

1. **Extravert/Introvert:** You run a weekly meeting in which your sales team brainstorms new leads. The Extraverts in your group comment on or ask questions about everything you say. You can't seem to make it through your agenda. At the same time, the Introverts rarely speak up, but you know they have good ideas. In fact, you often get e-mails from them days after the meeting. Although their comments are useful, you've already moved on to something else. How can you make these meetings more productive while appreciating the strengths and weaknesses of Extraverts and Introverts?

2. **Sensing/Intuitive:** Your employees need to learn a new office procedure. How do you present the information to maximize learning for both Sensing and Intuitive types?

3. **Thinking/Feeling:** The hiring committee has just completed candidate interviews. Two committee members want to choose someone based on the facts, such as résumés and responses to questions. Two others want to base their decision on the impression they formed of each candidate through eye contact, posture, appearance, and personal interactions. You've been asked to help the committee reach a resolution. What do you do?

4. **Judging/Perceiving:** Would you prefer to work with someone who likes to focus on only one project before starting another (Judging) or with someone who can multitask but may become distracted if he or she juggles too many projects (Perceiving)? What benefits and challenges would this type of coworker bring to your working relationship and job effectiveness?

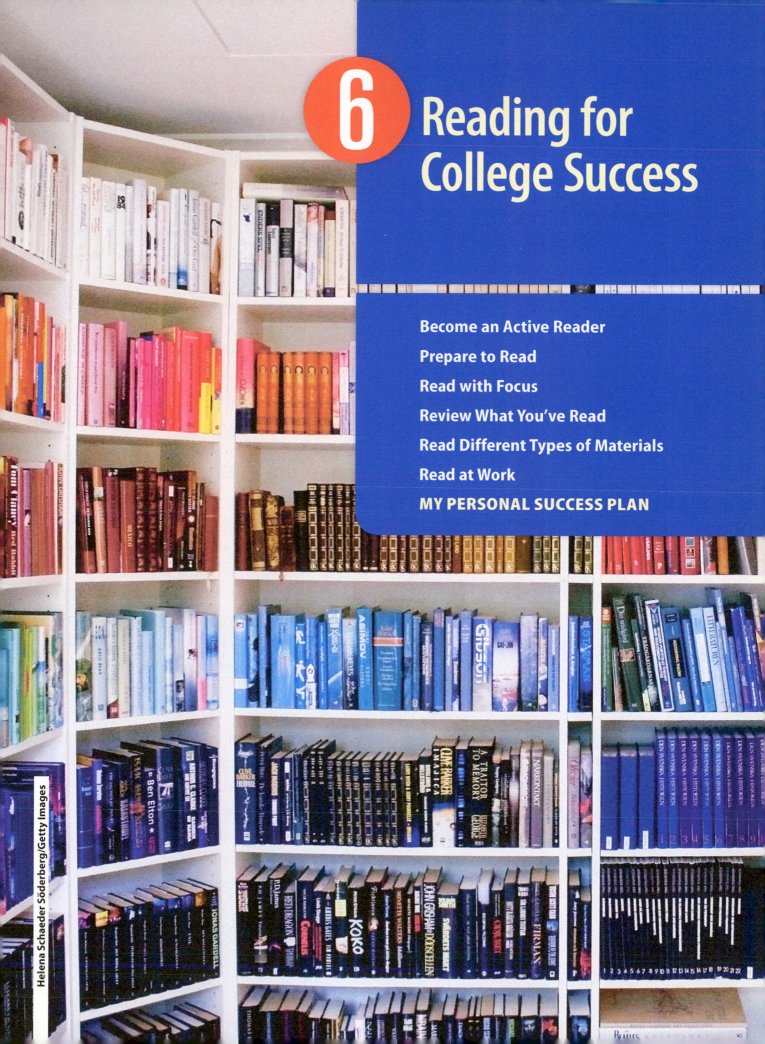

6 Reading for College Success

Become an Active Reader

Prepare to Read

Read with Focus

Review What You've Read

Read Different Types of Materials

Read at Work

MY PERSONAL SUCCESS PLAN

What you're doing this very second — reading — is one of the most powerful learning activities you'll do in college. And you'll be doing a lot of it. In fact, reading is the second most frequently used form of communication among college students, after listening.[1]

Do you wonder why your instructors assign so much reading? Consider this: A central reason you're in college is to acquire knowledge. In most of your face-to-face classes, you're in the classroom only a few hours each week, listening to lectures. In online, blended, practical, and discussion-based classes, you spend even less time listening to lectures. By adding reading assignments to the mix, your instructors can cover more material — and that benefits you in the long run. On top of all this, when you complete the assigned reading before class, you gain context for what is covered during the lecture; that makes your time in class all the more effective. So even if you're not a huge fan of reading, try to view it as a great opportunity to strengthen your learning.

Reading will play a critical role in your work life, too. After all, can you think of a job that requires no reading at all — none? It's not easy to do. Almost every job requires some kind of reading, whether it's e-mails or invoices, medical charts or memos, recipes or research reports. Sure, different jobs may call for different amounts of reading. But to excel at the job of your dreams, it's a safe bet that you'll have to know how to read, understand what you've read, and integrate that new knowledge into your work.

In this chapter we examine why reading is so important to your college career. We present a three-step process for getting the most from reading: preparing to read, reading with focus, and reviewing what you've read. We also describe strategies for reading effectively in math, science, and online classes; strategies for reading journal articles; and resources that can help if you're having difficulty reading. The chapter wraps up with tips on how to apply these concepts and practices on the job.

ACES Reflection:
Reading

Take a moment to reflect on your Reading score on ACES. Find your score and add it in the box to the right.

This score measures your beliefs about how well you read. Do you think it's an accurate snapshot of your current skills in this area? Why or why not?

■ **IF YOU SCORED IN THE HIGH RANGE** and you're confident that this score is accurate, then you can likely count reading among your strengths. This is excellent news, but as you know, even strengths can be improved. For instance, let's say you've developed some great strategies for reading your history textbook, but you find it more challenging to read your biology book. Using the information in this chapter, you can develop new strategies to increase your confidence in reading different types of materials, including your science texts.

■ **IF YOU SCORED IN THE MODERATE OR LOW RANGE**, take steps to improve your reading skills. Explore the ideas and practices in this chapter, and apply them to your course material. When you do, you'll find that you can become a more efficient and effective reader. Just give it a try!

ACES + ACTION

ACES paired with action is what leads to positive change. Now that you've reflected on your ACES results, how will you *use* what you learned about yourself to enhance your reading skills? Try these concrete suggestions, or get inspired and create your own!

▶ **Preview coming attractions.** To get a better sense of what you're about to read, flip through this chapter and examine each major heading. Based on these headings, what are the chapter's main themes?

▶ **Try a new strategy.** Try out one of the reading techniques recommended in this chapter that you've never used before. Afterward, write a summary of your experience. What best practices can you share with other students who want to try this technique?

▶ **Take time to review.** Find a classmate who wants to study class material together. Devote an hour of your time to reviewing and discussing what you've read for class.

Become an Active Reader

Reading is one of the most important skills that you'll be required to master in college. Why? Because reading is a central life skill: Successful people read to gain information and extend their learning. They read to learn how things work, discover insights into the past, and immerse themselves in a variety of cultures.

Reading is also a central study skill that sets the stage for the other study skills discussed in this book. Take a look at Figure 6.1, which illustrates how reading helps to kick off the learning experience: When you read, go to class, and take notes, you take in (or *input*) new information into your brain. You then *work actively* with that

FIGURE 6.1

How Academic Skills Connect

Photo: MapensStudio/Shutterstock

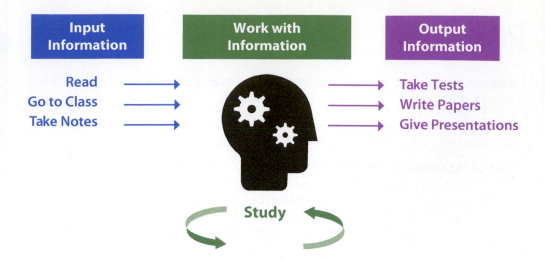

information by studying what you've learned, which helps you absorb and remember it. Finally, you demonstrate (or *output*) what you've learned through the tests you take, the papers you write, and the presentations you deliver. By weaving all of these skills together, you maximize your learning and become a stronger critical thinker—in every course.

Completing your reading is certainly important, but *how* you read also impacts your success. College work requires **active reading**, which involves interacting with the content you read, not just gazing at words on the page. When you read actively, you pay close attention. You think about the content carefully. You ask questions about what makes sense and why. These actions help you stay focused, which saves time in the long run: You learn and remember more of the material the first time around so you don't have to relearn it later. Active reading has three main steps: preparing to read, reading with focus, and reviewing what you've read (see Figure 6.2). We'll explore each of these steps in the following sections.

active reading: A reading strategy that involves engaging with the material before, during, and after reading.

Prepare to Read

FIGURE 6.2

Three Steps to Active Reading

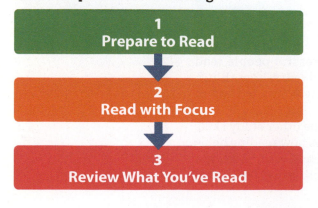

Mario and his family are taking a weeklong summer vacation. One morning, they get up, throw some clothes in a bag, get in the car, and drive west. They don't have a destination in mind—they just know that they want to end up somewhere fun. With that level of preparation, will Mario's family have a rewarding trip? It's certainly possible, but it's also a gamble. They didn't invest any time in research and planning, which would have given them a good sense of where they could go and what they could do on their journey. Now, they just have to cross their fingers and hope for the best.

Preparing to read in college works a lot like preparing to travel: It gives you an overall picture of what's to come, provides context for what you're about to do, and primes you to learn about something new—which ultimately makes it more likely that you'll have a rewarding experience. The tips in this section can help you prepare to get the most out of your reading.

Make a Plan for Your Reading

Before you read, start by making a plan. Assess how much material you have to get through, and estimate how long that reading will take. That way, you can build enough time into your schedule to complete your assignments.

It can be tricky to estimate time frames at first, but with experience you'll get more confident. Start by timing how long it takes you to read and understand five pages of material in each of your classes. As you do this, keep in mind that not every reading assignment will take the same amount of time and that each person reads at a different pace. For example, you might read novels in your English literature course relatively quickly, while reading chapters in your algebra book might take longer—or vice versa.

You can make a simple table like this one to figure out how much time you need for each class each week. Use this method to get control over your reading and make sure you're budgeting enough time to get things done.

Class	Time to read five pages	Number of pages in average week	Reading time for the week
English			
First-Year Experience			
Ecology			
Economics			

Preview the Material

Once you've made a plan for your reading, try *previewing* the material that you're about to learn. Previewing involves giving yourself a big-picture overview of what you'll be reading, and it's a technique you can use to read more actively, predict the subject matter that's to come, and consider how information you already know relates to what you're about to read.[2] The next time you open up your textbook, take these steps to preview what's coming.

- **Read the preface or introduction.** Take a look at the preface or introduction at the beginning of the book. Authors use these sections to describe the book's chapter structure and goals and to offer tips about how to use the material in each chapter. In the preface of this book, for example, we explain why we've included features such as Voices of Experience and Spotlight on Research in every chapter.

- **Read the table of contents.** At the beginning of any textbook is a table of contents listing the main and supporting headings for each chapter, and often the major features in each chapter. Before you begin an assignment, glance at the contents for the chapter you're about to read.

- **Read the chapter summary.** Many textbooks (including this one) provide chapter summaries, which give an overview of the

Get the Lay of the Land. Previewing material you're about to read helps you "get the lay of the land" so that you can predict what's coming and read the material more actively.
Byelikova Oksana/Shutterstock

contents of each chapter and highlight the main ideas. Scan the summary before you read.

- **Look for headings and key terms.** Skim through the chapter, looking at section headings, bold or italicized words, and definitions of key terms in the margins. All of these indicate the important concepts you'll be learning in the chapter.

Identify Purposeful Reading Questions

purposeful reading questions: Specific questions you want to be able to answer when you've finished reading.

After you preview the material, think of questions you expect to be able to answer once you've finished reading. These are called **purposeful reading questions** because your goal (purpose) in reading the material will be to answer them. Identifying these questions helps you focus your reading on what's most important. Purposeful reading questions vary in complexity; for example, you might want to know the definition of a term (low level of complexity) or the causes of an event (higher level of complexity).

How, precisely, do you go about identifying purposeful reading questions? You've got several options. Sometimes, the material itself provides questions you can use. For example, many textbooks include focus questions at the beginning of each chapter or review questions at the end of each chapter that spotlight which concepts the authors consider most important (see Figure 6.3).

You can also create your own purposeful reading questions. Keep it simple at first by drafting questions drawn from the chapter's headings and key terms. For instance, if a heading in your calculus book is "Polynomials," you could create the question "What are polynomials?" Then work up to more complex questions, such as, "What are

FIGURE 6.3
Creating Purposeful Reading Questions

Purposeful reading questions can come from questions in your reading, such as the outcomes in this textbook excerpt. Or create your own. Here, *informative speaking* is a key term, so you can ask "How do you define *informative speaking*?" From *Real Communication: An Introduction*, 4e, by Dan O'Hair, et al. Copyright © 2018 by Bedford/St. Martin's. All rights reserved. Used by permission of the publisher Macmillan Learning.

chapter outcomes

After you have finished reading this chapter, you will be able to

- Identify the goals of informative speaking
- Distinguish the eight categories of informative speeches
- Outline the four major approaches to informative speeches
- Employ strategies to make your audience hungry for information
- Structure your speech to make it easy to listen to

Like Neil deGrasse Tyson, the best informative speakers share information, teach us something new, or help us understand an idea. Clearly, Tyson has a talent for informative presentations. He knows how to analyze his audience members and tailor his presentations to engage them quickly. He organizes his information clearly and efficiently so that listeners can learn it with ease and presents information in an honest and ethical manner. In this chapter, we take a look at how you can use these same techniques to deliver competent informative speeches in any situation.

The Goals of Informative Speaking

As you recall from Chapter 13, the purpose of **informative speaking** is to increase the audience's understanding or knowledge; put more simply, the objective is for your audience to learn something. But to be a truly effective informative speaker, your presentation must not only fill your listeners' informational needs but also do so with respect for their opinions, backgrounds, and experiences. You need to be objective by focusing on informing your audience, not persuading them. You also need to be ethical by presenting relevant and reliable information. In this section, we examine these goals and investigate ways that you can ensure that your speech remains true to them at every phase of development and delivery.

different kinds of polynomials?," "How are polynomial equations solved?," and "How are polynomials used in mathematics and science?" Here are some additional examples of purposeful reading questions you might create in a variety of classes.

- "What were three causes of the War of 1812?" (American History class)
- "What's the difference between the unconditioned and the conditioned stimulus in classical conditioning?" (Introduction to Psychology class)
- "How do I diagram the components of a nerve cell and describe the major function of each component?" (Introduction to Biology class)
- "How can I apply the three steps in the active reading strategy?" (this class)

When you create purposeful reading questions, you use your critical thinking skills. For example, you gather information by skimming chapters, summaries, tables of contents, headings, and key terms. You evaluate the information when you figure out what questions to ask. And later, when you read, you apply the new information from the chapter as you answer your own questions.

Use Similar Strategies with All Your Reading Materials

What if you're preparing to read something other than a textbook chapter— something that doesn't have a preface, a table of contents, or boldfaced key terms? You can still use many of the same strategies. For example, you can estimate how much time you'll need to read the material, you can skim the first few paragraphs to get a sense of what the material will cover, and you can scan any headings to get a sense of key points and to create purposeful reading questions. The bottom line? Preparing to read is an effective strategy for all types of reading materials—not just textbooks.

Read with Focus

Once you're prepped and ready to go, take the next step: Complete your reading. Your goal is to absorb, understand, and remember information so you can use what you've learned to write papers, answer test questions, and gain insights into topics covered in your other classes. But you won't be able to remember every word in your reading assignments—no one can. So you need to read with focus: Figure out what information is *most* important, and concentrate on that. To do this, use your critical thinking skills to identify key information and to evaluate the quality of that information. And use your active learning and metacognition skills to select reading strategies that work best for you, depending on the subjects you're studying. The following tactics can help you focus on the most important information.

Mark Up Your Reading Material

Marking up a text helps you interact with the material you're learning, which in turn helps you understand and remember it. You can mark up reading material in several ways (see Figure 6.4), including annotating the margins of your text, highlighting and underlining key words and phrases, and taking notes.

Annotate. You can *annotate* your reading material by jotting down quick notes, inserting your own examples, drawing symbols ("DEF" might indicate a definition; "EX" might call out an example), and writing quick summaries in your own words— all in the margins of the book or article. Making notes and restating information in your own words requires you to process information more carefully than if you just

CONNECT TO MY EXPERIENCE

Think about a time you read the assigned material before class and a time when you showed up to class without reading beforehand. How were these experiences different? Did you feel better prepared for one than the other? Write a short paragraph about how you felt in each scenario.

FIGURE 6.4

Marking Your Textbook: A Sample Page

As you can see from this sample textbook page, you can use a number of techniques to mark your book: making annotations in the margins, highlighting main ideas, and underlining key points. You can also jot down purposeful reading questions and answer them on the page itself (if there's space) or in your notes. Text excerpt p. 147, from *Psychology*, 6e, by Dan and Sandra Hockenbury. Copyright © 2013 by Worth Publishers. Used by permission.

Purposeful Reading Question (PRQ): What's the difference between dreams and sleep thinking?

Dreams and Mental Activity During Sleep

Ex: Being chased through woods

☆ *Key Theme!*

KEY THEME

> A dream is an unfolding sequence of perceptions, thoughts, and emotions that is experienced as a series of actual events during sleep.

KEY QUESTIONS

More great purposeful reading questions!

> How does brain activity change during dreaming sleep, and how are those changes related to dream content?
> What roles do the different stages of sleep play in forming new memories?
> What do people dream about, and why don't we remember many of our dreams?

Dreams have fascinated people since the beginning of time. By adulthood, about 25 percent of a night's sleep, or almost two hours every night, is spent dreaming. So, assuming you live to a ripe old age, you'll devote more than 50,000 hours, or about six years of your life, to dreaming.

Wow. I will spend a ton of time dreaming.

SLEEP THINKING = SLEEP MENTATION

Although dreams may be the most interesting brain productions during sleep, they are not the most common. More prevalent is **sleep thinking,** also called *sleep mentation.* Sleep thinking usually occurs during NREM slow-wave sleep and consists of vague, bland, thoughtlike ruminations about real-life events (McCarley, 2007). Sleep thinking probably contributes to those times when you wake up with a solution to some vexing problem. But at other times, the ruminating thoughts of sleep thinking can interfere with your sleep. For example, on the night before an important exam, anxious students will sometimes toss and turn their way through the night as they mentally review terms and concepts during NREM sleep thinking.

DEF: SLEEP THINKING

WHEN I HAVE SLEEP THINKING:
– Wake up w/great idea
– Negative: toss and turn w/worry

In contrast to sleep thinking, a **dream** is an unfolding sequence of perceptions, thoughts, and emotions during sleep that is experienced as a series of real-life events (Domhoff, 2005). Granted, the storyline and details of those dream events may be illogical, even bizarre. But in the unique mental landscapes of our own internally generated reality, the bizarre and illogical are readily accepted as disbelief is suspended.

DEF: DREAM

Most dreams happen during REM sleep, although dreams also occur during NREM (Domhoff, 2011). When awakened during active REM sleep, people report a dream about 90 percent of the time, even people who claim that they never dream. The dreamer is usually the main participant in these events, and at least one other person is involved in the dream story. But sometimes the dreamer is simply the observer of the unfolding dream story.

So most people do dream.

PRQ:	Dream	Sleep Thinking
Answer	• Sequence of ideas, thoughts, emotions	• About actual events
		• General, unclear thoughts
	• Seems like real life	• Worry or great ideas
	• May be bizarre	• Normally during NREM
	• Mostly during REM	

highlight or underline (see the next section). Annotating takes some time, but it's worth it—you'll remember the material better later on, and you'll have notes that you can use to study.

Are you reading online? You can still use this approach, but instead of a pen or pencil, use digital tools to mark up the content (see the Read Online Course Materials section later in this chapter).

Highlight and Underline (But Proceed with Caution!). Highlighting and underlining help you identify main ideas and call out key content such as math formulas, diagrams, and definitions. These popular techniques offer a quick and easy way to spotlight important points and then locate that information later when you're studying. But research shows that when using these techniques, you should proceed with caution: If you highlight or underline mindlessly, then you're not processing the information carefully.[3] Later on, you might find it hard to remember what you've read. In addition, if you highlight or underline too much content, the page will become so busy that your markups will be useless.

To take a more focused approach to using these tools, read each section of the material before you make any marks. Ask yourself: What are this section's main ideas? Then go back to the material and highlight or underline *only* the content that's most important.

"I didn't read that scene, but I did highlight several passages."

A Note-Taking Tragedy. If you use highlighting to mark up your reading, do so in a focused way: Only highlight the most important information. Otherwise, you may get carried away and end up with many markings — and little learning.
Marty Bucella/CartoonStock.com

Take Notes. You can take notes while you read using a laptop or notebook, and you can return to these notes when it's time to study. If your goal is to read the material just once, take thorough notes (see the note-taking chapter for specific methods). Later, as you prepare for a test, you'll study directly from these notes. If you plan to reread the material, try taking broad notes as you read. For example, jot down key words with definitions, record where to find diagrams or charts in the chapter, or write a short summary of the material.

As you read and take notes, look for the answers to your purposeful reading questions, and write them down as you find them. For example, if one of your questions is "What are polynomials?" and you come across the definition of *polynomials* in the chapter, add it to your notes or mark it in your book so that later you can go back and study the definition.

Make It Personal

When you read, look for connections between what you're reading and your own life. As you saw in the learning chapter, this is a great way to strengthen your understanding of new material and really make concepts stick. Take Michelle, who's reading about eye contact and culture in her communications textbook. To connect the material to her own life, she thinks about how disconnected she felt on a recent first date when her date wouldn't look her in the eye, and how welcoming it feels when Andy, the barista at the coffee shop, looks right at her and smiles. Michelle also thinks about how one of her coworkers seldom makes eye contact with colleagues during meetings. He recently moved to the United States, and Michelle wonders if his behavior during meetings stems from the cultural norms he grew up with. By making these connections, Michelle is processing the material more deeply, a strategy that will help her remember what she learned later in the term.

Think Critically about What You Read

College would be simpler if everything you read was trustworthy, but that's not always the case. In fact, one of the best skills you'll develop in college is the ability to evaluate the quality, accuracy, and usefulness of information—that is, to think critically about what you're reading.

As you read, form your own conclusions about what you're reading, based on your evaluation of the information. For example, let's say your instructor assigns two readings about wage inequality between men and women. In one of the readings, the author argues that women are paid less because they're more likely to work part-time, take time off to have children, and enter occupations that pay less than more male-dominated ones. In the other reading, the author suggests that the pay gap stems from discriminatory practices in the workplace, such as male managers setting lower salaries for women or selecting other men for promotions. As a critical thinker and an active reader, you can evaluate the soundness of the arguments presented in each reading and the authors' credentials and then formulate your own thoughts about what's causing the gender pay gap.

What's *Really* Going On?
In the movie *The Wizard of Oz,* the "wizard" dispensing advice and warnings to Dorothy and friends is an illusion created by a man manipulating controls behind a curtain. This scene speaks volumes about how things aren't always as they appear. The lesson? Critically evaluate what you see — and read — so you don't get fooled. MGM/Photofest

Clarify Confusing Material

As you read, you'll inevitably run into material—a word, a concept, an example—that you don't understand. Try these techniques to clarify confusing content.

- **Carefully reread the material.** You might understand it better on the second or third try.

- **Expand your vocabulary.** Look up definitions of unfamiliar words, and use the words in sentences to grasp their meaning.

- **Move on.** Something you read later in the material might clarify things. Or simply giving yourself a few minutes away from the confusing content might help you see something you missed the first time.

- **Check your notes.** Take a look at your notes from class to see if they contain information that can help you better understand what you've read.

- **Ask questions.** Ask a classmate or a knowledgeable friend to explain the material, or talk with your instructor. His or her job is to help you learn, so don't be afraid to ask for clarification when you have questions.

- **Find help online.** Reading another author's interpretation of confusing content might help; so might watching a video of a particular concept, or listening to a podcast on the topic you're learning about. However, remember that not all Internet sources are trustworthy, so use your critical-thinking skills to evaluate what your search engine throws at you.

ASK FOR HELP WITH READING CHALLENGES

Many students find reading to be challenging but are uncomfortable asking for help. Is this true for you? If so, try thinking about your situation this way: Just as athletes, musicians, and business executives work with coaches to improve their performance, you can work with people on campus to improve your reading performance. Knowing when and how to ask for help is a valuable skill that will benefit you now and in the future. So take a moment to consider the following helpful resources.

Staff at the Learning Assistance Center. Most campuses have a tutoring or learning support center that focuses on helping students with reading, studying, and many other skills essential for college success. To find the office on your campus, browse your school Web site or type keywords such as "tutoring" or "academic support" into the site's search function.

Advisers. Advisers are used to working with students who need assistance, and they have likely helped others in your position. Talk with your adviser or someone in the advising office about how to approach reading.

Staff at the Disability Services Office. If you have a diagnosed learning disability or think you might have a reading disability, visit your school's disability services office to find out how the staff there can help.

CONNECT TO MY RESOURCES

List two individuals, departments, or offices at your college that could help you improve your ability to read course materials. How might they help you? For example, can they teach you how to read faster or mark up your texts more effectively?

Boost Your Reading Efficiency

Reading efficiently can help you stay focused on the most important material so that you don't waste time and effort on less relevant content. You can supercharge your reading efficiency by mastering the art of concentration and by increasing your reading speed.

Sharpen Your Powers of Concentration. Remaining focused while you read can help you avoid an all-too-common problem: realizing that your mind has wandered and that you have no idea what you just learned. Try the following tactics to enhance your concentration and stay "in the zone."

- **Set brief reading goals.** Create very short-term, focused reading goals if you're unfocused. Instead of trying to read for 90 minutes, for example, set a goal of reading four pages from your religious studies book and reading your marketing text for 15 minutes. Dividing your reading into small chunks and switching between topics can help you cover all of your reading assignments without feeling overwhelmed and losing focus.

- **Move around.** If you're bored with your reading and can't concentrate, get up and move. Take a 1-minute walk around the stacks in the library, grab 30 seconds of fresh air outside, or throw your book into your bag and head for a different study carrel. Then get back to reading.

- **Remove distractions.** If distractions—noises, people passing by, text message or e-mail pings—are preventing you from concentrating, remove them. For instance, turn off your phone, close the curtains or blinds so you can't see what's happening outside, or pop on some noise-canceling headphones. See the chapter on organization and time management for more ideas on creating a distraction-free zone.

Read with Speed. Increasing the speed at which you read is another way to make better, more focused use of your reading time. Reading faster is a skill that you can build with practice. Before you spend any of your money on a speed-reading class, try the following techniques.

- **Read in chunks.** Instead of reading one word at a time, try reading groups of words. (Here's how you could "chunk" the preceding sentence: "Instead of reading—one word at a time—try reading—groups of words.") As you focus on groups of words, your speed will increase.

- **Use a cue.** Place your fingertip at the middle of the first line of a paragraph. Slowly drag this "cue" down the middle of the paragraph, reading each line as you go. When you use a cue, your eyes follow your finger instead of moving left to right across each line. This forces your mind to read each line in chunks rather than each word individually. This technique may take some practice, but the more you do it, the easier it gets.

- **Skim.** If you have a lot of reading to do and not much time, skim the material. Move your glance quickly across each line or read the first and last sentence of each paragraph. Skimming isn't the most effective strategy for deep understanding of material—you'll likely trade some comprehension for speed—but it's better than not reading at all. Just try not to use this approach unless you're pressed for time.

> One thing I find helpful is to write in the margins of my book and make side notes.

NAME
Robert E. Moreno III

SCHOOLS
Glendale Community College; Northern Arizona University

MAJOR
Communication Studies

CAREER GOAL
Education Field

GAINING CONFIDENCE IN READING

Reading is something I've improved on greatly over the years, especially during my time at Glendale Community College (GCC). As a kid, I loved to read — it was fun. However, when I got to school, it became much more difficult. There was a lot to read! And in class they would make you read out loud. I always worried that my speech impediment would show. It wasn't until I attended GCC that I gained confidence in my reading, found my voice, and started to speak out more.

When I first got to college, I realized two things about reading. First, I'd have to do a lot more reading than I ever did as a kid. And second, I wasn't able to read things as quickly as the other students. However, I've implemented a few techniques to increase my reading speed and my retention of the material. One thing I find helpful is to write in the margins of my book and make side notes. If I don't know a particular word, I look it up so I'll understand what I'm reading. To increase my speed, I learned to first preview the chapter — to quickly look through the layout of the chapter, the headings, the pictures, and get an overall sense of what I'm going to read. Then I go back and fully read the chapter. This might take a little more time initially, but I found it's a great way to understand what I'm reading.

Now when I read out loud, I take my time and control my breathing. This helps me control my stuttering and speak fluently. I've found that reading has helped me become not only a better speaker but also a better writer. And as someone with a speech impediment, I enjoy expressing my thoughts, ideas, and passion in writing for others to read.

YOUR TURN Have you used any of the reading strategies Robert has used? If so, which ones? What benefits have these strategies provided for you? What challenges?

Review What You've Read

After you complete a reading assignment, you might be tempted to say, "Okay, check that off the list!" and continue on with your day. Do your best to resist that impulse: There's still work to be done. By revisiting what you've read, you'll improve your comprehension and recall of the information, and you won't have to relearn the material from scratch as you prepare for exams and assignments. Reciting, summarizing, and reviewing and studying are three potent techniques you can use.

Recite

After you read, take a few minutes to recite the main ideas, key words, and new information you've gained from the reading. When you *recite*, you state the information you've learned out loud (if you're by yourself) or in your head (if you're in the library). Reciting new knowledge helps you remember the information you've learned. And to really make the information stick, you can go beyond stating exactly what you've just read; recite answers to your purposeful reading questions, personal connections you've made, or notes you've written as well.

Summarize

Gather the central ideas from a reading, and write them down in your own words, either in your notes or at the end of each section of your textbook. Summaries can take different formats, including bulleted lists and short paragraphs. For example, you might write the following summary for this section of the chapter.

Reading Follow-up
- *State the main ideas out loud.*
- *Write a summary of the key concepts.*
- *Schedule time to review and study reading notes each week.*

Like reciting, summarizing requires you to think carefully about the material you've read, which boosts your comprehension of new concepts.

A Rave Review. Reviewing what you've read can help you remember the key concepts in the material. For example, try flipping through a textbook chapter, reciting to yourself the main ideas you've just learned. Give this and other reviewing strategies a try, and see what works best for you. Rei and Motion Studio/Shutterstock

Review and Study

There are many different ways to review and study the material you've read. If you took notes, look them over between classes. If you wrote summaries, study them while you eat breakfast. Here are some additional ideas.

- After you read a chapter, take 10 minutes to discuss the main ideas in it with a study partner.
- Recall the answers to your purposeful reading questions while you drive to school each morning.
- Make up your own test items for each chapter, and share them with members of your study group.
- Share your reading notes with a friend, ask for feedback, and fill in any information missing from your notes.
- Check out the learning chapter and the studying and memory chapter of this book, where you'll find a wide variety of additional tips you can use to review.

Read for Fun and Interest—
It's Good for You!

Did you know that motivation to read is connected to reading improvement? According to one study, students who are internally motivated to read have better outcomes than those who are externally motivated. In this study, researchers explored the reading motivations of 1500 students. Some students were motivated to read by internal factors — for example, they were interested in the material and they enjoyed the experience of reading. Others were motivated by external factors — namely, to become better readers than their peers.

After researchers tracked student reading performance over three years, they discovered the following:

▶ Students who read for enjoyment *and* because they were interested in the material had the most improvement in reading performance.

▶ Students who read for competitive reasons displayed no improvement in reading performance.

THE BOTTOM LINE

You'll have a lot of required reading in college, but if you also find time to read for fun, you might see your overall reading skills improve. Also, try looking for interesting topics in all your classes, even those that aren't your favorites — reading for interest can help keep you motivated and engaged.

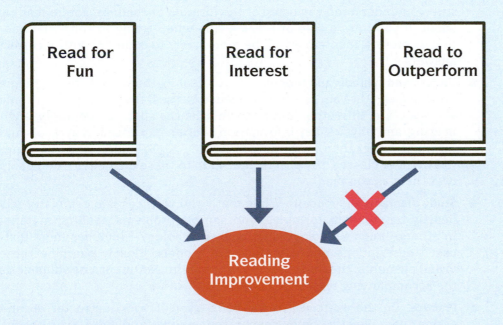

Reading for pleasure and to learn about topics that interest you may help you strengthen your reading skills.

Information from J. Retelsdorf, O. Koller, and J. Moller, "On the Effects of Motivation on Reading Performance and Growth in Secondary School," *Learning and Instruction* 21 (2011): 550–59. Photo: Jo karen/Shutterstock.

CONNECT TO MY CLASSES

Have you been doing a lot of reading in your other classes this term? Think about how the ideas in this chapter might help you with that reading. Write down two strategies you can apply immediately to the reading assignments for your other classes.

Read Different Types of Materials

The tips you've learned so far in this chapter can help you with any reading assignment in college. However, there are also more specific tips you can use for particular types of reading materials, such as math and science books, original research articles, and readings for online courses. Give these a try.

Read for Math and Science Classes

Math and science courses aren't identical—for example, chemistry isn't the same as calculus. That said, these courses share enough in common that you can use similar strategies for both science and math reading assignments.

- **Budget your time wisely.** Math and science reading tends to be dense, so schedule enough time to complete it by the due date.

- **Keep up with your work.** Many math and science classes are *linear*: To solve problems in week 2, you have to use what you learned in week 1, and so on. As you read, if you encounter a topic you don't understand, spend enough time on it to grasp it. If you're still struggling with it, get help before your instructor moves too far ahead.

- **Follow the rules.** Math and science have rules that must be followed, so be sure you understand each step of the formula or theorem you're reading about. If you miss a step or break a rule when trying to solve an equation or prove a theorem, you'll be more likely to come up with incorrect answers.

- **Understand symbols and formulas.** If you feel as though you're learning a new language in your math and science classes, that's because in some ways you are. In mathematics and in sciences such as chemistry, engineering, and physics, key information is often expressed in symbols and formulas rather than in words (see Figure 6.5). To understand the material in these classes, pay special attention to these elements—don't skip over them as you read.

- **Study diagrams and models.** While math and sciences like chemistry rely heavily on symbols, formulas, and sample problems, reading material in others—such as biology, anatomy, and geology—includes more text-based descriptions and diagrams and models. Closely examine these visual elements; the information they contain is often just as valuable as the accompanying text.

- **Practice.** Do the exercises in the book, even if your instructor doesn't assign them. Practice helps deepen your understanding of the material. Some texts include problems for you to complete, while others include sample quizzes that you can take to ensure you're comprehending the main ideas.

- **Use flash cards to memorize terms.** You'll encounter many terms in your science courses—for example, the names of organisms in a biology course or the parts of the human body in an anatomy class. Creating flash cards can help you learn and remember these terms. For tips on how to create flash cards, see the learning chapter and the memory and studying chapter.

Reading Science Textbooks

This page from an introductory chemistry textbook has been annotated to call out several types of information you might encounter while reading math and science material, including a sample problem, a practice exercise, a visual element, and a formula. Text excerpt p. 181, from Kevin Revell, *Introductory Chemistry*, 1st ed. © 2018 by W.H. Freeman & Worth Publishers.

Be sure to make note of formulas and practice using them.

7.1 Formula Mass and Percent Composition

Formula Mass

The masses of elements and compounds play a vital role in chemistry. Chemists use mass to identify unknown compounds and to understand and predict chemical reactions. As we saw in Chapter 3, the periodic table shows the average mass for atoms of each element. When working with compounds, we use these atomic masses to calculate the mass of a single molecule or formula unit. This is called the **formula mass**. For example, what is the formula mass of a water molecule? We know that a molecule of water, H_2O, contains two hydrogen atoms and one oxygen atom. Using the masses from the periodic table (**Figure 7.2**), we calculate the mass of water as follows:

$$\text{Formula mass of } H_2O = 2(1.01 \text{ u}) + 1(16.00 \text{ u}) = 18.02 \text{ u}$$

We found the formula mass by adding up the number and type of each atom, using the masses given in the periodic table. Chemists sometimes refer to the formula mass as the *formula weight*, or as the *molecular mass* or *molecular weight*.

Read the items in the margin. Here the information is important for solving the formula.

1
H
1.01

6
C
12.01

8
O
16.00

Figure 7.2 We use the average atomic masses from the periodic table to calculate formula mass.

Example 7.1 Calculating the Formula Mass of a Compound

Potassium carbonate, K_2CO_3, is a common water-softening agent. What is the formula mass of this compound?

To solve this problem, we add the atomic masses of each atom in the formula unit. •

$$\text{Formula mass of } K_2CO_3 = 2(39.10 \text{ u}) + 1(12.01 \text{ u}) + 3(16.00 \text{ u}) = 138.21 \text{ u}$$

Recall that we measure the mass of atoms in atomic mass units, abbreviated as *u* or sometimes as *amu*.

Look for examples that demonstrate how to solve problems.

TRY **IT**

1. Find the formula mass for each of these compounds:
   a. H_2CO **b.** Na_2CO_3 **c.** lithium nitrate   **d.** iron(II) bromide

   💻 *Check it*   💻 *Watch explanation*

Always work through the practice problems yourself to get comfortable with the concepts. Some texts, like this one, may even come with videos that walk you through the correct answers.

Read Journal Articles

Have you heard of the *New England Journal of Medicine, Science,* or *Nature*? These are examples of well-known *journals*—scholarly magazines that publish academic and scientific papers, many of which are written by college professors. In journal articles, professors describe research they're conducting, share new ideas or theories, summarize findings from a broad area of research, or present original works such as poetry or short stories. In fact, you've been reading information from journal articles throughout this book: Each Spotlight on Research describes findings that came from a journal article.

Journal articles are packed with useful information, but they can be more complex than other sources. To read and understand them, you have to know which parts of the article to focus on. Many articles, particularly research articles, have the following sections:

- *Abstract*: a paragraph summarizing the article
- *Introduction*: a review of previous research that supports the study and a description of the research questions, often called *hypotheses*
- *Methods*: a description of what the authors studied and how they studied it
- *Results*: a description of the statistical analysis used to answer the research questions
- *Discussion*: a written summary of the findings or answers to the research questions

You can follow these steps to understand the material in a research article:

1. Read the *abstract* and state the article's main idea in your own words. Once you can do this, you're ready to read the article itself.

2. Read the *introduction*, focusing on the hypotheses at the end of this section. Make sure you know what questions the authors are trying to answer.

3. Read the *discussion*, focusing on the first few paragraphs. The authors will likely state the answers to the research questions in prose form (as opposed to statistical form, which often appears in the results section).

4. Once you understand the research results from the discussion, read the *methods* and *results* sections to see more clearly how the authors came to their conclusions.

Journal articles are written primarily for other college professors, researchers, and experts in the field, so don't worry if you feel confused or overwhelmed at first: You're probably not the only one. Ask for help when you need it. Being able to read and understand even the basic ideas in a journal article is a useful skill, so it's worth investing the time now in learning how to do it.

Read Online Course Materials

If you're taking an online class for the first time this term, you may be a bit worried. Does the class have more required reading than your face-to-face classes? Is it a hassle to access the readings online? These are legitimate concerns, but here's good news: You can use a number of powerful strategies to handle your online course reading.

- **Be prepared to do more reading.** It's true that online classes require more reading, because you don't spend as much time in class listening to lectures. Now that you know, you can plan in advance how to complete all your reading on time.

- **Create your own schedule.** If your online class doesn't have regular reading assignments or quizzes to help you stay on track, build your own reading schedule—then stick to it.

- **Check your access.** If you have to access reading materials online, make sure you can do so when the class begins. If you run into any difficulties, ask the instructor for help right away. That way, you'll be confident you can access what you need to complete your assignments.

- **Learn how to mark up text online.** If you're reading online, learn how to mark up text using the tools available with your program or device.

⟩ CONNECT
TO MY CAREER

What types of materials would you need to read in your dream job (e.g., papers, manuals, blog posts)? If you're not sure, ask an instructor or do some research to find out. Then list two techniques from this chapter that you believe could help you read those materials more effectively.

Documents in PDF format, for instance, often allow you to highlight text and make notes in the margins. E-books frequently have the same features (see Figure 6.6). In addition, when you read electronically, you often have access to a search function, which allows you to find something you wrote in a note or to search for a specific term.

■ **Find an optimal device.** Depending on the platform you're using for your online classes, you may be able to access reading materials on a variety of devices (like your phone, tablet, and computer). Experiment to find what works best for you, given the task that you have to complete. For example, flipping through flashcards on your phone in between classes works well, but you'll likely want to read full chapters on a larger screen.

■ **Adjust your device to make reading comfortable.** Many e-books have customizable features, so look for ways to adjust the contrast on your screen and enlarge the font size so you can read without straining your eyes.

■ **Consider printing out materials.** If your reading materials are provided electronically but you prefer to annotate them in paper form, investigate whether you can print them out.

■ **Read and respond to online posts.** You'll often be required to read and respond to other students' online posts in discussion boards for the course. Take time to read and reflect on the posts. You can learn a lot from what others have to say.

FIGURE 6.6

Marking an E-book

When you're reading online, you can use tools to mark up the material. In this excerpt from a biology textbook, the student has used yellow highlighting to emphasize a key point. She has also included a note reminding herself to add a key term to the flash cards she's creating for the chapter.

FIGURE 5-11 presents an overview of the processes of transcription and translation. In transcription, which in eukaryotes occurs in the nucleus, the gene's base sequence, or code, is copied into a middleman molecule called messenger RNA (mRNA). (Because prokaryotes don't have a nucleus, transcription occurs in the cytoplasm.) This is like copying the information for the chocolate chip cookie recipe out of the cookbook and onto an index card. The mRNA then moves out of the nucleus into the cytoplasm, where translation allows the messages encoded in the mRNA to be used to build proteins.

c lembo   5/29/2018 5:03 PM

Key term! Add messenger RNA (mRNA) to flash cards.

Reply

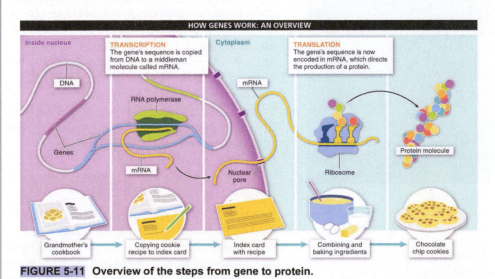

HOW GENES WORK: AN OVERVIEW

Inside nucleus

TRANSCRIPTION
The gene's sequence is copied from DNA to a middleman molecule called mRNA.

Cytoplasm

TRANSLATION
The gene's sequence is now encoded in mRNA, which directs the production of a protein.

DNA

RNA polymerase

mRNA

Genes

mRNA

Nuclear pore

Ribosome

Protein molecule

Grandmother's cookbook → Copying cookie recipe to index card → Index card with recipe → Combining and baking ingredients → Chocolate chip cookies

FIGURE 5-11 Overview of the steps from gene to protein.

Read at Work

Almost all jobs require *some* reading, and in many cases, reading is a key part of the job description. (If you want to be a textbook author, you won't get far without reading—trust us!) In fact, reading is so important that "reading comprehension" counts among the core skills needed to perform work in many professions.[4] In this section, we look at ways you can use reading skills on the job. As you work through the section, think about the profession (or professions) that interest you most. Do they involve a lot of reading? Or just a little? What kind of reading? How can you put the reading skills you're learning in this class to good use in your career?

Gather, Analyze, and Apply Information

Reading is a core activity in many jobs because you frequently have to gather, analyze, and apply information to get work done, and for all of those tasks you need strong reading skills. For example, suppose a pharmacist needs to dispense a new drug, but she's uncertain how it will interact with other medications a patient is taking. She has to read about the new medication, analyze whether it can be taken safely with the other medications, and then apply what she learned to this particular patient's situation. In positions like this one (and many others), reading relevant information—and thinking critically about that information—is a crucial part of performing your duties effectively.

Stay Current

Employers want to hire and promote people who keep up with the latest knowledge in their field, and reading can help you do this. Early in your career, identify the best sources of up-to-date, applicable information. As a psychologist, for example, you might consult a source like *Psychological Bulletin*. As a science teacher, you might go online to NASA's Web site to get a new lesson plan. Another way to learn the latest information is to join a professional association, such as the Society for Human Resource Management or the American Psychological Association. Many of these groups send out monthly or quarterly magazines containing articles about trends in the field. Finally, use reliable and reputable Web sites, blogs, and social media to stay up-to-date. For example, following various experts on Twitter can help you find out about articles, blog posts, and other reading materials you need to stay current and informed.

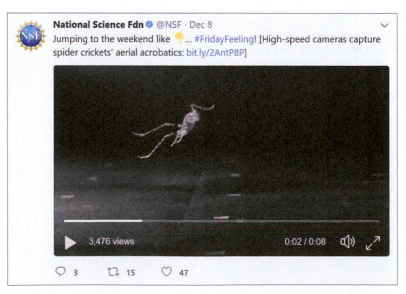

Use Twitter to Keep Current. Employers want to hire candidates who are well-informed about what's going on in their profession. One way to make sure you're up on the latest developments is to follow prominent organizations or individuals on Twitter, and read the articles they recommend. At the National Science Foundation page, for example, you'll find everything from groundbreaking research discoveries to amusing science-related memes.

Expand Your Skill Set

You can also use reading to build new skills that are valuable in your career. For example, do you want to learn more about how to use wind turbine technology, design more effective interventions for at-risk youth, or manage social media campaigns for your organization? Do you want to become a whiz

> **One of the main ways to grow in your profession is to read.**

NAME
Jeff Davis

PROFESSION
Director, Talent Acquisition

SCHOOL
Kansas State University

DEGREE
Bachelor's Degree in Business Administration

READING CRITICALLY FOR CAREER SUCCESS

I think many college students would be surprised to learn how important reading is for success in most careers. Reading is a core activity in most jobs — especially those that require a college degree. In my role as a talent acquisition director, reading is critical — reading e-mails, reading job applicant materials, and reading to recruit new employees.

It's not just the act of reading either — it's the act of reading *critically* that's important. For example, a supervisor might ask one of her employees to review data from competitor companies and prepare a report with recommendations. That requires critical reading and the ability to synthesize what you read from various sources. You need to be able to extract the information necessary to make important decisions — decisions that influence your professional success and the success of your company.

Reading is also important if you want to advance in an organization or career. Employees who focus on their own professional growth are highly valued by their employers, and one of the main ways to grow in your profession is to read. You're not going to advance in your career just by watching a bunch of YouTube videos. Professional workshops, webinars, and continuing education courses almost always include a heavy dose of reading. In our organization, for example, we've organized a leadership advancement book club.

Finally, getting a job may depend on how well you read and read critically. One of the first questions I ask every candidate on a job interview is "how did you prepare for this interview?" Successful candidates are those who have spent considerable time reading about our organization, its culture, values, and mission. That requires reading our Web pages, annual reports, and coverage of our organization in the local media — much of which is in print.

> **YOUR TURN** Do you currently have a job? If so, what kinds of reading are most useful for excelling in your job? If you're not currently employed but want to pursue a particular career, what kinds of materials will you likely need to read in order to do your job well and advance in your career?

at Excel or learn how to create a model of an erupting volcano before teaching a science lesson to your sixth-grade class? Reading can help you get it done. Pick up a book, browse relevant Web sites, or seek out a journal article on your topic of choice.

my personal success plan

READING

Based on your ACES results and what you learned in this chapter, are you inspired to set a new goal aimed at improving your reading skills? If so, the Personal Success Plan can walk you through the goal-setting process. Read the advice and examples; then sketch out your ideas in the space provided.

To access the Personal Success Plan online, go to the LaunchPad for *Connections*, Second Edition.

1 IDENTIFY A GOAL

Choose a reading goal to work toward this term. Here are some general ideas you might draw from; you can also create a goal of your own.

- ▶ Write purposeful reading questions for each assignment.
- ▶ Preview chapter headings before reading.
- ▶ Find a distraction-free place to read.
- ▶ Take notes while reading.
- ▶ Schedule time to review after reading.

2 MAKE YOUR GOAL SMART

Rewrite your specific goal so that it's SMART, and make sure to use the SMART goal checklist.

SAMPLE: I'll create purposeful reading questions before I read the next chapter in my economics book.

3 CREATE AN ACTION PLAN

Outline the specific steps you'll take to achieve your SMART goal, and note when you'll complete each step.

SAMPLE: Tomorrow night, I'll turn each bullet point from the chapter summary into a purposeful reading question.

4 LIST BARRIERS AND SOLUTIONS

Think about possible barriers to your action steps; then brainstorm solutions for overcoming them.

SAMPLE: I've never done this before, so I might have a hard time writing questions. If so, I'll ask my study partner Tejal to take a look at my questions before class on Friday.

5 ACT AND EVALUATE OUTCOMES

Now that your plan is in place, take action. Record each action step as you take it. Then evaluate whether you achieved your SMART goal, and make any adjustments needed to get better results in the future.

SAMPLE: My purposeful reading questions were mainly about definitions, which limited how much I learned from the chapter. Next time, I'll try writing more analytical questions.

6 CONNECT TO CAREER

List the skills you're building as you progress toward your SMART goal. How will you use these skills to land a job and succeed at work?

SAMPLE: Using purposeful reading questions helped me read with focus. I'd like to become a financial analyst, and I'll need that type of focus while I read annual reports and profit-and-loss statements.

my personal success plan

1 my general goal

2 my SMART goal

☐ Specific ☐ Measurable ☐ Achievable ☐ Relevant ☐ Time-limited

3 my action plan

4 my barriers/ solutions

5 my actions/ outcomes

6 my career connection

CHAPTER SUMMARY

This chapter explored a wide range of concepts and strategies for getting the most from your college reading. Revisit the following key points, and reflect on how you can use this information to support your success now and in the future.

- Along with attending class, note taking, studying, test taking, and writing and presenting, reading is a critical academic skill. Reading helps to set the stage for excelling at other study skills, so reading is foundational to your college success.

- To understand, remember, and apply what you've learned from reading class materials, you need to take a three-step active reading approach: (1) prepare to read, (2) read with focus, and (3) review what you've read.

- Strategies for preparing to read include making a plan for your reading; previewing your textbook preface, table of contents, chapter summary, and key terms; and developing purposeful reading questions — questions that you want to be able to answer once you've finished the reading.

- Strategies for reading with focus include marking up your reading materials, looking for personal connections to the material, thinking critically about what you're reading, clarifying material you don't understand, and boosting your reading efficiency by sharpening your concentration and increasing your reading speed.

- Strategies for reviewing what you've read include reciting key concepts in your own words, summarizing them in a bulleted list or paragraph, and reviewing and studying your notes.

- If you find reading to be challenging, you can contact the learning assistance center, an adviser, or staff at the disability services office for help.

- In addition to using the other strategies mentioned in the chapter, you'll want to master strategies for reading specific types of materials, such as math and science textbooks, journal articles, and readings assigned in your online classes.

- The critical-thinking skills you use to handle your college reading — including gathering, analyzing, and applying information — will prove just as valuable in your work life. By knowing how to get the most from your reading, you can excel at your job, stay up-to-date with knowledge in your field, and build new skills.

CHAPTER ACTIVITIES

Journal Entry

READING WITH A PURPOSE

Have you ever read something and then realized you were unable to identify or retain the key concepts? That's why being an active reader is so important. This chapter outlined three steps in active reading.

- Step 1 is preparing to read and it includes gathering materials, determining how much time to allot to a particular assignment, and previewing the material.

- Step 2 is reading with focus and it includes marking up your reading material, making personal connections, and thinking critically about what you read.
- Step 3 is reviewing what you've read.

Reflect on your experience with each step in this process. Be specific about the strategies you currently implement and the things you may not have thought about before today. Then identify the strategies outlined in this chapter, some of which might be new to you, that you could implement right now to improve your active reading.

Adopting a Success Attitude

DISCOVERING ENJOYMENT IN READING

Reading for pleasure has numerous benefits: It can build your knowledge, improve your vocabulary, boost your reading speed, enhance your creativity and imagination, and encourage attentiveness and focus. Moreover, reading for pleasure can relieve stress and promote positive emotions.

Choose four literary genres from the following list. For each genre you choose, identify a book that you might like to read. (Search online or go to a bookstore to get ideas.) Provide the full title of the book, the author's name, a brief description of the book (two to three sentences), and the reason it interests you.

Literary Genres

classic literature	horror	autobiography/biography
fantasy/adventure	mystery	nonfiction (factual information)
historical fiction	romance	poetry
crime/detective	humor	
science fiction	suspense/thriller	

Now set a goal for your reading. When will you read the titles you've listed?

Applying Your Skills

PREVIEWING YOUR READING

Preparing to read is a critical step in the active reading process, and previewing your reading is one method you can use to prepare. Previewing gives you a sense of what you'll be reading, prepares you to absorb new information, and helps you read with focus.

Preview one of the chapters in this textbook that you haven't read yet. Read the title, the chapter outline, and the first few paragraphs of the chapter (the introduction). Then look for the main headings and any boldfaced terms and read the chapter summary. Finally, write down five purposeful reading questions — ones you expect to be able to answer, or would like to answer, after you've read the full chapter. If you have trouble developing such questions, look at the examples in the Prepare to Read section of this chapter or try crafting Who?, What?, When?, Where?, How?, and Why? questions.

When you read the chapter later in the term, see if you can answer the purposeful reading questions you've developed.

College Success = Career Success

EXPANDING YOUR PROFESSIONAL VOCABULARY

Identify a professional journal or magazine related to your current career (if you're working), a future career (if you have one in mind), or a career that you're curious about (if you're undecided). If you aren't sure what journals or magazines relate to your career, do a Google search, ask an instructor in the appropriate department, contact a librarian at your college, or ask someone working in this field. Select an article from the publication, and use the tips you learned in this chapter to preview and read the article.

Write down five words from this article that are new to you or that seem important in the career you've identified. Next to each word, write down the definition. If the definition doesn't appear in the article, look the word up in a dictionary. Hold on to these words and definitions — if they're related to your current or future career, you can bet you'll see them again!

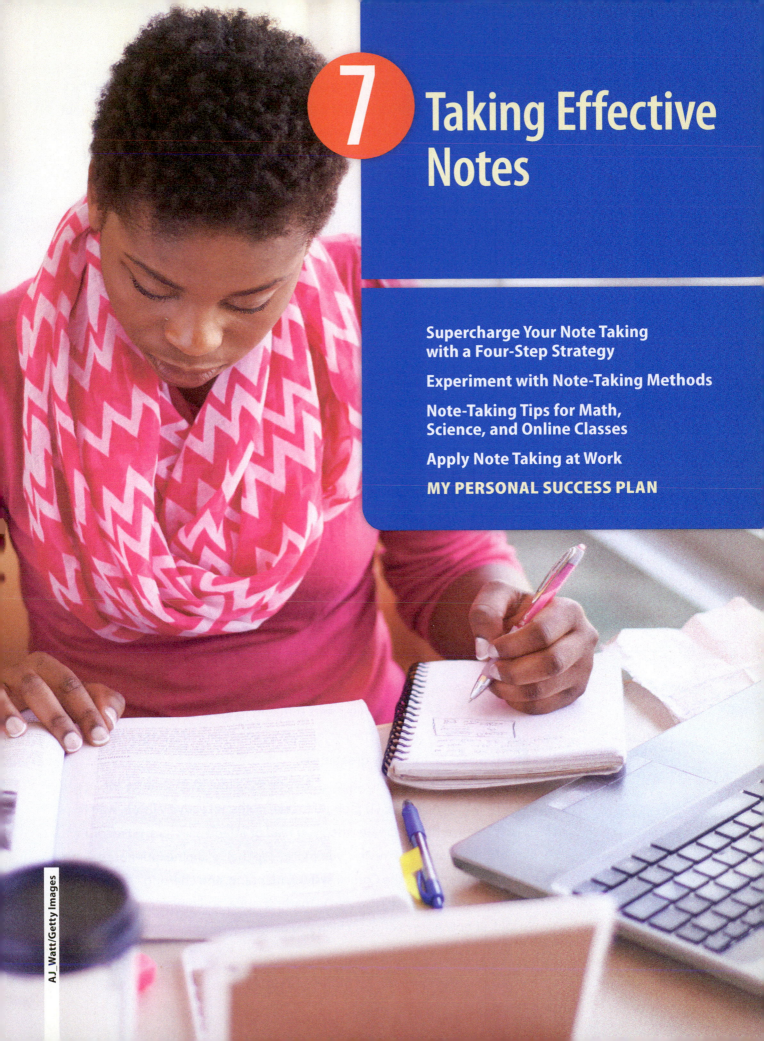

7 Taking Effective Notes

Supercharge Your Note Taking with a Four-Step Strategy

Experiment with Note-Taking Methods

Note-Taking Tips for Math, Science, and Online Classes

Apply Note Taking at Work

MY PERSONAL SUCCESS PLAN

Let's be honest: Note taking isn't the most exciting topic to study. In fact, you probably groaned at the thought of reading a whole chapter about taking notes. Now that we've got this out in the open, how can you approach this chapter with a positive attitude? Try to change your thinking about note taking.

At its heart, note taking is much more than writing or typing words: It's a way to record, organize, and manage information so that you can *learn* from and *use* it. To be a good note-taker, you need to recognize which information is most important, figure out how to record the information so it's clear, and use your notes to study. When you build these skills — as you'll do by using the strategies in this chapter — you'll better understand what you're learning and, as a result, perform better on exams and homework assignments. In short, note taking is a survival skill for college.

Note taking can also help you learn and manage information at work. For example, suppose you're meeting with team members to kick off a new project. During the meeting you take notes about your role in moving the project forward and how you'll interact with the rest of the team. Or let's say you work for an advertising agency. You're in charge of designing an ad campaign for a new client, so you call the client to talk about that company's product and its goals for the campaign. You take notes during the phone conversation. Later, when you start thinking in more depth about how to tackle the project, your notes serve as the starting point for many great ideas.

In this chapter we present a four-step strategy for taking notes: (1) prepare to take notes; (2) actively listen, watch, read, and participate when you read or attend a lecture; (3) record information; and (4) review your notes. We then examine four note-taking methods — outlining, the Cornell system, mapping, and charting — and explore specific strategies for taking notes in math, science, and online courses. Finally, we look at how note taking can help you excel at your job.

ACES Reflection:
Note Taking

Take a moment to reflect on your Note Taking score on ACES. Find your score and add it in the box to the right.

This score measures your beliefs about how well you take notes. Do you think it's an accurate snapshot of your current skills in this area? Why or why not?

■ **IF YOU SCORED IN THE HIGH RANGE** and you have a strong track record of effective note taking, then this is likely one of your strengths. Excellent! Now think about how you can enhance this strength. For instance, you might learn a new strategy that helps you stay focused during lectures. Or you might find a way to restructure your notes so they're easier to follow when you study for exams. The more strategies you have, the better you'll get at taking notes.

■ **IF YOU SCORED IN THE MODERATE OR LOW RANGE**, you've got the perfect opportunity: Use the strategies in this chapter to strengthen your note-taking skills. Sample some of the techniques presented, and figure out which ones help you most effectively record the information you need. Take control of your learning.

ACES + ACTION

ACES paired with action is what leads to positive change. Now that you've reflected on your ACES results, how will you *use* what you learned about yourself to build your note-taking skills? Try these concrete suggestions, or get inspired and create your own!

▶ **Pair and share.** Pair up with a classmate and ask that person to share two note-taking tips. Share two of your own in return. How are they similar? How are they different? Is there a new strategy you can try?

▶ **Instagram for inspiration.** Take a picture of a page of notes you're proud of and post it online for reactions from your friends and fellow students. What tips and tricks can they share with you?

▶ **Read to succeed.** As you read this chapter, write down two specific ideas that you'll try this week. Be prepared to report back on how these strategies work for you.

Supercharge Your Note Taking with a Four-Step Strategy

Note taking plays a key role in academic success.[1] When you combine it with other important study skills and activities—reading, going to class, studying, taking exams, and writing and speaking—note taking helps you absorb, think about, remember, and use the new information you're learning in your courses.

There is no "right" format for taking notes; you can choose from a variety of methods, depending on what works best for you. But no matter which method (or methods) you choose, you'll get the most learning power from your notes if

FIGURE 7.1
Four Steps to Effective Note Taking

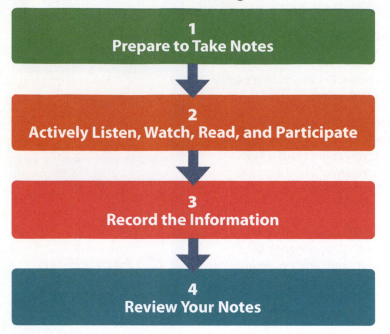

you approach note taking strategically. We recommend a four-step strategy: Get prepared; actively listen, watch, read, and participate; record the information you're learning; and review your notes (see Figure 7.1).

Let's take a closer look at each step.

Step 1: Prepare to Take Notes

When you *prepare* to take notes, you'll find it much easier to focus on the most important information once you actually *take* notes—for instance, when you're listening to a lecture, reading an assignment, or watching a video. Try these tactics to become a more efficient note-taker who can zero in on key content. The quality and usefulness of your notes is sure to improve.

- **Gather the materials you'll need to take notes.** For example, find your textbook and the previous notes you took for that class or project. Decide ahead of time whether to handwrite your notes or type them on a laptop or tablet (see the Spotlight on Research). If you choose to write by hand, make sure to have a notebook, pens, and a highlighter handy. If you're trying out a new note-taking app, which you can find with a quick search in your phone's app store, get comfortable with it before using it in class.

- **Create a system to label, organize, and store your notes.** That way, you can easily find and review your notes later when you want to use them to study for an upcoming exam or to complete a homework assignment. The chapter on organization and time management contains ideas for creating a system for labeling, organizing, and storing your notes.

- **Preview key concepts.** If you're preparing to take notes during a lecture, review the course syllabus and complete any required reading before class. If you're preparing to take notes while reading, use the previewing strategies described in the reading chapter, such as reviewing textbook chapter summaries, headings, and definitions to get a sense of the major ideas in the reading material.

- **Follow your schedule.** If you're attending a lecture, arrive a few minutes early to review your notes from the previous class. If you plan to take notes while reading, follow your study schedule and begin work at the time you had planned.

- **Review any handouts and bring them to class.** If an instructor provides materials ahead of time—for example, PowerPoint slides or a study guide—you can familiarize yourself with the key concepts that will be covered in class before you go. That way, during the lecture, you won't have to write or type what's already been provided in advance; instead, you can focus on the instructor's verbal explanation and take notes that expand on the information in the handouts. In fact, taking your own notes instead of relying solely on your instructor's handouts has huge benefits: You think more deeply about the information you're learning, so you stand a better chance of understanding, remembering, and applying it.

- **Bring unanswered questions to class.** If you have unresolved questions about your reading assignments, bring them to class. Your instructor may provide the information you're looking for—or you can ask the questions during or after class to get the answers you need.

- **Stay positive.** Remind yourself that note taking helps you maximize your learning.

Step 2: Actively Listen, Watch, Read, and Participate

To take good notes, you'll need to focus on the information you're receiving, whether it comes to you during a lecture, from something you're reading or discussing, or even from a video you watch for class. Focusing helps you identify the most important information in what you're hearing or seeing so that you can capture it accurately for later review and use.

To sharpen your focus on the key information, *engage* with that information by actively listening, watching, reading, and participating (depending on the note-taking situation). These techniques can help.

- **Eliminate distractions.** Even when you're trying hard to pay attention, it can be tempting to grab your phone, text with friends, or favorite their latest social media posts. But when you give in to distractions, you miss chunks of information you're supposed to absorb and record. So, take steps to eliminate distractions—for example, turn off your phone when you need to focus. The organization and time management chapter offers additional ideas for creating a distraction-free zone.

- **Empower yourself to concentrate.** If you're taking notes in class, sit in the front; you'll find it easier to hear your instructor and participate in class discussion. Plus, when your instructor is looking you in the eye, you'll be less likely to daydream or doze off. If you're taking notes while reading, find a quiet location in which to work.

Best Seat in the House? Right Up Front. At a concert or a sporting event, most of us try to sit as close to the stage or field as possible. That way, we're right in the heart of the action. Take the same approach to seating arrangements in your classes: Avoid the "nosebleed section" way in the back, and sit right up front near your instructor. It's a prime location for paying attention and taking quality notes.
Dmytro Aksonov/Getty Images

- **Look for written cues to important concepts in your reading.** When you take notes while reading, look for section headings as well as boldfaced terms. These signal important concepts in the material. (See the reading chapter for more information.)

- **Listen for verbal cues from your instructors about what's important.** In class, instructors' speech patterns can signal that certain information is especially crucial—for example, raising or lowering their voice when emphasizing points, or slowing down and repeating key concepts. Instructors might also use certain words and phrases alerting you to important material: "The main advantage . . . ," "Some of the challenges . . . ," "What we can conclude from this . . . ," "A key component . . . ," and (a student favorite) "People, this will be on the test."

- **Watch for nonverbal cues.** Pay attention to your instructors' gestures and movements during class. Some instructors step out from behind the lectern, stop moving, point to a PowerPoint slide, or make direct eye contact when emphasizing an important point. We know of one instructor who rang a cowbell each time he introduced an important concept. (Most instructors are subtler than this!)

- **Participate in class.** Get involved in what you're learning about in class. If your instructor encourages discussion, become an active participant: Contribute your thoughts about the topic of the day; ask questions about topics you're curious about; and volunteer responses to your instructor's questions. Participating in class can be intimidating—particularly if you're uncomfortable speaking in front of others, the class is large, or you find the topic of discussion confusing—but give it your best shot. By participating actively, you can clarify confusing concepts, gain additional insights into what you're learning, and stay focused on the material. And all of this helps you take better notes.

CONNECT TO MY EXPERIENCE

Think back to a time when you actively participated in class—for example, when you asked a great question, answered a question, or got your fellow classmates involved in a discussion. Briefly explain how it felt to contribute. Were you nervous? Excited? How do you plan to participate in your current classes?

Attention, Please! In real life, instructors seldom have audiences this attentive — watching their every move and writing down their every word. But imagine how good instructors would feel if audiences were this engaged. With that in mind, show courtesy to your instructors when you attend lectures. For instance, listen attentively and take every opportunity to participate actively.

Piero Tonin/www.CartoonStock.com

Step 3: Record Information

When it's time to record information you hear or read, do it quickly, accurately, and in a way that makes sense to you. Later in the chapter, you'll learn four specific methods for recording information, but these general strategies can also help.

- **Label your notes.** At the top of the page, include a label with the course title, date, and a page number. If you handwrite your notes, use only one side of the page, and start notes for each lecture or reading assignment on a new piece of paper. If you type your notes, create a new document or move to a new page for each lecture or reading assignment.

- **Resist the urge to write down *everything.*** Your instructors will talk faster than you can write, and not everything said in class or printed in a book is critical information. Instead, record only the main points and the most important details using the active learning techniques you just read about.

- **Learn to paraphrase.** Recording information *verbatim* (word-for-word) is important with chemical or mathematical formulas, definitions, dates, names, and diagrams because later you might need to reproduce these exactly on tests, in lab reports, or in papers. Often, though, it's best to **paraphrase** information by restating it in your own words.[2] For example, when you take notes as you read, if you just recopy the words on the page into a notebook, you're not interacting with the material. When you paraphrase, you have to think about what you're reading and then translate your understanding into your own words. Because you're interacting with the information, you're more likely to understand and remember it. Paraphrasing is also useful in class when you need to summarize the main points of a lecture or record key ideas from a PowerPoint slide. Table 7.1 shows an example of paraphrasing.

- **Use symbols and abbreviations to save time.** You can create your own shorthand using symbols and abbreviations that work for you. For example, you might use an asterisk (*) to flag important information and the approximately symbol (≈) to indicate approximate numbers. (See Figures 7.3 and 7.4 for more examples of useful symbols and abbreviations.)

- **Use metacognition to recognize when you don't understand information.** If you realize you have no idea what your instructor is saying or notice that you don't understand a sentence you just read, you're using metacognition. When you recognize that you're confused, you have information you can act on: Write down your questions and get clarification as soon as you can. You might use a star, an exclamation point, or a question mark to indicate the confusing material or leave space to jot down notes later when you get answers to your questions. Taking action to clarify concepts will get you the answers you need—*before* you see the material on a test.

- **Ask questions.** If your instructor allows questions during class (and most do!), raise your hand when you don't understand material. Asking

paraphrase: To restate information in your own words.

Ask Questions to Create Top-Notch Notes. As you're taking notes, notice when you don't understand something. If you're in class, ask questions to clear up any misunderstanding. That way, you'll be sure that you recorded information accurately—and you can study from your top-notch notes later on. Claudia Paulussen/Shutterstock

TABLE 7.1

Example of Paraphrased Content

Original content	Paraphrased content
"The first human beings to arrive in the Western Hemisphere emigrated from Asia. They brought with them hunting skills, weapon- and tool-making techniques, and other forms of human knowledge developed millennia earlier in Africa, Europe, and Asia. These first Americans hunted large mammals, such as the mammoths they had learned in Europe and Asia to kill, butcher, and process for food, clothing, and building materials. Most likely, these first Americans wandered into the Western Hemisphere more or less accidentally in pursuit of prey."	• First people in Western Hemisphere came from Asia • Thousands of years of knowledge and expertise: hunting, tools, weapons • Hunted mammoths—source of food, clothing, shelter • Probably accidental migration, searching for food

Source: James L. Roark et al., *The American Promise: A History of the United States,* 7th ed. (Boston: Bedford/St. Martin's, 2017), p. 4.

questions shows your instructor that you're engaged and that you care about what you're learning. If the instructor prefers to answer questions after class or during office hours, speak with him or her at the designated time and place.

■ **If you have a disability, make use of accommodations.** Depending on the type of disability you have, you may be able to audio- or video-record lectures or have another person take notes for you.

spotlight on research

Taking Notes?

Grab a Pen and Paper

With the popularity of laptops and tablets, more and more college students are coming to class with a computer. Typing notes is convenient, after all, and often neater and faster than writing by hand. But a question arises: When it comes to creating high-quality notes and learning information for tests, is one method more effective than the other? According to research, the answer may be "yes."

In one study, students watched a brief lecture and took notes using their preferred method: typing on a laptop or handwriting with pen and paper. After the note-taking activity, they were tested using two types of questions: fill-in-the-blank questions that required them to recall facts from the lecture and essay questions that required them to apply the ideas from the lecture.

Several interesting findings emerged.

▶ All students performed well on the recall test (fill-in-the-blank test questions).

▶ Students who handwrote their notes did much better on the application test (essay questions).

▶ Students who typed their notes recorded more information from the lecture — normally a good thing — but much of it was word-for-word. As you just read, paraphrasing is often the best way to learn and remember.

THE BOTTOM LINE

If possible, try writing your notes by hand. If you do, you're more likely to paraphrase information, which can lead to higher-quality notes and enhanced comprehension.

Students who handwrote their notes performed better on application tests and took higher-quality notes than students who typed their notes.

Information from P. A. Mueller and D. M. Oppenheimer, "The Pen Is Mightier Than the Keyboard: Advantages of Longhand over Laptop Note Taking," *Psychological Science* 25 (2014): 1159–68. Photos: Left: Alexandru Cristian Ciobanu/Shutterstock; Right: Jemastock/Shutterstock

Step 4: Review Your Notes

After you take notes, review them. Are they accurate? Complete? Do you have unanswered questions? If the information in your notes looks wrong or you don't understand it, your notes won't help you learn the material and use it to answer test questions or do class projects. Use these tips for reviewing your notes.

- **Review your notes when ideas are fresh in your mind.** After you've taken notes, spend a few minutes skimming them to check that the information still makes sense. If you find things that are questionable, mark them so you know to come back and get clarification. Try to review your notes within a day to fill in missing information; otherwise, you might come back to the material a few days later and have no idea what your notes mean.

- **Compare your notes with other students' notes.** See whether you're recording the same information and capturing the same level of detail as your classmates, and take the opportunity to clarify any concepts you found confusing.

- **Talk with your instructor.** Visit your instructor during office hours, and ask for feedback on the quality of your notes. If you have questions or don't fully grasp the material, ask for help.

- **Practice paraphrasing.** If you wrote something down word-for-word in your notes, try paraphrasing this content. Paraphrasing will help you understand the ideas more fully.

- **Compare your notes to the study guide.** If your instructor provides a study guide, compare your notes to the material it contains. Are the main ideas from your notes similar to those of the study guide? If not, add any missing content to your notes.

- **Clarify and reorganize your notes.** If your handwritten notes are hard to read, type them out. If your typewritten notes are confusing, retype them in a clearer form in a new document. Reorganize the content of your notes to clarify the connections between ideas. If your notes are incomplete, fill in the gaps. According to research, meaningful time spent reviewing and rewriting your notes more clearly may help you get higher scores on exams.[3]

CONNECT TO MY RESOURCES

Your instructors can be great resources for note-taking tips. Go to their office hours and ask them to share which note-taking methods they used in college. Ask for specific recommendations and try out one or two. Most people will be happy to share what worked for them when they were in your shoes.

Experiment with Note-Taking Methods

There is no single "best" note-taking method: Different methods work well for different people in different courses. In this section we describe four popular methods. As you read about each one, think about the note-taking methods you've used in the past. Which ones worked well for you? Which ones didn't? Keep in mind that note taking is a survival skill. As you gain experience and score more successes, your note-taking skill will improve, and your sense of self-efficacy will grow stronger.

Outlining

Creating an outline is a common, formalized way of taking notes (see Figure 7.2). Outlining helps you organize the material as you record your notes, making it easier to search for and review key information when you study. It works particularly well when instructors use a similar approach in their PowerPoint slides, but outlining can be used in any note-taking situation—inside and outside of class. You've probably used outlines to write papers; you can use the same format when taking notes.

FIGURE 7.2

Taking Notes in Outline Format

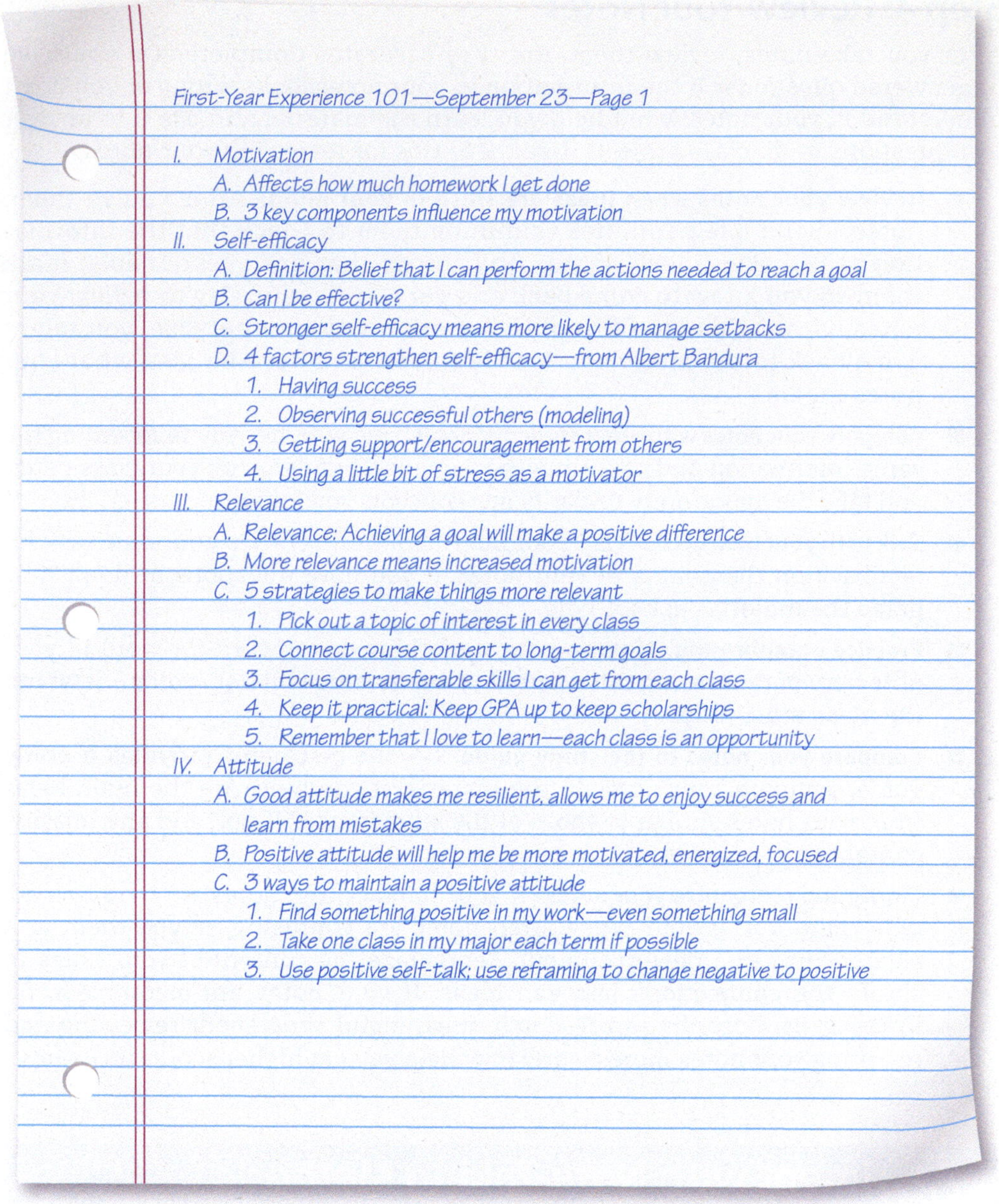

First-Year Experience 101—September 23—Page 1

I.   Motivation
   A. Affects how much homework I get done
   B. 3 key components influence my motivation
II. Self-efficacy
   A. Definition: Belief that I can perform the actions needed to reach a goal
   B. Can I be effective?
   C. Stronger self-efficacy means more likely to manage setbacks
   D. 4 factors strengthen self-efficacy—from Albert Bandura
      1. Having success
      2. Observing successful others (modeling)
      3. Getting support/encouragement from others
      4. Using a little bit of stress as a motivator
III. Relevance
   A. Relevance: Achieving a goal will make a positive difference
   B. More relevance means increased motivation
   C. 5 strategies to make things more relevant
      1. Pick out a topic of interest in every class
      2. Connect course content to long-term goals
      3. Focus on transferable skills I can get from each class
      4. Keep it practical: Keep GPA up to keep scholarships
      5. Remember that I love to learn—each class is an opportunity
IV. Attitude
   A. Good attitude makes me resilient, allows me to enjoy success and learn from mistakes
   B. Positive attitude will help me be more motivated, energized, focused
   C. 3 ways to maintain a positive attitude
      1. Find something positive in my work—even something small
      2. Take one class in my major each term if possible
      3. Use positive self-talk; use reframing to change negative to positive

- **First level.** Use uppercase Roman numerals (such as I, II, III) to represent the main ideas from a lecture or reading. You may be able to identify these before you read by previewing the chapter, or before class by reviewing lecture slides posted by your instructor.

- **Second level.** Use uppercase letters (such as A, B, C) to record the key points that support the first-level headings.

- **Third level.** Use Arabic numerals (such as 1, 2, 3) to record facts, details, or examples that support and illustrate the ideas in the second-level headings.

- **Additional levels.** You can add additional levels by indenting further and using alternating numbers and letters at each level.

- **Bullet points.** If you find letters and numerals too formal, use different levels of bullet points instead.

NAME
Nicole S. Williams

SCHOOL
Indiana University – Purdue University Fort Wayne

MAJOR
Business Management

CAREER GOAL
Financial Adviser or Accountant

OUTLINING AND OTHER NOTE-TAKING STRATEGIES

I've found the outlining technique to be a very effective note-taking strategy for me. I always use bullet points, main points, and subpoints. I came across this strategy in high school. My high school teacher really didn't write many notes on the board. She talked most of the time. So, when she did write on the board, I knew the information was important, and I chose it as the main point in my outline. Then I usually added the things she said afterward as my subpoints. I've been using this technique ever since.

I'm always ready to take notes. I always read assignments and books with a pencil in my hand so I can write down information. Also, I listen closely to speakers in class, because they don't always write down the key points. As a matter of fact, most of the important concepts are verbally stated, so you have to be an active listener.

I also review my notes for clarity, although I admit that I don't review as much as I should or would like to. But with a test coming around — say that my test is next week — I'll usually try to review my notes for at least an hour, then take an hour break, and then go back and review them again. I try to do this for the whole week until the test comes up. Then, if I have questions about my notes, I'll go to professors at least three days before the test. That's how I usually review.

YOUR TURN Have you used outlining to take notes? If so, what benefits has this method offered you? What challenges has it presented? If you haven't used outlining, what's the reason?

Courtesy of Nicole S. Williams

Cornell System

The **Cornell system** organizes each page of your notes into sections: Your initial notes go on the right, key points go in a cue column on the left, and a summary section goes at the bottom of the page (see Figure 7.3). This system helps you study because after attending class or reading, you return to your notes to expand on the material you just learned. To create notes using the Cornell system, follow these steps.

1. **Divide the page.** Draw a horizontal line about two inches from the bottom of the page. The space below the line is the *summary section*. Next, draw a vertical line about two and a half inches from the left side of the page, meeting the horizontal line across the bottom. The area on the left is the *cue column*. The area on the right is the *notes* section, where you'll write notes during class or while reading.

Cornell system: Method of note taking that organizes each page of content into sections: initial notes on the right, key points in a cue column on the left, and a summary section at the bottom of the page.

FIGURE 7.3

Taking Notes Using the Cornell System

First-Year Experience 101, Sept. 23, Page 1

Cue	Notes
★ Get motivated = succeed in college	Motivation — connected to my study and homework completion • 3 key components of motivation
Bandura = psychologist = self-efficacy	Self-efficacy — belief that I can perform actions needed to meet goal • Albert Bandura: 4 things build self-efficacy
Q: What is an example of self-efficacy beliefs? A: Me = Strong self-efficacy for speaking in class	• Experiencing success • Observing successful others (models) • Getting support/encouragement from others • Using a little stress to motivate (but not too much)
Relevance = the "R" in SMART!	Relevance — if things are important to me, I'm more likely to be motivated • Find a topic of interest in each class • Connect coursework to long-term goals • What transferable skills can I get in each class? • Practical things are more relevant • Remember that I love to learn
Positive attitude = powerful motivator	Attitude — having a positive attitude can help me stay motivated • Benefits: being resilient, enjoying success, learning from mistakes
"I've studied hard, so I'm confident I'll do well on this test."	• Always look for the positive • Take a class in my major each term, if possible • Positive self-talk and reframing are tools I can use

Summary:
A person's level of motivation can affect his or her success in college. Motivation includes three key components: self-efficacy (belief in one's ability to perform certain actions), relevance, and a positive attitude. Students can use a variety of strategies to strengthen self-efficacy, make tasks relevant, and stay positive.

⟫ **CONNECT TO MY CAREER**

Note-taking skills come in very handy at work. If you're currently employed, write down two strategies you're already using to take notes successfully on the job. If you're not employed, write a short paragraph about how note taking could help you excel in a career you're considering.

2. **Take notes.** Record information in the notes section in any form you like, such as an outline, paragraphs, or bullet points. Don't try to write down everything from the instructor's lecture or your reading material. Instead, focus on key concepts, supporting details, dates, formulas, and examples. Leave space between each idea in your notes. You can add information here later, or just use the space to keep your notes clean and easy to read.

3. **Write cues.** Once you finish taking notes, add cues to the cue column. Cues can be main ideas, key words, formulas, questions, diagrams, or examples that correspond to the notes you've already taken, or answers to any purposeful reading questions you've developed. (See the reading chapter.) Line up your cues with the corresponding content in the notes section. When it's time to study your notes, use the cues to find information quickly or to create flash cards, with the cue on one side and the content from your notes on the other.

4. **Summarize.** After you've created your cues, write a brief summary at the bottom of the page that restates the main ideas from your notes. To summarize, you have to understand the material, so writing the summary proves that you've grasped what you've read or heard. When it's time to study, use the summary as a quick review of the ideas from that page of notes.

Mapping

A *map* is a graphical depiction of course material. It includes *nodes* and *branches* that show the connections among concepts. Detailed maps also incorporate symbols and other markings that further describe the content (see Figure 7.4). Maps can be particularly useful if you're a Visual learner. Some students sketch their maps before class with main ideas from a textbook chapter and then fill in content while listening to the lecture. For others, maps work best as study tools. The key to effective mapping is to create a consistent system and focus on key words rather than trying to cram in too much detail. With practice, you can learn how to use nodes, branches, and symbols to organize material and make course concepts come alive.

- **Nodes.** Nodes represent the main topics and key ideas from the lecture or reading assignment. Create a system of nodes that works for you, either with one main node (topic) in the center of the page or several large nodes on each page. When you create one central node, you can add smaller nodes to represent concepts that support the center node's main topic. For instance, in Figure 7.4 "Motivation" is the central node, and "Self-Efficacy," "Relevance," and "Attitude" are smaller nodes that introduce supporting concepts.

FIGURE 7.4
Sample Notes Map

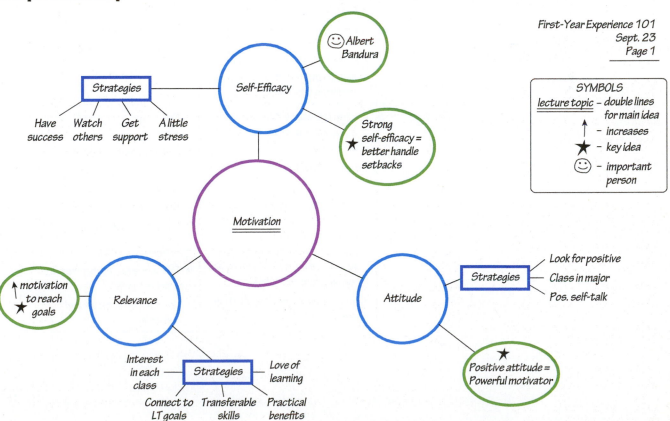

- **Branches.** Branches represent supporting details, such as examples, formulas, and dates. Branches might be smaller circles, squares, or simply a straight line pointing to information. Their shape and location show how the details connect to specific nodes and how different pieces of supporting information relate to one another. For instance, in Figure 7.4 the rectangular branches indicate strategies that can help strengthen each of the three components of motivation.

- **Symbols.** You can use symbols such as stars or exclamation points to emphasize important concepts in your map. For example, a number inside a box might represent an important date; a smiley face might indicate an important person (see Figure 7.4). You can also use different kinds of lines, like solid or dotted, to reflect the nature of the connections between nodes and branches.

Charting

A chart is a series of rows and columns designed to organize main ideas, key concepts, and supporting details. Charts allow you to record information in a way that's easy to study from later. Consider the sample chart from a first-year experience class shown in Figure 7.5. The main topic is found in the left-hand

FIGURE 7.5

Using Charts to Take Notes

Motivation Comparison Chart, First-Year Experience 101 Sept. 23 page 1

Topic	Features	Strategies
Self-efficacy	• Related to my belief that I can perform the actions needed to meet a goal • Strong sense of self-efficacy means I'm more likely to manage setbacks effectively	• Experience success • Watch successful others • Get support/encouragement • Have just a little stress as a motivator
Relevance	• When I believe that achieving a goal will make a positive difference • Helps motivate me to reach for goals	• Pick a topic of interest in each class • Connect class to long-term goals • Build transferable skills in all classes • Keep things practical • Focus on love of learning
Attitude	• Benefits include becoming resilient, enjoying successes, and learning from mistakes • Motivation and positive attitude are connected	• Always look for the positive • Take a class in my major each term, if possible • Use positive self-talk and reframing

column, and the other two columns highlight defining features and strategies related to the main topic. Charts work particularly well in classes where your instructor always presents course content in the same way. You can sketch out a rough draft of the chart before you go to class and then fill it in during the lecture.

Note-Taking Tips for Math, Science, and Online Classes

The basics of note taking apply in most learning situations: You need to prepare, focus, record, and review information, whether you're taking computer science or composition. But science, math, and online classes have unique characteristics, so additional, specialized strategies can come in handy. In science and math classes, for example, you'll come across a lot of formulas, diagrams, and equations. You'll need to record these quickly if you're in a lecture, and record them accurately both in class and while reading. And most online classes don't have traditional lectures at all, so you'll take notes on other types of information. By adjusting your strategies to account for these differences, you can record the information you need efficiently and effectively.

Taking Notes in Math and Science Classes

Whether you take one math or science class or ten over your college career, try these strategies for taking good notes.

- **Be ready to record formulas and equations.** Formulas and equations are sentences written in mathematical notation. When you write down a formula or an equation, carefully record and label each of the components or steps in the process. Where appropriate, also note how the formula or equation is used.

- **Leave space in your notes.** Leave enough room in your notes to draw diagrams, write formulas and equations, and copy down problems. Also leave space to record each step as you solve problems and to show your work (see steps 1–4 in Figure 7.6).

- **Use good scientific laboratory practice.** If you think you've made a mistake in a formula, an equation, or a diagram, don't erase or scratch out everything you've written. Instead, draw one or two lines through the part containing the mistake. These lines will help you trace your thinking later and find errors that need fixing. To create a clean version, rewrite the material on a new page of notes.

- **Record different solutions.** In math, there is often more than one way to solve a problem. If your instructor presents different possible solutions, record each one in your notes; that way, you'll understand the reasoning behind the results more fully.

◗ CONNECT TO MY CLASSES

Identify your most challenging class. Which of the note-taking methods described in this chapter would work best for you in that class? Jot down two reasons you think this method would be a good fit for that course.

A Winning Formula. When you take notes in math and science classes you often need to record formulas and equations. To do this effectively, try these best practices: Copy down formulas and equations neatly and carefully, leave plenty of space in your notes, and if you make a mistake, draw a clean line through the error. UpperCut Images/ Getty Images

FIGURE 7.6

Sample Page of Math Notes

Math and science notes include lots of diagrams and problems. Give yourself plenty of space to write things out and show your work, and if you make a mistake, neatly cross it out. Carefully written notes can be useful when you run into problems and need to ask for help—others can see what you've done and help you identify the correct answers.

Algebra I - Sept. 23

Topic: Plotting the slope of a line using a linear equation

Equation: $y = 2x - 1$

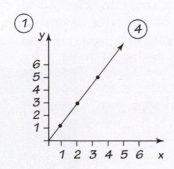

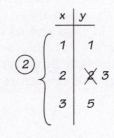

③

$x = 1$	$y = 2(1) - 1$	$x = 2$	$y = 2(2) - 1$	$x = 3$	$y = 2(3) - 1$
	$y = 2 - 1$		$y = 4 - 1$		$y = 6 - 1$
	$y = 1$		~~$y = 2$~~		$y = 5$
			$y = 3$		

Process:

Step ① Draw x + y axes   Step ③ Solve for y

Step ② Identify #s for x   Step ④ Plot x + y values on grid

- **Keep writing if you get off track.** If you fall behind the lecture when writing down a problem or a diagram, mark where you got off track and keep writing down what your instructor is saying. You want to record as much of the information as possible—you can always go back later to fill in what you missed.

- **Learn the shorthand.** In your math or science classes, learn the shorthand for those fields. For instance, if you know that Hz = hertz and d = distance in physics, or that BTU = British thermal unit in chemistry, you'll take notes faster and better understand what the information means.

- **Practice the problems.** In math and sciences like chemistry, it's crucial to practice the problems you learn in class and in your reading. After you've recorded a problem in your notes, grab another piece of paper, cover up your answer, and try to solve it again. This repetition and practice will show that you've got it figured out—or that it's time to get some assistance (see the next strategy).

- **Ask for help when you need it.** If you don't understand a concept, talk with a tutor or your instructor to get clarity. Because math and science classes tend to be linear (meaning information builds from class to class), you need to clear up any confusion immediately to stay on track. Moreover, forming a good relationship with your instructors will help you succeed in these classes.[4]

Taking Notes in Online Classes

The note-taking strategies you use for traditional classes are the same for online classes and *hybrid* classes (a blend of face-to-face and online). But online classes don't meet as regularly as face-to-face classes, so students sometimes fall behind and cut out time to take notes. To avoid this scenario, make sure you spend as much time taking notes in your online class as you do in your other classes. For example:

- When you watch videos or listen to audio recordings of lectures, take notes.

- When you read online, take notes.

- When someone makes an important point on the class's discussion board, take notes.

And don't forget to manage your time. When your instructors post recorded lectures online, resist the impulse to spend less time (or no time) taking notes, on the assumption that you can always go back and view the lectures again. You can—but it's more efficient to view lectures just once and take good notes rather than having to watch them several times because your notes are incomplete.

Write While You Watch. Taking notes while watching a lecture your instructor has posted online is a smart move: If you don't take notes, you might have to watch the video several times to grasp the content, and you'll have no recorded information to use while studying for exams. Jose Luis Pelaez Inc/AGE Fotostock

Apply Note Taking at Work

By this point in the chapter, you've definitely started to think critically about how note taking can help you master what you're learning in school. Now, though, let's take a look at how the ideas in this chapter can also help you in another area: your career. Here are several ways that taking stellar notes can set you up for professional success.

Demonstrate Accuracy and Attention to Detail

Paying attention to details and accurately recording information—two hallmarks of good note taking—are just as important in the workplace as they are in college. How an employee captures information can make or break an organization or a business—and can even have life-and-death consequences. Think about it: If a nurse writes down incorrect details about a patient's drug allergies, then that patient could become very ill or even die if prescribed the wrong drug. If a baker mistakenly writes down that a couple wants a chocolate wedding cake instead of vanilla, then those unhappy customers could write a negative online review—driving potential new customers away. For almost all employees, the ability to capture information accurately is a key job requirement.

Transform Information

Have you ever explained something computer-related to a relative who has no experience with technology? Have you ever studied with a friend and found yourself explaining a complex idea in a way that made the concept more understandable—for your friend *and* yourself? In scenarios like these, you're *transforming* technical or complicated information by restating it in a way that others can understand. You practice this skill every time you paraphrase while taking notes.

Transforming information is particularly useful in *STEM* fields (science, technology, engineering, and math), but it's also useful in sales, education, and many other careers. The more comfortable you feel with absorbing information and restating it in an accessible way, the more effectively you can communicate this information to others in the workplace.

Good Notes, Good Care. If you work in an emergency room, taking accurate notes is crucial. When patients arrive, you may need to interview them and write down their symptoms, medications, and allergies. By taking detailed, accurate notes, you can help provide the right care for patients. Kate Kunz/AGE Fotostock

Use the Information You Record

At its heart, note taking involves accurately recording, organizing, and managing information so you can learn from and *use* it. How might you use the information

> Understanding crime scenes, finding and arresting suspects, writing reports, and getting convictions all require good notes.

NAME
Rob Hawkins

PROFESSION
*Police Lieutenant /
U.S. Army Sergeant
First Class, Retired*

SCHOOL
*American Military
University*

DEGREES
*Associate of Arts;
Bachelor of Arts*

MAJORS
*Personnel
Administration;
Criminal Justice*

TAKING NOTES ON THE JOB

Accurately taking notes and recording information is critical to effective police work. Understanding crime scenes, finding and arresting suspects, writing reports, and getting convictions all require good notes. When I get a call and start to gather information, one of the first things I do is to create a map of the situation. Each node of the map is a different person involved in the case, and I use branches to indicate the relationships among these individuals. I write down information near each node, including what the person observed or what he or she told me. I also put stars next to critical pieces of information and cross things out when I can eliminate a suspect or determine that certain information doesn't apply. These maps are very useful when I write up case reports—I can look at the maps and understand each situation better. Sometimes maps help me make connections between pieces of information or think of other questions to ask an individual. They stimulate my thinking on the case.

Maps are useful in all kinds of situations, not just during an investigation. I used the same system in the military to create operations orders. Also, when I was training an Afghan battalion commander during my last deployment, I used maps to help him create an organization and structure for the five hundred men he was leading.

YOUR TURN If you currently have a job and use note taking in your work, explain how you use it and how it helps you. If you don't currently have a job, identify a job that interests you, and brainstorm how note taking might help you in that job.

you've collected? In the work world, you might use information captured in notes to create slide presentations, press releases, research reports, *infographics* (which present ideas and data in a visual format), ad campaigns, business plans, and other documents. Each time you do any of these things, you get a chance to communicate what you've learned in a clear, understandable, and creative way.

my personal success plan

NOTE TAKING

Based on your ACES results and what you learned in this chapter, are you inspired to set a new goal aimed at improving your note-taking skills? If so, the Personal Success Plan can walk you through the goal-setting process. Read the advice and examples; then sketch out your ideas in the space provided.

To access the Personal Success Plan online, go to the LaunchPad for *Connections*, Second Edition.

1 IDENTIFY A GOAL

Choose a note-taking goal to work toward this term. Here are some general ideas you might draw from; you can also create a goal of your own.

- ▶ Try the Cornell notes system.
- ▶ Build note-taking skills in math class.
- ▶ Go to the academic support center for help with notes.
- ▶ Share notes with a classmate.
- ▶ Switch to handwritten notes for all classes.

2 MAKE YOUR GOAL SMART

Rewrite your specific goal so that it's SMART, and make sure to use the SMART goal checklist.

SAMPLE: I'll use the Cornell system to take notes for the next two weeks.

3 CREATE AN ACTION PLAN

Outline the specific steps you'll take to achieve your SMART goal, and note when you'll complete each step.

SAMPLE: By Wednesday, I'll format twenty pages of notes using the Cornell system. I'll use these pages to take notes in class for the next two weeks.

4 LIST BARRIERS AND SOLUTIONS

Think about possible barriers to your action steps; then brainstorm solutions for overcoming them.

SAMPLE: If I have any trouble getting used to the Cornell system, I'll remind myself that it takes practice to get comfortable with a new note-taking method.

5 ACT AND EVALUATE OUTCOMES

Now that your plan is in place, take action. Record each action step as you take it. Then evaluate whether you achieved your SMART goal, and make any adjustments needed to get better results in the future.

SAMPLE: I used different formats (outlines, paragraphs, bullet points) to record information on my Cornell pages. That ended up being confusing, so I'll use a more consistent format from now on.

6 CONNECT TO CAREER

List the skills you're building as you progress toward your SMART goal. How will you use these skills to land a job and succeed at work?

SAMPLE: I want to become a nurse practitioner, so I'll need to collect information from patients about their health concerns and present it in reports to health care providers. Using the Cornell system will help me do that effectively.

my personal success plan

1 my general goal

2 my SMART goal

☐ SPECIFIC ☐ MEASURABLE ☐ ACHIEVABLE ☐ RELEVANT ☐ TIME-LIMITED

3 my action plan

4 my barriers/ solutions

5 my actions/ outcomes

6 my career connection

CHAPTER SUMMARY

This chapter described the skills needed to take good notes in all types of classes, introduced four note-taking methods, and explored how note taking can help you excel at work. Revisit the following key points, and reflect on how you can use this information to support your success now and in the future.

- To take good notes, you need to follow a four-step process: prepare to take notes; actively listen, watch, read, and participate to focus on the information you're hearing or reading; record information; and review your notes.

- You can use a number of methods to take notes. This chapter describes four such methods: outlining, the Cornell system, mapping, and charting.

- Outlining is a structured way to take notes that involves recording information at different levels using letters and numerals or bullet points.

- In the Cornell system, you record notes, cues, and summaries on a single page. You first make notes and then go back to write cues and summaries that will be useful for studying.

- Mapping presents information visually. Nodes, branches, and symbols help you organize and depict relationships among ideas.

- Charts organize a large amount of information in a series of rows and columns.

- To take good notes in math and science classes, you need to be especially thorough in noting formulas, equations, and diagrams. Learning math and science shorthand (such as abbreviations) will help you take notes quickly and accurately.

- When taking notes for online classes, keep up with class material, schedule enough time for note taking, and take notes on all the information you're exposed to (such as recorded lectures, videos, and discussion board posts).

- At work, taking good notes can help you demonstrate accuracy and attention to detail, transform information so it's easy for others to understand, and use information to develop a wide range of documents and presentations and to complete important projects.

CHAPTER ACTIVITIES

Journal Entry

ASSESSING YOUR NOTE-TAKING STRATEGY

This chapter presented a four-step strategy for taking notes.

- Step 1 is preparing to take notes and it includes gathering the note-taking materials you need and previewing concepts.

- Step 2 is actively engaging with the material, which also involves concentrating and eliminating distractions.

- Step 3 is paraphrasing and recording information.

- Step 4 is reviewing your notes.

Reflect on some of the challenges you've had with each step in the process, and consider the different strategies outlined in this chapter that you could implement to improve your note taking. Has this reflection had any impact on your note-taking confidence? In what way? Based on this reflection, will you adopt a different strategy for taking notes in the future? Try different methods? Revise your current strategy? Explain your decision.

Adopting a Success Attitude

BUILDING CONFIDENCE IN IDENTIFYING KEY POINTS

It takes time to build strong note-taking skills. This activity focuses on building your confidence in one component of note taking: identifying key points of a message.

First, in a notebook, create three headings across the top of a page: "Advertiser," "Product," and "Key Selling Points" (see the example). Under the headings, add numbers 1 through 10. Now watch a series of commercials on television or online. For each commercial, write down the name of the advertiser, the product, and the key points the ad is making to interest you in the product. For example, the advertiser may be an insurance company that's trying to sell car insurance, and the key selling points are the company's low-cost premiums and fast processing of claims. If you're watching these commercials with other people, ask them to help. Have fun with it!

Advertiser	Product	Key Selling Points
1.		
2.		
3.		
Etc.		

Applying Your Skills

IMPROVING YOUR NOTE-TAKING SKILLS

Select a note-taking method described in this chapter (outlining, the Cornell system, mapping, or charting) that you haven't used before but would like to try. During the next week, use this method in a specific class to take notes during lecture, for reading assignments, or both. After each note-taking session, review your work within twenty-four hours and respond to the following questions:

- What are the main ideas of the lecture or reading you took notes on? What material was unclear? What questions do you have? (Talk with your instructor to clarify any confusing concepts.)
- Overall, what did you like about this note-taking method? What challenges did you encounter?
- Will you continue to use this method? Why or why not? If not, what other method(s) will you try instead?

College Success = Career Success

TAKING EFFECTIVE NOTES AT WORK

At work, taking good notes enables you to record instructions, deadlines, action items, ideas, and questions. In long meetings, note taking can help you stay alert, focused, and actively engaged. It can also communicate your interest in and commitment to your work, as well as your desire to succeed.

For this activity, pretend that your boss has sent you to a professional conference. She wants you to attend a presentation at the conference, give her a one-paragraph summary of the main ideas, and report what you learn to your colleagues at the next staff meeting. To do this exercise, follow these steps:

1. Go to the TED Talk Web site (**www.ted.com**) and watch a video on a topic that interests you or is related to your future career. TED Talks are "ideas worth spreading" — short presentations designed to share information and opinions and to inspire viewers.

2. As you watch the TED Talk, pretend you're at the conference, sitting in the audience. Take notes that capture the speaker's main ideas, and write down any questions or ideas you have about the topic. (If you were at an actual conference, you'd have an opportunity to ask the speaker questions or share your own ideas.)

3. After watching the TED Talk, write a one-paragraph summary of the talk. Consider having someone review your notes and summary paragraph to give you feedback on whether you've captured the main ideas. (Note: This person doesn't need to have watched the TED Talk. If you took good notes, the information you've recorded will be clear.)

4. Now pretend that you're back at work and that you have to report to your colleagues on what you learned from the talk. With a partner or a small group (in or outside of class), briefly describe the TED Talk, highlight the speaker's main points, and share your questions and observations.

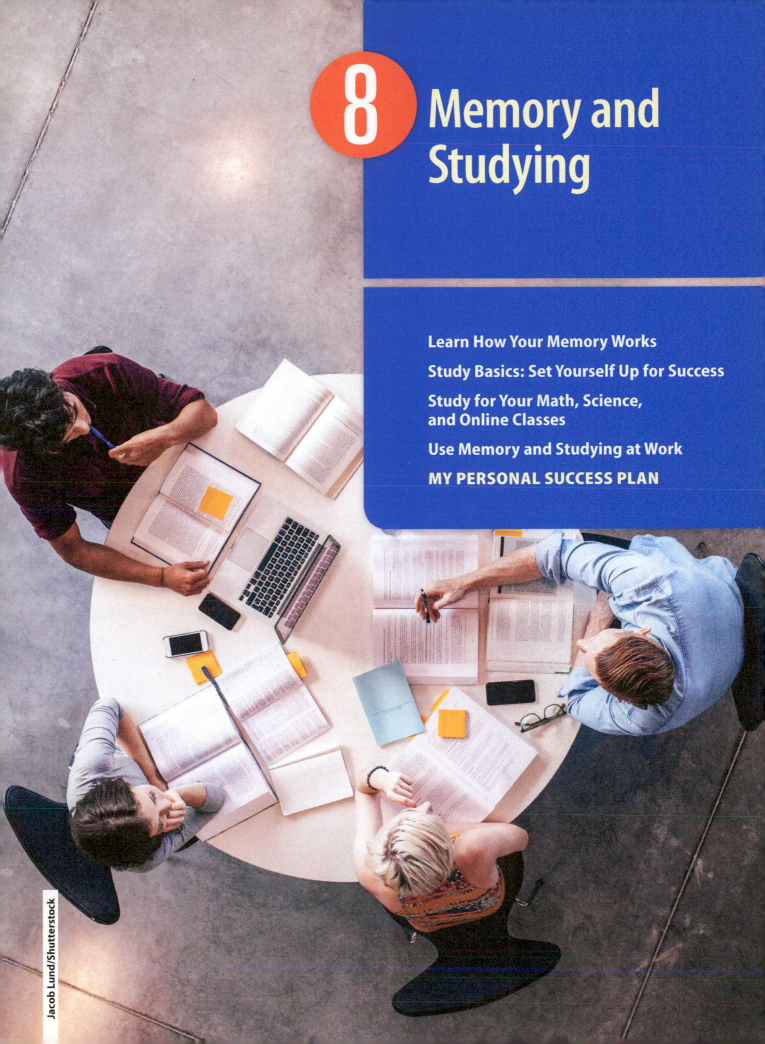

8 Memory and Studying

Learn How Your Memory Works

Study Basics: Set Yourself Up for Success

Study for Your Math, Science, and Online Classes

Use Memory and Studying at Work

MY PERSONAL SUCCESS PLAN

Picture a student sitting in the library, eyes half open, staring blankly as he slowly turns pages of handwritten notes. He seems to be studying, but his mind isn't focused, and he's just going through the motions. How well do you think this student will perform on his upcoming exam? Chances are, he'll be disappointed with the results: When you don't pay attention to and think actively about what you're learning, it's hard to remember that information and use it to answer test questions, contribute to discussions, or complete projects. Information doesn't magically end up in your brain. That's why you need study strategies that help you remember — strategies you'll learn in this chapter.

There's no question that studying effectively and remembering what you study will help you excel in college, but guess what: These skills are also important in the workplace. Today, jobs change rapidly, and the most successful people know how to learn and remember new information and then use it at work. Think about your instructors: They know their fields of study so well that they can share their knowledge in their job — teaching — without having to read straight from a book or their notes. They also use their knowledge to excel at other types of work, such as conducting research or publishing articles.

No matter what career you end up pursuing, knowing how to absorb and retain new information will come in handy. For instance, if you're in information technology (IT), you might study software specifications so that you can integrate a new application into your company's IT system. Or if you're in marketing, you might study regional demographics to determine where your company should launch its next product. Knowing how to study and remember information helps you learn continuously — and that's exactly what employers want.

With these points in mind, we start this chapter with memory basics, including how people take in information, create memories, and forget. Then we consider strategies that help you stay focused and productive while you're studying and help you remember what you learn. Finally, we offer ideas for how you can use these strategies on the job.

ACES Reflection:
Memory and Studying

ACES
Academic & Career Excellence System

Take a moment to reflect on your Memory and Studying score on ACES. Find your score and add it in the box to the right.

This score measures your beliefs about how well you study and remember information. Do you think it's an accurate snapshot of your current skills in this area? Why or why not?

- **IF YOU SCORED IN THE HIGH RANGE** and you're confident that this score is accurate, then memory and studying may be strengths for you. That's great news. Remember, though, that even strengths can be improved. For instance, maybe you routinely create review sheets — a tool that helps you study and remember information. If you learn how to create other kinds of do-it-yourself study tools, too, you'll be in a better position to switch tools as needed to suit the subject matter or the settings in which you're studying.

- **IF YOU SCORED IN THE MODERATE OR LOW RANGE**, focus on finding new strategies. This chapter — in fact, your entire college experience — gives you a powerful opportunity to build your memory and study skills. You can strengthen these skills with time and practice, and this chapter is filled with ideas to help you do so.

My ACES Score ....
- ☐ High
- ☐ Moderate
- ☐ Low

To find your **Memory and Studying score**, go to the LaunchPad for *Connections*, Second Edition.

LaunchPad
macmillan learning

ACES + *ACTION*

ACES paired with action is what leads to positive change. Now that you've reflected on your ACES results, how will you *use* what you learned about yourself to study and remember information? Try these concrete suggestions, or get inspired and create your own!

- ▶ **Read with purpose.** Write down three purposeful reading questions for this chapter before you start reading. When you finish the chapter, be sure you can answer each one.

- ▶ **Work together.** Pair up with a friend and brainstorm different strategies you can use to remember information for class.

- ▶ **YouTube to improve.** Search YouTube for a quick video on improving your memory. Try the techniques suggested in the video for a week and report your findings to the class.

Learn How Your Memory Works

Think of memory and studying as partners who walk hand in hand. After all, if you can't remember the information you're studying, you won't learn it. As a result, you won't be able to use it later to get work done for class. To understand how memory works, and why it sometimes fails, it helps to think about how your brain takes in the information coming from your textbooks and instructors — and then turns that information into memories. Memory involves three processes:

1. **Encoding**, or taking in information and changing it into signals in our brain
2. *Storing* the information in our memory
3. *Retrieving* the information when we want to remember it

encoding: Taking in information and changing it into signals in our brain.

To get a basic sense of how memory works, consider what happens when you run out of milk. You open the door of the fridge, and you see a milk carton on the shelf. You pick it up and realize it's almost empty. This information from your senses of sight and touch is *encoded* into your brain as an idea: You need to pick up milk on the way home. You repeat this thought several times as you head to class ("Don't forget to buy milk"), and this repetition *stores* the idea in your memory. Later, on your way home, you *retrieve* your memory about the milk and stop at the store to pick up a carton.

How You Remember

Making memories is incredibly complex, and scientists have many theories about exactly what occurs and why. According to one common model, which we'll focus on here, there are three stages of memory: sensory memory, short-term/working memory, and long-term memory.[1] The processes of encoding, storage, and retrieval connect these three stages together. In the following section, we'll look at how this relationship works—and how it helps us remember what we learn.

sensory memory: Process that uses information from the senses to begin creating memories.

Sensory Memory. In the first stage, **sensory memory**, you take in information through your five senses and form fleeting memories based on those experiences. In college, for example, information can come in through your ears (when you listen to lectures) and your eyes (when you read textbooks). In some classes you might also use touch as you perform experiments or use equipment. A few lucky students, like those of you taking culinary classes, will also get to smell and taste in class. As you absorb information through your senses, you form sensory memories of these experiences.

But sensory memories last only a split second. Our senses are constantly bombarded with information, and our brains can't take in everything.[2] It's only when we pay attention to information that it is *encoded* and moves to the next stage of memory: short-term/working memory (see Figure 8.1).

short-term memory: Memory that stores a small number of items for a short period of time.

Short-Term/Working Memory. Our **short-term memory** is quite limited in how much information it can hold and for how long it can hold it. Research shows that most people can hold about four to seven things in their short-term memory at once, and that information lasts for only 20 to 30 seconds.[3] Have you met someone new, only to forget his or her name when you start chatting? Blame your short-term memory.

FIGURE 8.1

The Basics of Memory

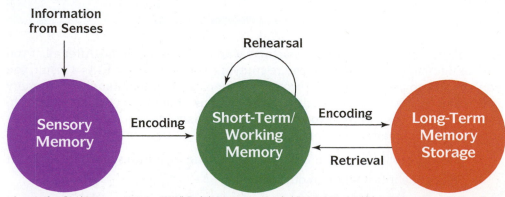

Information from David G. Myers and C. Nathan DeWall, *Psychology in Everyday Life*, 3rd ed. (New York: Worth Publishers, 2014), p. 194.

To make information "stick," you need to put effort into remembering the information. For example, when you are first introduced to another student, you might repeat (or *rehearse*) his name in your head five times as soon as you hear it. In addition, you might make a mental note to ask him if he wants to be your study partner for the next exam. When you put this kind of effort into remembering someone's name, you're engaging your **working memory**—the part of your short-term memory that actively processes memories and information. Thinking about, applying, rehearsing, and connecting new information to your existing memories are all ways to use your working memory, and they help your brain encode the information and move it to the next stage: long-term memory.

working memory: The part of short-term memory that actively processes memories and information.

Long-Term Memory. Unlike sensory or short-term memory, the storage capacity of your **long-term memory** seems limitless, and memories here can last forever (although they don't always).[4] This is where you *store* the record of your life, such as your earliest childhood memories, your tenth birthday party, and your wedding day. Long-term memory is where you keep the facts, ideas, procedures, and skills you learn in college, such as the circumstances that led to the American Revolution and the process of cell division. It's also the place from which you *retrieve* your memories when you need them—for instance, when you're taking a history or biology quiz or when you run into a new acquaintance and greet him by name.

long-term memory: Memory that stores a potentially limitless amount of information for a long period of time.

Putting It All Together. How do the three stages of memory work together? To understand this, it's helpful to compare them to the process of creating a spreadsheet. Suppose you're trying to save money to pay next term's tuition, so you decide to create a spreadsheet showing how much you spent last month. You take the following steps.

- First, you gather information about your income and expenses, such as paycheck stubs and credit card statements. When you see the information in front of you, you create a *sensory memory* of the facts and figures.
- Next, you create a spreadsheet file on your computer and enter your expenses into it. The process of typing numbers is similar to your memory's

Unforgettable Experiences. Many years from now, the memories you have of graduation day — of putting on your cap and gown, getting your diploma, and celebrating with family and friends — will be stored in your long-term memory. Long-term memory is where you keep the record of your life, and it's also the place from which you retrieve your memories when you need them. Image Source TAC/Getty Images

Think back to a time when you successfully remembered information that you used to complete a test or work on a project. Perhaps you recalled dates from the Civil War on a high school exam, or product specs at a previous job. In writing, briefly describe the strategies you used to memorize that information. How effective were these strategies? Will you use them to study for your classes now?

encoding process—it's how information gets into the file. As you're typing, you realize that you haven't saved the spreadsheet on your computer. The unsaved spreadsheet is like your *short-term/working memory*: Until you make the effort to save it, you could lose the information if you had a power outage or your hard drive crashed.

- Finally, you save the spreadsheet file, which is like *storing* information in your *long-term memory*. Later, you open the file and *retrieve* the data.

Of course, your brain is much more complex than any computer program. For example, a computer shouldn't "forget" unless it experiences a mechanical failure, but a human brain can forget with normal age wear and tear. Still, this analogy gives you the basic idea of how the memory processes and stages work together.

Why You Forget

We've seen how memory works, but what happens when it *doesn't* work? Why do we forget? Forgetting occurs when there's a breakdown in one of the memory processes. Imagine that you meet a new acquaintance named Julio, but when you run into him a week later, you can't remember his name. What happened? There are several possibilities. If you didn't hear his name when he first told you, then that information never made it into your sensory memory. Or you might have heard his name, but it slipped away because you didn't pay enough attention to keep it in your working memory. This represents an *encoding failure*: The information got lost or wasn't in your mind long enough to move to your long-term memory.[5] The other possibility, and certainly the more frustrating one, is that you did create a long-term memory for Julio's name but you still can't remember it. This is a *retrieval failure*.[6]

To further understand forgetting, let's revisit the budget spreadsheet analogy. Imagine two different scenarios.

Scenario 1: When you finish working on the spreadsheet, you don't give it a meaningful file name. Instead, you call it "Document 1." You don't pay attention to where you save it on your computer. And finally, you don't open the file for nine months. When you finally want to look at the spreadsheet, you'll probably have a hard time finding it.

Scenario 2: This time, you look closely at the computer screen as you name the file "Monthly Budget." You save the file in your "Finances" folder. Then you access the file weekly for nine months, adding new expense and cost data at the end of each week. You'll probably find it much easier to locate, open, and use the file in this scenario than in scenario 1. Why? Because you paid attention when you named the file, you saved it in an accessible folder, and you worked with it repeatedly. By doing this, you used all the memory processes. You took in the information using your senses, and you worked with and retrieved the information many times, which helped the memory stick.

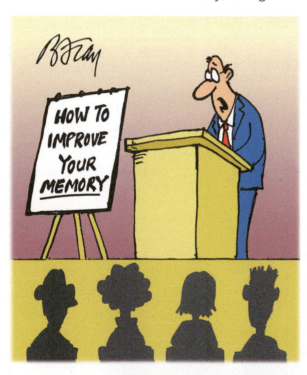

" DANG, I FORGOT MY NOTES! "

Memory Mastery. When you forget information, you might feel frustrated—or even embarrassed. Do your best to master key memory strategies, like making meaningful memories and repeatedly accessing the information; that way, you can retrieve what you've learned when you need it! Brian Fray/CartoonStock.com

When you learn material for your classes, the ability to encode, store, and retrieve information is crucial. Think about it this way: Scenario 1 is similar to reading a textbook chapter only once and then trying to remember information from the chapter while you're taking a test a few weeks later. If you don't put effort into studying the chapter, you won't create strong memories of what you read, and you'll have trouble remembering the information when you need it. By contrast, actively thinking about the new information, making meaningful memories of the information, and repeatedly accessing the information by studying and reviewing it will move that information from your sensory memory to your short-term/working memory, and from there to your long-term memory. In this way, you'll remember what you've learned, both at test time and far into the future.

Study Basics: Set Yourself Up for Success

Now that you understand how memory works, let's shift our focus to study strategies that help you remember and use your newfound knowledge. But first, ask yourself how you feel about studying. Do you dread it? Find it boring? Feel anxious about it?

If you have negative views of studying, try changing how you think about it. Instead of seeing studying as a task that you have to do, consider it an *opportunity* for you to build valuable skills and work toward your goals. For example, if you want to become the first person in your family to get a college degree, each hour of studying gets you one step closer to achieving your long-term goal. By thinking positively and working to develop a growth mindset, you'll remain focused on developing your study skills and mastering the assigned material.

In addition, remember that studying isn't a one-size-fits-all activity. It's a *metacognitive* process, which requires you to think carefully about what you're learning and how you're learning it. As you saw in the motivation chapter, metacognition involves three steps: planning and organizing; monitoring your progress; and evaluating results and making adjustments. You can use these steps to assess how well your study techniques are working for you:

1. **Plan and organize** the strategies you'll use to study for each class.
2. **Monitor your progress** as you try out your selected techniques. Are you recalling key points more quickly? Is material becoming easier to master?
3. **Evaluate your results and adjust as necessary.** If you do well on your first test, that's a positive sign that your study techniques are working; if you don't do well, it may be time to adjust your approach and try out a new technique or two.

To help you maximize your options, this chapter includes a wide variety of study strategies you can pick from. Give some (or all!) a try as you build study plans for each class.

Manage Your Time and Monitor Your Environment

To study for classes effectively, you have to be in control of your time and take steps to ensure that your environment is distraction-free. Here are several strategies that you can use to make the most of every minute.

Space Out Your Studying. What's the most productive way to learn new material? As you saw in the learning chapter, it's when you space out your studying across multiple days or weeks and study in small blocks of time.[7] For a reminder about why this strategy is so effective, think back to the budget spreadsheet example earlier in this chapter: The more you work with the material, the more you remember about it. By contrast, trying to "cram" large amounts of information into your brain all at once (especially late at night) leads to poor performance on tests.[8]

Switch Up Your Study Topics. As you also saw in the learning chapter, mixing up the topics you're studying (interleaved practice) is one of the most efficient ways to learn and remember material.[9] Moving from economics to anatomy to math over the course of an hour is one way to switch up your studying. Another method is to mix up the type of material you're studying for a single class. For example, let's say that you're preparing for a psychology final where you'll need to match famous psychologists with their associated theories, explain types of conditioning, and identify different structures in the brain. You can spend a few minutes with your theory flash cards, then switch to review sheets for operant and classical conditioning, and finally study your Cornell notes to work on brain structures. By mixing up the topics and types of material you're studying, you'll be making the best use of your study time.

Maximize Study Opportunities. To make the most of study opportunities identify brief periods of time that are going to waste and turn them into quick study sessions. For instance, if you have 30 minutes between classes, use some of that time to review your chemistry notes. If you have a 15-minute break at work, use it to look over flash cards. Thanks to mobile technology, studying anywhere is easier than ever: You can put your notes on your smartphone and review them while you're waiting in the doctor's office or commuting on the bus.

No Grumpy Cats Allowed. When you're studying, it's easy to let distractions creep in — like surfing online to see how Grumpy Cat's Las Vegas book signing went. (Yes, she really had a book signing!) But distractions can impair your concentration and prevent you from remembering information. So catch up on Grumpy Cat's latest antics — but only *after* you've finished studying.
MediaPunch/REX/Shutterstock

Minimize Distractions. As useful as technology is as a study aid, take care that it doesn't become a distraction. If you send text messages while you're supposed to be reading notes on your phone, you'll have trouble creating long-term memories of the information you're trying to study. Although multitasking may seem like a good idea, your mind isn't truly capable of focusing on more than one thing at a time, so distractions prevent you from giving your full attention to the material you're trying to learn.[10] For tips on how to eliminate distractions while you're studying, see the organization and time management chapter.

Make Connections

As we've noted throughout this book, one great way to make lasting memories is to link new information to something you already know or to personal experiences you've had (see the motivation and learning chapters). This technique can come in very handy when you're studying for an exam.

As an example, let's look at Cecily, who is studying for a biology midterm exam and needs to remember the main parts of an animal cell. As Cecily studies, she sees that one part of the cell, the Golgi apparatus, is made up of flat, oblong shapes that are connected and stacked on top of each other. Their function is to process carbohydrates and proteins and sort them for transportation throughout the body. To Cecily, the Golgi apparatus looks a lot like stacked pancakes. She thinks about her favorite breakfast foods, pancakes and bacon, which provide the body with carbohydrates and protein. Now that she's made an association between that breakfast and the Golgi apparatus, it will be easier to remember what she learned when she takes the midterm.

Study Strategy of Champions. When you connect new information with previous knowledge or experiences, you'll make lasting memories through elaborative rehearsal. Cecily is an expert at this strategy: She makes the connection between breakfast food and biology to better reinforce concepts. Even better? Cecily pictures a plate of warm, fluffy pancakes each time. By using dual coding *and* elaborative rehearsal, she sets herself up for studying success. 5 second Studio/Shutterstock

When you make connections and apply information to other situations, you're using a powerful process called **elaborative rehearsal**. In elaborative rehearsal, you associate the meaning of new information with other information already stored in your memory, making it easier to recall the new information later. As an added bonus, making connections involves critical thinking—a vital skill that helps you evaluate, learn, and use new information at school and at work. And as a double bonus, if you visualize an image of whatever connections you're making, you'll also be using dual coding—another top-notch strategy that can help strengthen your learning.

elaborative rehearsal: The process of making connections between new ideas and other information already stored in your memory.

Draw a Mental Picture

Another way you can use visualization to remember information is by creating a mental picture of the material you're studying. Start by looking at the image you want to re-create in your mind. It might be a figure from your chemistry text showing the molecular formula for benzene, or the parts of a blueprint for your construction course. Cover up the original image and try to picture what it looks like in your mind. Then look back at the actual image: How well does your mental picture match the image? Repeat this activity until the image in your mind matches the image you see on the page.

Join a Study Group

Have you ever heard the saying "There's strength in numbers"? When it's time to study, working with other students can help you learn and improve your performance on tests.[11] There are several types of study groups. Many schools offer **Supplemental Instruction** for especially difficult classes, which consists of study groups led by students who did well in those classes in the past. Your instructors might also set up study groups for their classes to encourage students to work together. Alternatively, you can create your own study group with classmates who want to support one

Supplemental Instruction: A student-led study program for especially difficult classes.

Strength in Numbers. Joining a study group is a great way to master material. Group members can help one another grasp difficult course content. And when you explain a topic to other members, you deepen your understanding of that topic. That deeper understanding will pay off during tests. Jacob Lund/Shutterstock

another and work together. If you set up a study group yourself, create an agenda to help the group focus on particular topics at each meeting. Without some kind of direction, group members may end up wasting valuable study time.

Before attending a group meeting, spend time studying on your own and identify specific questions you'd like help with. For instance, if you're struggling to understand the ins-and-outs of interest groups in your American Government class, ask the study group leader or your study partners for help. And be prepared to teach others in the group about topics you understand well. One of the most powerful ways to truly understand material (not just memorize it) is to teach it to someone else. A study group gives you that opportunity.

Test Yourself on Key Concepts

Answering practice test questions is a great way to get ready for an exam and increase your confidence, and it can have a significant impact on your performance. Try these tips to create self-tests and check your understanding of key concepts.

Make Flash Cards. As you saw in the learning chapter, one easy way to test yourself is to use flash cards. Flash cards are a blank slate—you can put anything you want on them. For instance, you can put key words on one side of the card and definitions on the other, or write historical events on one side and the dates when they occurred on the reverse side. You can also use them to quiz yourself on broad concepts, themes, or theories.

rote rehearsal:
Memorization of specific information or facts by studying the information repeatedly.

As you flip through the flash cards over and over, you use **rote rehearsal**, which means you memorize specific information or facts by studying the information repeatedly. This approach is valuable when you need to remember specific facts, such as the parts of the human body or mathematical formulas. In general, flash cards are less useful when you need to demonstrate comprehension of more complex information, such as how the Ottoman Empire changed from the thirteenth to seventeenth centuries. So, for a well-rounded study strategy, use flash cards in addition to other techniques in this chapter.

> ## "You have to think of your brain as a muscle—if you don't challenge it, it will become weaker!"

voices of experience
student

NAME
James Lawrence

SCHOOL
Mississippi Gulf Coast Community College

MAJOR
Psychology

CAREER GOAL
Clinical Psychologist

USING STUDY TOOLS TO SUCCEED

When I first started junior college, I was nervous about my classes and really didn't know what to expect from my professors. I had heard that college was harder than high school and required more studying — something my mama called "burning the midnight oil." I honestly didn't know how to study because in high school I never had to. I just went to class, listened to the teacher's lecture, completed my worksheets, and passed the test.

It was the second week of classes when the difference between high school and college really sank in. I realized that there were no more worksheets and that just attending class wasn't going to allow me to succeed. Most of my classes included four exams — each covering material from up to six chapters — and I needed to do more than just memorize the material in all those chapters. I panicked, then made friends in each of my classes. We formed study groups, and in those groups I picked up some new strategies for learning. Some students in the group used flash cards to help them study, and others would make their own test questions to practice understanding the material.

Making flash cards worked best for me because it made me act on the material rather than just reading it over and over. I had to identify and write a concept on one side of the card and write the explanation on the other side. Having to write the material down was a concrete way for me to interact with the content. Then I could quiz myself using the cards no matter where I was on campus. You have to think of your brain as a muscle — if you don't challenge it, it will become weaker!

> **YOUR TURN** Have you ever created flash cards as a method of self-testing? If so, how well did this study tool work for you? What were the advantages? The challenges? Have you tried creating other types of practice tests for yourself?

As you use your flash cards, keep these tips in mind.

- Shuffle the cards regularly and review them multiple times. Recognizing the content once won't help you master it.
- Go through the cards twice a day for the entire week before an exam.
- If you find yourself flipping through the cards mindlessly, set them aside for a few minutes and come back to them when you can stay focused.

Design Practice Exams. You can also design a practice test that looks more like an exam your instructor would give. To get an idea what types of questions should go on your test, review your notes from class and the notes you took while reading your textbook. Then, build the test itself. You might create matching questions for dates and events in history class, essay questions for economics class, multiple-choice questions for accounting or biology, and practice problems for chemistry or math. Create answers for each question; then take the test yourself, and trade tests with a friend for even more practice.

Answer Purposeful Reading Questions. If you've created and answered purposeful reading questions while taking notes on a textbook chapter or other reading assignment (see the reading chapter), you have a ready-made self-test. Review the questions in your notes, cover up the answers, and answer the questions out loud to yourself or with a study partner. Or combine your purposeful reading questions with other study tools. You might make flash cards with a question on one side and the answer on the other. If you like the Cornell notes system, write your questions in the cue column on the left and your answers in the notes section on the right; then use the summary section at the bottom to restate in your own words the key ideas you want to remember (see Figure 8.2).

Take Practice Quizzes. Creating your own practice tests is hugely helpful, but you can also make use of the ready-made resources that are included with your textbooks. Some textbooks include practice quizzes at the end of each chapter or section, while others come with online quizzes you can use to test yourself on different chapter concepts. With this book, for example, you likely have access to LearningCurve adaptive quizzing, which you can use to check your understanding of key concepts in each chapter. Make use of any available instructor- or publisher-provided quizzing resources, online or in your textbook; the more you practice answering questions, the more confident and well-versed you'll be in the book's main ideas.

FIGURE 8.2

Using Purposeful Reading Questions and Cornell Notes to Study

Introduction to Nursing

Purposeful reading questions:
What are the three levels of preventive care? What is an example of each level?

1. Primary prevention: prevent healthy individuals from acquiring illness
   Example: educate people on use of sunscreen
2. Secondary prevention: illness/disease has occurred, but person wants to slow its progress
   Example: individual visits dermatologist regularly and has suspicious growths removed
3. Tertiary prevention: treat illness/disease to limit impact
   Example: treat individual with skin cancer

Summary:
Preventive care has three levels: primary (preventing healthy people from getting sick), secondary (slowing progress of disease), and tertiary (limiting disease's impact through proper treatment).

At the end of each chapter, many textbooks provide study or practice questions. These questions are there for a reason: According to research, if you're using them to study, you're more likely to get better grades.

In one study, researchers gave a large group of students 500 practice questions to help them prepare for an exam at the end of the class. These were short-answer essay questions, designed to help students focus on the main topics from their reading (e.g., "What are the basic components of the central nervous system?"). At the end of the class, the researchers examined the relationship between the number of study questions the students answered and how they performed on the exam. They found the following:

▶ The students who passed the exam answered an average of 81 percent of the 500 study questions before taking the exam.

▶ The students who failed answered an average of 41 percent of the study questions before taking the exam.

The researchers also asked the students how the questions were helpful. The students said that the study questions helped them plan their studying, better understand the course material, and prepare for the exam.

Answer Practice Questions to
Master Your Material

THE BOTTOM LINE

Answering more practice questions before taking an exam can help you pass the exam.

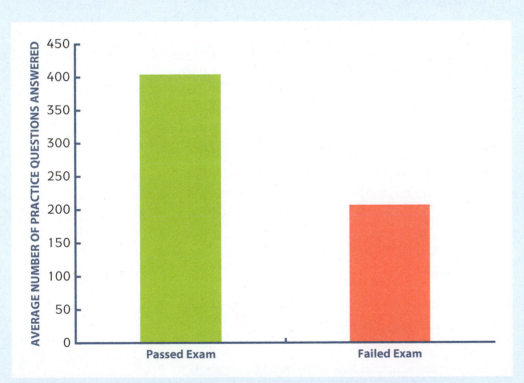

Students who passed the exam answered almost twice as many practice questions as those who failed the exam.

Information from P. Wilhelm and J. M. Pieters, "Fostering Effective Studying and Study Planning with Study Questions," *Assessment and Evaluation in Higher Education* 32 (2007): 373–82.

Create Review Sheets

As you record information from lectures and reading assignments, you'll find yourself building up mounds of pages and stacks of bulging notebooks. To manage all this information, try creating a review sheet by condensing pages of detailed notes into a one-page document (see Figure 8.3). When you condense material, you include only the information you really need, such as the main ideas from your notes, annotations you made while reading a textbook chapter, problems from your math class, or dates from your history class.

While it's a good idea to try to whittle down the main points to just one page, do give yourself some flexibility: If a single page is too limiting, create a separate review sheet for each chapter or reading that will be covered on a test. For example, you might decide to create a separate review sheet for each book you read in your American Literature class, which would involve developing a template that includes the main characters, the genre of the book, major themes, and any connections between that book and the other texts you're reading for the course.

And as with self-tests, crafting review sheets gives you a great opportunity to reach out to classmates: You can exchange review sheets and compare your documents with one another, and each person can offer ideas for improving the study tools and filling in any gaps.

FIGURE 8.3

Excerpt of Sample Review Sheet

REVIEW SHEET   Oct. 10
                                                Ch. 8: Memory and Studying
Memory

3 Processes:
1. Encoding: Moving info from environment to brain
2. Storage: Keeping info in memory
3. Retrieval: Getting info back out of memory/storage

Sensory memory → Short-term (working) memory → Long-term memory

Forgetting:
- Encoding failure (Never got into memory)
- Retrieval failure (Can't get it out of memory!!)

Studying

It's all about metacognition: thinking about how you learn.

Plan → Monitor → Evaluate

Tips:
- Space out studying—study chem 20 min <u>each day</u>
- Interleave—switch off between chem and bio
- Cut down on distractions/use free moments wisely
- Make connections/use elaborative rehearsal

Use Mnemonics

If you want to memorize specific material you can create a **mnemonic** (pronounced "neh mon ik"), which is a trick or strategy to remember information. For example, the rhyme "Thirty days hath September, April, June, and November . . ." is a mnemonic for remembering the number of days in each month. Mnemonics help you remember specific information you need to recall for an exam or to solve a problem. Creating a mnemonic requires critical thinking, as well as some creativity. Try the following popular mnemonic strategies.

Acronyms. Make an *acronym*, a word created from the first letter of each word you want to remember. For example, the acronym HOMES can help you remember the five Great Lakes (Huron, Ontario, Michigan, Erie, Superior). In your Introduction to Psychology class, the acronym OCEAN can help you remember the five major personality traits (openness, conscientiousness, extraversion, agreeableness, neuroticism). In this class, the acronym SMART can help you remember the steps of the goal-setting process (specific, measurable, achievable, relevant, and time-limited).

Associations. Create associations between new information and things you already know. Let's say you want to memorize a list of Greek gods for your art history course. You start with Zeus, king of the gods, whom you associate with your uncle, who happens to be a large and powerful man. Zeus's wife, Hera, you associate with your aunt Helen. (Both names start with *H*, which is easy for you to remember.) Next you associate Ares, the son of Zeus and Hera, with your cousin. You might take the association even further and imagine how all of these gods would interact at your family reunion. As you create these associations, you're practicing elaborative rehearsal and building long-term memories of this new information.

Acrostics. An acrostic is a phrase or sentence in which the first letter of every word corresponds to a list of words you want to remember. Acrostics are especially useful when you want to memorize words in a particular order. Some common acrostics are "Every Good Boy Does Fine" (E, G, B, D, F) for lines on the treble clef, or "Kids Prefer Cheese Over Fried Green Spinach" (kingdom, phylum, class, order, family, genus, species) for the order of taxonomy in biology. Can you think of what the acrostic "My Very Energetic Mother Just Served Us Nachos" represents? Here's a hint: We all live on "E."

mnemonic: A learning strategy that helps you memorize specific material.

Hungry for Acrostics? Acrostics are potent memory boosters. For example, the acrostic "Kids Prefer Cheese Over Fried Green Spinach" can help you remember the order of taxonomy in your biology class (kingdom, phylum, class, order, family, genus, species). You can make up acrostics yourself to remember information, especially terms that go in a specific order.
Left: Isuaneye/Shutterstock
Right: littlenySTOCK/Shutterstock

Method of Loci. Associate words you need to remember with locations that are familiar to you. For instance, suppose you're trying to remember the sequence of early U.S. presidents. You could associate each president with the sequence of actions you perform while getting from your apartment to school. You wake up and say good morning to George Washington (the first president), whom you imagine sitting on your dresser. Next you see John Adams (the second president) at the breakfast table. Then you greet Thomas Jefferson (the third president) as you leave your apartment. Finally, you see James Madison (the fourth president) at the end of your driveway. The memory links you choose don't have to make sense. In fact, it's better if they're funny, outrageous, or off-the-wall: They'll capture your attention, making them easier to remember.

Study for Your Math, Science, and Online Classes

Math and science classes differ in some important ways from classes in other disciplines; for example, they emphasize solving problems. And online classes differ from traditional face-to-face classes; for instance, in online classes you can usually watch lectures or respond to discussion posts whenever you want. To learn and remember information effectively, adapt your study strategies and tools to the unique characteristics of these classes.

Math and Science Classes

Many of the study strategies you've already learned in this chapter can be used in all your courses, but several additional suggestions will be particularly helpful in your math and science classes.

- **Get plenty of practice solving problems.** Complete all the problems in your textbook, even if your instructor doesn't assign them, and do any problems provided by your instructor. If a study guide or a tutor gives you additional problems, solve those too. Many Web sites also offer practice math, physics, or chemistry problems. Your textbook may even come with access to such online practice problems (see Figure 8.4).

- **Check your answers when solving problems.** Do your answers make sense? Are they what you expected? For example, if you're calculating the amount of force acting on a moving object, it wouldn't make sense to have a negative value as an answer. Testing yourself in this way can help you determine how well you understand the formula or equation featured in the problem. In addition, evaluate whether you're making similar or repeated mistakes when you solve problems so that you have time to correct these mistakes before an exam.

- **Write down units when solving problems.** As you work on a problem, make sure you're using the correct units of measure. If your solution is supposed to be in hertz (Hz) and instead it's in seconds, you know you've made a mistake. By making this a habit, you can catch a lot of simple mistakes.

- **Create lists of theorems, formulas, symbols, and vocabulary.** Review these lists during your study time.

- **Explore Khan Academy (www.khanacademy.org).** This free, online resource provides brief lectures and demonstrations of many math and science concepts.

CONNECT TO MY RESOURCES

Your adviser, instructors, and the staff at the tutoring center are just a few of the many people on campus who can help you strengthen your study skills. Write down the office location, phone number, contact person, and Web site for two study resources on campus. How will you use these resources?

8.4 Continuous Probability Models

31. Generate two random real numbers between 0 and 1 and take their sum. The sum can take any value between 0 and 2. The density curve is the shaded triangle shown in **Figure 8.13.**

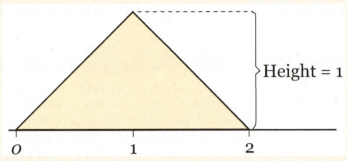

Figure 8.13 The density curve for the sum of two random numbers, for **Exercise 31.**

(a) Verify by geometry that the area under this curve is 1.

(b) What is the probability that the sum is less than 1? (Sketch the density curve, shade the area that represents the probability, and then find that area. Do this for part (c) as well.)

(c) What is the probability that the sum is less than 0.5?

Show Answer

32. Suppose two data values are each rounded to the nearest whole number. Make a density curve for the sum of the two roundoff errors (assuming each error has a continuous uniform distribution).

33. On the TV show *The Price Is Right*, the "Range Game" involves a contestant being told that the suggested retail price of a prize lies between two numbers that are $600 apart. The contestant has one chance to position a red window with a span of $150 that will contain the price. On one episode, the price of a piano is between $8900 and $9500. If we assume a uniform continuous distribution (i.e., that all prices within the $600 interval are equally likely), what is the probability that the contestant will be successful?

Show Answer

Online Classes

Whether you're studying for online classes or traditional face-to-face courses, most of the same techniques can help you master material in both environments. The following tips, though, are particularly useful in studying for online courses.

- **Study all class materials.** In an online class, you may have to watch recorded instructor lectures or online videos. Add the notes you take during these lectures or videos to your study materials for the class.

- **Set up an online study group.** Create an online discussion group with your classmates to share information or practice questions. Your online course-management system might offer videoconferencing so you can hold a virtual study group.

- **Explore online study resources at your school.** Your school may have online tutors, extra recordings of lectures, or other resources specifically designed for students taking online classes. Investigate your options.

FIGURE 8.4

Solving Practice Problems

Completing plenty of practice problems, like the ones shown here, is a great way to study for math and science classes. So try your hand at all the problems provided in your textbook—even those your instructor hasn't assigned—and check out Web sites offering practice problems. Information from COMAP, *LaunchPad for For All Practical Purposes: Mathematical Literacy in Today's World*, 9th ed. (New York: W. H. Freeman, 2015).

⸦ CONNECT TO MY CLASSES

Take a minute for metacognition: Now that you've read about a number of different study strategies, which ones do you think would work best in each of your classes? Write down the classes you're currently taking and note one or two strategies that would be a good fit for each one. Then, monitor your progress, evaluate your results, and adjust as necessary!

Use Memory and Studying at Work

The ability to study and remember information is just as valuable *outside* the classroom as it is *inside* the classroom: Employers want to hire and promote people who keep learning and growing, and mastering memory and study strategies can help you do exactly that.

Use Your Memory to Build Personal Connections

Have you ever walked into a restaurant where the server knows your regular order? Has a supervisor in another department ever called you by name? If so, you know that it creates a feeling of personal connection when people remember details about you. You can use your memory to build such connections yourself. Remembering details about others shows that you're interested in their lives and helps to forge positive relationships. It's rewarding on a personal level to make connections in a work setting, but these connections can also have business-related benefits: The people you connect with may be the source of your next sale, or they might help you network to get a promotion.

Communicate Using Elaborative Rehearsal

As you saw earlier, elaborative rehearsal involves making connections between new information and things you already know. Elaborative rehearsal helps you not only learn and remember information but also explain complex ideas to other people, such as customers and colleagues. Suppose that you're a computer systems analyst and you need to explain the concept of computer bandwidth to a client, including how small and large bandwidths differ. You explain that small bandwidth is like a garden hose (it has low data flow) and that large bandwidth is like a fire hose (it has large data flow). You're connecting a new concept, computer bandwidth, with something most people know about: the difference between garden and fire hoses. As a result, the client "gets" the concept because you've communicated it effectively.

Expert Communicator. When you excel at learning and remembering information, you can become a subject matter expert. Being an expert makes you valuable in the workplace, especially when you communicate your knowledge to others. Here, human rights lawyer Amal Clooney shares her expertise at a professional conference. FABRICE COFFRINI/Getty Images

Become a Subject Matter Expert

When you're motivated to learn and study, you'll continue to build knowledge about your chosen field. You may even become a *subject matter expert*: someone who constantly learns new information to build a deep understanding of his or her field, whether it's banking regulations, solar panel design, or software development. Being an expert is a big advantage in the workplace, as employers value go-to individuals who have the knowledge and skills the organization needs to succeed.

Be a Lifelong Learner

One of the best benefits of memory and study strategies is that you can use them to become a *lifelong learner*. Lifelong learners—who keep

"For me to be successful, I had to keep studying and learning."

NAME
Deborah Bobbio

PROFESSION
Software Engineer

SCHOOL
Miami Dade College

DEGREES
*Associate in Arts;
Associate in Science;
Bachelor of Science*

MAJORS
*Computer Art Animation;
Computer Engineering
Technology; Electronics
Engineering Technology*

LIFELONG LEARNING

During college I focused mostly on the hardware side of computers and engineering. When I got my first job out of college, it was as a software engineer, which is a field I had little experience with before my senior year. Fortunately my employer didn't expect me to be an expert right away — I developed my skills during the first few months on the job. I was very preoccupied with being able to keep up, but I was also excited to learn about something I didn't have much experience with. I knew that, for me to be successful, I had to keep studying and learning.

My employer put me on a big project right away, so I started looking for free online classes and reading up on the programming language I needed. I also learned that it's okay to ask for help. When I got stuck with something, I would do some research or talk with a fellow developer. Taking small breaks was extremely important; it helped me focus so I wouldn't just stare at the information and then forget what I learned.

Just like in school, at work there are deadlines, projects, and problems to solve — some of which are easier than others. As with homework, I've learned that it's all about practice. The more work I do, the more I learn. No one will expect you to be an expert right out of school, but if your employers see you utilizing all your resources to get the job done, they'll recognize it. I'm motivated to keep learning, and this job has given me the incredible opportunity to do that.

> **YOUR TURN** If you currently have a job, how do you learn and remember the information you need to perform your job? If you're not employed but are interested in a particular job or career, what kind of information will you need to master to excel in that role? How will you master it?

Courtesy of Deborah L. Bobbio

building their knowledge and skills long after graduation — tend to be curious about the world around them, apply study skills when they encounter something they don't know, and look for new skills to develop. Lifelong learning keeps your brain active, makes life more interesting, and has benefits for your career: It helps you develop your skills, making you more valuable to your organization — and more marketable if you decide to look for a new job or ask for a raise.

my personal success plan

Based on your ACES results and what you learned in this chapter, are you inspired to set a new goal aimed at improving your memory and study skills? If so, the Personal Success Plan can walk you through the goal-setting process. Read the advice and examples; then sketch out your ideas in the space provided.

To access the Personal Success Plan online, go to the LaunchPad for *Connections*, Second Edition.

1 IDENTIFY A GOAL

Choose a memory or studying goal to work toward this term. Here are some general ideas you might draw from; you can also create a goal of your own.

- ▶ Make flash cards as a self-test.
- ▶ Join a study group.
- ▶ Revise my study schedule to space out studying.
- ▶ Practice mixing up studying between subjects.
- ▶ Complete practice test questions for each class.

2 MAKE YOUR GOAL SMART

Rewrite your specific goal so that it's SMART, and make sure to use the SMART goal checklist.

SAMPLE: This week I'll create flash cards for each course and use them to test myself for 10 minutes a day between classes.

3 CREATE AN ACTION PLAN

Outline the specific steps you'll take to achieve your SMART goal, and note when you'll complete each step.

SAMPLE: I'll use the first 20 minutes of my next study session to create flash cards.

4 LIST BARRIERS AND SOLUTIONS

Think about possible barriers to your action steps; then brainstorm solutions for overcoming them.

SAMPLE: If I forget to review my flash cards between classes, I'll set a reminder on my phone to help me remember.

5 ACT AND EVALUATE OUTCOMES

Now that your plan is in place, take action. Record each action step as you take it. Then evaluate whether you achieved your SMART goal, and make any adjustments needed to get better results in the future.

SAMPLE: I made so many flash cards that I didn't have time to review all of them between classes. I'll pare them down to just the most important information.

6 CONNECT TO CAREER

List the skills you're building as you progress toward your SMART goal. How will you use these skills to land a job and succeed at work?

SAMPLE: My ability to remember specific pieces of information will help me if I become a tax accountant. I'll be able to understand and apply the many changes in tax law that occur each year.

my personal success plan

1 my general goal

2 my SMART goal

☐ SPECIFIC ☐ MEASURABLE ☐ ACHIEVABLE ☐ RELEVANT ☐ TIME-LIMITED

3 my action plan

4 my barriers/ solutions

5 my actions/ outcomes

6 my career connection

CHAPTER SUMMARY

In this chapter we looked at how memory works and explored strategies and tools you can use to study. Revisit the following key points, and reflect on how you can use this information to support your success now and in the future.

- Memory involves three processes: encoding, storing, and retrieving information. Creating a memory begins with taking in information through your five senses (sensory memory). Information resides briefly in your short-term memory, and you can use your working memory to move it into your long-term memory.

- Forgetting occurs when there is a failure to encode or retrieve information.

- Learning how to study effectively is a metacognitive process. It involves planning and organizing your study strategies, monitoring your progress, and evaluating your study results and making adjustments.

- Studying is most effective and efficient when you space out studying for each class, switch up the topics you're studying, make use of available study opportunities, and minimize distractions. Best practices also include using elaborative rehearsal to enhance your studying, making mental pictures, and joining a study group.

- You can build your own study tools like flash cards, practice exams, purposeful reading questions, review sheets, and mnemonics. Also take advantage of tools from your instructor or textbook like online quizzes or practice questions.

- Completing as many practice problems as possible, checking your answers, using correct units of measure, making lists of formulas and terms, and using online resources can help you study for math and science classes.

- Good study strategies for online classes include studying all course materials, accessing online resources, and creating virtual study groups.

- You can excel in your job and advance your career by using memory and study strategies and tools to become a subject matter expert and a lifelong learner, as well as to communicate information and build personal connections at work.

CHAPTER ACTIVITIES

Journal Entry

ENHANCING YOUR CURRENT STUDY STRATEGY

This chapter introduced you to multiple strategies for studying and remembering material. Up to this point, what has been your overall strategy in studying for exams? Reflect on the strengths and weaknesses of this approach. Questions to aid in your reflection include:

- How far in advance of the test do you begin to study?

- How much time do you spend studying? Do you study with other people?

- Do you study in small doses or prefer longer study sessions?

- What types of distractions do you encounter when studying? How do you typically deal with these distractions?

- How do you test yourself on the material or try to remember it?

- After reading this chapter, what study strategies seem important to implement? What new memory techniques will you try?

Adopting a Success Attitude

FINDING MOTIVATION TO STUDY

Motivation is a study aid: It can help you stay focused and accomplish tasks efficiently and effectively. Your attitude can affect your level of motivation: When you feel negatively about a class, a test, or studying in general, you risk setting yourself up for failure. Select one class that you find particularly challenging; then respond to the following questions to adopt a more positive attitude toward studying for that class.

1. What long-term goals do you want to achieve by attending college? How will studying for this class help you achieve your goals?

2. What is one positive statement you can tell yourself over and over (a mantra) to get through this class?

3. What are some specific good things that will come from studying for this class? For example, what knowledge, abilities, attitudes, relationships, or study skills will you build as a result? How will these good things be useful in future classes or in your career?

4. In what ways are you in control over how and when you study for this class? What are the benefits of having this control?

5. What negative thoughts or beliefs do you have about studying for this class? Play devil's advocate and challenge each thought or belief.

Applying Your Skills

USING MNEMONICS TO ENHANCE MEMORY

When you use mnemonics to remember new information, you take personal responsibility for your learning by improving your chances of moving information from your short-term memory into your long-term memory.

Choose a class in which you need to remember a string of words or ideas for an upcoming exam. Then complete the following steps to create your own acrostic (a type of mnemonic). We've provided an example to get you started.

1. Select a list of words or ideas you need to remember. Write these words in a column (vertically) and underline or highlight the first letter in each word.

2. Identify words that begin with each of the underlined or highlighted letters.

3. Put the words together to create a short phrase or a sentence. This is your acrostic.

4. Use your acrostic, and then assess how well it worked. Did it help you remember the information? If not, you may need to change the words in step 2 to create something more fun, interesting, or memorable.

Example: Remembering Piaget's four stages of cognitive development in children.

Step 1	Step 2	Step 3
Sensory Motor Stage	Six	Six Penguins Cooked Falafel
Pre-operational Stage	Penguins	
Concrete Operational Stage	Cooked	
Formal Operational Stage	Falafel	

College Success = Career Success

FORMING STUDY GROUPS

Study groups have an important place in college and at work. In college, members of study groups offer each other moral support and share ideas. At work, colleagues may form groups to study for a licensing exam, learn about a new product, design a marketing campaign, or prepare for a big meeting or presentation. Forming a study group at school can help you build teamwork skills — skills that many potential employers value.

With these advantages in mind, build a plan for forming a college study group by answering the following questions:

1. For which class(es) will you form a study group?

2. Who will you ask to be in your study group? Why?

3. How many people will be in your group?

4. How often will the group meet? Where? For how long?

5. If the study group is for an online class, how will the group differ from a study group created for a face-to-face class? How will you communicate with group members?

6. Who will be in charge of creating the agenda for each study group session?

7. How will you study as a group? What strategies from this chapter will you use? Why?

Now that you have a plan, don't wait — start building your study group today so that you can begin meeting this term!

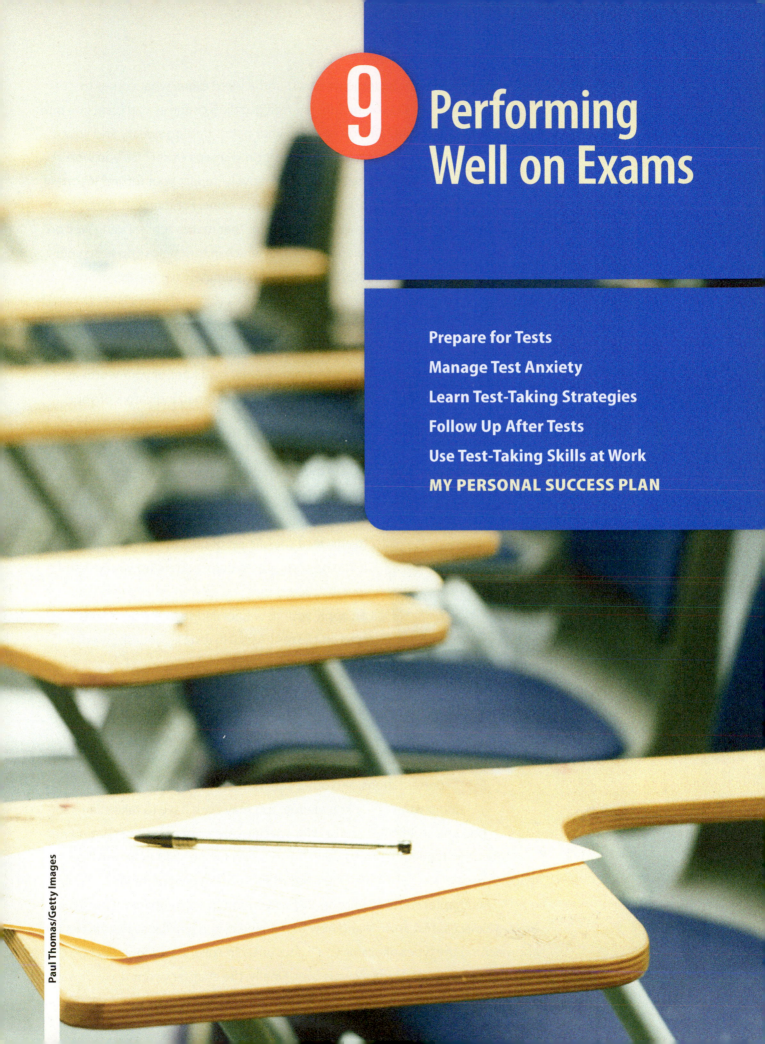

9 Performing Well on Exams

Prepare for Tests

Manage Test Anxiety

Learn Test-Taking Strategies

Follow Up After Tests

Use Test-Taking Skills at Work

MY PERSONAL SUCCESS PLAN

When you hear the word *test* or the word *exam*, what comes to mind? Do you picture yourself guzzling coffee as you cram late into the night? Do you envision your palms getting sweaty and your heart starting to pound as test time creeps closer? Do you worry that failing an exam could negatively impact your future? If you answered "yes" to these questions, you're not alone. For many students, tests have tremendous power and meaning. That makes sense: Doing well on tests helps you get good grades, which in turn helps you keep your financial aid, stay in college, and ultimately get the job of your dreams.

Before you start hyperventilating, though, let's put exams in their proper perspective. Yes, doing well on them matters, but exams are *not* measures of your worth as a human being. They're *not* broad indicators of your intelligence. They don't even completely measure your knowledge of a given topic. A single exam will *not* dictate the future direction of your life, and often it won't make or break your grade for a course.

Rather, an exam is a snapshot of your ability to answer a specific set of questions on a given topic. It's an opportunity to demonstrate (to yourself and your instructor) that you've studied and that you can apply your new knowledge to the questions posed on the test. As such, tests let you "show what you know."

When you do well on a test, you demonstrate that you understand complex information — a skill that's important not only for school but also for any career you pursue. In your work life, you'll encounter projects, presentations, and other situations in which you need to demonstrate your knowledge. You may even have to take exams to become certified or licensed for specific careers or as part of continuing education requirements. By building your test-taking skills now, you'll be ready to dazzle later, whenever you need to show mastery of material.

This chapter starts off with strategies you can use to prepare for exams. Next, we discuss test anxiety and how to manage it, and you'll discover tactics for approaching the types of exams you'll encounter in college and for reflecting on your performance once the exam is over. Finally, the chapter wraps up with ways to use your test-taking skills at work.

ACES Reflection:
Test Taking

ACES

Academic & Career
Excellence System

Take a moment to reflect on your Test Taking score on ACES. Find your score and add it in the box to the right.

This score measures your beliefs about how well you take tests. Do you think it's an accurate snapshot of your understanding? Why or why not?

■ **IF YOU SCORED IN THE HIGH RANGE**, this is great news; you're likely a strong test taker. But you can still build on this talent. For instance, if it's harder for you to take essay tests than multiple-choice tests, you can use the strategies you find in this chapter to make essay tests more manageable. As you read, jot down tactics you'll try out to improve your performance on exams.

■ **IF YOU SCORED IN THE MODERATE OR LOW RANGE**, remind yourself that tests can intimidate even the most prepared student, and you're probably facing many of the same challenges as your classmates. Like all the other success skills in this book, performing well on exams is a skill you can build in college. Read on to find out how.

My ACES Score ....
- ☐ **High**
- ☐ **Moderate**
- ☐ **Low**

To find your **Test Taking score**, go to the LaunchPad for *Connections*, Second Edition.

LaunchPad
macmillan learning

ACES + *ACTION*

ACES paired with action is what leads to positive change. Now that you've reflected on your ACES results, how will you *use* what you learned about yourself to become a stronger test taker? Try these concrete suggestions, or get inspired and create your own!

▶ **Reach out.** Lots of people experience test anxiety and nearly everyone gets stressed about tests. Exchange ideas with two other classmates about how to handle stress or test anxiety. Take notes on their suggestions so you can try them out yourself.

▶ **Find a resource.** Explore campus resources and identify two places where you can get help in preparing for exams or evaluating your test-taking strategies after a test.

▶ **Ask an expert.** Before your next exam, talk with your instructor about how to prepare for and answer the upcoming test questions. What preparation suggestions does your instructor recommend for multiple-choice questions? What about essay questions?

Prepare for Tests

According to an old saying, "Success is 90 percent preparation and 10 percent perspiration." The idea that preparation leads to success isn't a new concept—throughout the book we've stressed that investing time up front helps you learn and retain more information—but it's equally relevant in this chapter. Why? Because taking the time to prepare is one of the most *crucial* parts of taking tests successfully.

You can use many test-preparation strategies to set yourself on the right path; in fact, some of them may already sound very familiar. Let's explore them in more depth.

CONNECT
TO MY EXPERIENCE
Think about a time when you studied effectively for a test and earned a good grade. Write down everything you did to study, and put a star next to the things you'd like to do to prepare for your next exam. Also, write down any new strategies you'll try next time, including how you'll adjust your schedule if needed.

Build a Sensible Study Schedule

The road to successful test taking begins on the first day of class, when you receive your syllabus and start creating your personal study schedule. The chapter on organization and time management is packed with strategies you can use to create and follow a schedule for studying for each exam. For example, if you space out your studying over time, rather than cram it all into the day before the test, you'll retain more information[1] and feel less stressed when exam time approaches. Build a sensible schedule that gives you plenty of time to prepare, to learn, and to remember.

Use Your Study Skills

The many study-skills strategies you've already learned about in this book—including reading, note taking, strengthening your memory, and studying—can also help you prepare for tests and exams. In some cases, the strategies you use will depend on what type of test you'll be taking. For example:

- Flash cards can help you get ready for true/false and matching questions and for classes where you need to memorize formulas.
- Review sheets work well to prepare you for essay questions.
- Completing practice problems can prepare you for math and science exams.

There are also strategies that you can use no matter what type of test you're taking. For example, it's always smart to retake the practice tests you've created the day before an exam and to meet up with study group members for a review session—they'll provide support and encouragement, and they're a great source of information if you have questions.

Know the Exam Format

cumulative exams: Exams that cover everything you've learned in the course up to that point in the term.

Knowing the exam format is critical to getting ready for a test. It also takes some of the anxiety out of the test-taking experience. Early in the term, find out what kinds of questions your instructors will include on their exams. (Multiple-choice? Essay? A mix?) Some instructors put this information in the syllabus; in other classes, you may have to ask. In addition, figure out whether the exams are **cumulative** (covering all the material you've learned so far in the course) or whether they include only new material you've learned since the previous test. This information will affect how you prepare.

Review Previous Exams

If your instructors provide their previous exams as a study aid, use them to get some practice and familiarize yourself with the types of questions you'll see on tests. Your instructors may make these tests available online, in a study guide, or in their offices. If your instructors don't mention previous exams, ask them if these exams are available—the worst they can say is "no." Also, even if an instructor doesn't let students review previous exams, he or she may review test material during the class period before the exam or host a study session. Take advantage of all of these opportunities.

CONNECT
TO MY RESOURCES
Answering practice test questions is a great way to build test-taking skills. You can get these questions from your instructor, your textbook, Supplemental Instruction or tutoring on campus, or (your best option) you can write your own. Make a "practice question plan" for your next test: Write down where your questions will come from and how many you'll answer. Then, build this practice time into your schedule.

Stay Healthy

The week leading up to an exam can be stressful, and you may find yourself skimping on sleep, devouring junk food instead of taking time to prepare meals, and cramming for the test rather than hitting the gym. These behaviors may be understandable, but they can backfire and sap your energy. As a result, when test day comes, you may deliver a less-than-stellar performance.

Resist any urge to change your routine right before a test. Instead, make a plan to stay healthy. Try to stick to your normal exercise, diet, and sleep routines—going into a test well rested is vital to performing your best. Also, give yourself a wake-up insurance policy: If your exam is first thing in the morning, set your regular alarm plus a second alarm as backup.

Talk with Your Instructor

Your instructors want to help you succeed—that's why they teach—so visit them during their office hours if you have questions or concerns about exams. Sometimes students feel intimidated by in-person visits, but office hours are designed so that students can meet and talk with instructors and learn one-on-one. A subject matter expert will be sitting in the room with you, ready to clarify questions and provide advice—what a great opportunity!

Healthy Test Prep. As tempting as it may be to gulp down caffeine and cram late into the night to prepare for a big exam, this behavior could leave you tired and unfocused at test time. To keep your energy levels up, stick to your normal routines: Get plenty of rest, eat right, and keep exercising. That way, you'll deliver your best possible test performance. **PeopleImages/Getty Images**

To get the most from these visits, prepare a list of questions beforehand. For example, you might ask, "What will the exam format be?," "How much time will we have to complete the exam?," or "How would you recommend preparing for the test?"

Most instructors' office hours are first-come, first-served, so consider making an appointment before you go. Also, if you can't make it to office hours, don't give up: Ask your instructor if he or she is willing to meet with you before or after class so you can get the answers you need.

If you're taking an online class, you may not be able to visit your instructor in person, but you can still find ways to communicate. Some professors hold "virtual" office hours, during which they're available to chat or answer questions online. Alternatively, use e-mail or contact your instructor to schedule a phone call.

Manage Test Anxiety

If you experience some level of **test anxiety** (nervousness or worry) before or during an exam, guess what? You're normal. Research has found that between 25 percent and 40 percent of students have experienced test anxiety.[2] In fact, a mild level of test anxiety is actually a *good* thing: It helps you stay attentive and focused while you prepare for and take the test. Intense test anxiety, though, can cause damaging, obsessive thoughts of failure ("I'm going to bomb this test"; "I know I'll fail this class"). It can also spawn feelings of doom and dread following

test anxiety: Nervousness or worry about performance on an exam.

TABLE 9.1
Reframing Negative Messages

Negative thought	Positive reframe
I'm going to forget everything I've studied.	I'm well-prepared and I know the material.
I'm terrible at taking tests.	I'm getting better at taking tests.
If I fail, I'll get kicked out of college.	It's only one test, not my whole college career.
I'm not smart enough.	I *am* smart enough and I belong here.

⸮ CONNECT
TO MY CAREER
Do you have a job now, or have you had one in the past? If so, write down a time when you experienced anxiety on the job. How did you manage those feelings? How might you manage similar feelings if they occur again? Select two strategies from this chapter, and explain how they could help you.

the test ("I just know I gave the wrong answer on question 9"). If you have intense test anxiety, you might experience physical reactions such as sweating, nausea, shortness of breath, or headaches. Your mind might even "go blank" during the exam.

The good news is that you *can* manage test anxiety and its negative effects—both before and during exams. To do so, try these tactics.

- **Breathing.** Breathe in to the count of three ("one, two, three") and breathe out in reverse ("three, two, one"). Repeat this pattern several times. Note how calm you feel as you exhale.

- **Muscle relaxation.** Choose a muscle group, tense those muscles for a count of 10, and then relax them. For example, curl your toes tightly and then relax. Repeat or move on to another muscle group, such as your lower leg muscles and then upper leg muscles.

- **Reframing.** Reframe any negative thoughts about failing the test as positive thoughts. For example, if you're thinking, "I'm going to freeze up," write that down; then rewrite it as "I've worked hard, and this test will let me demonstrate my knowledge." (See Table 9.1 for more reframing examples and the Spotlight on Research for more on the power of positive thought.) Put your positive statements in a prominent place you can see every day, and repeat them to yourself whenever you think about your next exam.

- **Visualization.** Envision a place that relaxes you—a beach, a meadow, a forest—and visualize yourself in it. "Visit" this place in your mind to relax before or during an exam.

Your Happy Place? If you have test anxiety, visualizing a place that relaxes you, and imagining yourself in that place, can help calm your nerves. You can visit this place anytime you want—when you're studying hard for an exam and starting to feel anxious, or even during the test if your stomach suddenly twists into knots. yellowdog/AGE Fotostock

> # "I calm myself down by breathing easily and slowly."

Courtesy of Stephanie Young

NAME
Stephanie Young

SCHOOL
Oklahoma City Community College

MAJOR
Diversified Studies

CAREER GOAL
Dental Hygienist

PREPARING FOR TESTS AND OVERCOMING TEST ANXIETY

When I was taking college algebra, I learned that I need to breathe. I would hold my breath through a portion of my tests because I had test anxiety, and one night I just told myself I have to get over this — it's not going to work. Now, before an exam I make sure to set aside ten minutes just to look over my notes, to assure myself that what I've been studying isn't anything to be afraid of. During this time, I calm myself down by breathing easily and slowly. I also run a lot, and I feel calmer when I run. I try to stay positive, because I know I'm not going to do well if I tell myself I'm not going to do well.

When I first started school, I would cram before tests, and it wouldn't work. Cramming made my anxiety issues worse. I would also feel really burnt out, and then I wouldn't do well. Now, I break up my studying. If there are ten things I have to learn for a test, I'll focus on two things each day. Also, I'll rewrite my notes and read over them throughout the day. If I can tell my husband how something works, then I feel comfortable about it, and I move on. I'm a mom and I have a four-year-old who needs my attention, too, so it works for me to study in small amounts.

I have a study buddy, and that makes preparing for tests a lot easier. I also use the biology lab at school. The lab assistants there are students, too, and are really knowledgeable. It's reassuring to know that they're learning what I'm learning and that I can move on like them. They'll sit and tutor you, too, if you need a tutor. It's hands-on in the biology center, and I really like that. Mingling with other students in the lab helps because sometimes what they're learning is being taught in a different way.

> **YOUR TURN** If you experience test anxiety, have you used any of the strategies for managing it that Stephanie describes? If so, which ones? How have they worked for you? What (if any) other strategies have you found helpful?

- **Preparation.** If you feel especially anxious about tests when you're not sufficiently prepared, add more time to your study schedule. Take practice tests to get comfortable with the test format.
- **Worry time.** This strange-sounding technique has helped many people manage anxiety: Plan 20 minutes each day for worrying about an upcoming test. During this "worry time," focus as hard as you can on your worries. Set the timer on your phone, and at the end of the 20 minutes, stop worrying and go on with your day. If you feel anxious at other times during the day, put those thoughts and feelings aside until your next scheduled worry time.

- **Worry journal.** Record all your worries in a journal. Write down what you're afraid of, along with the emotions and physical sensations you're experiencing. Then close your journal to symbolize that you're setting aside your worries for the rest of the day. Or when you're done writing, rip the page out of your journal, crumple it up, and "throw away" your worries.

- **Campus resources.** Talk with a counselor about test anxiety or any other issues affecting your ability to succeed in school. If you experience test anxiety because you have difficulty understanding course material, work with a tutor to establish a regular study schedule and boost your confidence.

spotlight on research

Think Positively to Overcome Test Anxiety

Not surprisingly, people who suffer from test anxiety tend to get lower scores on exams than those who don't,[3] and they often experience negative feelings and expect to perform poorly. But there is good news: According to one study, you can combat these effects by harnessing the power of positive thought.

Researchers asked more than one hundred students to engage in a brief writing task and then take a quiz. Students in one group wrote about a recent successful experience, focusing on a time when they overcame a challenge and felt good about themselves. Students in another group wrote about what they did in a typical morning. Students then answered questions about their feelings, how they manage stress, and any anxiety they felt about the upcoming quiz. Then they took the quiz. Students in the positive-thoughts group:

▶ Had more positive feelings, a more optimistic attitude, and less test anxiety than students in the routine-thoughts group

▶ Had greater confidence in their stress-management skills than students in the routine-thoughts group

▶ Performed better on the quiz than students in the routine-thoughts group

THE BOTTOM LINE

Simply remembering successes and thinking positive thoughts can help you reduce anxiety and perform better on exams.

The group of students who had strong positive thoughts performed better on the quiz than the group of students who had routine thoughts.

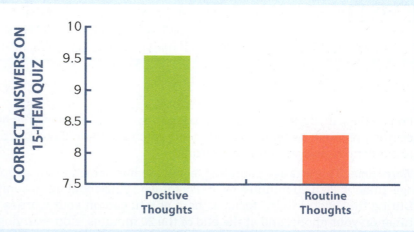

Information from D. W. Nelson and A. E. Knight, "The Power of Positive Recollections: Reducing Test Anxiety and Enhancing College Student Efficacy and Performance," *Journal of Applied Social Psychology* 40 (2010): 732–45.

Learn Test-Taking Strategies

CONNECT TO MY CLASSES

When test day rolls around, you can go into the exam knowing that you've spent time preparing, and now it's time to perform. Most of your success depends on the hard work and learning you've done before the test, but during the test you can use the strategies in this section to maximize the benefits of this preparation.

Start Smart

It's "go" time: The exam is in your hands (or on your screen). Get a solid start by taking these steps.

- **Write your name or student ID.** Depending on your instructor's instructions, put your name or student ID number on the test documents. These documents might include the test questions, an electronic answer sheet, or a booklet where you'll write essay responses.

- **Read the directions.** Instructors design their tests in different ways, so carefully read the test instructions before answering any questions. For example, some instructors discourage guessing by giving *negative* points for an incorrect answer and *zero* points if you leave the answer blank. Others ask you to choose more than one answer to a question. Find out what the rules are before you start.

- **Preview questions and budget your time.** Quickly review the types of questions on the test and the points assigned to each. For instance, a 50-point test may have ten multiple-choice questions worth 1 point each and two essay questions worth 20 points each. Knowing this helps you budget your time and might reduce feelings of anxiety.[4] If you have 50 minutes to complete the 50-point test, spend no more than 1 minute on each multiple-choice question and about 20 minutes on each essay question. Also, use all the time provided. If you finish early, take advantage of the remaining time to check your answers.

- **Start with easy questions.** Tackle the questions you know the answers to first. If you're especially well-prepared for an essay question, start with that. If you can easily answer fifteen true/false items, begin with those. Responding to questions that are easy for you can help you gain confidence. Be sure, though, to keep in mind the overall points; leave enough time to answer the high-value questions, whether they're hard or easy.

- **Manage any test anxiety.** If you tense up as you start the test, use the relaxation techniques described earlier. In particular, remind yourself that you're prepared, and it's time to show what you know.

Answer Multiple-Choice Questions

Exams during your first term and those in larger classes will likely contain multiple-choice questions. To answer them, you have to accurately recall information, evaluate multiple options, and eliminate poor choices. Try these strategies to improve your performance on multiple-choice questions.

- **Read the directions carefully.** Often, you'll be prompted to pick the single best answer for a multiple-choice question, but occasionally you may have to select more than one response. In addition, sometimes a multiple-choice question will ask you to identify which of the options is *incorrect*. Finally, check whether your instructor gives negative points for incorrect answers.

CONNECT TO MY CLASSES
Think about the exams you've taken so far in each of your classes. Were there any similarities among these exams? What were the differences? Write down the test-taking strategies that are working best so far in each class. Be sure to note if there are effective techniques in one class that might also help in another.

"We prefer to call this test 'multiple choice,' not 'multiple guess.'"

Choose; Don't Guess. Try answering each multiple-choice question in your mind before looking at the answer options. That way, you're thinking rather than guessing — and you can *choose* the correct response.

Chris Wildt/CartoonStock.com

- **Answer the question in your mind *before* reading the answer choices.** Before you look at the response options, answer the question in your mind if you can. Then look through the options for a choice that matches your answer. If you find one, you can be relatively confident it's correct.

- **Mark any questions you skip.** If you don't know the answer to a question and want to come back to it, clearly mark the question you skip so you can easily find it later. If you're using an electronic scoring form, leave that response blank and return to it later.

- **Cross out all wrong answers.** As you read through each answer option, eliminate all choices that you know are incorrect. Crossing out wrong answers will help you focus on the options you're seriously considering.

- **Read all the options.** Before marking your response, read all the answer options carefully. Instructors may use tricky language to make sure that you're paying attention and that you really know the material. They may also include several items with similar wording.

- **Look for mismatches in how the question and the answer options are worded.** Response options that don't match the question in some way may be incorrect. For instance, if the question names a category and one of the answer responses contains something that doesn't fit in that category, that response is likely wrong. As an example, the following question asks about organs.

  Which organs can be susceptible to cancer? Check all that apply.
  - ____ A. Lung
  - ____ B. Brain
  - ____ C. Uterus
  - ____ D. Foot

  Answer D (foot) is not an organ, so it is incorrect.

- **Look for clues in other questions.** From time to time, you'll find the answer to one question in the wording of another question.

- **Look for conditional and unconditional language.** Answers that use conditional language (such as *frequently*, *mostly*, and *typically*) tend to be correct. Answers with unconditional language (such as *always*, *forever*, *totally*, *never*, and *only*) are often wrong.

- **Consider "all of the above."** If at least two of the answer options are correct, then "all of the above" or "all of the choices" is often your best response.

- **Look for the longest answer option.** All things being equal, if you don't know the answer to the question, then choose the longest answer option. Test-question writers tend to make the correct responses longer than the others.

Answer Matching Questions

Matching questions require you to connect test items in one list with the correct answer in a second list (see Figure 9.1). These questions allow instructors to cover a great deal of information in a single test question. One challenge of these questions is that if you get one pair wrong, it keeps you from getting another right. Try some of these ideas to answer matching questions.

- **Read the directions or question prompt very carefully.** Be sure you know exactly what the question is asking you to match.

- **Read through all the options.** Take time to read all the items in both lists. Getting familiar with both lists will ensure that you know everything the question covers.

FIGURE 9.1

Sample Matching Question

Match the therapy theory with the correct theorist.

1.	Gestalt	a.	Perls
2.	Person-centered	b.	Skinner
3.	Cognitive	c.	Freud
4.	Behavioral	d.	Beck
5.	Psychoanalysis	e.	Rogers

FIGURE 9.1

Sample Matching Question

- **Start at the top of one list.** Matching questions are most commonly presented as two columns. Start with the first item in one of the columns, and search through the other column to find the correct answer. After you find the answer, move on to the second item in the column. If you don't find the correct answer, skip it and move to the next item, and so on.

- **Answer questions you know first.** First make any matches you're confident are correct. Skip over the ones you're not sure about.

- **Match all the items.** Matching questions usually have the same number of items in each column. Make sure you match all the items.

- **Draw a line between items.** If you're taking a written test rather than an online test (and you have a pencil that you can erase), draw a line between answers in the two columns. This approach allows you to see which items you've matched and which options remain. It also prompts you to match all the items.

- **Quickly double-check your answers.** After you've matched all the items, briefly review your answers to make sure you've used all the items and you haven't duplicated any answers.

Answer Fill-in-the-Blank Questions

Fill-in-the-blank questions can be more challenging than multiple-choice questions because you don't have several responses to choose from. Instead, you have to produce the answer yourself. The following strategies can help.

- **Think about the key concepts, dates, and main topics of the class.** These are often the answers to fill-in-the-blank questions. For example, suppose a major topic covered in your U.S. history class is the Civil War. On a test, you see the question "On November 19, 1863, President Abraham Lincoln gave an address dedicating the Soldiers' National Cemetery in Gettysburg, the site of a significant battle in the [blank]." The answer that goes in the blank would be "Civil War."

- **Write something.** Unless there is a penalty for guessing, write something in each blank provided in the question.

- **Check grammatical fit.** For example, if the blank in the sentence requires a noun, make sure your answer is a noun. If the blank requires the past-tense form of a verb, be sure your answer takes that form.

- **Check your work.** After you've filled in all the blanks in a sentence, reread the sentence to make sure your responses make sense and are grammatically correct.

Tools for Tackling Tough Test Questions. A potent set of strategies can help you tackle difficult test questions. For instance, with a true/false question, unconditional language (such as *all* and *only*) often indicates a false statement. For fill-in-the-blank questions, your answers should be in the correct grammatical form — for example, use a noun if the blank calls for a noun. David Schaffer/Getty Images

Answer True/False Questions

True/false questions can be challenging to answer, particularly when they're long and include language that seems designed to trip you up. On the positive side, you always have a 50 percent chance of being correct. Consider these strategies for answering true/false questions.

- **Look for conditional and unconditional language.** As with multiple-choice questions, conditional terms (including *sometimes*, *often*, *generally*, *seldom*, or *some*) suggest that the statement is probably true. Unconditional language (such as *all*, *only*, *invariably*, or *entirely*) often indicates a false statement.

- **Choose "false" if any part of the answer option is incorrect.** For example, the statement "The noble gases include helium, neon, argon, krypton, xenon, radon, and hydrogen" is false because hydrogen is not a noble gas.

- **Guess "true."** If you have no idea whether the item is true or false (and your instructor doesn't deduct points for guesses), then select "true" as your response. As instructors, we can tell you that it's easier to write test items that are true than those that are false.

Answer Essay Questions

You'll often encounter essay questions on college tests, particularly in upper-level and smaller courses with fewer students (and thus fewer essays for instructors to read). Most essay questions require you to describe topics in detail, make arguments, or analyze information. For these questions, you need to use your critical-thinking skills. In fact, your answers may need to show a mix of the levels of learning represented in Bloom's taxonomy (see the critical thinking chapter), which range from remembering, understanding, and applying to analyzing, evaluating, and creating. Here are some suggestions for answering essay questions effectively.

- **Read the question carefully.** Essay questions often include one or more of the following terms: *define*, *summarize*, *apply*, *explain*, *compare/contrast*, *critique, illustrate, justify, outline, describe, review.* Circle these terms in the question, and make sure you're answering the question that's being asked. For example, if a question asks you to compare and contrast two theories and your response merely defines them, you're not answering the question.

- **Budget your time.** If you have 30 minutes and three essays to write, give yourself 10 minutes for each.

- **Organize your response.** Before you start writing, briefly outline your response. Decide on a main point and supporting details for each paragraph in your essay. Use your outline to ensure you're answering the question completely. Also, leave space at the end of your answer in case you have time to return to the essay and want to add a few more supporting details.

- **Write neatly.** If you have poor handwriting, take time to write legibly so that your instructor can read your response.

- **Proofread.** If possible, leave yourself time to proofread each essay so that you can fix any problems with grammar and spelling, flow of ideas, and accuracy of content. Draw a line through any problem areas, and neatly write your revision above the crossed-out material.

"Will Mr. 'No Comment' please remain after class."

"No Comment"? No Dice. Answering essay test questions takes careful thought about what the question is asking for. You won't get away with just jotting down careless or silly responses. Instead, you need to review the question's wording, and use critical thinking to generate a strong answer. Martha Cambell/CartoonStock.com

Take Math and Science Tests

In your math and science classes, test questions often are about solving problems—for example, showing a proof, solving for a variable in an equation, or drawing the electron configuration of a copper atom. Consider these strategies when you answer problem-solving questions.

- **Show your work.** Write out each step of your answer. This will help you double-check your work and show your instructor how you arrived at your answer.

- **Check for basic errors.** Review your work to catch and fix simple mistakes, such as mixing up positive and negative signs, rounding a number incorrectly, or calculating operations out of order.

- **Tackle hard problems last.** If you encounter a difficult problem, skip it and do the easier ones first. Return to the hard one later.

- **Answer all the questions.** Write down something for each question. Even if you can't solve an entire problem, you might get partial credit for the work you show.

- **Make your answers legible.** Make sure any diagrams and proofs you write are clear and neat. Sloppy or unreadable work will hurt your grade.

Take Tests Online

During your college experience, you'll probably take at least a few exams online (see Figure 9.2). Even traditional classes that meet face-to-face may have online tests. Use the following strategies to take online exams successfully.

- **Use your notes sparingly.** Most of your online tests will be open book/open note but they'll also be time-limited. During an open book/open note test, you can use the book and your notes as a resource. However, you won't have time to look up the answer to every question. Study as you would for any other type of test, and use your notes and book to verify answers for just a few questions.

- **Check your browser.** Make sure that your computer's browser works with the test-taking platform. Your instructor may recommend a specific browser, or you may need to check the login procedure to confirm you can access the test-taking system.

- **Test your Internet connection.** Before starting the exam, check that you have a secure, stable Internet connection. If you lose your Internet connection during the test, don't close the browser. Instead, reestablish the connection and try to continue. A broken connection or closed browser may cause the system to mistakenly conclude that you've finished taking the test. If this occurs, contact your instructor immediately and explain the situation.

- **Reserve a quiet space.** Find a quiet, distraction-free space to complete the exam. If necessary, make arrangements ahead of time with roommates or family members.

- **Don't start until you're ready.** Most online exams are *forced completion*, meaning that once you start, you can't stop and return later to finish. Wait until you're ready; then begin.

- **Enable pop-ups.** Sometimes questions appear as pop-ups, so before you start, make sure your browser will allow pop-ups during the exam. Use the browser's Help feature to find out how to disable the pop-up blocker.

- **Record your answers.** If your instructor allows it, write down your answers as you complete the exam. Record the question number and your response to multiple-choice, true/false, matching, and fill-in-the-blank questions. For essay questions, copy and paste your answers into a Word document. That way, if your answers somehow get lost, you can use your saved responses to re-create them.

FIGURE 9.2

Sample Online Question

To prepare for an online test, practice *taking* an online test. This question comes from LearningCurve, an online self-assessment system that you may have access to with this textbook. Questions like these will help you get comfortable with course material and an online testing environment.

In the first stage of memory, _____ memory, you take in information through your five senses and form fleeting memories based on those experiences.

- ○ short-term
- ○ long-term
- ○ working
- ○ sensory

Take Tests with Integrity

Throughout your college career, you and your classmates will have many opportunities to act with **integrity** by being honest and demonstrating behavior that reflects your values. You'll take personal responsibility for and ownership of your education, which you likely value highly. For example, you'll spend time studying when you'd rather be doing something more fun, and you'll do your own work on papers and class projects instead of plagiarizing (see the information literacy and communication chapter). Taking tests is another critical opportunity to act with integrity—again, by doing your own work rather than cheating. When it comes to test taking, cheating can involve anything from peeking over a neighbor's shoulder and copying down her answers to looking at a copy of a stolen exam.

Students decide to cheat for a variety of reasons: They're overwhelmed by college demands, they don't have enough time to prepare effectively, they're not sure how to study for tests, or they simply don't want to put in the effort to succeed. But cheating comes with some high costs. For one thing, if you cheat, you're cheating *yourself* out of the opportunity to learn—so you're wasting your tuition money. You're also being unfair to all the students who put in the effort to learn the material. And if you decide to cheat and you get caught, you may fail the exam, fail the entire course and have to repeat it, and have a written record of the event permanently attached to your student file. You might have to go in front of a student panel at the college, or you could even be expelled. These risks just aren't worth the possibility of scoring a few more points on an exam by cheating.

Also, take care to avoid any *appearance* of cheating during exams. For instance, if you're taking a closed-book exam, pulling out your phone or rummaging in your bag for gum, an extra pen, or scratch paper is asking for trouble. If you need to do any of these things, let your instructor know. If you have study materials with you, put these in your bag before you enter the classroom, and turn off your phone. If your instructor *believes* you've cheated, even if you haven't, you may be severely penalized. Don't put yourself in a position to be questioned.

integrity: Being honest and displaying behavior that is consistent with one's values.

Choose Integrity. Tempted to cheat on a test? Don't go there. You'll cheat yourself out of an opportunity to learn, and if you get caught, you could be expelled from school. Are those risks really worth the possibility of scoring a few extra points on an exam? ESB Professional/ Shutterstock

Follow Up After Tests

Have you ever taken a test, walked out of the classroom, and then never thought about the experience again? As tempting as that might be—particularly right after the test ends—once you've completed a test, you have a valuable opportunity to follow up by thinking metacognitively about your results and how to make improvements in the future.

Evaluate Your Preparation and Performance

As you've seen throughout this book, metacognition is an important process that involves planning and organizing, monitoring progress, and evaluating results and making adjustments. After you take an exam, engage your metacognitive skills: Spend time evaluating how well you prepared for the exam and whether you're pleased with the results. A great way to approach this evaluation is to ask yourself two questions: "How did I perform on the exam?" and "How did I *expect* to perform on the exam?" Your answers to these questions can help you figure out what to do next (see Table 9.2).

Performed Well, Expected to Do Well. If you end up with this result, then your preparation, studying, and test-taking skills are likely working—well done! Here are several questions you can ask yourself to prompt additional reflection:

- What specific strategies did you use to study for this test? Which of these helped you the most? Which helped the least?
- Are these strategies likely to be effective in all your classes on all types of tests, or will you need to try new strategies next time?

As you continue using these proven study approaches, keep monitoring how well they work for you. Decide if it makes sense to change your approach for different types of tests in different classes, or whether you'll stick with these same strategies in multiple settings.

Peformed Well, Expected Poor Performance. If you end up with this result, the good news is that you performed well; the not-so-good news is that your performance

TABLE 9.2
Evaluating Test Performance

	Performed well	Performed poorly
Expected to perform well	• Keep doing what works. • Assess whether changes are needed. • Give yourself credit for success.	• Employ growth mindset. • Evaluate your study schedule. • Apply effective study strategies.
Expected to perform poorly	• Use metacognition to assess what went well. • Focus on the most helpful strategies. • Give your confidence a boost.	• Analyze what happened. • Make a new plan for next time. • Commit to making a change.

caught you off guard. Enjoy your pleasant surprise, but at the same time, consider why your expectations and the outcome didn't match. Consider these questions:

- Did you get lucky? Was the exam a lot easier than you expected?
- Do you tend to be hard on yourself or expect too much? Do you lower your expectations just in case you don't do well?

Take a close look at what you did well this time and continue using the strategies that helped you most. In addition, do your best to be honest with yourself in the future so you can better align your expectations with your end result.

Performed Poorly, Expected Poor Performance. Focus on the positives here: Since you weren't surprised by this outcome, you likely have some idea what you need to do to improve. The answers to these questions can help you determine your next steps:

- How did you study for this exam? Why weren't these strategies effective?
- What questions did you get wrong? Were they mostly questions of a certain type (multiple-choice, true/false)? Were they mostly questions about specific content?
- What convinced you that you weren't going to do well? Did you know you needed more study time? Were you confused by the material? What steps can you take next time to make sure you expect and obtain that positive end result?

Performed Poorly, Expected Good Performance. If you find yourself in this position, take a few deep breaths and acknowledge that it's perfectly natural to feel disappointed or upset. Next, adopt a growth mindset and view this as an opportunity to make a change. By identifying what led to the disappointing results, you can figure out how to do better next time. These questions can help you stay focused on improvement:

- Did you devote enough time to studying? If you simply underestimated the time you needed to study, perhaps you were underprepared.
- Did you study the right things for this type of class and this type of test? For example, did you spend a lot of time memorizing dates for your history exam, when you should have prepared for essay questions on the causes of the Revolutionary War?
- Are your study skills effective? Did you spend a lot of time rereading the material and not as much time engaged in proven strategies like elaborative rehearsal or self-testing?

Get Help to Make a Change

Once you've conducted your evaluation, the next step in the metacognitive process is to make adjustments. If you have an exam that doesn't go as well as you had hoped, consider reaching out to your instructor, an adviser, or the academic success center on campus. For example, share with your instructor how you prepared for the exam and get his or her feedback on what you might do differently next time. Work with a tutor or a study group to learn other test-preparation strategies. And definitely make use of the Personal Success Plan by writing a positive goal focused on improving your test results the next time around. When you're open to feedback and honest about what you could do better, that's a great first step toward making a change.

Use Test-Taking Skills at Work

If you think that test taking has nothing to do with the work world, think again. The skills needed to excel on tests in college courses are just as valuable in any job or career you pursue. As in college, effective test taking lets you "show what you know" at work.

Answer Questions Confidently

In any job you'll need to respond to questions from your supervisor and coworkers, and possibly customers and suppliers. Of course, these people won't ask you multiple-choice, fill-in-the-blank, or true/false questions or demand that you write an essay. But the preparation and thinking skills needed to respond effectively to their questions are the same skills you use to answer questions correctly on college tests.

For example, suppose your boss asks you to evaluate proposals from five marketing agencies that want to handle the advertising campaign for your company's new product. You'll need to recall detailed information about the product, evaluate the different options presented by the agencies, and eliminate poor choices (such as agencies that charge high fees). These are the same skills you use to respond to multiple-choice questions on exams.

Or let's say a patient asks about the side effects of his medication or a coworker wants to know which part to replace to fix a wind turbine's gearbox. To answer these questions, you "fill in the blank" by providing a precise, accurate response. If you're in human resources, a coworker might ask you about the health care options in your company's benefits plan. You'll need the same critical thinking skills—in this case, comparing and contrasting several options—that you draw on when taking essay tests.

The test-taking abilities you're developing can help you respond to all types of questions in the workplace, which, in turn, can help you do everything from demonstrating product knowledge, to boosting sales, to building relationships.

Take Exams for Work

Besides helping you answer questions at work, test-taking skills can be useful for taking work-related exams. These skills can help you pass licensure or certification exams required to enter professions ranging from landscaping, paralegal work, and real estate to counseling and graphic design. In some careers, employees also have to take annual performance assessments to show whether they're functioning at the required level in their job.

In addition, many professions require individuals to earn continuing education credits, which provide evidence of ongoing learning and professional development. Large organizations might also provide educational opportunities such as online tutorials, which often conclude with tests to show what you've learned from the training. For example, suppose

Licensed to Serve. Are you interested in a career that requires you to pass a licensure or certification exam, like becoming a landscape architect? If so, the test-taking skills you build in college can help you pass that exam, demonstrating that you have the expertise needed to effectively serve your clients or customers.

Toa55/Shutterstock

> "Knowing how to prepare for exams has been critical to my success—both inside and outside of school."

TAKING TESTS ON THE JOB

NAME
Amy Hildreth

PROFESSION
Registered Nurse

SCHOOL
Des Moines Area Community College

DEGREE
Associate Degree in Nursing

MAJOR
Nursing

I went back to school when I was thirty-four to become a registered nurse. In nursing school you're evaluated on written exams and skills. The written exams may have several correct answers, but you have to learn how to choose the best answer. Also, you need to be able to perform skills/scenarios in front of instructors. It was a tough curriculum—each term our class size got smaller and smaller—but I learned how to prepare for exams so I could make it through.

This regular evaluation of my skills and knowledge continued even after I graduated from the nursing program. After graduation, you have to sit for a national licensing exam with the board of nursing in order to demonstrate competency as a registered nurse. To prepare for this exam, I enrolled in a week-long review class and purchased books and CDs with hundreds of practice questions so I could test myself. Those practice questions were a huge help.

After I passed the board of nursing exam, I had more testing to complete. Before I could start my first job as an RN, I had to perform math calculations for drug conversions and IV pumps and take a pretest to assess my basic nursing knowledge. Also, now that I'm an RN, there are continuing education and recertification requirements. We have practice skills and scenarios we have to attend yearly, and there are multiple tests and worksheets to complete for the unit I work in. There are also continuing education requirements to renew my license, and I'm working on becoming certified in my nursing specialty (critical care), which is similar to preparing for my licensure exam. I'll go to a study course and take practice tests in order to get ready.

Knowing how to prepare for exams has been critical to my success—both inside and outside of school. Figuring out how to prepare for exams in college helped me become an RN, and now these same skills are helping me move forward in my career.

> **YOUR TURN** Are you interested in pursuing a job that will require you to pass certification or licensure exams? If so, which preparation strategies described by Amy sound most useful to you? If you've already passed such exams, what strategies helped you most? If you've had difficulty passing these exams, what might you do differently in the future?

you're a new manager, and you take an online course on how to create a budget. After finishing the tutorial, you complete a test that checks your knowledge. The results include feedback on course content you need to review to address any weak areas—information you can use to get the most out of your learning experience.

my personal success plan

Based on your ACES results and what you learned in this chapter, are you inspired to set a new goal aimed at improving your test-taking skills? If so, the Personal Success Plan can walk you through the goal-setting process. Read the advice and examples; then sketch out your ideas in the space provided.

To access the Personal Success Plan online, go to the LaunchPad for *Connections*, Second Edition.

1

IDENTIFY A GOAL

Choose a test-taking goal to work toward this term. Here are some general ideas you might draw from; you can also create a goal of your own.

- ▶ Find ways to reduce test anxiety.
- ▶ Build a schedule that spreads out study time.
- ▶ Ask my instructor for test-taking advice.
- ▶ Write better responses to essay questions.
- ▶ Evaluate how I perform on my next test.

2

MAKE YOUR GOAL SMART

Rewrite your specific goal so that it's SMART, and make sure to use the SMART goal checklist.

SAMPLE: To reduce my test anxiety, I'll practice breathing techniques and visualization for 10 minutes each night.

3

CREATE AN ACTION PLAN

Outline the specific steps you'll take to achieve your SMART goal, and note when you'll complete each step.

SAMPLE: Starting tonight, I'll use breathing techniques for various amounts of time and visualize different kinds of images until I find the right combination.

4

LIST BARRIERS AND SOLUTIONS

Think about possible barriers to your action steps; then brainstorm solutions for overcoming them.

SAMPLE: Muscle relaxation didn't work for me before. If these new techniques don't work, I'll visit the counseling center to get more help with relaxation skills.

5

ACT AND EVALUATE OUTCOMES

Now that your plan is in place, take action. Record each action step as you take it. Then evaluate whether you achieved your SMART goal, and make any adjustments needed to get better results in the future.

SAMPLE: The visualization/breathing combination worked great. When I tense up, I picture a waterfall, breathe deeply, and start to relax.

6

CONNECT TO CAREER

List the skills you're building as you progress toward your SMART goal. How will you use these skills to land a job and succeed at work?

SAMPLE: I'm learning to relax in difficult situations, so things will go more smoothly when it's time for me to interview for a job or give a big presentation.

my personal success plan

1 my general goal

_____
_____
_____
_____
_____
_____

2 my SMART goal

_____
_____
_____
_____

☐ **S**PECIFIC ☐ **M**EASURABLE ☐ **A**CHIEVABLE ☐ **R**ELEVANT ☐ **T**IME-LIMITED

3 my action plan

_____
_____
_____
_____
_____

4 my barriers/ solutions

_____
_____
_____
_____
_____

5 my actions/ outcomes

_____
_____
_____
_____
_____

6 my career connection

_____
_____
_____
_____

CHAPTER SUMMARY

In this chapter we explored a range of ideas for succeeding on your college exams. Revisit the following key points, and reflect on how you can use this information to support your success now and in the future.

- ■ Each exam you take is a snapshot of your ability to answer a specific set of questions on a particular day. Performance on any one exam will not make or break your college career.

- ■ Key strategies for preparing for tests include building a study schedule, using study strategies, learning the exam format, reviewing previous exams, sticking to your routines to stay healthy, and talking with your instructor about how best to prepare.

- ■ Moderate worry about a test can improve your performance, but intense test anxiety can lead to lower test scores. Strategies for managing intense test anxiety include breathing exercises and muscle relaxation, reframing negative thoughts into positive ones, visualizing a relaxing place, preparation, scheduling worry time, and using a worry journal. Most campuses have additional resources for managing anxiety.

- ■ When exam time arrives, it's important to first read the instructions and determine the points for each section, and then budget your time. Answering the easier questions and the highest-value questions first is a good strategy.

- ■ You can use a wide variety of strategies to take tests with multiple-choice, matching, fill-in-the-blank, true/false, and essay questions. You can also use specific strategies to prepare for problem-solving tests in math and science and for tests administered online.

- ■ Deciding not to cheat on tests reflects integrity. But you also need to avoid behaviors that give the appearance of cheating, such as looking at your phone while taking a test.

- ■ After taking an exam, you can use metacognition to assess the effectiveness of your approach to preparing for and taking the test. Based on this evaluation, you can apply successful strategies to other exams or change your approach to get better results in the future.

- ■ The test-taking skills you develop in college can help you enter and advance in a job or career, by enabling you to answer questions from others in the workplace and to complete licensure or certification exams and continuing education credits.

CHAPTER ACTIVITIES

Journal Entry

WORKING THROUGH TEST ANXIETY

As you read in this chapter, many students experience nervousness or worry (test anxiety) before or during an exam. Have you ever experienced test anxiety? If your answer is "yes," try to think about a specific experience and then reflect on the following questions:

- ■ What type of test caused you the anxiety?

- ■ What feelings did you have about the test and your preparation for the test? How did your body experience the anxiety? For example, did you have trouble sleeping, eating, or concentrating?

- Did you engage in any negative self-talk about the test, the content you needed to learn for the test, or your study strategies? If so, what types of things did you tell yourself?
- Based on your reading of this chapter, give yourself three to five pieces of advice for preparing for future tests, staying healthy before the test, and managing test anxiety.

If you've never experienced test anxiety before, reflect on why using the following questions:

- Is there a certain perspective or attitude that you take regarding the nature or purpose of exams? Do you typically feel confident in your preparation for exams?
- Describe your test preparation strategies. Do you enlist the support of anyone else in helping you prepare for exams — for example, an instructor, peer leader, or study group?
- How do you stay healthy during the week leading up to the exam?
- Based on your reading of this chapter, give yourself three to five pieces of advice for preparing for future tests, staying healthy before the test, and continuing to keep any test anxiety in check.

Adopting a Success Attitude

REFRAMING NEGATIVE SELF-TALK ABOUT EXAMS

Have you ever said anything negative to yourself before taking an exam? Thoughts are powerful — they can influence how you perform. To positively affect your performance, let's practice reframing negative thoughts about exams into thoughts that reflect optimism, hope, personal responsibility, and empowerment.

Read the negative thought on the left, and then create a more positive thought on the right, using the categories to guide you. The next time a negative thought about an exam creeps into your mind, see if you can reframe it as a positive thought.

Negative thought	Positive thought
Pessimistic	**Optimistic**
"I don't think I'll do well on this exam."	Example: "This exam will be challenging, but I'll study and do my best."
Blame	**Ownership**
"The instructor created an impossible exam!"	_____
Inability	**Empowerment**
"I'll never be able to memorize all this material!"	_____
Victim	**Master of my destiny**
"I don't think the instructor likes me; he'll probably give me a lower grade than everyone else."	_____
Hopeless	**Hopeful**
"I'm never going to pass this exam! Why even study?"	_____
Crisis	**Opportunity**
"My life will be ruined if I flunk this test!"	_____

Applying Your Skills

ANTICIPATING ESSAY QUESTIONS

In college, your instructors will probably tell you if an exam will include essay questions, but they likely won't give you the exact questions in advance. So you'll need to anticipate the types of essay questions you'll see on the test. Let's practice.

Pretend you'll be taking an essay exam on this chapter. Review the chapter and your notes, looking for important concepts that could be turned into essay questions. Then create one essay question using each of the following verbs: *describe*, *summarize*, *explain*, *compare/contrast*, *critique*, and *outline*. To get you started, here's an example: "*Explain* how the test-preparation and test-taking skills presented in this chapter can be used in the workplace." Finally, test yourself on chapter concepts by answering two of the questions you created.

College Success = Career Success

EVALUATING YOUR PERFORMANCE

This chapter described the importance of using metacognition to analyze what went right and what went wrong after taking a test. At work, regularly evaluating your performance helps you identify strengths and weaknesses, set goals, make adjustments, and, ultimately, become a more effective, efficient, and valuable employee. In fact, you may be asked to provide a self-evaluation in a performance review or discuss your approach to self-evaluation in a job interview.

To practice self-evaluation, number your paper from 1 to 10 and provide a self-rating for each item using the following scale:

Never	Infrequently	Sometimes	Frequently	Always
0	1	2	3	4

_____ **1.** Attends class (in person or online)

_____ **2.** Demonstrates a positive attitude

_____ **3.** Participates in class discussions

_____ **4.** Completes assigned readings

_____ **5.** Asks for help when necessary

_____ **6.** Sticks to a study schedule

_____ **7.** Is open to instructor feedback

_____ **8.** Checks spelling on written assignments

_____ **9.** Turns in homework on time

_____ **10.** Takes the lead in small group discussions

Choose two behaviors you rated lower than the others, and describe the steps you'll take to increase your ratings in the next two weeks. Turn in this self-evaluation to your "supervisor" (your instructor) for feedback.

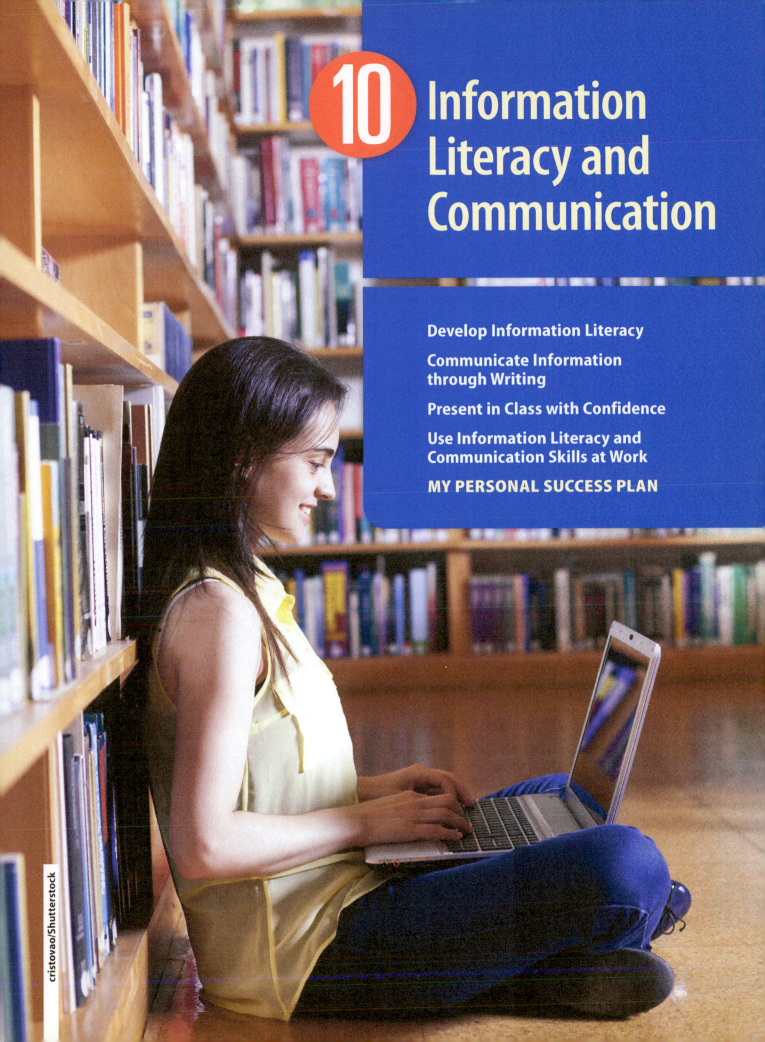

10 Information Literacy and Communication

Develop Information Literacy

Communicate Information through Writing

Present in Class with Confidence

Use Information Literacy and Communication Skills at Work

MY PERSONAL SUCCESS PLAN

When you work on a class assignment, is the information you need already in your head? When you begin to write, do the words flow easily onto the page? When you deliver a presentation, do you calmly stroll up to the front of the room and wow the crowd? These scenarios might happen occasionally — and isn't it great when they do! But for many of us, tracking down the right information and communicating what we've learned through writing and speaking can be difficult. For example, you might have trouble locating useful sources for a paper and clarifying your thoughts in writing, or maybe you suffer from stage fright when presenting in class. If so, here's good news: Although researching and communicating information takes work, you can build these skills — and college is the perfect place to do it.

As a college student, you'll use these skills all the time: You'll write papers that reference outside sources and give class presentations on various topics. You'll also use these skills in your job: Police officers, for instance, need to write reports and speak with authority during daily briefings, while civil engineers must record the results of structural tests or explain the design needs of a new bridge. Many careers rely heavily on information gathering and communicating (criminal attorneys, sales representatives, reporters), but to excel in almost every job, you'll need to work with information and express your ideas effectively through speaking and writing.

The ability to find, evaluate, and communicate information is called *information literacy*, and in this chapter we focus on all three components. First, we look at how to find the information you need and evaluate the quality of the information you've found. Then we explore how to communicate that information to others, which involves navigating the writing process, avoiding plagiarism, and giving strong class presentations. Finally, we conclude the chapter by looking at the many ways you can use these skills to succeed in your career.

ACES Reflection:
Information Literacy and Communication

Take a moment to reflect on your Information Literacy and Communication score on ACES. Find your score and add it in the box to the right.

This score measures your beliefs about how well you work with and communicate information. Do you think it's an accurate snapshot of your current skills in this area? Why or why not?

■ **IF YOU SCORED IN THE HIGH RANGE** and you're confident that this score is accurate, you may excel at working with and communicating information. This is great news, but don't stop there: Use the information from this chapter to become an even stronger researcher and communicator. For example, learn how to track down new, reliable sources of information for research papers; take steps to sharpen your writing skills; or try out tips for delivering a persuasive presentation.

■ **IF YOU SCORED IN THE MODERATE OR LOW RANGE**, seize the day! Use the strategies from this chapter and this course to grow as a researcher, writer, and speaker. With time, practice, and a positive attitude, you can build your skills and develop confidence in each of these three areas.

To find your **Information Literacy and Communication score**, go to the LaunchPad for *Connections*, Second Edition.

LaunchPad
macmillan learning

ACES + *ACTION*

ACES paired with action is what leads to positive change. Now that you've reflected on your ACES results, how will you *use* what you learned about yourself to work with and communicate information more effectively? Try these concrete suggestions, or get inspired and create your own!

▶ **Go beyond Google.** Web searches can provide countless sources of information, but not all of this information is trustworthy or useful. Go beyond Google and search an online database at your college's library instead. Select a topic, conduct a search for that topic, and write down three of the sources you find. Where do these sources come from? Are they trustworthy?

▶ **Dig deeper.** Plagiarism can be difficult to understand. Talk with your instructor to get a clear understanding of what is and what isn't considered plagiarism. Bring one of your writing assignments to get feedback on how you've cited sources.

▶ **Get comfortable.** Partner with someone from class and practice giving a short presentation to one another on a topic of your choice. Evaluate whether practicing with a peer lessens your anxiety about presenting to the full class.

Develop Information Literacy

Meet Destiny, who is several weeks into her first term of college. She has two weeks to write a short paper about one form of government for her political science class, and the paper must reference five academic sources. She isn't sure where to start, so she Googles "dictatorship." Instantly, she has pages and pages of information at her fingertips. As the options fill her screen, Destiny's confidence grows—she's well on her way to getting this paper done!

FIGURE 10.1

Key Elements of Information Literacy

information literacy:
Finding information, evaluating its quality, and effectively communicating it to others.

Destiny selects paragraphs from the first five Web sites that show up in her search results and pastes them into her paper. Since she knows that copying someone else's work is cheating, she rewrites the paragraphs in her own words. She includes references to the sites where she got her information, as well as a few images to jazz things up. She feels good when she hands the paper in, but later she receives the bad news: She got a D. Confused and upset about what happened, she asks herself: What did I do wrong?

To answer this question, Destiny needs to understand **information literacy**. Information literacy includes a number of elements, but we'll focus on three of the most essential: finding information, evaluating its quality, and effectively communicating it to others (see Figure 10.1).

Destiny had trouble with all three elements. First, she didn't locate the type of information the assignment required (academic sources). Instead, she used the first sources that showed up in her Internet search, without considering whether they were appropriate for an academic paper. Second, she used the information without checking whether it was reliable. Third, the patchwork of paragraphs she stitched together from five different Web sites and then rephrased didn't communicate a clear, smoothly flowing message.

Destiny wasn't information literate, so she made some serious mistakes in her paper. But you don't have to go down the same road. Let's look closely at each element of information literacy, beginning in this section with the first two: where to find information and how to evaluate the quality of the information you've found.

Find the Information You Need

When you write a paper or presentation, you'll need to conduct research on a particular topic—either a topic your instructor assigns or one that you select yourself based on what you've found interesting in class. Using a simple Google search to find this information may be tempting (as it was for Destiny), but try this alternative instead: Visit your college's library. Although the Internet may make libraries seem outdated, they're hugely valuable. Not only do they contain countless resources, including many electronic ones, but they also have staff who can answer questions and help you find what you need.

As an added bonus, you don't have to be *in* the library to take advantage of its resources. Whether you're sitting in the library itself, at your desk, or at your kitchen table, you can access the library's Web site. From there, you can explore a wealth of physical and electronic resources you'll need to write papers and complete assignments, including the following:

cite: To give another author credit when you include his or her ideas in your paper or project.

- **Books.** Books provide more depth and detail than many other information sources. Prominent book authors are usually experts in their subject matter, and they add credibility to your writing when you acknowledge, or **cite**, their ideas in a paper. Use the library Web site's search tool to look for books by topic, title, or author. If the library doesn't have a book you need, check whether an electronic version is available or whether you can borrow the book from another library.

- **Journal articles.** Instructors and other experts often publish research findings, theories, and literature reviews in professional journals. Journal articles are typically *peer-reviewed*, meaning that other experts review, comment on, and approve the articles before they're published. Peer review is part of the scientific process, and it helps to ensure that the journal's information is useful and trustworthy. Journals are a good source for facts and other information you need. However, you might find it more difficult to read articles than books because articles are generally written for other professionals in the field.

- **Newspapers and magazines.** Information in newspapers and magazines is often timely because these periodicals are published more frequently than books or journals. Look to newspapers and magazines for descriptions of recent events or in-depth reporting. These articles have less technical detail than what you'll find in journal articles, but they're easier to read.

- **Encyclopedias, archives, and historical documents.** Encyclopedias provide broad overviews of many topics and are a good starting place for gathering basic information. Archives and historical documents can also be valuable sources of information. For instance, to write her paper on dictatorships, Destiny might have quoted from or described part of the Declaration of Independence.

- **Databases.** Using databases on your library's Web site, you can find collections of journal articles, magazine and newspaper articles, videos, government reports, and images on specific topics. If Destiny had started with databases rather than with Google, she could have found articles about dictatorships from highly respected sources such as the *Journal of International Affairs* and the *Economist*. Many libraries organize their databases by field, so you can search by specific topics of interest.

- **Course reserves.** Some instructors create a set of physical or electronic readings for a course that students can access through the library's Web site. When your instructor puts extra time into making these materials available, you know that he or she considers the information important, so be sure to take advantage of what's been provided.

- **Web sites.** Web sites can be excellent sources of information; in fact, many of the sources we've just mentioned are available on Web sites, from in-depth newspaper pieces to scholarly journal articles and searchable databases. Because there's so much information available on the Web, however, you're also bound to come across results that are of questionable quality if you do an open search — for example, blogs written by nameless authors, press releases that subtly push certain products, or even articles designed to look like real news sources that are completely made up. When in doubt check with your instructor or someone at the library who can help you determine if a specific Web site will be a good information resource, and follow the tips in the next section to check the quality of your sources.

⚲ CONNECT
TO MY CAREER

To learn more about a career that interests you, find and read one article in a peer-reviewed journal or professional magazine related to this career. (For example, a geology major might read the *Journal of Geophysical Research*.) What was most intriguing about the article you chose?

Access Academic Sources. With a quick search of your library's databases, you can find a wide array of academic sources on any number of topics. To give this a try, pick a topic and enter key words into the search box (e.g., "wage gap" and "trends"). What types of resources are returned to you? How might these differ from the results of a Google search?

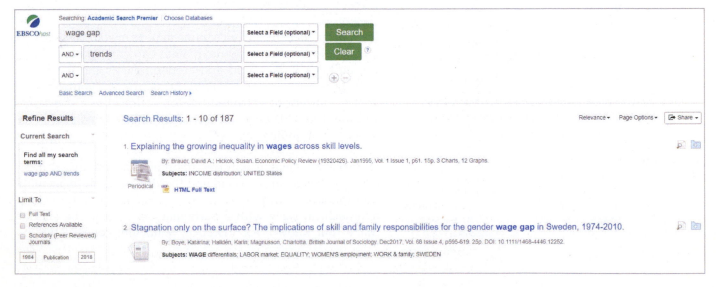

Evaluate the Information You've Found

Once you've found information that seems appropriate for your project, the next step is to evaluate the quality of that information. As you've seen throughout this book, evaluation is a key component of critical thinking, and it requires higher-level thinking skills. To prompt reflection and analysis, ask yourself probing questions such as "Can I trust what I'm reading right now?" and "Does the author's argument make sense?"

In some ways, evaluating the quality of the information you find is like examining the quality of ingredients when you're baking. Just as you wouldn't put a rotten apple into a pie, you don't want to include weak or questionable information in your papers. Recognizing bad information isn't as easy as picking out a rotten apple, but the strategies in this section can help you make sound decisions about the quality of your sources.

Basic Quality. When you locate a source, begin your analysis of that source by asking some simple questions about the basic quality of the information. For example, when looking at a book, check the name of the publisher. Have you heard of the company? Does the publisher have a well-developed Web site? With the rise of self-publishing, anyone can write and print a book.

If you're examining a journal article in the library, see if it includes a list of professionals who edit and review articles for the journal. If you've found an article through your library's Web site or another online database, do a quick search to make sure the journal is peer-reviewed.

When you're evaluating Web sites, keep in mind that trustworthy sources will clearly state who maintains the site and will often be linked to other well-known, respected sites. Sites ending in *.edu* (educational institutions), *.gov* (government sites), or *.org* (often not-for-profit organizations) may be more appropriate for research purposes than *.com* (commercial) sites. Ads and pop-ups are another way to evaluate the quality of a Web site. Sites that are crowded with ads or pop-ups may be more interested in generating clicks—and making money from advertising revenue—than in providing reliable information. (For a list of questions you can use to evaluate the quality of online articles, see Table 10.1.)

Author Credibility. To determine an author's credibility, investigate the answers to these questions: Do you recognize the author's name? Has your instructor referred to the author in class, or does the author's name appear in your textbook in a list of citations or the index? What can you find out about the author's background and credentials? Is he or she an expert on the topic? As you read the source, ask yourself how well the author has covered the topic. Does he or she seem well-informed? Do trusted Web sites refer to this person as an expert or quality source?

Objectivity. Quality sources maintain objectivity by presenting all sides of an issue and backing up their ideas with information from other outside sources. If the author does approach an issue with a particular bias, he or she should make that known. For instance, politically conservative or

"I just read an online article that says you should never believe anything you read online."

Online Articles: Trustworthy — or Not? It's important to think critically about any information you read, but it's especially important to evaluate information published online. Why? Because anyone can post anything they want — without undergoing a peer-review process. So put extra care into assessing an online article's trustworthiness. Marty Bucella/CartoonStock.com

TABLE 10.1

Questions to Ask When Evaluating Web Sites and Articles Online

Basic Quality	• Who maintains the Web site on which the article is posted? • Is the site linked to other well-known, respected sites? • Does the URL end in *.edu, .gov, .org,* or *.com*? • Are there lots of ads or pop-ups?
Author Credibility	• Do you recognize the name of the author who wrote the article? • What can you find out about the author's background and credentials? Is he or she an expert on the topic? Does he or she seem well-informed? • Has your instructor referred to the author in class? Does the author's name appear in your textbook or on quality Web sites?
Objectivity	• Does the author present all sides of the issue he or she is writing about? • If the author has a particular bias, is he or she up front about this view? • Has the author backed up his or her ideas with information from outside sources? • Is the author or Web site selling something or promoting a specific agenda?
Currency	• When was the article posted? • Does the article reference other recent events? • Do other quality sites reference the page?

liberal writers should be up-front about their point-of-view. A bias doesn't mean that the author's writing is flawed or useless, but you do need to be aware of it and consider how well the author has supported his or her ideas. If the author merely states a biased view without backing it up, you probably shouldn't include this information in your paper or presentation. Also, if your source is a Web site, consider whether that site is trying to sell something or promote a specific agenda; this might compromise the objectivity of the material.

Currency. Check the publication date of books and journals. How current is the information you're evaluating? How current does it need to be? A description of the Internet written in the mid-1990s might be a great resource for a project on the history of the Internet, but not for a project focused on today's Internet-related issues. Also check the dates of the citations in articles or books. If the dates of the citations are close to the article's or book's date of publication, the authors were using current information. With Web sites, look for the dates when articles were posted and for references to more recent events so that you can see whether the content is refreshed regularly. Also check to see if other quality sites reference the page or organization. However, don't assume that older content is worthless; a thirty-year-old book for a geology class might still be a good source if it's an important work in the field.

Wikipedia. Using information from Wikipedia in papers and presentations has long been a controversial topic on college campuses, and many instructors don't consider it an acceptable academic source.[1] Why is there so much controversy over a site that's so popular? Wikipedia is an information source created by thousands of volunteer editors, so anyone who wants to can contribute content to the site.[2] This combined brainpower means that a huge volume of information is available on Wikipedia, which is an advantage. But it also means that the site's information might be inaccurate or purposefully misleading, since the people making revisions may not be experts on the content they're altering. With peer-reviewed journal articles or edited textbooks, on the other hand, people who are experts on the subject matter have read and reviewed the information. Peer review doesn't guarantee complete accuracy, but it does make the information more trustworthy than content in Wikipedia articles.

Before you use Wikipedia, follow two rules of thumb. First, investigate the wealth of electronic resources available through your library: In using these resources and in consulting with a librarian, you'll find content you know you can count on. Second, ask your instructors for their thoughts about the site, and follow their lead. They'll let you know whether they consider Wikipedia an acceptable starting point for research—provided you confirm your information through other sources—or a site that you should stay away from altogether.[3]

Communicate Information through Writing

After you conduct research by finding sources and evaluating their quality, you're ready to move on to the next element of information literacy: communicating what you've learned. In college, students often communicate their learning in writing. In fact, as you've likely seen for yourself, almost every college course includes some type of writing assignment, from essay questions and research papers to creative writing and lab reports.

Why do instructors assign so much writing? It's not to torture you—remember, they have to read everything they assign! Rather, writing assignments help instructors answer two important questions: (1) Do my students understand the key concepts we're covering in class? and (2) Can they think critically about the material? You use all aspects of critical thinking when you write in college, from gathering, evaluating, and applying information to reviewing outcomes. The strategies in this section can help you apply those skills to your writing assignments—especially your research papers.

Prepare to Write

Before you can actually begin to write, you need to prepare yourself. Preparing effectively for your writing assignment will help you stay on track later when you write the first draft and make revisions. As you read this section on preparation, think back to Destiny's experience. If you had fourteen days to write a paper on dictatorships, how would *you* prepare?

Clarify Your Purpose. When you understand *why* you're writing—your purpose—you can more easily organize the information and ideas in your written piece and focus on the points you want to convey. Consider these different purposes for writing:

- **To inform.** One reason for writing is to inform the reader about a particular topic. Most of your papers in college will serve this purpose, including research reports, annotated bibliographies, review papers, and lab reports.

- **To persuade.** In persuasive writing, you might start by conveying information about a topic and then seek to persuade your reader to view the topic in a particular way. Editorial assignments in a journalism class, policy papers in a government course, or advertising plans in a marketing course fit into this category.

- ■ **To express or entertain.** In expressive writing or writing for entertainment, you convey your thoughts and ideas or tell stories to enlighten an audience. Examples include writing poems or short stories for a literature course, plays for a theater course, and song lyrics for a music course.

Make a Plan. Writing assignments often take longer than you expect, so schedule plenty of time to complete them. Plan out each part of the process: preparing, writing your first draft, revising, and polishing. As an example of what a writing plan might look like, see Figure 10.2, which shows a schedule for a short research paper (about two to five pages). Not only does this schedule build in time to write the first draft, but it also includes seven and a half hours of preparation (reading, researching, and outlining) and then four and a half hours of revising and polishing. While not everyone spends the same amounts of time on each part of the process, significant chunks of time are usually required for each step. Building a plan helps you manage and get the most from that time.

The Magic of Writing. Anything you write has a purpose, such as informing, persuading, or entertaining. When J. K. Rowling wrote the Harry Potter series, she set out to entertain her readers. And entertain she did — so much so that people waited in line until midnight to get the next volumes in the series. Some fans, like this one, even dressed up as characters from the books. Lisa Maree Williams/Stringer/Getty Images

FIGURE 10.2
Sample Plan for Each Step in the Paper-Writing Process

Monday, 6:00–8:00 p.m.	Read/Research: Find two journal articles and two book chapters. Read and take notes from one journal article.
Tuesday, 9:00–10:00 a.m.	Read/Research: Read and take notes from second article.
Wednesday, 1:00–4:00 p.m.	Read/Research: Read and take notes from both book chapters. Find additional articles or chapters if necessary.
Saturday, 9:00–10:30 a.m.	Outline: Write an outline for the paper.
Sunday, 9:00–11:00 a.m.	Write draft 1: Use outline to write first draft.
Tuesday, 8:00–9:30 a.m.	Revise to create draft 2: Review and edit draft 1.
Wednesday, 1:00–3:00 p.m.	Revise to create draft 3: Review and edit draft 2. Ask a friend to read and provide feedback.
Thursday, 6:00–7:00 p.m.	Polish: Use feedback to make last edits and polish draft 3 (final draft) several days before it's due. Schedule time over weekend to celebrate hard work!
Monday, 8:00 a.m.	Hand in final draft.

**❥ CONNECT
TO MY EXPERIENCE**
Think briefly about the most successful writing assignment you've completed. How much planning did you put into that assignment? What planning techniques worked well for that paper that you can repeat as you write papers this term?

Create an Outline. An outline helps you organize your ideas before you start writing. You can use it to sketch out the structure of your entire paper and ensure that you have all the required components of the assignment, such as an introduction, citations (if required), main and supporting ideas, and a conclusion. The sample outline in Figure 10.3 has two levels of headings, but you can add as many headings and as much detail as you want. You can also include examples or quotations that you plan to use in your paper—or you can keep it simple and leave such details for the writing step. For more on the benefits of outlining, see the Spotlight on Research.

FIGURE 10.3

Sample Outline

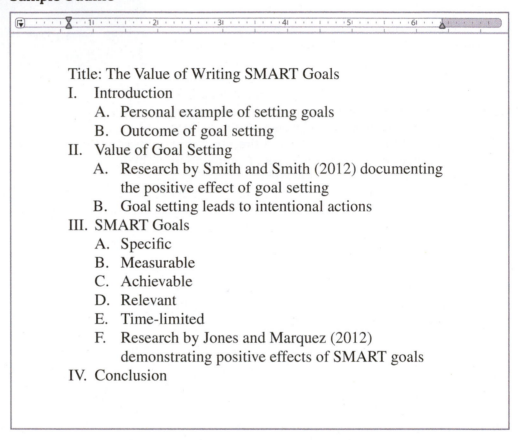

Title: The Value of Writing SMART Goals
I.   Introduction
     A. Personal example of setting goals
     B. Outcome of goal setting
II. Value of Goal Setting
     A. Research by Smith and Smith (2012) documenting the positive effect of goal setting
     B. Goal setting leads to intentional actions
III. SMART Goals
     A. Specific
     B. Measurable
     C. Achievable
     D. Relevant
     E. Time-limited
     F. Research by Jones and Marquez (2012) demonstrating positive effects of SMART goals
IV. Conclusion

Write Your First Draft

Once you've taken time to prepare, you're ready to write your first draft. For some students, all the preparation makes this part easy. For others, writing a draft can be intimidating or overwhelming. If you find it challenging to get started, think of writing like rolling a boulder down a hill: The hardest part is the first push to get the massive object moving. Once you put those first few words on paper, the rest of the process comes more easily. As you sit down to write, use the techniques in this section to craft a strong draft.

thesis: The main idea or argument of a paper or an essay.

Develop a Thesis Statement. A **thesis** statement is the main idea or argument you want to convey, and it sets the stage for your entire paper. You can create your thesis at various points in the writing process. You might draft it during your research to organize your thoughts, and include it in your outline to give clarity to that document. Or you might choose to write a thesis statement once your research and outline are done.

spotlight on research

Create an Outline to Improve Your Writing

Can creating an outline improve the quality of your written work? According to an experiment conducted by researcher Ronald Kellogg, the answer is "yes!" In his study, college students read arguments for and against outfitting city buses with equipment to serve individuals with disabilities. Then they wrote a paper in which they expressed support for the idea. Some students were instructed to create an outline first, while others were told to just start writing. Researchers then examined the length of the paper, the time spent writing, the writing speed, and the writing quality.

What did they discover? Students who created an outline before writing:

▶ Wrote longer papers than those who didn't create an outline (an average of 139 more words).

▶ Spent more time writing (about 7 minutes longer).

▶ Wrote faster (11.3 compared to 8.5 words per minute).

▶ Produced papers that were rated as higher quality by two judges.

THE BOTTOM LINE

Creating an outline can result in greater productivity during the writing process and a higher-quality paper — which may lead to improved performance in college.

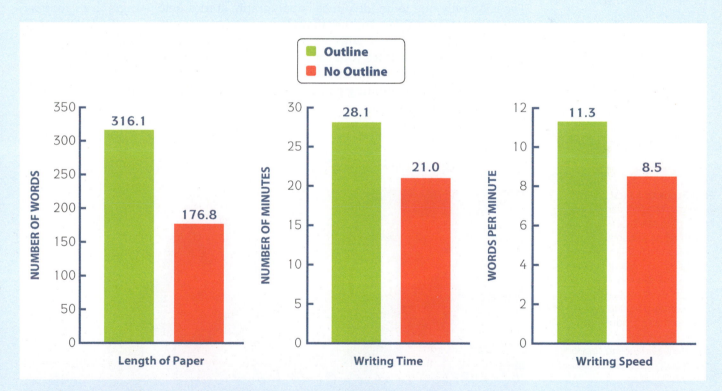

Creating an outline has a positive impact on writing.

Information from R. T. Kellogg, "Attentional Overload and Writing Performance: Effects of Rough Draft and Outline Strategies," *Journal of Experimental Psychology: Learning, Memory, and Cognition* 14 (1988): 355–65.

How you word your thesis depends on your writing purpose. For example, if you write a thesis statement about SMART goals, it might vary according to purpose.

- ■ **To inform:** Learn how to set and achieve your goals using SMART criteria.
- ■ **To persuade:** You should try SMART goals to improve your note-taking skills.
- ■ **To express:** This is how I used a SMART goal to improve my note-taking skills and succeed in college.

Structure Your Paper Carefully. Each paper needs a clear structure: an introduction, followed by the body of your argument, and a conclusion.

For the introduction, focus on something compelling that grabs your reader's attention right from the start. Imagine, for example, that you're writing an essay on hunger. A perfectly serviceable—but dull—introductory sentence might read: "Hunger is a serious problem in the United States." Compare that statement with this one: "One out of the next six people you meet will go to bed hungry tonight." Wouldn't that second sentence make you want to keep reading much more than the first?

As you move from the introduction to the body of your argument, pay attention to how you structure each paragraph. The most common approach is to start with the main idea and then follow it with supporting ideas, examples, facts, or details. Focus on only one main idea in each paragraph; start a new paragraph as soon as you begin writing about another main idea.

Finally, end your draft with a conclusion that pulls your thoughts together. A strong conclusion restates your thesis, revisits the major findings or recommendations of your paper, or summarizes your argument. To come full circle, you might even connect the concluding paragraph to the catchy introduction you created at the start of your paper.

First Steps to a First Draft. Writing a first draft can be intimidating, but the best way to get started is just to begin. Once the words start to flow and you feel increasingly confident in your writing, you can focus on making sure your draft contains all the right elements (including a thesis statement, an introduction, and a conclusion) and presents important evidence to support your main points. James Woodson/ Getty Images

Think Critically. You'll have the opportunity to demonstrate your critical-thinking skills many times as you write your draft. Here are just a few examples of how you can incorporate critical thinking into the writing process:

- **Provide evidence.** Incorporate citations and ideas from your sources into your draft. A paper on poverty that simply says "poverty is bad" shows you haven't really thought about your topic. But if you include statistics on the number of children in poverty who go to school hungry each day, you'll demonstrate that you found and applied evidence. Just be sure to credit others when you use their ideas to support your point. (More on this below.)

- **Interpret information and draw conclusions.** As you write, interpret and draw conclusions from the information you're working with, and incorporate these into your paper. For instance, suppose that a key source for your paper is an article about how national economies have become increasingly interconnected. You could think up three of your own examples showing the impact of globalization and work these into your draft. Then, at the end of the paper, you could identify what you see as the positive or negative effects of globalization.

- **Consider alternative explanations.** An important part of thinking critically is considering alternative explanations. For example, let's say you're writing a short paper on drowning deaths for a public health class. You've found an article whose author claims that eating ice cream causes drowning. The author backs up this claim with numbers showing that ice-cream consumption and drowning rates increase together. If you neglected to use your critical-thinking skills, you might say, "Makes sense—people eat ice cream, get cramps, and drown." But if you had your critical-thinking hat on, you would be open to alternative explanations, such as this one: Both swimming (and hence drowning) and eating ice cream increase during the warmer summer months. So, although it may appear that one event causes the other, something else—the warm weather—is actually causing both events to increase.

- **Compare and contrast.** If appropriate for the writing assignment, describe similarities and differences between topics. For instance, for a political science class, you might compare and contrast the reasons the United States entered the wars in Iraq and Afghanistan.

- **Generate new ideas.** For some writing, you'll have an opportunity to generate original ideas—for example, in forms such as poetry, essays, or short stories in an English class, or by brainstorming new ways to use an existing product or tool in a design or engineering class. This gives you a chance to use both critical and creative thinking as you work.

Examine Alternatives. When you examine sources for a paper, it pays to think critically by considering alternative explanations for what you read. That way, you don't make assumptions—like concluding that ice cream causes drowning because ice-cream consumption and drowning rates increase together, when it's really a third factor that causes both numbers to spike: the hot summer weather. stockcreations/Shutterstock

Avoid Plagiarism

As you write, it's crucial to work with information carefully and take steps to avoid **plagiarism**. Plagiarism, which is a very serious issue in college,[4] occurs when one person uses another person's words or ideas and presents them as his or her own. In some cases, plagiarism is intentional. When a student takes a paper off the Internet, puts his or her own name on it, and turns it in, that's a clear case of plagiarism. When a student knowingly copies information into a paper without putting it in quotation marks and citing the original author of the information, that's also intentional plagiarism.

plagiarism: When one person presents another person's words or ideas as his or her own.

⟆ CONNECT
TO MY CLASSES

Plagiarism can have serious consequences. Examine the syllabi for your courses. Find and write down the consequences of plagiarism as listed on one of your course syllabi. List any additional consequences you can think of that aren't shown on the syllabus you've selected.

But plagiarism isn't always intentional. Let's say a student copies a sentence from a source and puts it in his paper, planning to go back later to credit the author, but then forgets. Is this plagiarism? At many schools the answer would be "yes"; often, instructors don't distinguish between intentional and unintentional plagiarism. If you do get caught plagiarizing, whether you meant to plagiarize or not, you may have to rewrite your paper. Even worse, you might automatically fail the course, have to meet with the dean of your college, or even be expelled.

We assume that since you're in college, you value your education and will honor your values by not plagiarizing intentionally. But what's your best defense against accidental plagiarism? Develop good research and writing habits by applying the following strategies.

- **Take notes in your own words.** When reading books, articles, or original documents, avoid copying large sections of material. Instead, paraphrase these sources (see the chapter on note taking) by taking notes in your own words, and then use these notes to write your paper. Give credit to the original author by citing the source where you got the information.

- **Use quotation marks for direct quotations.** If you use someone else's exact words, which you should do only in moderation, always use quotation marks and cite the source from which you took the quotation.

- **Keep track of where your information comes from.** You might use one color of ink to copy a sentence from a book and a different color for your own words. Be consistent so that you always know which notes and ideas are yours and which are those of others.

- **When in doubt, give credit.** If you aren't sure whether you need to cite a source, err on the side of caution and include the citation to the original work.

- **Use a style guide for your citations.** The MLA (Modern Language Association) and APA (American Psychological Association) have established guidelines for formatting papers and citing sources. These style guides will help you with some of the "nuts and bolts" of writing a paper—such as the format to use for the title page, line spacing, margins, paragraph indents, headings, page numbers, and citation style. Including citations is especially important for avoiding plagiarism; just ask your instructor which style guide is most appropriate for your particular class.

- **At the end of your paper, include a bibliography or reference list.** This list shows that you've done research and that you're giving appropriate credit for the ideas in your paper.

- **Seek guidance.** If you have any concerns, ask your instructor or someone from the campus writing center to review your paper before it's due and give you some guidance on avoiding unintentional plagiarism.

Revise and Polish Your Paper

Once you've completed a first draft of your paper and made sure to cite your sources, it's time to revise and polish what you've written. Consider these ideas for editing and finalizing your work:

- **Include transitions.** Transitions connect your paragraphs and smooth the flow of ideas throughout your entire work. (For instance, the first sentence under the heading "Revise and Polish Your Paper" serves as a transition from the preceding section.) If your paper sounds choppy, adding transitions between paragraphs can help.

- **Read your paper out loud.** You can identify language that sounds awkward and then revise as needed to make your writing more fluid.

> I enjoy being critiqued by as many people as possible, and I find it helpful to gain multiple perspectives.

Courtesy of Michael J. Wicht

NAME
Ashley J. Willey

SCHOOLS
Highland Community College; University of Nebraska

MAJOR
Advertising and Public Relations

CAREER GOAL
Copy Writing

GETTING FEEDBACK ON YOUR WRITING

I've learned that the best way to become a good writer is to read good books. These books inspire me to try to emulate as many styles as possible until my own style shines through. I find myself playing around with different narration styles that I would typically never have used. I'm also blessed to have had a very good English professor, who taught me how to appreciate the knowledge I've gained and encouraged me to use methods of revision that have been amazing learning tools for me.

One of the best things I've done as a writer is to attend creative writing workshops. I enjoy being critiqued by as many people as possible, and I find it helpful to gain multiple perspectives. It's important to go to your professors for their opinion, and not only to other students. Your professors are professionals who can provide you with the most experienced, educated opinion. I follow their advice to the best of my ability, until I get feedback that my work is creating the impression that I was aiming for. This allows me to learn from my mistakes and perfect my craft.

I'm comfortable building professional relationships with my professors and going to them after-hours for advice. I'm not ashamed to ask for help, because I know that my professors are there for me. Many students fail to take advantage of the resources available in the college setting because they're closed off and are so focused on their goals that they miss out on opportunities. I'm getting my degree not for me but, ultimately, for my daughter. In order to go to college, I first had to obtain my GED without the help of my daughter's father, who was not supportive of my obtaining my education. I began community college as a single mother and am now attending the University of Nebraska. I want to set the bar as high as I possibly can for my daughter.

> **YOUR TURN** Have you used any of the approaches that Ashley describes for improving your writing? If so, which ones? How useful have these approaches been? Have you found any other approaches helpful?

- **Have someone else read your paper.** Ask a friend or classmate to give you honest feedback. Someday you can return the favor.
- **Use campus resources.** Use any resources your school offers to help with writing. Make an appointment at the writing center, work with a tutor, or ask your instructor to review a draft of your writing.
- **Polish and proofread.** Once you've revised your draft several times to address macrolevel issues of structure, flow, and clarity, give your written piece a final polish. Then step away from your paper and take a break, returning with fresh eyes to revisit and proofread it carefully. Fix any spelling, grammar, and punctuation errors, and make sure it reads just as you want it to.

**CONNECT
TO MY RESOURCES**

Your campus probably has a wide variety of resources that can help you improve your writing. Find and write down the name, location, and hours of a writing resource at your campus.

Write in Online Classes

You can use the strategies we've just explored to write papers in both face-to-face and online classes. However, what if you're writing something that's not as formal as a complete paper? In online classes, for example, instructors often require other types of writing assignments in addition to papers, such as blog posts or written comments on other students' posts. These posts and comments will be graded, so you'll want to make sure they're high quality. To excel at these types of online written assignments, try the following tips:

- **Write in complete sentences.** Shorthand and slang are fine for Facebook and Twitter, but use more formal and thoughtful language when writing for your online classes.

- **Watch your tone.** Writing posts in online classes can feel conversational—there is a back-and-forth exchange of information—but remember that in online conversations you don't have nonverbal cues and tone to provide context, so the tone you had in mind doesn't always come through. As you type posts for online classes, read them out loud and listen to how they sound. Could readers interpret your tone in a more negative way than you intended? If so, rephrase your comments so that they're more positive and constructive.

- **Pay attention to your emotions and how quickly you respond in these classes.** If you're having a heated discussion on a controversial topic, consider writing out your post on a piece of paper and coming back to it 20 minutes later to make sure it conveys your message appropriately.

Present in Class with Confidence

In addition to communicating your ideas in writing, you'll likely also need to prepare and deliver a class presentation at some point during your college career. Colleges consider verbal communication skills to be part of a well-rounded education, and employers value these skills as well.[5] Just as writing a paper does, authoring and delivering a presentation demonstrates your understanding of course content and also shows off your critical-thinking skills: To speak intelligently about a topic, you have to gather information about it, evaluate that information, use it in your presentation, and then afterward review the outcomes of your talk—all key components of critical thinking.

As valuable a skill as public speaking is, however, for many people it's utterly terrifying. What can you do if the thought of standing in front of the class gives you stomach butterflies and sweaty palms? You can practice and build your skills to increase your confidence. It won't happen overnight, but any student can become a successful public speaker.

Know Your Purpose — and Your Audience

To begin, give yourself plenty of time to plan your presentation. Use that time to figure out the purpose of the presentation and the major points you want to make. For example, if you have to demonstrate a medical procedure in your nursing class, you may design your presentation to *inform* your audience about how to perform the procedure. If you're going to show a new smartphone application you developed in your mobile computing class, your purpose may be to *persuade* classmates that the app is worthwhile. You might even perform a one-act play to *entertain* classmates in your drama course.

To plan your presentation properly, you also need to consider your audience. Ask yourself:

- **How many people will be there?** If you're presenting to a small group (fewer than thirty people), you can move around the room and involve your audience. You can pose questions, have listeners complete tasks and report back to the larger group, or even stimulate discussion among audience members. With larger groups, this interactive style is more difficult, so you may decide to spend your time addressing the audience as a whole.

- **How much do they know about your topic?** If your topic is new to the audience, share what you've learned while researching your presentation. If your topic is covered in the textbook, your listeners probably know the basics, so use your presentation to provide new information or discuss the topic in more depth.

- **How can you capture the audience's interest?** Brainstorm ideas for grabbing your audience's attention at the start of your presentation—for example, by developing a funny (and tasteful) anecdote or joke, a personal story, or an example that will engage the audience while also setting the stage for your topic.

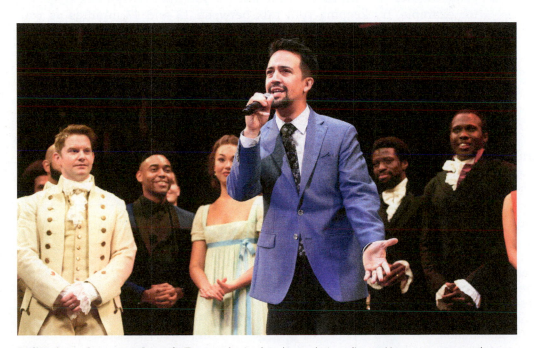

Delivering a Superstar Speech. Top-notch speakers know their audience. Here, composer and actor Lin-Manuel Miranda is surrounded by fellow performers and a theater full of *Hamilton* fans, but he knows they're only part of his audience. The other part is made up of people who watch videos of his speech on social media, read articles in which he's quoted, or see clips of his appearance on television. Is he nervous? Probably a little. Chris Pizzello/Invision/AP

Craft Your Presentation

Many of the same strategies you use to write papers can also help you create presentations. Like written work, most presentations have a thesis statement, an intriguing introduction, a well-structured multipart argument, and a clear conclusion. As with papers, you'll develop several drafts of your presentation as you work to create the finished product.

Presentations usually use more visual aids than written pieces do, so consider what types of visuals will strengthen your message. You can use slides containing text and images (PowerPoint, Prezi, and Google Slides are popular slide-creation tools) or physical objects that demonstrate a process (such as taking blood pressure) or clarify a key concept (such as how electrons move during a chemical reaction). As you weigh your options, pay attention to the visuals your instructors use in class, and consider your own preferences. What types of visuals capture *your* attention the most? Whatever visuals you decide to include, keep in mind that such aids work best when they convey main ideas and aren't overly complex (see Figure 10.4).

Practice Your Presentation

Fear of speaking in public is very common,[6] and practicing your presentation is the best way to become more comfortable, confident, and calm. Once you've crafted your presentation, rehearse it several times to polish the following elements of your talk:

- **Time.** Work to stay within the time limit. If you have 20 minutes to speak, for example, try keeping your talk between 15 and 17 minutes as you practice. That way, you'll know that your presentation isn't too short or too long, and you'll have a few minutes left for questions from your audience.

FIGURE 10.4

Lecture Slides: Cluttered and Clean

A text-heavy slide (left) is more effective when it's been pared down, broken into bullets, and jazzed up with an image (right). Sergey Nivens/Shutterstock

Introduction to Human Resource Management

The first step for HR professionals is to hire new employees. After new employees are hired, the second step is to onboard these individuals. Onboarding is the process of orienting individuals to the policies and culture of the organization. After that, HR professionals are responsible for overseeing the training and development of these individuals. Another task for the HR professional is administering the pay and benefits systems as well as developing new policies and procedures related to working at the organization.

Introduction to Human Resource Management

- Essential HR functions
  - Hiring new employees
  - Onboarding new employees
  - Training and development
  - Performance management
  - Administering pay and benefits
  - Developing policies and procedures

- **Voice volume.** Make sure you're speaking loudly enough. If you'll be using a microphone to give your presentation, practice talking at the same volume you'd use when sitting next to another person. If you won't have a microphone, practice speaking loudly enough so that people at the back of the room can hear you. And vary the volume and pace of your voice to keep everyone energized—speaking in a monotone is a sure-fire way to put your audience to sleep.

- **Body language.** Practice showing confidence and authority through your posture and other body language. Stand up straight, make eye contact, and imagine conversing with your audience—glancing only briefly at your notes or slides if needed. Also practice using hand gestures to emphasize points, and avoid nervous gestures that will distract your audience (like tugging at your hair or wringing your hands).

To practice your presentation, consider asking trusted friends, colleagues, or classmates to watch you. They can provide feedback on how you can improve. Or record your practice sessions on your smartphone or computer and critique your own performance. It may be hard to hear critical feedback or watch yourself on video, but these techniques will help you strengthen your presentation—and boost your confidence.

Deliver a Great Presentation

When the big day arrives, you can do several things to present successfully.

Stage-Fright Antidote. Would you give a toast at your best friend's wedding without rehearsing it beforehand? Probably not. So why would you give a class presentation without practicing it first? Rehearsing can give you the confidence you need to fight stage fright. That way, you can focus on delivering your message. Lucy Clark/Shutterstock

- **Look the part.** Even if your appearance isn't factored into your official grade for the presentation, your instructor and audience will notice what you're wearing. So, approach class presentations as you would a job interview. Ditch the shorts and flip-flops in favor of business casual or nicer clothes. Professional apparel gives you an air of credibility and conveys to your audience that you take the assignment seriously.

- **Arrive early.** By arriving early, you'll have time to get set up and organize your presentation, notes, and any materials you plan to use.

- **Breathe and visualize.** Take deep breaths and visualize yourself being successful. Settling your nerves in advance will help you deliver a smooth presentation.

Harness the Power of Technology: Present Online

Increasingly, online classes require students to prepare presentations and deliver them using technology tools such as videoconferencing or smartphones. Many of the strategies for giving successful presentations also apply to online presentations, but you may have to master some new technology skills to make your presentation a success—for example, adding narration to a slide presentation or setting up conferencing tools such as Skype or WebEx on your laptop. If you have concerns about using any required technology to deliver your online presentation, ask your instructor for help. And be sure to schedule some extra time during the preparation phase to try out any technology and make sure it's running smoothly.

Use Information Literacy and Communication Skills at Work

The information literacy and communication skills you build in college will continue to be valuable assets after you graduate. Not only will you use them during the job-application process, but they're also important for accomplishing tasks and sharing your ideas with others once you're on the job.

Sell Yourself to Potential Employers

No matter what your occupation, being able to write and speaking intelligently about your own skills and experiences can help you "sell" yourself to potential employers. You'll likely need to write a résumé and a cover letter as part of the job-application process and you'll need to go on interviews. If you have weak writing and speaking skills, you'll find it hard to convince potential employers that you're the ideal candidate. In addition, many organizations ask employees to complete an annual self-evaluation, which often involves writing and presenting a summary of your accomplishments. You'll need information literacy skills in order to pull together, evaluate, and present that information.

Work with Information Effectively

Information literacy and communication skills can help you work with information effectively once you're on the job. In fact, in a recent survey employers listed oral communication, writing, and information literacy as three of the top six skills colleges should emphasize for new graduates.[7] Look at Table 10.2 for ideas about how people in various occupations might use the skills in this chapter. Then ask yourself: "How will I use information literacy and communication in *my* desired field?"

Communicate Your Great Ideas

Your experiences on the job can inspire you to develop big, creative ideas—for example, plans for new products that will boost sales or new processes that will increase efficiency. To showcase your creativity or share your ideas, you need to communicate them verbally or in writing. For example, if you're a software

TABLE 10.2

Using Information Literacy and Communication Skills in Different Careers

Career	Example
Nonprofit campaign manager	Research past campaigns, identify best practices used by successful campaigns, and communicate ideas for a new campaign to the project team.
Computer systems administrator	Find and evaluate software options in response to a new security threat. Write a report describing the benefits and drawbacks of each option.
Occupational therapy assistant	Write down therapy progress, communicate this information verbally and in writing to occupational therapists. Communicate treatment plans to patients.
Market research analyst	Gather and evaluate data on consumer habits and trends, product pricing, and competitor positioning. Conduct an analysis, write reports, and create graphs communicating that information to clients.
Radiologic technologist	Stay up-to-date on scanning procedures, explain them to patients, and direct patients' actions during scans.

> Clearly communicating information . . . helped improve the efficiency of the factory and cut our mistakes down to nearly zero.

NAME
Matt Mahler

PROFESSION
Production Supervisor

SCHOOL
Southern New Hampshire University

DEGREE
Associate of Arts

MAJOR
General Studies

MANAGING AND COMMUNICATING INFORMATION

Writing and communicating were among my strongest areas in college, and I continue to use these skills on the job. Before my recent promotion to Production Supervisor, I served as the Interim Production Manager at the bread factory where I work. Obtaining ingredient information, determining its quality, and creating a way to manage and then communicate that information were all skills I used to do my job.

Before I took this position, people had to guess how many ingredients to order each week, and this caused us to fall short a lot. The ordering process was also problematic, as orders were written on a form and faxed to the supplier. To improve the quality of information we were working with, I started using Excel to track our daily ingredient usage to be more precise in weekly ingredient ordering. I also changed the ordering procedure: I e-mailed our order, which eliminated the problem of lost or unreadable faxes and created a record of our weekly orders.

Closely monitoring ingredient usage also helped me communicate more effectively with the mixers. I could see when there was an overscaling of ingredients, and I had tangible data to show the mixers while I coached them. Being able to quantify the ingredients that were being overscaled into dollar amounts gave the mixers a clear picture of what was happening and how important it was to avoid waste.

Overall, managing information and then clearly communicating information to my production team and supplier helped improve the efficiency of the factory and cut our mistakes down to nearly zero.

YOUR TURN If you're currently employed, what kinds of information do you need to find and evaluate, and in what ways do you communicate that information? If you're not employed but have a particular career in mind, how will knowing how to find, evaluate, and communicate information help you excel in that career?

Courtesy of Matthew Mahler

developer, you might give a presentation about how your new app will revolutionize social networking. As an astronomer, you might write a scientific paper to detail your discovery of a distant galaxy. When you know how to express your ideas effectively, you can make a meaningful contribution to your company or organization, your community, your customers—and even your own professional development.

my personal success plan

1 IDENTIFY A GOAL

Choose an information literacy or communication goal to work toward this term. Here are some general ideas you might draw from; you can also create a goal of your own.

- ▶ Write outlines for all my papers.
- ▶ Build critical-thinking skills to better evaluate resources.
- ▶ Make a plan for getting my next paper written.
- ▶ Use a style guide to cite my sources correctly.
- ▶ Practice presentations out loud at least two times.

2 MAKE YOUR GOAL SMART

Rewrite your specific goal so that it's SMART, and make sure to use the SMART goal checklist.

SAMPLE: I'll create an outline for my economics paper that's due next week.

3 CREATE AN ACTION PLAN

Outline the specific steps you'll take to achieve your SMART goal, and note when you'll complete each step.

SAMPLE: I'll spend one hour this Sunday night writing my outline.

4 LIST BARRIERS AND SOLUTIONS

Think about possible barriers to your action steps; then brainstorm solutions for overcoming them.

SAMPLE: Outlines have always been hard for me. If I get stuck, I'll take my outline to the writing center on Monday and get feedback.

5 ACT AND EVALUATE OUTCOMES

Now that your plan is in place, take action. Record each action step as you take it. Then evaluate whether you achieved your SMART goal, and make any adjustments needed to get better results in the future.

SAMPLE: For this big paper I didn't leave enough time to develop my outline, so for my next assignment I'll build more time into that phase of the writing process.

6 CONNECT TO CAREER

List the skills you're building as you progress toward your SMART goal. How will you use these skills to land a job and succeed at work?

SAMPLE: Using outlines will help me organize my writing. When I become a public relations specialist, I'll use them to write effective press releases.

my personal success plan

1 my general goal

2 my SMART goal

☐ SPECIFIC ☐ MEASURABLE ☐ ACHIEVABLE ☐ RELEVANT ☐ TIME-LIMITED

3 my action plan

4 my barriers/ solutions

5 my actions/ outcomes

6 my career connection

CHAPTER SUMMARY

In this chapter you learned about information literacy and communication skills. Revisit the following key points, and reflect on how you can use this information to support your success now and in the future.

- Information literacy is the ability to find, evaluate, and communicate information through writing or speaking.

- Information sources include books, journal articles, newspapers, magazines, encyclopedias, databases, course reserves, and Web sites.

- Critically evaluating the quality of information involves considering whether your source is credible, objective, and current.

- Preparing to write includes clarifying your purpose, scheduling time for each step in the writing process, and creating an outline.

- A well-written, multidraft piece has a clear thesis, an engaging introduction, focused paragraphs with smooth transitions, and a strong conclusion. It also meets requirements for proper formatting and citations and is polished and free from grammatical errors.

- Writing in college requires you to demonstrate your critical-thinking skills by providing evidence, interpreting information, drawing conclusions, considering alternative explanations, comparing and contrasting, and generating new ideas.

- Plagiarism occurs when one person takes credit for another person's words or ideas, accidentally or deliberately. By citing sources and developing good research and writing habits, you can avoid plagiarism.

- In your online classes, you can communicate effectively by keeping your blog posts professional and providing constructive comments on discussion boards.

- Creating a strong classroom presentation involves planning what you want to say, crafting the content, practicing thoroughly, and taking steps to prepare yourself the day of the presentation. In online classes, it also involves using technology tools such as videoconferencing.

- Information literacy and communication skills can help you excel in your career by enabling you to "sell" yourself during the job-application process, work with information effectively on the job, and communicate your ideas.

CHAPTER ACTIVITIES

Journal Entry

SPEAKING CONFIDENTLY IN PUBLIC

Describe an experience in which you spoke in public. It might have been a persuasive speech you delivered to classmates, a sales pitch to customers, a pep talk to the soccer team, or a proposal to the city council. How did this experience affect your feelings about public speaking? What strengths do you have as a public speaker? What are your opportunities for growth as a public speaker? What tips from this chapter can you use to enhance your public-speaking skills?

Adopting a Success Attitude

OVERCOMING WRITER'S BLOCK

For some people, negative thinking and self-doubt can create a mental block, making it difficult to even begin writing an assigned paper. If this happens to you, try using freewriting to break through this writer's block. With freewriting, you write as much as you can about a specific topic for a set period of time without any constraints. Let's give it a try.

Sit down at a computer and type your topic at the top of the page (or write it on a piece of paper). You may want to choose a topic that relates to a writing assignment for another class. Set a timer for 10 minutes, and then type or write whatever comes to mind about this topic — thoughts, feelings, beliefs, questions, arguments, experiences, and so on. Don't worry about organization, grammar, punctuation, or spelling. Type or write as fast as you can, and don't stop until the timer goes off. When it does, congratulate yourself — you've overcome writer's block! Now review what you wrote. Did you generate any new ideas that might help you with your writing assignment? If not, it's okay — you may need to try freewriting a few more times to start seeing results. Don't give up on this technique after only one try!

Applying Your Skills

FINDING INFORMATION AND CITING SOURCES

For many college writing assignments, you'll need to find information from various sources and accurately cite those sources. This activity gives you practice developing these skills using the many resources of your campus library, and challenges you to compare and contrast these library resources with sources found online.

1. First, identify a topic you find interesting or even controversial. For help, type "controversial essay topics" into your Web browser, or select a topic that you'll be writing about for an actual class assignment this term.

2. Go to the Web site for your college or university library. Locate the library's general search engine (typically a box you can type in), which often appears on the library's home page. (If you need help locating the search engine, reach out to the library staff — helping you find resources is their job!)

3. Use the library search engine to find five different sources for your topic. Sources may include a full book, book chapter, magazine or newspaper article, scholarly journal article, published dissertation, conference proceedings, technical report, film/video, or other Web documents or reports. To find these sources, type a series of search terms into the search engine. For example, let's say you choose to investigate whether performance-enhancing drugs should be accepted in sports. In this case, you'd enter the key words "performance-enhancing drugs" and "sports" into the search engine.

4. Provide citations for five of the sources you find during your search. Depending on your instructor's preference, use either MLA (Modern Language Association) or APA (American Psychological Association) style to cite each source. For example, let's say you locate the book *Steroids: A New Look at Performance-Enhancing Drugs* by Rob Beamish and the newspaper article "There Are No Sound Moral Arguments against Performance-Enhancing Drugs" by Chuck Klosterman. Your instructor requires APA style for citations, so you cite these sources as follows:

Beamish, R. (2011). *Steroids: A new look at performance-enhancing drugs*. Santa Barbara, CA: Praeger.

Klosterman, C. (2013, August 30). There are no sound moral arguments against performance-enhancing drugs. *New York Times*. Retrieved from **http://www .nytimes.com.**

5. Once you've finishing citing your library sources, conduct a general Internet search on the same topic. Type the same key words into your Web browser (such as "performance-enhancing drugs" and "sports") and select two Web sites that come up. As with your library sources, cite these two Web sources using your instructor's preferred citation style.

6. Reflect on the information you've collected from both searches by responding to the following questions.

   ■ What are the advantages of using the library to find sources of information for your topic? Were there any disadvantages to locating information this way — for example, was there anything about this process that you found challenging or that you'd like to do differently next time? Did you ask for help?

   ■ What are the advantages and disadvantages of conducting a general Internet search for information? Were the sources you found online different from those you found in the library catalog? If so, how?

   ■ How can you evaluate the quality of the sources you find online? List at least three ways to evaluate source quality.

College Success = Career Success

PROVIDING INSTRUCTIONS EFFECTIVELY

Presentation skills can be quite valuable in the workplace, and one way you can use these skills is to train others. For example, your boss may ask you to explain to new employees how to complete a multistep task. If you break down a complicated task into small, specific steps, you'll find it easier to explain the task to others.

To practice this skill, follow these steps:

1. Find a partner, and gather two sheets of paper and a pencil.

2. Without showing your partner what you're doing, draw something simple on one piece of paper, such as two lines or an abstract shape.

3. Without showing your partner your drawing, give him or her instructions for how to draw your design on the other piece of paper. Be specific about where to begin ("Hold the piece of paper horizontally, and begin two-thirds of the way down the left-hand side of the page . . ."), and specify how long and how big to make each shape or line.

4. If your partner can't understand your instructions, ask him or her to erase part of the drawing. Then give your partner alternative instructions.

5. Once your partner is finished, compare his or her drawing against your original drawing. How well do they match?

Reflect on this activity. What did you learn from this process about giving instructions and communicating effectively?

11 Connecting with Others

Enhance Your Communication Skills

Build Emotional Intelligence

Resolve Conflict

Grow and Sustain Healthy Relationships

Embrace Diversity

Connect with Others at Work

MY PERSONAL SUCCESS PLAN

magine how you would respond to the following scenarios:

■ While your significant other is talking, your mind starts to drift. Suddenly your loved one snaps, "You never listen to me!" and stomps out of the room.

■ You review your psychology syllabus on the first day of class, and you see that there will be a group assignment. You don't know anyone else in the class.

■ In a job interview, the interviewer explains that the company wants to hire employees who respect people's differences and treat each other fairly. She asks you to give examples of how well you work with people from diverse backgrounds.

If you can easily imagine an effective way to respond to each of these scenarios, you may have a natural ability to connect with other people—and to maintain those connections. And if you had difficulty responding to these scenarios? You can learn how to build and strengthen connections, even in challenging or emotionally charged situations. In fact, no matter how confident you are in your abilities, there is always room for growth, and it's worth investing the time to strengthen your skills.

Why is connecting with others so important? Because healthy connections form the foundation of a successful, satisfying life, both while you're in school and after you graduate. For example, the connection skills we explore in this chapter may help you communicate more effectively, understand and manage emotions, and resolve conflicts productively. In addition, you can use these skills to build and sustain healthy, positive relationships with a diverse array of people—from group members and instructors in college to supervisors, colleagues, and customers in the workplace.

With that in mind, this chapter begins with a look at two vital aspects of effective communication: listening actively and speaking effectively. We then explore how to strengthen your *emotional intelligence* (including how to recognize, understand, and manage emotions in yourself and others) and manage conflict. Next, we examine how connecting with others can enhance your existing relationships, help you build new ones, and strengthen your relationships with people from different backgrounds. Finally, we consider the benefits of transferring these skills to the workplace.

Hector Mandel/Getty Images

ACES Reflection:
Connecting with Others

Take a moment to reflect on your Connecting with Others score on ACES. Find your score and add it in the box to the right.

This score measures your beliefs about how well you connect with others. Do you think it's an accurate snapshot of your current skills in this area? Why or why not?

■ **IF YOU SCORED IN THE HIGH RANGE** and you're confident that this score is accurate, you may be great at making connections. Still, consider how you can strengthen this skill. You can probably think of at least one interpersonal interaction — a job interview, a disagreement with a classmate — that you could have handled more effectively if you had better understood and managed the emotions that arose during that interaction. As you read this chapter, you'll learn new techniques you can use to build on your current connection skills.

■ **IF YOU SCORED IN THE MODERATE OR LOW RANGE**, try something different. This chapter is filled with tips and strategies you can use to connect more effectively with others. Use these approaches to boost your confidence and build rewarding relationships with the people in your life.

ACES + ACTION

ACES paired with action is what leads to positive change. Now that you've reflected on your ACES results, how will you *use* what you learned about yourself to improve your connections with others? Try these concrete suggestions, or get inspired and create your own!

▶ **Practice small talk.** Talking to strangers isn't always easy, but it does get easier if you practice. Strike up a conversation with someone new at school, work, your church, the gym, or elsewhere. How did it feel to make this connection?

▶ **Maintain connections.** Call, e-mail, instant message, text, or handwrite a note to a family member or friend you haven't spoken to recently but want to maintain contact with. Ask how this person is doing and share something about yourself — for example, what you're learning in school. Maintaining communication will ensure you have support when you need it most.

▶ **Experience different cultures.** Attend a campus or community event in which you interact with people who differ from you in some way. Doing so can promote insight and help you feel more comfortable connecting with people you might not typically meet.

ACES
Academic & Career Excellence System

My ACES Score ....
- ☐ High
- ☐ Moderate
- ☐ Low

To find your **Connecting with Others score**, go to the LaunchPad for *Connections*, Second Edition.

LaunchPad
macmillan learning

Enhance Your Communication Skills

Communication is at the heart of connecting with others. When we communicate, we engage in a back-and-forth exchange that helps us learn information and build relationships with the people around us. In college you'll communicate with a wide variety of people, in many different situations. Some of the most important conversations will be one-on-one: For example, you might clarify concepts with an instructor, discuss project plans with a classmate, or exchange first-year survival tactics with a friend. Communication experts call this active exchange of information between two people (and sometimes more) **interpersonal communication**.

interpersonal communication: An active exchange of information between two or more people.

Interpersonal Communication

Ideally, a speaker conveys a clear message to the receiver. The receiver hears the complete message, overcoming any barriers; interprets it accurately; and then gives the speaker feedback. The receiver may also contribute substantial content to the conversation, thus becoming the speaker. szefei/Shutterstock

Interpersonal communication is a two-way street, where each person takes turns speaking and receiving. When you're the speaker, your goal is to convey your message clearly to the person on the receiving end. When you're the receiver, your goal is to listen actively to the speaker's message and to provide short responses called *feedback* that show you've heard and understood the message—or to ask for clarification if you haven't. (See Figure 11.1.) The roles of speaker and receiver may quickly reverse if the receiver has something more substantial to contribute to the conversation.

In this section we focus on your role as the receiver of information, including how to listen and how to respond when barriers to a conversation prevent you from hearing or understanding the full message. Then we touch on ways you can communicate your message effectively when you're the speaker—a topic we continue to explore throughout the chapter.

Become a Better Listener

Strange as it may seem, one of the best ways to become a good communicator isn't to speak—it's to listen. As we discuss in the note taking chapter, during *active listening*, you pay close attention to a speaker and focus on his or her message so that you can take accurate, useful notes. In interpersonal communication, active listening demonstrates your respect for others and helps you grasp their meaning when they speak. Active listening involves communicating nonverbally as well as providing verbal feedback.

Nonverbal Communication. Your body language says a lot about how well you're listening to another person, and the following techniques can help you stay engaged and attentive:

- **Make eye contact.** Maintain an appropriate amount of eye contact with the person who's talking. Preferred levels of eye contact vary according to culture or context, but most Americans prefer eye contact of moderate intensity—enough to show interest, but not so much that the other person feels like you're staring.

- **Maintain open body posture.** Convey attentiveness by using an *open posture*—face the speaker, sit up straight, relax your shoulders, and keep your arms at your sides or folded in your lap. Avoid any temptation to cross your arms because this *closed posture* may convey irritation, anger, discomfort, or disagreement with the speaker or his or her message.

- **Watch your body movement.** Lean slightly toward the speaker to show that you're ready to listen or want to hear more. Nod occasionally to encourage the person to continue, or to convey your understanding of (or agreement with) what he or she is saying.

- **Stay focused.** Maintain your focus on what the other person is saying; for instance, try not to glance at your phone or give in to other distractions.

Provide Feedback. In addition to nonverbal communication, you can show that you're listening to someone and that you understand his or her message by providing verbal feedback.[1] Here are several ways to provide feedback effectively:

- **Give brief encouragement.** When used occasionally, brief responses such as "yes," "uh-huh," and "okay" indicate that you're paying attention to the message. (Although when used too frequently, they may give the impression that you want the speaker to hurry up and stop talking.)

- **Paraphrase.** If you summarize or *paraphrase* what the speaker said by restating it in your own words, you can check your understanding of the message ("So, what I hear you saying is . . .").

- **Manage barriers.** Interpersonal communication isn't perfect, and sometimes barriers—everything from noise to confusion to distractions—can cause communication to break down. To overcome barriers, address them tactfully by asking a follow-up question, providing information, or sharing your own insights (see Table 11.1). You may also contribute to the conversation by helping manage the other person's emotions and defuse heated situations using *emotional intelligence*, which we'll explore later in the chapter.

CONNECT TO MY CAREER

Ask a friend or relative to pretend to interview you for your dream job. Shake hands with the "interviewer." As you answer his or her questions, be mindful of your eye contact, body posture, and body movement. Afterward, ask for feedback on the messages you conveyed nonverbally.

TABLE 11.1

Using Feedback to Manage Communication Barriers

Communication barrier	Examples of possible feedback
You couldn't hear what the speaker said because of a loud noise.	"Sorry, but I couldn't hear what you said. Can you explain again?"
You didn't understand what the speaker said.	"I'm not sure I get what you're saying. Can you clarify what you mean?"
You zoned out for a minute and lost track of the conversation.	"I apologize. I lost focus for a second. Could you repeat what you just said?"
The speaker seems distracted.	"I may be wrong, but you seem a bit distracted. Do you want to pick this up later, when things have calmed down?"
The speaker is telling you one thing, but his or her expression and body language convey something else.	"I know you're telling me that everything's fine, but you look sad."

Become a Better Speaker

Feedback shows that you're listening to a conversation, but what do you do when you want to communicate something more substantial—to become the speaker yourself? Throughout the rest of this chapter we'll look at specific techniques that will help you express your message thoughtfully, effectively, and honestly—during both pleasant and not-so-pleasant conversations. We begin by discussing emotional intelligence, which you can use to speak with others openly and sensitively.

Build Emotional Intelligence

emotional intelligence: The ability to recognize, understand, and manage your own and others' emotions.

Emotional intelligence—the ability to recognize, understand, and manage your own and others' emotions—is a critical part of communicating and connecting effectively with others (see Figure 11.2).[2] It can also help you learn about yourself and better manage how you respond to others. Thus, emotional intelligence is both *interpersonal* (between people) and *intrapersonal* (within ourselves).

To see how emotional intelligence works, let's say your friend Gustavo just broke up with his significant other. He's weeping as he tells you about the breakup, so you *recognize* that he's sad, and you might seek to *understand* the reason for his sadness by saying, "Did you think things were going better than they really were?" You might then try to help Gustavo *manage* his sadness by offering a sensitive response: "I'm so sorry, Gustavo. That must be hard. Is there anything I can do to help?"

During conversations, recognizing, understanding, and managing your *own* emotions can also help you communicate more effectively. For example, suppose a coworker tells you excitedly that she just received the employee of

FIGURE 11.2

Components of Emotional Intelligence

Source: Synthesized from the work of Mayer and Salovey (2008; 1997).

the month award. You always arrive for work early and talk enthusiastically with customers, so you feel strongly that you deserve the award more than your coworker, who spends all day on her phone and takes too many breaks. You recognize that you feel unappreciated, and thanks to this understanding, you can rein in your emotional reaction and respond appropriately. Instead of shouting, "You don't deserve that award!", you can manage your emotions and politely congratulate your coworker. Later, you can look up the criteria for the award and schedule a meeting with your boss to discuss his perceptions of your work performance.

Let's take a closer look at how you can handle situations like these in healthy ways by mastering the three key elements of emotional intelligence.

Recognize Emotions

The first step in exercising emotional intelligence is recognizing emotions—identifying what you or another person is feeling and labeling it.[3] Is it sadness? Excitement? Anger? Embarrassment? Joy?

Your Emotions. To better recognize your own emotions, there are a number of strategies you can try, including the following:

- Find and use words that designate emotions. Google the phrase "feeling word list," and select specific words that describe how you feel. Avoid generic words such as *happy*, *sad*, *mad*, and *glad* and instead choose words that depict the intensity of your emotions. For example, if you're unhappy, would you describe yourself as *slightly disappointed* or *completely devastated*?

- Consider how your body is reacting physically to an emotion. Is your heart pounding? Are you sinking in your chair? Are you becoming hot? Clenching your teeth? Getting teary-eyed? Physical responses can provide clues to our feelings.

In some cases, you might have various conflicting feelings about the same situation, and that's okay—feelings are complicated. However, denying feelings (especially negative ones) can cause problems. For example, if you're stressed out and you don't recognize it, you can't manage the stress. As a result, you might develop headaches, high blood pressure, or ulcers; feel overwhelmed or unmotivated at school or work; or start experiencing conflict in your personal relationships. Recognizing that you feel stressed is the first step to doing something *about* that stress.

Others' Emotions. There are also strategies you can use to recognize emotions in other people. For example:

- Ask the person what he or she is feeling.
- Pay attention to what others tell you. Notice when someone says he or she is feeling "excited," "thankful," "sad," or "frazzled."
- Notice what the person's body language seems to be saying. If a friend says he's "fine" but he's wringing his hands, you might conclude that he's actually feeling nervous or worried.
- Pay attention to **paralinguistics:** changes in the voice that convey emotion. When people are angry or anxious, for example, their throat muscles may tense up, giving their voice a higher pitch. If they're excited, their voice might get louder.

⟩ CONNECT TO MY EXPERIENCE
Select a feeling you've had today (good or bad) and rate the intensity of this feeling on a scale of 1 (low intensity) to 10 (high intensity). As you reflect on this feeling, record your reactions. What thoughts or words do you associate with this emotion? What physical reactions?

paralinguistics: Changes in the voice (such as volume or pitch) that convey emotion.

Name That Emotion. When you're trying to recognize which emotions other people are feeling, look at their gestures, facial expressions, and other clues. What emotion do you think the people in the photo on the left are experiencing? What about the person on the right? What cues led you to arrive at your interpretations?

Left: DreamPictures/Getty Images
Right: antoniodiaz/Shutterstock

Understand Emotions

Once you've recognized your own emotions or those of another person, the next step is to understand why these feelings are occurring. Then you can manage the emotions effectively.

Your Emotions. When it comes to understanding your own emotions, let's start with an example: Suppose you just got your paper back in English class, saw that you got a D, and reacted by feeling angry. To better understand yourself, ask "Why do I feel this way? What's making me angry?" Maybe you think you're angry at your instructor because you believe you deserved a B, and the grade you got makes you wonder whether your instructor respects you. As you engage in metacognition, though, you may realize what's actually happening: You're really angry at *yourself* for not putting more effort into your work.

Understanding where your feeling of anger comes from can help you think before you act. That way, you can manage the emotion and respond constructively to the situation. For instance, if you conclude that you're angry at yourself for not putting more effort into your work, you'll probably adopt more effective strategies the next time you write a paper for class—rather than storming into your instructor's office and demanding to know why she doesn't like your writing.

empathy: The ability to understand another person's emotions.

Others' Emotions. When you understand another person's emotions, you have **empathy** for that person, even if you haven't had the same experience that triggered his or her feelings. For example, suppose your coworker Rashida tells you she just completed her first marathon. You hate running and have never completed a marathon. But by imagining yourself in her shoes or recalling one of your own experiences that gave you a similar sense of accomplishment, you can feel some of the same pride and excitement that Rashida is feeling. That empathy can help you respond appropriately, with feedback such as "That's great news, Rashida! You must feel fantastic about achieving your goal!"

Manage Emotions

In the personal and financial health chapter, we explore how to manage stress, depression, and anxiety so that they don't affect your academic performance. In this section we focus on managing the emotions you might have toward a speaker, as well as the emotions of those around you.

Your Emotions. How can you manage your own strong emotions? As an example, let's take another look at anger. If you find yourself getting angry with someone because of something he or she said, what can you do? Once you *recognize* your anger and *understand* where it comes from, you can manage it using a number of techniques.

- Take a deep breath and count to ten.
- Use empathy to put yourself in the other person's shoes, or ask the other person questions to try to understand his or her perspective.
- Calmly let the person know you're reacting intensely to what he or she is saying.
- Take a brisk 5-minute walk to blow off steam.

These tactics can help dial down the intensity of your emotion, enabling you to think more clearly and respond more appropriately to the situation.

Others' Emotions. When you see other people experiencing strong emotions, you can help them manage these feelings in a sensitive and respectful way. Your goal isn't to change or control what they feel, but to provide empathy and, if appropriate, to help them work through their feelings or suggest professional resources. The following strategies may be useful:

- Let them know you recognize that they may be having a hard time.
- Invite them to share their feelings with you, and listen to them actively.
- Put yourself in their shoes and provide a compassionate response.
- If you've had a similar feeling or experience, share it and let them know what helped you through it.
- Instill hope that their situation can change.
- Offer assistance and connect them to appropriate campus or community resources if needed.

Managing emotions is a key step toward resolving interpersonal conflicts and restoring healthy connections between yourself and others—a topic we'll turn to now.

Erupting Emotions. If you don't effectively manage your emotions (especially negative ones), they can cause problems: Similar to lava inside a volcano, these emotions can intensify over time, and without any release, they'll eventually blow. Are you about to erupt in anger over something someone said? If so, adopt the emotion-management strategy that works best for you—even if it's just taking a quick walk to let off steam. LukaKikina/Shutterstock

⟩ CONNECT
TO MY RESOURCES

Let's say that your classmate, who is going through a difficult breakup, has been feeling sad and lonely. Research and record the resources that are available on your campus to help this student. How might you suggest in a sensitive way that this person contact these resources?

Resolve Conflict

Conflict arises when two or more people disagree. Arguing with a friend about which movie to see, disputing your grade on a pop quiz, receiving a customer complaint—these types of disagreements can all lead to conflict, which makes it an inevitable, and normal, part of life. But not all conflict is the same. In cases where the disagreement is minor, the incident may end with a quick compromise; in cases where you feel that compromising would go against your values, however, the conflict may be harder to resolve.

Conflict can be scary, and we all deal with it differently. Some people deny there's a problem or give in to the other person to maintain harmony, while others fight ferociously for what they believe in or compete to "win" every time. But the ideal outcome of any conflict is a resolution that's agreeable to everyone involved, and that often requires collaboration among the parties.

As we saw earlier, communicating effectively and honing your emotional intelligence can help you work through difficult situations. As you'll see now, you can also use assertiveness and "I" statements.

Be Assertive

Being *assertive* means stating your thoughts, feelings, and opinions and advocating for yourself without disrespecting other people or their views. Although being assertive can feel intimidating, it's good for your mental health and your relationships.[4] For example, by letting an instructor know you need help in class, you can gain access to resources that will help you succeed. By asking your boss for clarification on a work assignment, you can complete the assignment more effectively. By telling your romantic partner you want more intimacy, you can start a conversation where you both brainstorm ways to feel more connected.

Assertiveness differs from *passivity*, in which people keep their thoughts and feelings to themselves to "avoid causing trouble." Some situations call for passivity: For example, it would be inappropriate to express your negative opinions about someone at his or her funeral. However, your ideas, opinions, feelings, and needs matter. If you don't speak up for yourself in situations where doing so is appropriate, your needs may go unmet.

Assertiveness also differs from *aggression*, which involves humiliating, criticizing, blaming, attacking, or threatening others. Aggressive communicators provoke feelings of fear or dislike. By contrast, assertive communicators are respectful. They take responsibility for getting their needs met, address issues as they arise, and speak openly and honestly.

To be an assertive communicator, you must first value yourself and your own feelings and opinions. Not everyone will like what you have to say, but by being honest, you'll likely earn their respect. Consider these assertiveness strategies.

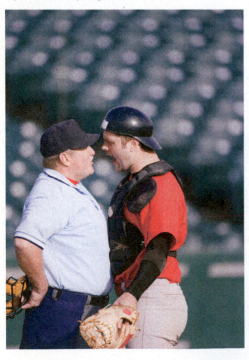

Assertiveness—or Aggression?
Assertive behaviors help you express your thoughts and feelings and pose questions in respectful ways. Assertiveness works far better than aggression in interpersonal conflict because it invites honest conversation rather than triggering defensiveness. Considering the aggressive stance these two men have adopted, do you think they'll resolve their conflict productively?
Koji Aoki/Aflo/Getty Images

- Before making a request, know what you want to ask for.
- Rehearse what you plan to say. You may even want to role-play the scenario with a friend.
- Show confidence in your feelings and opinions by making eye contact with others and demonstrating confident nonverbal behavior, such as an open posture.
- Speak clearly and concisely. Emphasize the key points you're communicating.
- If you're making a statement, end it with a downward inflection in your voice. Ending with an upward inflection will make your statement sound like a question, signaling uncertainty.
- If the situation is too fresh and you're feeling angry or emotional, wait a day or two to have the conversation when you feel calmer and more in control.
- If you didn't do anything wrong, don't apologize.
- Remind yourself that you have the right to say "no" and to change your mind.
- Take the strongest stance on issues that matter most to you. For less significant issues, practice the vital art of knowing when to let it go.

Use "I" Statements

Statements beginning with "I" show that you're taking ownership of your thoughts and feelings—such as "I felt hurt when you didn't respond to my text" or "I think I'm confused by your behavior." By using "I" statements, you express your thoughts and feelings clearly, honestly, and constructively[5] and create a respectful environment in which you can explain how something the other person said or did has affected you. During disagreements or conflicts, "I" statements give the receiver the chance to respond or clear up any misunderstanding and give the speaker a chance to request the receiver's help in finding a solution.

For example, suppose Petra, your housemate, keeps leaving dirty dishes in the sink before heading off to work. You're angry, and your first impulse is to say, "You're such a slob" or "You're the most inconsiderate person I know." Such blaming or judging statements tend to make other people feel defensive.[6] Instead, you might say calmly: "I get frustrated when you leave dirty dishes in the sink because I feel like I have to spend extra time scraping them off, and it's harder for me to get to school on time. I'd like to talk about this so we can find a solution." By sharing your feelings, Petra has a chance to reflect on her behavior and how it affects you. She may feel motivated to start rinsing the dishes herself, but if not, you might respectfully suggest a solution: "Perhaps we could each be responsible for washing our own dishes. What if we agree to do this at least four times a week?"

Together, using "I" statements like these, being assertive, and drawing on the other skills you've learned about in this chapter (active listening, providing feedback, exercising emotional intelligence) can help you resolve conflicts and handle sensitive situations with care.

"So Much for Crashing on the Couch." You just got home after a tough day at school and work. You go to crash on the couch—and find yet another pile of laundry left by your housemate. You're furious. What "I" statements could you make to productively express your feelings about the situation and arrive at a solution that works for both of you? Africa Studio/Shutterstock

Grow and Sustain Healthy Relationships

All the connection skills we've discussed so far—effective communication, emotional intelligence, conflict resolution—have an overarching purpose: helping you build and sustain healthy relationships while you're in college. These relationships are important because to succeed in school, you need a strong *social support network*—a group of people who encourage you when things get tough and join in celebrating your accomplishments. This network can include people outside of school, as well as classmates, faculty members, members of study groups, and people you meet in campus clubs, professional organizations, or even online. In this section we look at how to connect with the important members of your social support network.

Getting to Know You . . . Meeting classmates is a great way to start building a network of people who can support you and connect you to the resources you need to succeed in school. So take every opportunity to strike up conversations with fellow students. Who knows? Some may become lifelong friends. Sam Edwards/Getty Images

Connect with Classmates

Getting to know your classmates can help you build a network of people who—whether they become good friends or just study partners—can keep you motivated and connect you to information and other resources you need to succeed in class.

To forge connections in face-to-face classes, notice which students seem motivated to learn. Strike up a conversation with these students before or after class, and ask if they might be interested in organizing a study group.

If you're taking an online class, look for other opportunities to get to know your classmates. For example, some online classes may require students to introduce themselves in a discussion forum and respond to one another's introductory posts. And online classes often provide separate discussion forums in which students can get to know each other and share resources related to the class, the college, or other common interests.

Connect with Instructors

When you feel connected to your instructors, you'll feel more comfortable asking them for help. And when they know you, they'll be more likely to give you career advice, point you to internship or job opportunities, and write you letters of recommendation. So try chatting with your instructors before class, after class, or during their office hours—although take care to maintain an appropriate degree of professionalism in these conversations. Telling an instructor you saw a great concert last night is fine; describing how wild and crazy you got at that concert isn't a good move.

Also keep in mind that you communicate with your nonverbal behavior in addition to your words. In a face-to-face class, getting to class on time, sitting near the front of the room, making eye contact, shutting off your phone (no texting), and taking notes shows your respect for your instructors and your interest in the class material. In an online course, your instructor will assess other aspects of your communication, including the quality and frequency of your discussion board posts and your e-mail etiquette. Be sure to follow the guidelines in the following box when crafting e-mails to your instructors.

> ## HOW TO COMMUNICATE WITH YOUR INSTRUCTOR VIA E-MAIL
>
> 1. Use the subject line to indicate the content and purpose of your e-mail ("Question about deadline extension for English literature paper").
> 2. Address your instructor formally by his or her appropriate title—for example, "Dear Dr. Jones. . . ."
> 3. If you don't know the instructor personally, explain who you are. For example, "I am a student in your 8:00 a.m. English literature class."
> 4. Be courteous in your tone, even if you're stating a complaint.
> 5. Use complete sentences, proper sentence structure, and correct spelling and grammar. Proofread your message and use the spell checker before you hit "Send."
> 6. Keep your message brief and to the point. If something requires a long explanation, set up an in-person meeting.
> 7. Never use all capital letters in an e-mail. That's considered shouting.
> 8. Review your e-mail to make sure you've included all relevant details and any required attachments.

Connect with Your Campus Community

Connecting with the larger campus community is another great way to meet people and build relationships. Your school may have a number of student-led clubs and organizations to fit your interests, values, and affiliations—everything from a Ballroom Dance Club and a Campus Vegetarian Society to a Korean American Student Association and an Accounting Club. Additionally, you may want to get involved in student government to develop leadership skills or volunteer in the local community. For example, if you like sports, you may want to coach for the Special Olympics. If you enjoy technology and engineering, you may want to get involved with the First Lego League and help young people learn how to build and program robots.

Your college may even offer trips or classes that combine instruction with volunteer experience in the community, which is called **service learning**. For example, you may want to join an "Alternative Spring Break" trip to learn about and help restore the coastal ecosystem in Arcata, California. Or you might want to register for a class to understand the political, economic, social, and environmental changes in Cuba and then travel to Cuba as a class to explore grassroots changes occurring at the community level. With so many opportunities, your options for meeting and connecting with other people are endless!

CONNECT TO MY CLASSES
Which of your current instructors seem most approachable? Why? For those who don't seem approachable, forge a connection by visiting them during their office hours or contacting them by e-mail. Then write a short paragraph about your experience, including how it affected your impressions of these instructors.

service learning: Classes that combine classroom instruction with volunteer experience in the community.

The Value of Getting Involved on Campus

You may be thinking, "Joining a campus club sounds fun, but I need to focus on getting good grades." Absolutely, you need to fulfill your obligations, but research shows that getting involved on campus has benefits.

In one study, researchers at a large state college tracked the extracurricular activities of almost fifteen thousand first-year students to determine how active involvement on campus related to their grades and how long they stayed in college. The students were divided into two groups: those who participated in extracurricular activities (student clubs, student government, orientation) at least once during their college career and those who never participated in any extracurricular activities. The researchers discovered some interesting facts:

▶ Students who participated in campus activities achieved higher cumulative GPAs than those who didn't.

▶ Students who participated in campus activities remained in college at higher rates than those who didn't.

Why might this be so? Other research provides some clues. First, getting involved on campus can make college more fun and interesting, thus motivating students to invest more time and energy into their studies.[7] Second, participation in campus activities can help students connect with others on campus, increase their social support network, and develop confidence and social skills—which in turn may make it easier to ask for help from instructors, advisers, or other college resources.[8] Finally, feeling like a valued member of the campus community may instill a sense of pride and belonging that further serves as motivation.

THE BOTTOM LINE

Participation can lead to good things! Getting involved on campus may help you connect to people and resources at your school—and ultimately help you succeed.

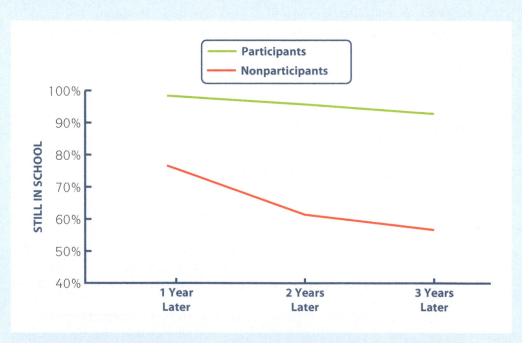

In this study, students who participated in campus activities remained in school at higher rates after one, two, and three years than students who didn't participate in campus activities.

Information from J. Wang and J. Shiveley, *The Impact of Extracurricular Activity on Student Academic Performance* (Sacramento: California State University, Sacramento, Office of Institutional Research, 2009).

Connect with Others Online

Joining online communities and networks that fit your interests and needs can also help you build relationships.[9] For example, through social media sites such as Facebook and Twitter and professional networking sites such as LinkedIn, you can meet others and stay connected through activities like wall posting, picture sharing, and instant messaging. If you want to meet people who share your interests, you can join an online discussion forum. If you want to make changes in your life, such as losing weight or stopping drinking, you can join an online support group.

While online interactions can be fun and rewarding, do use caution in how you present yourself and who you meet. Use these tips to be professional and stay safe:

- Reflect on what you're posting. Five years from now, would you be embarrassed by the photo of yourself you just shared? If a potential employer saw the image, could it jeopardize your chances of getting your dream job? (Yes, some recruiters will search your name on the Web.)

- Think critically about others' posts, including their trustworthiness: Is the information accurate? Is its source reliable and respectable?

- If you arrange a face-to-face meeting with someone you met online, practice personal safety: Let someone else know about the meeting, get together in a public place, and consider bringing a friend along with you.

Stay Connected with Friends and Family

It takes time and effort to maintain relationships, but even as a busy college student you can use active listening, emotional intelligence, and assertiveness skills to show the people in your life *off* campus just how special they are. Here are a few strategies for preserving meaningful relationships with friends and family while in college.

- Stay connected with your loved ones through e-mail, texting, Facebook, phone calls, or face-to-face visits.

- Actively listen to any concerns or fears they might have for you.

- Share your hopes and dreams with them.

- Let them know how they can support you emotionally while you're in school.

- Don't be afraid to share disappointments, frustrations, or loneliness. Your family members and friends want to be there for you. And they may surprise you with some good advice.

- Invite them to campus or show them your online coursespace so that they feel they're part of your college experience.

- Communicate your needs assertively. Don't assume they can read your mind.

- Develop empathy—try to understand what it's like for them to spend less time with you.

- Let minor disagreements go.

- If tensions build, address the issue in a calm, respectful way using "I" statements.

- Try to negotiate mutually beneficial solutions to any conflicts that arise.

Embrace Diversity

School and work can provide wonderful opportunities to build relationships with people who are different from us in any number of ways. Some of these differences might be visible, such as gender, skin color, age, and physical ability. Other differences, such as income, religious affiliation, ethnicity, and sexual orientation, may only become apparent when we get to know someone better.

diversity: Characteristics or attributes that make us different from one another and that can be the basis for membership in a group.

The term **diversity** refers to characteristics or attributes that make us different from one another and that can be the basis for membership in a group. Differences are important to acknowledge and understand as they're elements of who we are and they help to form our identity. Differences make the world a more vibrant and interesting place. Imagine how boring life would be if everyone was exactly the same! There is great value to living, working, and socializing with people who differ from us:

- We gain new perspectives.
- We develop a deeper understanding and appreciation for others and their life experiences.
- We recognize that each person is a unique individual, not just a member of a particular group.
- We engage in metacognition to rethink false beliefs we may have held about individuals from certain groups.
- We learn more about ourselves by reflecting on our own diversity, experiences, and attitudes.

If we're open to differences, they can stimulate and inspire us. Let's explore this topic in more detail.

Recognize Differences

If you were asked to describe yourself, what would you say? Would you talk about physical characteristics, such as your hair color or height? Would you mention your age, where you grew up, or your life goals? When we describe ourselves, we can draw from many characteristics, including physical appearance, personality traits, interests, family background, values, and skills. All of us are *multidimensional*—we're defined by many different aspects of our identity.

culture: Shared concepts, ideas, values, norms, and rules of behavior of a specific group of people.

Some aspects of our identity are shaped through our **culture**. Culture includes the shared beliefs, customs, rituals, language, food, clothing, values, goals, and practices of a racial, religious, or social group.[10] As you think about the culture or cultures that influence your own identity, take a moment to reflect on the defining characteristics of each one. Are there particular foods, clothing, customs, or rituals that make up this culture? How do these cultural influences impact your identity and, as a result, your interactions with people from different cultural backgrounds?

As you go through life, there may be times or environments in which one aspect of your identity is stronger or more important to you than another. For example, you may notice that you're the only woman in a work group of men, and you may wonder how your gender impacts your overall experience in the group. At other times, gender may stand out less than other aspects of your identity: Maybe your identity as a student athlete or a person with a disability will become more relevant at some point.

As you think about your own identity and the diversity you see on your campus, at work, and in your personal life, reflect on the characteristics that make each of us unique and shape our experiences. Just some of these many characteristics are listed in Table 11.2.

TABLE 11.2
Common Elements of Diversity

Element	Description	Did you know?
Race	A way to classify people into groups according to physical characteristics such as skin color, hair color, facial features, and body build.	Guessing someone's race based on physical features is risky because appearances may be deceiving. Further, many people are multiracial, which may not be clear from physical appearance alone.
Ethnicity	A way to identify a group of people with a common ancestral heritage and, often, a shared history and culture.	In the United States, people who identify as Hispanic or Latino (from places such as Mexico, Puerto Rico, and Cuba) are the largest and fastest-growing ethnic group.[11]
Gender	Refers to characteristics that a society or culture defines as masculine or feminine. Gender is different than *sex*, which refers to biological rather than cultural differences.[12]	Gender can also refer to one's own experience of being a man or a woman (gender identity), how a person presents him- or herself to the world (gender expression), or expectations others have for an individual based on their perception of the person's gender (gender roles).[13]
Sexual orientation	Refers to an enduring pattern of attraction to others, such as persons of the opposite sex (heterosexuality), the same sex (homosexuality), or both sexes (bisexuality).[14]	You may never know someone's sexual orientation unless the person tells you. If someone shares his or her sexual orientation with you, don't assume that it's been shared with everyone else.
Mental and physical ability	Refers to a person's ability to perform one or more major life activities, such as caring for oneself, walking, speaking, breathing, and thinking.	Mental or physical impairments, or disabilities, can limit someone's ability to perform major life activities. Sometimes it's clear that someone has a disability (such as when a person uses a wheelchair). Other times, the disability isn't so visible (such as when a person has dyslexia).
Religion	An organized system of spiritual beliefs, traditions, and practices agreed upon by a group of individuals.	Many colleges offer classes on world religions. These classes can be a great way to learn more about different belief systems.
Socioeconomic status	Refers to social standing or prestige based on income, occupation, or education.[15]	Visible status symbols, such as the way a person dresses, don't always accurately reveal socioeconomic status. Some wealthy people spend modestly, for instance, while some people in financial trouble spend lavishly to build their image.
Age	Indicates how old a person is, which determines the social, political, economic, and technological events the individual is exposed to in his or her lifetime.	Terms such as *Baby Boomers* (born 1946–1964), *Generation X* (born early 1960s to early 1980s), and *Millennials* (born early 1980s to early 2000s) are used to classify people who were born during different time periods.

Develop Multicultural Competence

In order to connect meaningfully and communicate effectively with others, it's not enough to simply recognize differences; we need to strive to understand, appreciate, and respect others' differences as well. *Multicultural competence* is a transferable skill that involves being aware of your own cultural background, values, and biases; respecting others' cultural backgrounds, values, and beliefs; and using culturally sensitive interpersonal skills.[16]

Know Your Own Background and Biases.
The first component of multicultural competence involves developing an awareness of your own cultural background, values, and biases. In the section above, we explored ways to become more aware of your identity and cultural background. In this section, we'll focus on becoming more aware of your biases and where they might come from.

No doubt you've seen or read about people looking down on, or even mistreating, those who are different from them. Reactions like this can occur when a person has inaccurate beliefs about a particular group, or has had a certain experience with a member of a group and then generalizes that experience to the larger group ("I don't trust teenagers because a teenager vandalized my car last year"). Lack of exposure to a particular group can also cause reactions like these, because people can be suspicious of what's unfamiliar. Have you personally ever felt uncomfortable talking or working with any groups of people? If so, what might have caused this discomfort? Was it any of the reasons just listed? How might your own background and life experiences have influenced these feelings?

Inaccurate beliefs or lack of exposure to particular groups of people can lead to *stereotyping*, or assigning real, imagined, or exaggerated characteristics (negative or positive) to all members of a particular group—for example, "All American tourists are rude" or "Everyone from the East Coast is well educated." When we exhibit these kinds of fixed, overgeneralized beliefs, we fail to see individual differences, and we abandon critical thinking in favor of a lazy thinking process where we place people in simple categories—sometimes even "us" and "them" categories. Our distorted thoughts may then influence our behavior in negative ways, and, in some cases, can even lead to acts of discrimination.

discrimination: Treating people less favorably because of their membership in a particular group.

Discrimination involves treating people less favorably based on their membership in a particular group—in other words, taking actions based on negative stereotypes or sweeping judgments. For example, it's considered discrimination if a manager avoids hiring well-qualified job candidates because of their age (*ageism*), race (*racism*), gender, religion, or sexual orientation. Colleges and workplaces have established policies against all forms of discrimination, so report any incidents of discrimination you witness. Doing so will help make these environments safe places for diverse ideas, interests, beliefs, opinions, and lifestyles. If you've ever experienced discrimination, you know firsthand how important it is to combat it.

Respect Others' Backgrounds.
The second component of multicultural competence is respecting and trying to understand others' cultural backgrounds. We can do this by practicing *tolerance*. When we're tolerant, we acknowledge, value, and respect what makes someone different from us. We may not always agree with other people, but we use empathy to try to understand their perspectives by putting ourselves in their shoes. Being tolerant means treating people with dignity and respect, and accepting that not everyone thinks or acts like we do.

Be Culturally Sensitive.
The third component of multicultural competence is using culturally sensitive interpersonal skills. We've covered numerous interpersonal skills in this chapter, so you may already be able to brainstorm ways to

ensure your communication is appropriate. In addition, here are several specific suggestions:

- Make sure your eye contact is respectful by not staring or rolling your eyes at anyone because they are speaking another language or wearing clothing that is customary in their country of origin or their faith.

- Try to maintain an open body posture and watch your body movements so they don't convey distrust, disgust, or a lack of acceptance to ideas that may be new or different.

- When speaking, avoid terms that are derogatory to a particular group or considered outdated and offensive. Do research to understand how people prefer to be addressed or, if you're unsure, assert yourself and ask.

- Respect physical space and boundaries. For example, don't lean on someone's wheelchair or assume that because someone has a disability, he or she needs to be taken care of. Asking if people need help is one thing, but assuming they aren't capable is another.

- Finally, be curious and ask questions about other cultures, but don't ask people to speak on behalf of their gender, race/ethnicity, religion, or another element of their identity. Remember that although a person may belong to a particular cultural group and endorse some of that group's values, beliefs, and customs, he or she still maintains uniqueness. Thus, in addition to recognizing and respecting differences *between* cultural groups, we can't forget that there are differences *within* groups as well.

Learn and Advocate

To build relationships with a wide variety of people, it's important to have an open mind and a willingness to learn. By interacting with people who differ from you in some way, you may gain new perspectives, find you have much more in common than you originally thought, and lessen any misconceptions or preconceived notions that could lead to discrimination. Let diversity enrich your relationships by using these strategies.

- **Gain information.** Learn more about people who are different from you, including how other groups have been treated throughout history. For example, take a class such as Men and Masculinity or Comparative Religions. Attend public events offered by your school, such as a Martin Luther King Jr. celebration. Learn how to create a safe space for lesbian, gay, bisexual, transgender, queer, and questioning (LGBTQQ) individuals by attending a Safe Zone Training Program.

- **Seek personal contact.** The more you interact with people who have different backgrounds, the more comfortable you'll feel. Talk together about the same things you would discuss with other friends. Explore what you have in common. Discover how you differ, and identify what's interesting or valuable about those differences.

- **Be open to feedback.** As you interact more with people who are different from you, you may unintentionally offend them through word or action. If this happens, use active listening to understand their viewpoint, and remain open to their feedback. Apologize, and thank them for the opportunity to learn from the experience.

- **Assert yourself.** Use your assertiveness skills to stand up for others whom you see being treated unfairly because of something that makes them different. Let people know that you don't want to hear offensive language, jokes, stereotypical remarks, or insults directed toward a particular group of people, including any groups you're a member of. Report illegal discrimination, hate crimes, and other abuse to authorities.

- **Advocate for social justice.** Certain groups of people have been and continue to be marginalized and oppressed in our country. Injustices and inequalities do exist, and *social justice* is a term used to identify a process and a goal that we can work toward individually and as a society. As one definition explains, "The goal of social justice education is full and equal participation of all groups in a society that is mutually shaped to meet their needs. Social justice includes a vision of society that is equitable and all members are physically and psychologically safe and secure."[17]

Advocate for Issues You're Passionate About. Getting involved in social issues is a great way to help people who may not otherwise have a voice. This advocacy can also help you build connections with other students and gain new skills. What social issues are important to you? What is one way you could make a difference? Joseph Reid/Alamy

> # Campus is a place where all students are welcome and we all belong.

NAME
Alexis Arellano

SCHOOL
California State University San Marcos

MAJOR
Human Development with a Concentration in Children's Services

CAREER GOAL
Teacher

APPRECIATING DIVERSITY

Now that I'm a senior, I see that I'm more aware and more open-minded than I was when I started college. Some of my classes have been very useful in helping me look at the world from different perspectives. I've had classes in anthropology, sociology, and digital media where we looked at different artifacts and I got to appreciate many different cultures. One class in particular stands out. I had a medical anthropology class where we learned that the American Medical Association's approach to medicine is really the youngest form of healing. Tibetan, Chinese, and Native American medicine all have much longer histories, and this class really helped me look at different cultures and appreciate their history and contributions.

I try to help other students appreciate this as well through my work as a peer adviser. I get to serve as a bridge between students and the resources available to them on campus, which means I get to show them how our campus works to meet their needs. I answer general questions and help students with major and schedule changes. I've really come to appreciate the many different cultural backgrounds of students on campus. We've got student centers on campus for many different cultural groups. I encourage students to go check these out, to learn about others who are different from them. Campus is a place where all students are welcome and we all belong. It's a great place to explore and learn about others.

> **YOUR TURN** To what degree do you identify with Alexis's experience of becoming more open-minded in college? Have you had classes that have helped you look at the world from different perspectives? Have you learned anything new about yourself or another culture by interacting with students from different cultural backgrounds? If you haven't had either of these experiences yet, challenge yourself to take a class, meet someone new, attend an event, or join a club that will broaden your perspective culturally.

We can work toward social justice by helping empower individuals and groups, and if we have power and privilege, we can be a voice for those who need it and actively confront injustice and inequality in society. For example, issues such as homelessness, poverty, hunger, unclean water, domestic abuse, and unequal treatment based on race, sex, age, or sexual orientation affect people around the globe, and in many cases, right in your neighborhood. To become an advocate, you might attend a rally or march for or against a particular issue; call or write your congressperson; donate money or help with fundraising efforts; or provide direct service by volunteering at a homeless shelter, being a Big Brother or Big Sister, or picking up trash in the local park.

Connect with Others at Work

Connecting with others not only benefits you in college but is also crucial to career success. When you know how to build and maintain healthy, positive relationships with other people in a work setting, you're more likely to get the job of your dreams—and then excel at it once you're hired.

Impress an Interviewer or Employer

Try these tips for making a good impression when you're looking for a job and once you've joined an organization's ranks.

- **Ace the interview.** Arrive early for a job interview, make good eye contact, and use a firm handshake to communicate your interest, enthusiasm, and respect. In addition, listen actively to the interviewer, ask relevant questions, and clearly state your skills and career goals.

- **Maintain professionalism through social media.** Potential employers may review your posts on social media to assess your professionalism, integrity, and ethics, so make sure they'll like what they see if they access your profile.

- **Leverage your existing relationships.** For instance, a classmate might know of a job opening that interests you, or your instructors may give you letters of recommendation to share with interviewers.

- **Further your career.** Once you have a job, use your connection skills to advance in your career. For example, to negotiate a raise with your boss, use assertiveness to explain what value you bring to the organization. Or clearly describe your career goals, including a promotion you're eyeing, and ask for "stretch assignments"—challenging work that lets you build the skills needed for the higher-level role you want.

Work Effectively with Colleagues

In a work setting, differences in personality, goals, work styles, and ability can spark disagreements. Supervisors know that conflict can erode productivity, so they expect coworkers to get along. The skills laid out in this chapter can help you manage these conflicts. Here are some suggestions:

- **Bridge cultural gaps.** Your colleagues or clients may come from many places around the globe. Learn about their homelands and customs, such as holidays and cuisine. If you sense that you may have offended someone unintentionally, apologize and ask for feedback on your behavior. Use this feedback to improve. And if someone unintentionally offends you, use "I" statements to gently enlighten him or her.

- **Offer feedback sensitively.** At some point in your career, you may be asked to supervise someone or manage a project. In this role you'll need to give others feedback so that they can improve their performance. To provide such feedback, let them know what they're doing well before offering criticism. And frame your feedback in terms of behavior they can change ("I need you to arrive at meetings on time") versus a character attack ("You don't care about this project"). Offer support and suggestions for how they can make the desired change in behavior.

- **Avoid gossip.** It's fun to talk and laugh with people at work, but try to steer clear of office gossip. Gossip erodes morale and can get you in trouble. So talk about entertaining topics with your coworkers, but don't repeat confidential news or make fun of others behind their back.

The Workplace Connection. Connecting with others at work can help you collaborate productively with your colleagues, boss, and employees (if you're a manager). Result? Workers deliver their best performance on the job. Productive connections at your job can also help you advance your career and forge enduring friendships. Chicasso/ Getty Images

NAME
Alan Geans

PROFESSION
Village/City Manager

SCHOOL
Indiana Wesleyan University

DEGREE
Bachelor's Degree in Business Administration

Courtesy of Lauren Flanigan

INTERPERSONAL SKILLS FOR WORKPLACE SUCCESS

As an employer responsible for hiring and supervising employees, I'm regularly challenged with identifying and securing talent for my office and managing and developing employees. One thing I've learned over time is that trust is an important component to success. You have to trust that your employees are invested in their work and the success of their organization. Communicating that trust and giving your employees the freedom to succeed promotes a healthy workplace climate. At the same time, however, I'm a strong believer in having measures in place to help identify when employees aren't performing as they should—that way you can identify problems early and provide the support necessary to help them succeed.

I've also learned to deal more effectively with conflict at work. Whenever I experience conflict or see it in my employees, I have to remind myself that we're not here at work to like each other! We're here to get a job done and everyone in my office has a passion for their work and the goals of our organization. I focus on acting professionally: I'm open and honest with my coworkers when we disagree and I encourage my employees to act similarly. Sometimes disagreement reveals new ways of looking at a problem or reveals an interesting solution.

Finally, I think students today will find themselves working in a more diverse world than people my age did when they first entered the workforce. It's important to consider multiple dimensions of diversity—like age, gender, race/ethnicity, and ability—and to recognize that people are in different places with how they think about and embrace issues of diversity and inclusion. Some people might welcome diverse people, backgrounds, and opinions, whereas others might find a diverse workplace challenging or intimidating. As with conflict, I think it's important to have open and honest conversations when diversity issues hinder workplace success.

Having self-awareness of your own attitudes, beliefs, and skills and being able to effectively communicate with others is a recipe for success at work, and college is an excellent place to develop awareness and communication skills.

> **YOUR TURN** Alan understands that conflict in the workplace can be beneficial. In what ways do you think conflict can be beneficial? What experiences have you had with conflict in the workplace? If you don't have work experience yet, what types of conflict do you imagine might happen in the workplace? In addition to approaching conflict with a positive mindset, Alan said he tries to remain professional. What might that look like? What are the attitudes, behaviors, and communication skills that contribute to professionalism when dealing with conflict in the workplace?

my personal success plan

CONNECTION SKILLS

Based on your ACES results and what you learned in this chapter, are you inspired to set a new goal related to connecting with others? If so, the Personal Success Plan can walk you through the goal-setting process. Read the advice and examples; then sketch out your ideas in the space provided.

To access the Personal Success Plan online, go to the LaunchPad for *Connections*, Second Edition.

1 **IDENTIFY A GOAL**

Choose a connection-related goal to work toward this term. Here are some general ideas you might draw from; you can also create a goal of your own.

- ▶ Resolve conflict with friends or loved ones.
- ▶ Learn how to recognize my emotions by journaling about them.
- ▶ Sign up for a service-learning class.
- ▶ Visit one of my instructors during his or her office hours.
- ▶ Learn more about people with different backgrounds by reading a book, attending a public event, or taking a class.

2 **MAKE YOUR GOAL SMART**

Rewrite your specific goal so that it's SMART, and make sure to use the SMART goal checklist.

SAMPLE: For one week I'll make a conscious effort to use "I" statements whenever a disagreement arises between me and someone else.

3 **CREATE AN ACTION PLAN**

Outline the specific steps you'll take to achieve your SMART goal, and note when you'll complete each step.

SAMPLE: During all my interactions with others next week, I'll notice if I'm using blaming or accusatory language and will reframe my comments as "I" statements.

4 **LIST BARRIERS AND SOLUTIONS**

Think about possible barriers to your action steps; then brainstorm solutions for overcoming them.

SAMPLE: If I get so upset during a disagreement that it's hard to transform blaming language into "I" statements, I'll count to ten and try again.

5 **ACT AND EVALUATE OUTCOMES**

Now that your plan is in place, take action. Record each action step as you take it. Then evaluate whether you achieved your SMART goal, and make any adjustments needed to get better results in the future.

SAMPLE: Counting to ten didn't help me reduce my frustration as much as I had hoped. The next time my emotions get away from me, I'll try taking a short, brisk walk instead.

6 **CONNECT TO CAREER**

List the skills you're building as you progress toward your SMART goal. How will you use these skills to land a job and succeed at work?

SAMPLE: In any career I pursue, learning how to manage conflict effectively will help me work well with others and stay productive on the job.

my personal success plan

1 my general goal

2 my SMART goal

☐ SPECIFIC ☐ MEASURABLE ☐ ACHIEVABLE ☐ RELEVANT ☐ TIME-LIMITED

3 my action plan

4 my barriers/ solutions

5 my actions/ outcomes

6 my career connection

CHAPTER SUMMARY

This chapter introduced you to fundamental skills for connecting with others in college, work, and life. Revisit the following key points, and reflect on how you can use this information to support your success now and in the future.

- In interpersonal communication, ideally a speaker conveys a clear message to the receiver. The receiver hears the complete message, overcoming any barriers; interprets it accurately; and then gives the speaker feedback. The receiver may also contribute more substantial content to the conversation, thus becoming the speaker.

- The three steps to exercising emotional intelligence are recognizing, understanding, and then managing your own and others' emotions.

- Assertive communication can help you constructively resolve conflicts by sharing your thoughts, feelings, and needs in an honest, respectful way.

- Using "I" statements can also help you resolve conflicts effectively. By showing that you're taking responsibility for your feelings and reactions, you're less likely to trigger defensiveness in the other person.

- Communication skills, emotional intelligence, and the ability to constructively work through conflicts with others can help you build and sustain positive, healthy relationships.

- Knowing how to interact effectively with people from diverse backgrounds is valuable in college and the workplace because it helps you change and grow.

- Knowing how to connect with others can help you impress interviewers, advance in your career once you get a job, and interact effectively with colleagues.

CHAPTER ACTIVITIES

Journal Entry

RECOGNIZING DIFFERENCES

In order to truly embrace diversity and develop empathy for the values, beliefs, and lived experiences of others, we must first develop self-awareness of our own background. Describe who you are and what makes you unique in ten to twelve sentences. You may want to include elements of diversity found in Table 11.2, and you'll likely want to describe the customs, traditions, rituals, food, clothing, and other characteristics that embody your cultural background. You could even talk about values, beliefs, experiences, or accomplishments that are unique to you. Feel free to be creative as you describe yourself; for example, if you could bring in an item or two that speaks to your identity (anything from a photograph to a food dish), what would you bring? You can describe this in your journal.

Once you've completed the first part of the assignment, reflect on your experience by answering these questions:

- What was it like for you to think about and write about your identity?

- What aspects of your identity are probably known by others? What positive or negative reactions have you had to these aspects of your identity?

- What aspects of your identity do others know only if you choose to share with them? What positive or negative reactions have you had to these aspects of your identity?

- How has thinking about your own identity changed the way you think about interacting with those who are different from you?

Adopting a Success Attitude

BUILDING EMOTIONAL INTELLIGENCE

Everyone is entitled to feelings — good, bad, or ugly. When we have negative feelings, it's important to recognize them, try to understand them, and respond to them in healthy ways. This exercise will help you reflect on negative feelings you've had and how you reacted. If you find that your reaction had negative consequences, you can think about how you'll handle things differently in the future.

From the following list of feeling words, choose five emotions that you experienced in the last week. Then, on a separate piece of paper, respond to the questions below for each emotion you've identified. An example is provided.

Feeling Words

irritated	aggressive	resentful	provoked	disappointed	helpless
embarrassed	shy	distrustful	pessimistic	discouraged	lonely
sorrowful	crushed	offended	anxious	preoccupied	fearful

What emotion did you experience?	Embarrassed
What caused this emotion?	I answered a question incorrectly in class.
How did you respond?	I left class early and skipped the next class.
What was the consequence?	I missed a quiz and was given 0 points.
If appropriate, provide an alternate response	If this happens again, I'll tell myself it's okay to be wrong and will remain in class to seek the right answers.

Applying Your Skills

COMMUNICATING ASSERTIVELY

Respond to the following scenarios by using an "I" statement to convey your feelings, the situation's impact on you, and your interest in arriving at a solution to the problem.

1. You're working on a group project for class. You show up at the second group meeting with your part of the project complete. No one else has done any work yet. You feel angry and disappointed.

   "I" message: _____

2. You like to bring your lunch to work, but the office refrigerator is disgusting! It's full of forgotten leftovers and rotten fruit. You decide to say something to your coworkers.

   "I" message: _____

3. You have a big test tomorrow and need to study. No one else in the house seems to care. The television is blaring, the phone keeps ringing, someone's blasting a stereo, and the dog is scratching at the door to go outside.

"I" message: _____

College Success = Career Success

WRITING PROFESSIONAL E-MAILS

Effective e-mail communication is important both in college and in the workplace. The best e-mails are brief and focused and have an informative subject line that helps the receiver quickly determine your e-mail's purpose and whether your message needs immediate attention. Rewrite the following e-mail messages to ensure that they convey the most important information. If necessary, edit to make the tone more professional, the subject line more informative, and the message more efficient.

> To: Instructor
> From: Student
> Re: Class
>
> How's it going? I'm thinking I'm going to be late to class tomorrow night. We have a sales meeting at work tomorrow at 3 p.m. which will probably go until 4 p.m. My boss is a talker, so maybe even later. Since my car died, I've been taking the bus. I'll have to look at the schedule to tell you when I'll be able to get to class. Maybe around 4:45 or 5:00 if I don't miss the bus. Be sure to let me know if you talk about anything important before I arrive. See you then!

> To: Boss
> From: Employee
> Re: Important — Impending Vacation
>
> I remember you saying we should check with you to schedule our vacation. I am thinking about going somewhere warm this year — maybe Florida or Arizona. If I go to Florida, I might drive. If I go to Arizona, I might fly there. Either way, I would like to go sometime in the next six months — maybe in late February when it is still cold. Maybe I could take the last week of February? If not, the second to last week of February would be good too. Let me know what you think so I can begin to plan my vacation. Thanks!

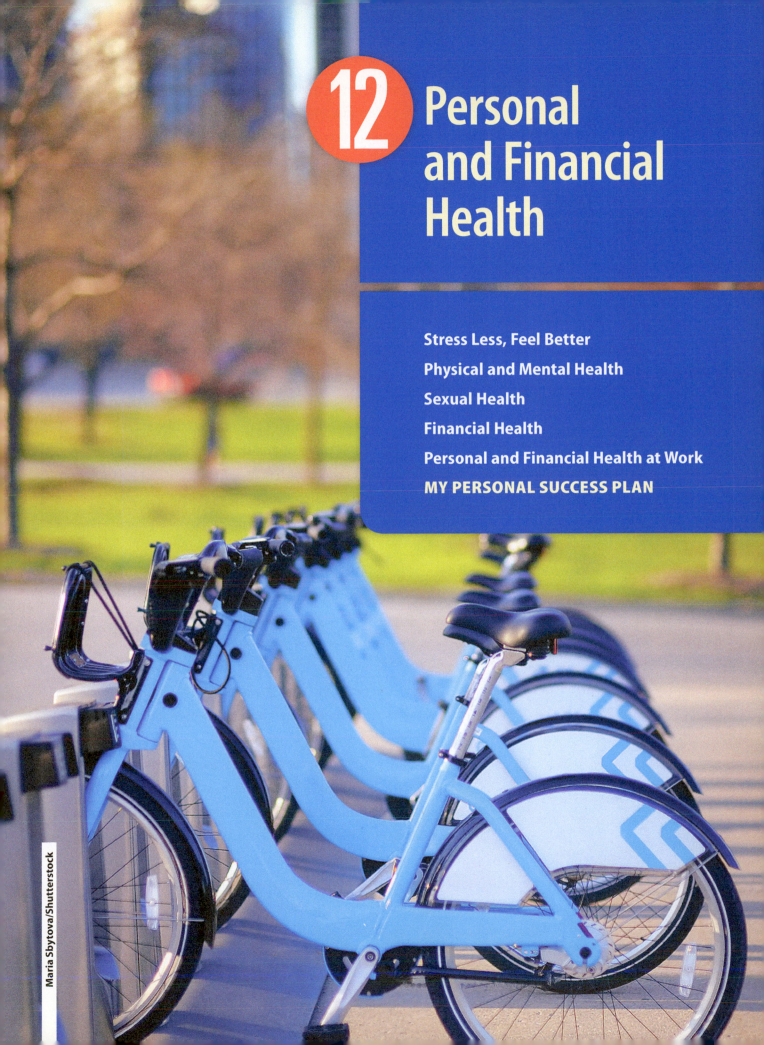

12 Personal and Financial Health

Stress Less, Feel Better

Physical and Mental Health

Sexual Health

Financial Health

Personal and Financial Health at Work

MY PERSONAL SUCCESS PLAN

Close your eyes, and create a mental image of what stress feels like to you. Perhaps you're picturing a 20-pound weight in your backpack, and you can almost feel it pulling on your shoulder straps. Maybe you're imagining an itchy sweater that's three sizes too small, a metal vise squeezing your head, or a dark storm cloud following you around, ready to dump rain on you at any moment. Is your image as awful as any of these? Not as bad? Worse?

Now think about the relationship between feelings of stress and your personal and financial health. If you're like many people, there's a clear connection between how stressed you are and how good you feel — and even between how stressed you are and how well you manage your money. For example, if you're anxious about presenting in class, your blood pressure might rise and you might lose sleep. And high stress levels might prompt you to engage in a little "retail therapy" and splurge on things you don't need (or can't afford) in an effort to distract yourself from your troubles.

Conversely, your personal and financial health choices can affect how stressed you feel. For instance, if you don't get enough sleep, eat nothing but French fries every day, and never exercise, you'll probably experience stress in the form of exhaustion and anxiety. If you don't manage your money carefully, you may run out of funds for everyday expenses, further ratcheting up your stress levels.

The good news about this connection is that if you make the right decisions about your personal and financial health, you can control your stress levels — and this chapter shows you how. First, we examine stress in more detail. Then we explore key aspects of your physical well-being and mental health and consider ways to manage both. Next, we present strategies for maintaining sexual health and explore how to enhance your financial health through budgeting, understanding financial aid, and managing credit. Finally, we look at how strengthening your personal and financial health can benefit you in the workplace.

ACES Reflection:
Personal and Financial Health

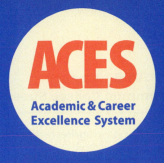

ACES
Academic & Career
Excellence System

Take a moment to reflect on your Personal and Financial Health score on ACES. Find your score and add it in the box to the right.

This score measures your beliefs about how healthy you are physically, mentally, and financially. Do you think it's an accurate snapshot of how you feel in this area? Why or why not?

■ **IF YOU SCORED IN THE HIGH RANGE** and believe this score is accurate, then staying healthy and financially stable may be one of your strengths. Excellent! But remember: You can always work to improve strengths. For instance, if you're already getting enough exercise, explore how you could also improve your diet. Or if you've built an effective budget, identify ways you could reduce your spending to free up funds for tuition and other important expenses.

■ **IF YOU SCORED IN THE MODERATE OR LOW RANGE**, use the suggestions in this chapter to better manage your health and to stay on track financially. Once you identify and implement strategies that work for you, you'll feel better physically and mentally, as well as more fiscally secure.

My ACES Score ....
- ☐ **High**
- ☐ **Moderate**
- ☐ **Low**

To find your **Personal and Financial Health score**, go to the LaunchPad for *Connections*, Second Edition.

LaunchPad
macmillan learning

ACES + ACTION

ACES paired with action is what leads to positive change. Now that you've reflected on your ACES results, how will you *use* what you learned about yourself to improve your personal or financial health? Try these concrete suggestions, or get inspired and create your own!

▶ **Find a friend.** Invite a friend to go with you to the health center to exercise. If you've never been there before, ask someone who goes there regularly to show you the ropes. Exercise is easier to do consistently when you have a partner.

▶ **Compare notes.** Talk with two or three peers about creative ways they've saved money since they got to college. In return, share one way that you've cut expenses. Then try out two of the ideas you get from your friends; how did they work for you?

▶ **Try an app.** Look for an app or online tool to help you budget and track your spending. Try out one tool for a month and see how it helps you manage your money.

Stress Less, Feel Better

Why is stress such a major factor in our lives? To answer this question, let's explore how stress works and how it affects us. When you feel stress, your body releases stress hormones, such as cortisol and adrenaline.[1] Such hormones can speed up your heart rate and breathing. In addition, your muscles tense up, and your body readies itself for a fight-or-flight response—a primitive reaction in which you either combat the danger facing you or run away from it.

FIGURE 12.1
Common College Stressors

____ Starting/Restarting College

____ Significant Change in Income

____ Disruption to Sleeping Pattern

____ Illness

____ Major Paper/Assignment/Exam

____ Start/End of a Dating Relationship

____ Problems with Family Members

____ Choosing a Major

____ Job Change

____ Making a Presentation in Class

____ Balancing School, Work, and Family

____ Other Stressors: _____

The fight-or-flight response was useful long ago in our evolutionary history. If a lion chased you, a surge of adrenaline would give you the strength to whack the animal over the head with a club or run away. Either move could boost your chances of survival. Today, many of us don't regularly face the kinds of perils that call for a fight-or-flight response. However, if we keep *experiencing* that response, we get bombarded with the resulting physical changes, which can lead to health problems such as anxiety, ulcers, fatigue, weight gain, and depression.[2]

How can you avoid these problems? Start by understanding your own personal stressors, which are events and situations that tend to freak you out. To get a better sense of your stressors, look at the list of some common college stressors in Figure 12.1 and check off any items you experienced during the last year. Note that any event that intensifies your emotions and physical reactions—whether distressing or joyous—can be a stressor. For example, you can feel stress when you end a relationship or when you start a new one.

The good news is that you *can* manage stressors, and the most potent strategies for doing so involve keeping your mind and body healthy and your finances under control. We'll look at these strategies in more detail now, beginning with two vital components of personal health: your physical and mental well-being.

Physical and Mental Health

Feeling unwell (either physically or mentally) can hurt your academic performance by making it hard to go to class, pay attention, study, and get your assignments done. If you do whatever you can to maintain your well-being—including eating right, staying active, and getting enough sleep—you'll be way ahead of the game. Let's explore strategies for staying healthy and feeling good.

Eat Right

Have you ever come home after a stressful day and gobbled up a pint of ice cream or a giant bag of potato chips—only to realize that you felt just as stressed, and maybe a bit ill, once all the goodies were gone? Guess what: What and how much you eat has a big impact on your health (in the short *and* long term), your energy level, and even your mood.

That said, always eating healthy isn't easy in college. If you're juggling family responsibilities, a job, and coursework, you're probably on the go from morning until night. Finding time to prepare nutritious meals may seem impossible. And if you live on campus, you may have access to dining halls and food trucks that offer an array of fast foods with high amounts of fat, salt, and sugar.

Let's consider some ideas for navigating these environments and discuss the consequences of eating too much—or too little.

Master Healthy Eating. When you make healthy dietary choices, you give your body the sustenance and energy it needs for you to function effectively. To learn about healthy eating, visit the U.S. Department of Agriculture's MyPlate program at **www.choosemyplate.gov**. An updated version of the food pyramid, MyPlate

offers guidelines on issues such as what proportions of the different food groups should be included in every meal and how to eat healthy on a budget. There's even MyPlate On Campus, which spotlights strategies students can use to adopt a healthy lifestyle.

In addition, take advantage of other information sources to learn about healthy eating. For example, read the nutrition facts on foods you buy and ask dining services on campus for information about the calories, fat, sodium, and sugar in the available meal choices. The more you know, the better choices you can make about which foods to pick and which to skip.

Finally, try these strategies for selecting foods that deliver a powerful, healthy-eating punch:

- Start your day with a light, nutritious breakfast, such as fruit and yogurt, instead of calorie-laden breads and meats. This kind of breakfast energizes you, kick-starts your metabolism, and helps you concentrate.

- Keep healthy snacks in handy places, such as your backpack, car, and refrigerator or pantry at home.

- Eat more fruits and vegetables. If you change from fewer than three servings a day to more than five servings, you can cut your risk of heart disease by 17 percent![4]

- Stay away from processed foods and beverages. They have a lot of preservatives, sugar, and fat.

- Avoid supersized meals. Instead, take a smaller plate and say "no" when someone offers a larger portion. These easy steps will reduce your calorie intake.[5]

- Carry a water bottle with you, and keep drinking from and refilling it. You'll stay hydrated—essential for feeling well both physically and mentally.

Get Help for Eating Disorders. People often use healthy eating strategies as part of a plan to lose weight or maintain a certain weight. Managing your weight can be a good thing if you do so in a balanced, careful way. But if weight

The Five-Minute Workout.
You don't have to be an elite
long-distance runner to get the
benefits of this form of exercise. In a 2014 study published
in the *Journal of the American
College of Cardiology*, researchers
concluded that running just 5
minutes each day can add years
to your life.[9] That's a lot of bang
for your jogging buck! Cultura RM
Exclusive/Edwin Jimenez/Getty Images

**♦ CONNECT
TO MY CLASSES**
Have you set up a sleep
schedule that supports
your course schedule? For
example, do you go to bed
earlier the night before your
early-morning classes? Write
down the ideal sleep schedule
for your current classes.
Compare this to your current
sleep schedule. What's one
change you can make to
better align these schedules?

loss becomes your main focus in life and you start to
engage in dangerous eating behaviors, you risk serious
health problems. Severely restricting food intake and
having an irrational fear of gaining weight are symptoms of *anorexia nervosa*. Engaging in binge eating followed by intentional purging (vomiting), obsessively
overexercising, and abusing diuretics are symptoms of
bulimia nervosa. These disorders can make you seriously
ill—and even kill you.[6] If you show symptoms of these
disorders, or you know someone who does, support is
available: Seek help now at your campus's health and
counseling centers.

Stay Active

Get more exercise! We've all heard this before, and
there's a good reason why: Exercise helps build muscle strength and improves cardiovascular fitness. It's
also a great way to manage the stress of being a college student.[7]

Every week, try to get at least 150 minutes of moderate exercise or 75 minutes of vigorous exercise.[8] If you
have difficulty following an exercise routine or if you
hate gyms, build an exercise schedule that works for
you. For instance, break the 150 minutes into 30 minutes
of exercise, five days a week. Or do a 45-minute workout
two days a week and squeeze in several 10- to 15-minute
walks to get the additional hour.

You can also take advantage of everyday tasks and events to get more exercise.

- If you have a car, park some distance away from class, your job, or the gro-
  cery store, and walk to your destination.
- Take stairs instead of elevators.
- During study breaks, take a walk around the library or do jumping jacks in
  your room.
- Sign up for a fitness class at the recreation center.
- Ask a friend to work out with you. Having company can keep you motivated.
- Join an intramural sports team.

Don't Skimp on the Z's

Do you often stay up until 1:00 a.m. playing video games, scrolling through your
Facebook news feed, or texting friends? Do you frequently stay up late studying or
doing laundry after putting your kids to bed? Getting enough sleep affects our ability to function each day;[10] when we're overtired, dealing with stress is much more
difficult. If you usually get less than seven to eight hours of good-quality sleep each
night, you're probably exhausted. To get enough Z's and feel your best each day, try
these strategies:

- Avoid late-night cramming. Organize your time so that you can get a full
  night's sleep before exams and can finish assignments on time.
- Stay away from caffeinated or energy drinks in the late afternoon or evening.

> ## Exercise has made a world of difference to me this semester.

NAME
Mathew Schneider

SCHOOL
University of Texas at Arlington

MAJOR
Biology

CAREER GOAL
Physician Assistant

STAYING HEALTHY AND COPING WITH STRESS

In my second year of college, I was struggling to balance my schoolwork, family life, and work. I also felt alone at school—I'm forty-three years old and almost retired from the military, so I felt different from this young crowd I now call my classmates. This was stressful. When I'm stressed, I find it difficult to accomplish things, I feel irritable, and I lose my appetite. Sleep becomes a huge issue for me; at night I'll just toss and turn and get rings under my eyes from not sleeping.

This semester, I was determined to change my sleep habits. In my Human Physiology class, I learned that sedentary activities, such as just going to class and studying, reduce energy levels and metabolism rates. When I found this out, I developed a goal of living healthier. This is an ongoing battle, but I've found that exercise helps me sleep better. It has also built up my energy level and helped me cut back from a pot of coffee a day to two cups (never after 6:00 p.m.). I've gone from restless sleep, which gave me no energy for the day, to quality sleep after exercise, which helped me feel fully functional and energized. Exercise has made a world of difference to me this semester.

In order to get control of my stress, it has also helped to get support. My wife has been supportive when I feel stressed out. When my stress is school-related, my classmates, study groups, and student organizations have been the most comforting. I created a support group where I made friends and improved my grades. This tool helps me handle even my hardest and most stressful classes. I'm well known in the biology department as the study-group king, and I've found that so many others have been helped by this group as well.

YOUR TURN To what degree do you identify with Mathew's experiences with exercise and with getting support for managing stress? For example, what role does exercise play in your life as a college student? Whom do you turn to for moral support when you're feeling overwhelmed?

- Get enough exercise, particularly earlier in the day.
- Don't nap during the day; napping only makes it harder to fall asleep once you're in bed for the night.
- Establish a regular sleep schedule—then stick with it.
- If you have trouble falling asleep, try relaxation techniques such as deep breathing, tensing and releasing muscles throughout your body, or envisioning peaceful scenes.

CONNECT
TO MY RESOURCES

Many campuses have mental-health services, such as counseling centers, that can help students manage a wide range of challenges. Even if your school doesn't have a fully staffed counseling center, it can still refer you to the appropriate health care professionals. Find out what mental-health services are available on campus, and record their contact information.

Take Care of Your Mental Health

Taking care of your mental health is just as important as nurturing your physical health. If you're feeling down or worried, just going to class or reading a textbook chapter might seem as impossible as climbing Mount Everest. Depression, anxiety, eating disorders, substance abuse, and other mental-health issues are all too common among college students.[11] The good news, however, is that you *can* get better if you experience these challenges, and there are people who can help.

In this section we look at anxiety and depression, two of the most common mental-health problems affecting college students.

Anxiety. If you experience excessive worry, dread, or fear, you may have anxiety. For some people anxiety is a general, all-encompassing sensation. For others it's more specific; for instance, they might feel anxious in social settings or while taking tests. Anxiety can also express itself as panic attacks, during which your heart starts racing in your chest for no apparent reason, you can't catch your breath, and you feel as though you're having a heart attack. If you suffer from anxiety that's far beyond everyday worry, reach out for help. The counseling center, an adviser, a clergy member, or another person you trust can connect you with the resources you need, on or off campus.

Depression. Depression is common among college students, particularly since adjusting to college can result in feelings of loneliness, loss of previous friendships, or discomfort in being in a new environment. Left untreated, depression can affect your appetite, causing you to lose or gain weight; keep you awake at night or make

Many Ways to Reach Out. If you're experiencing feelings of anxiety or depression, you're not alone: Help is available. Your college may have counselors on staff or provide referrals to community groups. In addition, organizations like the National Institute of Mental Health have a presence on campuses across the country, which serves as another way to connect students with the help they need. Megan Farmer/ Omaha World-Herald via AP

it hard to get out of bed in the morning; and leave you feeling listless, with little interest in activities you used to enjoy.

Depression can range from very mild (feeling down a couple of days a month) to severe (feeling suicidal). If you experience symptoms of depression that last for more than two weeks or that make it hard for you to get through the day, or if you have experienced depression in the past and experience its symptoms again—including thoughts of hurting yourself—get help immediately. To manage feelings of depression, reach out to others who can help you: a clergy member, friends, family, or a therapist.

To get help, call, e-mail, or simply walk into a counseling service on campus or in your community, express that you have concerns and would like to talk with someone, and arrange to have a confidential conversation with a mental health professional. Your first session will probably involve the counselor asking you questions such as "What brought you here today?" "How long have you been experiencing this concern?" and "Have you been to a counselor before?" The counselor and you can then create a plan for what you'll work on together and how often you'll meet. These sessions are an opportunity for you to explain what you're experiencing in more detail and work with the counselor to find new and effective strategies to improve your mental health. Remember: You *don't* have to go it alone.

Prevent Substance Abuse

One of the most important things you can do to stay healthy—and stay safe—at college is to limit your consumption of alcohol and drugs. Alcohol and drug abuse are serious health problems on many college campuses. Why do students use drugs and alcohol? Some do so because they think it will help them manage stress. Others think that it's an expected part of being a college student and that "everyone's doing it." (Actually, many college students *overestimate* the amount of binge drinking that goes on at their school, so the assumption that "everyone's doing it" is wrong.[12])

At worst, abusing alcohol and drugs can lead to addiction and cause health problems (such as liver damage) and death from overdose. At best, it costs you money you could spend on other, more useful things. The healthy choice? Avoid illegal substances altogether; if you choose to use legal substances, adopt an "everything in moderation" mindset. In addition, follow these rules to protect your physical safety—as well as your professional reputation:

- When you go out with friends, designate a responsible member of the group to stay sober and make sure that everyone gets home safely at the end of the night.

- Remember why you're in college and your goals for the future. You'll be less likely to let your partying get out of hand.

- Don't post photos online of yourself drinking or taking drugs. Potential employers may find them and pass you over for a job.

- If your use of alcohol or drugs prevents you from attending or doing well in your classes, if you feel that you can't control it, or if important people in your life express concerns about it, you may have an addiction problem. Seek out confidential help at the counseling center.

Practice Self-Care

The key theme underlying all the tips in this chapter is that taking care of yourself and your health is important. In keeping with this theme, our final suggestion of the section is to practice *self-care*. Self-care involves using your metacognitive skills to monitor how you feel—both emotionally and physically—and take specific steps to give yourself a boost if you're down, exhausted, or overwhelmed. Self-care isn't meant as a substitute for professional help, but it can be an important part of staying healthy.

Take a look at the list of self-care suggestions below and consider which options you might use to stay centered and engaged in college. Many of these strategies are most effective when you apply your metacognition during and after the activity: Pay attention to your thoughts and feelings as you act, and then evaluate how you feel right after the activity and again later in the day. For additional ideas or for help with any of these strategies, look online, ask your friends, or check out the recreation center at your college.

- Meditate for 10 minutes when you get up in the morning or before you go to bed at night.
- Take a yoga class.
- Journal for 15 minutes each day.
- Practice deep breathing.
- Turn off social media for an hour.
- Learn a new mindfulness activity.
- Get a cup of coffee with a friend or on your own.
- Sit in the sun for 15 minutes.
- Volunteer at the local animal shelter or spend time with a friend's pet.
- Write a self-affirmation (something positive about yourself), and post it where you can see it each day.

Creative Self-Care. On the lookout for a promising new self-care activity? Consider giving "goat yoga" a try. These classes are popping up across the country as a way to exercise, be mindful, and make friends with miniature goats, all at the same time. What's not to love? J. Kyle Keener/The Pharos-Tribune via AP

Sexual Health

For students who choose to be sexually active, practicing safe sex helps minimize stress and promotes overall health. Reducing your risk of sexually transmitted infections and using effective birth control if you're not ready to start a family are two ways to take control of your sex life and adopt healthy sexual behavior.

Avoid Sexually Transmitted Infections

There are many types of **sexually transmitted infections (STIs)**, which are illnesses spread through the exchange of bodily fluids during sexual activity. These include human papillomavirus (HPV) (an estimated 14 million new cases per year), chlamydia (over 1.5 million new cases), genital herpes (over 750,000 new cases), and HIV/AIDS (more than 37,000 new cases per year).[13] If you're sexually active, it's important to be well-informed and to take steps to reduce your risk. For example:

- Have sex with only one partner at a time—a person you know well.
- Always use condoms.
- Get tested for STIs regularly, even if you don't have any symptoms. You can pass an STI to someone else without even knowing you have one.
- Have your partner get tested regularly.

Issues of sexual health are very personal, but if you have any questions or concerns about STIs, talk with someone you trust who can advise and support you—for example, a counselor, a clergy member, your physician, or a mentor. This person can connect you with the information you need to stay safe and healthy.

sexually transmitted infections (STIs): Illnesses, some treatable and some incurable, that are spread through the exchange of bodily fluids during sexual activity.

Practice Birth Control

If you're a woman having sex with a man and you don't want to start a family now, practicing birth control can give you peace of mind and prevent the stress that can come with an unplanned pregnancy. If you're a man having sex with a woman, using a birth control method designed for men is a good idea, especially if you're not certain that your partner is using birth control. There are many birth control options. Some require prescriptions; others are sold over the counter; still others involve behavior choices. Most don't protect against STIs. Physicians can share information about each method's risks and benefits, which can help you choose what's right for you.

- Birth control pill: a pill a woman takes orally at the same time each day.
- Patch: a skin patch a woman wears. She applies a new patch each week for three weeks and wears no patch during the fourth week, when she should get her menstrual period.
- Intrauterine device (IUD): a small device inserted in a woman's uterus by a health care provider. Some IUDs can be used for up to ten years.
- Vaginal ring: a small ring inserted in a woman's vagina for three weeks and removed during the fourth week, when she should get her menstrual period.
- The shot: an injection of pregnancy-preventing hormones that lasts for three months.
- Condoms: sheaths that are worn over the penis or inserted into the vagina.
- Abstinence: choosing not to engage in sexual intercourse.[14]

Financial Health

If you're like most students, one big reason you're in college is to graduate, get a job, and make enough money to pay your bills and plan for the future. When you earn a college degree, you make a tremendous investment in yourself and your future financial health. As Figure 12.2 shows, people with an associate's degree earn, on average, $127 more per week than those with only a high school diploma, and those with a bachelor's degree earn $464 more per week. That translates into roughly $6,600 to $24,000 of additional income each year for the rest of your life, depending on the degree you get. Imagine what you and your family could do with that added income! Plus, as Figure 12.2 also shows, people with a degree are less likely to be unemployed.

As important as it is to your financial future to get a degree, you will likely face at least a few financial challenges while you work toward your goals. In fact, in one recent survey, seven out of ten Americans identified money as a significant stressor in their lives,[15] while in another, almost 60 percent of the college students surveyed worried about paying for school.[16] As a college student, you may be worrying right now about how you'll pay next term's tuition, pay for child care next week, or whittle down your student loan and credit card debt. But if these and other financial worries keep you up at night, you *can* take steps to take control of your finances—starting with creating a budget.

Create a Budget

budget: A plan that documents income and expenses for a specific period of time.

A **budget** is a critical survival tool for your financial health. It is your financial plan: It documents your income and expenses over specific time periods (such as a week, month, or year). Creating and sticking to a budget lets you take control of your money, live within your means, and achieve your financial goals. To create a budget, follow these steps.

FIGURE 12.2

Earnings and Unemployment Rates by Educational Attainment, 2016

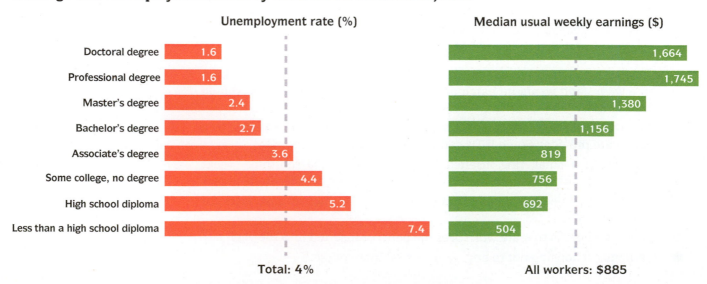

	Unemployment rate (%)	Median usual weekly earnings ($)
Doctoral degree	1.6	1,664
Professional degree	1.6	1,745
Master's degree	2.4	1,380
Bachelor's degree	2.7	1,156
Associate's degree	3.6	819
Some college, no degree	4.4	756
High school diploma	5.2	692
Less than a high school diploma	7.4	504
	Total: 4%	All workers: $885

Note: Data are for persons age twenty-five and over. Earnings are for full-time wage and salary workers.

Information from Current Population Survey, U.S. Bureau of Labor Statistics, U.S. Department of Labor, http://www.bls.gov/emp/ep_chart_001.htm.

Step 1: Gather Information. For one month, collect your bank statements, loan and scholarship information, pay stubs, and any regular bills. Track *all* of your spending over the course of the month, and keep all of your receipts in one place, such as a desk drawer. If you spend $2 on a cup of coffee and don't get a receipt, jot down "$2 coffee" and the date on a piece of paper and save it. You'll need all this information to build your budget.

Step 2: Record Your Income and Expenses. Using a form or spreadsheet like the one in Figure 12.3, enter into the "Last Month" column all the income and expense information you gathered for the previous month (in step 1). Then subtract your total expenses from your total income to obtain your balance for the past month. If your income was greater than your expenses (a financially healthy situation), your balance will be positive. If you spent more than you made (a financially unhealthy situation), your balance will be negative. Once you see where your money's coming from—and, more importantly, where it's going and if you're spending more than you make—you can decide whether you need to manage your money more effectively.

Step 3: Use Your Insights to Make Changes. If you discover that you aren't managing your money as effectively as you'd like, you can create a new budget reflecting the changes you need to make. For example, you might take a part-time job to earn more, or cut back on unnecessary spending. Return to your budget, and record your expected income and expenses in the "Next Month" column.

Step 4: Track Your Results and Refine Your Budget Further. At the end of the next month, see how closely your actual income and expenses match what you budgeted for the month. Use any differences to further tweak your budget to bring your actual earning and spending in line with your goals. The sections that follow provide ideas you can try.

❥ **CONNECT**
TO MY EXPERIENCES

When you were growing up, how did your family manage the household's income? Was there a budget for monthly income and expenses? If so, how useful was the budget? If not, what were the consequences? Write one page about what your early experiences taught you about budgeting.

FIGURE 12.3

Recording Your Income and Expenses

	Budget Worksheet	Last Month	Next Month
3	**Income**		
4	Scholarships		
5	Work		
6	Support from family		
7	Loans		
8	Savings		
9	Other		
10	**Total Income**		
11			
12	**Expenses**		
13	Tuition		
14	Books/supplies		
15	Housing		
16	Utilities		
17	Electricity		
18	Internet		
19	Cable		
20	Food		
21	Meal plan		
22	Groceries		
23	Dining out		
24	Phone		
25	Car payment		
26	Child care		
27	Debt payments		
28	Entertainment		
29	Other		
30	**Total Expenses**		
31	Total Income:		
32	– Total Expenses:		
33			
34	Balance:		

Reduce Your Spending

If you usually spend more than you make or you just want to save some money, try reducing your spending. You may find some easy ways to do this. For example, if Callista wants to cut her spending by $100 a month, she can brew her own coffee each morning instead of buying coffee on the road, and she can eliminate one night out each week. Other solutions may require more sacrifice. If Callista's goal is to graduate with less than $5,000 in debt, she may have to take fewer classes per term so that she can work more hours and pay more tuition up-front.

To make it easier to reduce your spending, distinguish between your must-haves (needs) and nice-to-haves (wants). For instance, Jerome *needs* a car to get from work to class, but he *wants* to keep his new SUV, which comes with a monthly payment he can barely afford. As tempting as it is to keep that SUV, Jerome could boost his financial health by trading it in for a car that doesn't break his budget.

Being honest with yourself about your needs and wants and cutting your expenses can be hard, but here are some ideas that can help:

- If you live on campus, change to a less expensive meal plan. If you live off campus, shop smart by using coupons and buying products on sale.

- Drop your cable plan.

- Find a cheaper Internet service.

- Explore housing options. Is it cheaper to live on campus? Would you save money by selling your house and renting? Can you find a roommate to share expenses?

- Cancel your gym membership and use campus facilities or exercise outdoors.

- Go an extra two weeks between haircuts.

- Explore options at your school for taking more classes each term. Full-time students can often take one or two more classes each term without paying more, which adds up to substantial savings. But take care that you don't get overloaded: Talk with your adviser and family about how to make this work.

Get a Job to Boost Your Income

Working is a fact of life for most college students. According to the National Center for Education Statistics, 43 percent of full-time students and 78 percent of part-time students work while attending college.[17] Working has important advantages. You make money, gain valuable experience, build your skills, apply what you're learning in class to the real world, and build your résumé.

However, there are potential risks associated with working, and it's good to be mindful of these as you schedule your time. Students who work more than fifteen hours a week and those who work off campus are more likely to have lower grades and leave school before graduating.[18] If you have a stressful job and work long hours, you might also have trouble putting enough time into your studies.

If you're balancing work and school effectively now, continue taking good care of yourself so that you don't get overwhelmed. If doing both is becoming problematic, consider taking fewer classes or getting more financial aid. You can talk about possible solutions with an adviser, your family, and your school's financial aid office.

spotlight on research

Do you sometimes make poor decisions about your money? Do you occasionally splurge on things you don't need or use your credit card when you probably shouldn't? If this sounds like you, don't lose hope: instead, head straight to your college's financial aid office for a money management workshop.

In one study, a group of researchers examined how a brief workshop on positive financial habits impacted college students' thoughts about their financial choices. Students participated in a 90-minute seminar on budgets, tracking spending, saving, and credit, and they completed a pre- and post-test survey of their positive and negative financial choices. When they analyzed the results, the researchers found a statistically significant change in students' behavior before the workshop compared to what they planned to do afterward, including:

▶ An increase in planned healthy behaviors like creating a budget.
▶ A decrease in planned risky behavior such as taking out a cash advance on their credit card.

THE BOTTOM LINE

Knowledge of good financial practices can help you make better decisions about saving and spending. Seek out resources like money management and financial aid workshops to keep yourself informed and aware.

Money Matters:

Get Informed about Finances

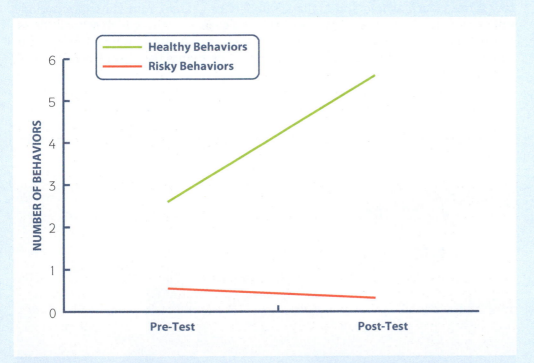

After taking a brief financial workshop, students planned to engage in fewer risky behaviors and more healthy behaviors related to money management.

Information from L. M. Borden, S. Lee, J. Serido, and D. Collins, "Changing College Students' Financial Knowledge, Attitudes, and Behavior through Seminar Participation," *Journal of Family and Economic Issues* 29 (2008): 23–40.

Navigate Financial Aid

It's no secret that college is expensive and that financial aid is a lifesaver for students who couldn't otherwise afford to go. According to the U.S. Department of Education, 86 percent of full-time students at four-year schools and 79 percent of full-time students at two-year schools receive financial aid,[19] in forms such as public or private loans, grants, scholarships, or work-study programs.

Many sources of aid are available, but learning about and applying for aid can be stressful. A good place to start is with the basics: how to apply for aid, what types of aid exist, and how to keep your aid once you receive it.

FAFSA. If you're currently receiving financial aid, then you've already completed a form called the Free Application for Federal Student Aid (FAFSA). If you haven't yet applied for financial aid, start with the FAFSA. This tool assesses your (or your family's) financial situation and calculates how much the federal government believes you can afford to pay for college, which determines how much aid you qualify for. To learn more about the FAFSA, go to **www.fafsa.ed.gov** or visit your college's financial aid office.

Grants. One common type of financial aid is a *grant*, which is money provided by the government or your college that you're not expected to repay. The federal government gives grants based on financial need (such as Pell Grants) as well as military service (such as Iraq and Afghanistan Service Grants). Your state government might provide grants to in-state residents who earned a strong high school GPA or those who graduated in the top half of their class and attend a two- or four-year college in the state. Your college may also provide grants based on financial need or past accomplishments.

Scholarships. As with grants, you don't have to repay scholarships. Scholarships come from different sources and are awarded for different reasons, such as financial need, talents or accomplishments, membership in a cultural or religious group,

Dialogue for Dollars.
Navigating the complex world of financial aid is challenging, so talk with someone in your college's financial aid office. Ask questions about what types of aid are available, how to apply for aid, and how to keep it. One meeting with a financial aid officer could make a world of difference for your academic and financial future. Hero Images/Getty Images

or a student's area of study (e.g., education or health science). Your high school or college may award scholarships, or you can earn them through your community, private organizations or businesses, and sometimes even your employer. Web-based services can help you find scholarships, but be sure to start with secure sites that don't charge a fee. You can also get started by completing a scholarship search activity at the end of the chapter.

Student Loans. Many students take out loans to help pay for college, but it's crucial to understand the pros and cons of borrowing that money before you accept the terms of a loan. Some students simply sign up for the maximum loan they can get, without considering whether they'll be able to repay the money when they graduate. Before you sign on the dotted line, take the following steps to be certain that you understand, and can meet, your obligations:

1. **Know your options.** First and foremost, you'll want to research the types of loans that are available to you. Common loans available to students include the following:

   ■ **Direct subsidized loans.** The federal government provides these loans. They usually have a lower interest rate than other types of loans, and interest doesn't *accrue* (get added to the loan) while you're in school. Students qualify for these loans based on financial need.

   ■ **Direct unsubsidized loans.** These government-provided loans tend to have higher interest rates than subsidized loans, and interest accrues while you're in school. All college students are eligible for unsubsidized loans, regardless of financial need.

   ■ **Direct PLUS loans.** PLUS is a federal loan program that lets parents borrow money for the college expenses of a dependent student. PLUS loans have a higher interest rate and charge more fees than other federal loans.

   ■ **Private loans.** These loans are issued by institutions such as banks, credit unions, or colleges. Compared to federal loans, they often have higher interest rates and fewer repayment options.

2. **Talk with an adviser.** Make sure to speak with an adviser about course options and credit hours. For example, you'll want to confirm that you're taking all the courses you need to graduate on time. Spending an extra year, or even an extra term, in college may mean more loans, which means more money that you have to pay back. In addition, talk with your adviser about the number of credit hours you can and should be taking. As noted earlier in the chapter, many colleges allow students to take fifteen or eighteen credits (five or six classes) before paying an overload fee. If you can take more credits for the same amount of money, you'll maximize your loan and tuition dollars. At the same time, give this option some serious thought: Taking five or six classes is a lot of work and may not be your best option for academic success.

3. **Avoid surprises: Know what you'll owe.** Whenever you take out a loan, you have to pay back the money you borrow, along with interest. To prepare yourself, calculate how much your loan payments will be when you complete college, and consider your options for repayment. (For federal loans, you can find a repayment calculator and an array of information about repayment options at **https://studentaid.ed.gov** or by searching for "Federal Student Aid.") Often, the faster you pay off the loan, the less interest you'll end up paying in the long run, which can save you big bucks.

CONNECT TO MY RESOURCES

If you've taken out student loans, it's not too early to craft a strategy for repaying them. Visit the financial aid office and ask about (1) your expected total debt upon graduation, (2) the average debt of graduates at your school and the percentage of students who can't repay their loans, and (3) options for reducing your loans.

4. **Visit the career center.** Visit the career center to learn how much you can expect to earn if you graduate with your intended degree. Will your future income be enough that you can repay your loans and still afford to eat?

5. **Meet with a financial aid counselor at your college.** Set aside time to talk with a financial aid professional about any and all questions you have about your financial aid package. Consider taking someone with you to that meeting—ideally a trusted friend or family member who understands loans in college. This person can consult with you about what types of questions to ask and what your best course of action will be. Specific questions might include:

   ◾ What types of loans am I eligible for?

   ◾ When do I have to start paying back my loans?

   ◾ What is the interest rate for each of my loans?

   ◾ Is the interest deferred (meaning interest isn't added to the loan) while I'm in school?

   ◾ What will my monthly payment be when I have to start repaying my loans?

   ◾ If I spend an extra term or an extra year in college, how much larger will my loans be?

◗ **CONNECT**
TO MY CAREER

Are you currently working? If so, you can build valuable skills, even if your current job isn't in your future career field. List three skills you'll need in your future career, or a career that interests you, that you can develop in your current job. How will you build these skills?

Work-Study Programs. If you receive a work-study award, you can apply for an on-campus job that's been set aside for someone with financial need. Positions fill up quickly, and placement isn't guaranteed, so talk with someone in the financial aid office if you want to explore what's available. Sure, the work-study job you get may not be perfect or exciting—you may find yourself making copies or delivering mail. Still, every job offers learning opportunities, and some work-study jobs can even give you experience in your field of study. For instance, if you want to be a journalist, a work-study job that involves helping your journalism professor write a book could teach you a lot about your dream profession.

Keeping Your Financial Aid. After all the time and energy you put into applying for and securing financial aid, take the following steps to keep it—or even increase it.

◾ **Fulfill requirements.** Understand and fulfill all the requirements for keeping your financial aid. For example, if your GPA falls below a certain level or if you drop a class and become a part-time student (which colleges and funding sources define differently), you may lose your aid.

◾ **If your financial situation changes, see if you qualify for more aid.** For instance, if you or a primary wage earner in your family loses a job, talk with your school's financial aid office about what has changed and how that affects your aid eligibility.

◾ **Keep looking for aid.** You may qualify for different scholarships as you progress through college. For instance, a donor may have established a scholarship for junior and senior engineering students who want to go into public service. Regularly research emerging opportunities like these.

◾ **Apply for financial aid each year.** Be sure to complete the FAFSA and any other required applications on time so that you can keep your aid every year.

Control Your Credit Cards — So They Don't Control You

When you buy something with a credit card, you're taking out a short-term loan from the credit card company and promising that you'll pay for the purchase later. Like student loans, credit cards come with interest rates. You have to pay that interest if you don't pay off your credit card balance in full every month, and credit card interest rates can be shockingly high—as much as 20 percent or more.

To grasp how this high level of interest can affect your financial health, meet Jason. He has a $3,000 balance on his credit card, which charges 18 percent interest. If he makes only the minimum payment of $75 each month (and doesn't spend any more on the card), he'll end up paying more than $4,500 over five years!

If you have a credit card, look at one of your statements. Credit card companies are required to tell you how much you'll pay in the long run if you make only the minimum monthly payment on your balance. Once you start racking up big credit card debt, it's very hard to whittle it back down, so keep that number in the forefront of your mind. It could motivate you to whip out that "plastic" less often—and maybe even cut up your card and throw it away.

If you're going to use credit cards, try these tactics for keeping your debt under control:

The Smart Approach to Credit. It pays to keep an eye on your spending and limit how much you charge. If you overspend and you don't pay your credit card balance in full every month, the interest can start piling up, and you can get buried under a mound of debt. High credit card balances can also hurt your credit score, making it hard for you to take out loans in the future. Betsy Streeter/CartoonStock.com

- Use only one card. If you have several cards, pay off and close all except one.

- Pay off the entire amount every month— on time.

- Consider getting a debit card. This functions like a credit card when you make purchases, but it's tied to your checking account and withdraws money that you already have.

- Understand how credit cards and other debt can impact your *credit report*, which is a document that records information about your borrowing and repayment history over time. Each time you get a credit card or take out a loan, credit-reporting agencies Equifax, TransUnion, and Experian track how much you've borrowed, your credit card limit, and your history of making payments. By keeping low or zero balances on your cards and making your payments on time, you'll get a better rating on your report, which will make it easier to borrow money at competitive rates in the future.

- Because credit is so important, you'll want to be sure you check your credit report for errors. Each year, you can get a free copy of your credit report from each of credit-reporting agencies at **www.annualcreditreport.com**.

Personal and Financial Health at Work

Behaviors that nurture your personal and financial health at school will help you do the same at work. That certainly benefits you: When you're healthy and financially secure, you'll likely enjoy your job more. It's also a good thing for your employer: Organizations want healthy, financially stable employees, because these employees tend to be the happiest and most productive.[20] Consider these ideas for staying healthy at work—and reaping the rewards.

Boost Your Productivity

Eating smart, staying active, and managing stress (including financial pressures) can have a positive impact on your productivity at work. After all, when you feel well and in control, you can get more done. Here are some simple but powerful ideas you can use to stay healthy and boost your performance:

- **Brown-bag it.** Packing your lunch gives you complete control over your diet—and it's a lot cheaper than buying food at work.

- **Get moving.** If you have a sedentary job, make an effort to move around. Take the stairs rather than the elevator, or park your car far from the front door. Go for short, brisk walks during breaks. If your job involves a lot of repetitive motion, such as operating a piece of equipment over and over in the same way, occasionally flex your muscles and stretch to avoid getting tendinitis or repetitive-movement injuries.

- **Take breaks.** It's hard to stay productive at work without taking short breaks. Spend a few minutes throughout the day relaxing and taking deep breaths. Step outside for some fresh air. Or chat with a coworker for a few minutes while you're refilling your mug at the water cooler.

- **Manage your mental health.** If you're in a job that generates a great deal of emotional stress (such as social work or medicine), that stress can erode your productivity if you don't take steps to stay healthy. Take extra care to manage your mental health—talk with a therapist, practice relaxation techniques, or spend quality time with people who support you.

- **Use your company's wellness plan.** Many companies offer a wellness plan as part of their employee-benefits package. Wellness plans can include a variety of services, such as help with quitting smoking or a discounted gym membership. If you take advantage of these options, you might even get a break on your health insurance premiums.

Manage Work Budgets

The budgeting skills you use to manage your own money—and keep your finances solid while you're in school—can also come in handy in the working world. Employees in many jobs are expected to keep an eye on the "bottom line" and watch out for the financial health of their particular team, group, or organization.

For instance, suppose you own a small business. If you find creative ways to cut travel costs, you might free up funds you can channel into your marketing budget—and boost sales as a result. Or let's say you're a manager responsible for tracking your group's revenue and expenses. If your organization wants to boost profitability, you might scour your departmental budget, looking for places where your team can cut spending or increase revenue.

Escape the Sedentary Work Life. Sitting at a desk all day can lead to back and neck problems, as well as stress and anxiety from lack of exercise. One way to fight back is to try treadmilling at a stand-up desk. What are some other ways to get up and get moving during the workday?
AP Photo/Michael Conroy

> ## "Using stress-management techniques has been a crucial part of my success.

Courtesy of Nadine Hernandez

MANAGING STRESS

It's taken me many years, but I've figured out how to manage stress, and I am much more successful today because I've learned that I have to take care of myself first. I was the first in my family to go to college, and during the many years I spent working on my A.A. degree, I had the thought in my head that "people like me don't go to college." As a first-generation college student and single mother, I had no educational support from an adult, like a role model or mentor. I also had child-care issues, and I worried about my daughter's and my younger sister's and brothers' well-being — and this was in addition to dealing with family finances and balancing part-time work, school, and parenting. All of these things were incredibly stressful and made it challenging to stay in school. One day I decided to go to the counseling center on campus, where I learned ways to manage the anxieties and fears I was experiencing.

I now work as an EOPS (Extended Opportunities Programs and Services) Program Specialist, where I get to work with educationally and economically disadvantaged students by supporting them with guidance from start to finish through the community college process. I also plan and conduct workshops for economically and educationally disadvantaged single mothers who live below the poverty line and are going to college. I teach my students the same stress-management skills that I continue to use today: Take care of yourself first, prioritize your tasks, eat healthy, and get rest and regular exercise. I also encourage students to use the counseling center if they need more help. Using stress-management techniques has been a crucial part of my success, and I enjoy helping others use these tools to succeed.

> **YOUR TURN** If you're currently working and have experienced stress on the job, have you used any of the stress-management techniques Nadine found useful? If so, which ones? What, if any, additional strategies have you found helpful? If you're not currently working but have a career in mind, what might be the most difficult stressors associated with that career? How will you manage them?

Employees of all kinds can take part in brainstorming ways to enhance revenue and reduce costs. In fact, because staying financially sound is so important to most organizations, you may find that being financially responsible and reducing spending is a requirement of your position. Many employees include money management in the professional goals that they strive to reach each year.

my personal success plan

Based on your ACES results and what you learned in this chapter, are you inspired to set a new goal aimed at improving your personal or financial health? If so, the Personal Success Plan can walk you through the goal-setting process. Read the advice and examples; then sketch out your ideas in the space provided.

To access the Personal Success Plan online, go to the LaunchPad for *Connections*, Second Edition.

1 IDENTIFY A GOAL

Choose a personal or financial health goal to work toward this term. Here are some general ideas you might draw from; you can also create a goal of your own.

- ▶ Get more exercise.
- ▶ Improve diet and see how it impacts your energy level.
- ▶ Get to sleep at a consistent and reasonable time for a week.
- ▶ Build a budget for the next month.
- ▶ Spend a few minutes each week looking for new scholarships.

2 MAKE YOUR GOAL SMART

Rewrite your specific goal so that it's SMART, and make sure to use the SMART goal checklist.

SAMPLE: Starting next week, I'll increase the amount of time I exercise from one hour to two and a half hours each week.

3 CREATE AN ACTION PLAN

Outline the specific steps you'll take to achieve your SMART goal, and note when you'll complete each step.

SAMPLE: Tomorrow I'll find out where the on-campus gym is located and go check it out.

4 LIST BARRIERS AND SOLUTIONS

Think about possible barriers to your action steps; then brainstorm solutions for overcoming them.

SAMPLE: I know gyms are often crowded, so I'll find out which time slots are least busy at the on-campus gym and schedule my exercise time for those slots.

5 ACT AND EVALUATE OUTCOMES

Now that your plan is in place, take action. Record each action step as you take it. Then evaluate whether you achieved your SMART goal, and make any adjustments needed to get better results in the future.

SAMPLE: I wasn't able to find enough non-busy time slots at the gym to increase my exercising to two and a half hours per week. So I'll add a few 20-minute jogs around my neighborhood to fill in the gap.

6 CONNECT TO CAREER

List the skills you're building as you progress toward your SMART goal. How will you use these skills to land a job and succeed at work?

SAMPLE: Working out is great for stress management. Getting the recommended amount of exercise each day will help me manage stress when I start a new job after college.

my personal success plan

1 my general goal

_____
_____
_____
_____
_____
_____

2 my SMART goal

_____
_____
_____

☐ **S**PECIFIC ☐ **M**EASURABLE ☐ **A**CHIEVABLE ☐ **R**ELEVANT ☐ **T**IME-LIMITED

3 my action plan

_____
_____
_____
_____

4 my barriers/ solutions

_____
_____
_____
_____
_____

5 my actions/ outcomes

_____
_____
_____
_____
_____

6 my career connection

_____
_____
_____
_____
_____

CHAPTER SUMMARY

In this chapter we examined many strategies for nurturing your personal and financial health. Revisit the following key points, and reflect on how you can use this information to support your success now and in the future.

- Safeguarding your personal and financial health can help you manage stress. Constant severe stress can lead to physical, emotional, and mental-health problems.

- Your personal health includes your physical well-being and your mental health. Eating a healthy diet, staying active, and getting enough sleep can all enhance your physical well-being and mental health, enabling you to stay sharp in class and get the most value from your studies.

- Anxiety and depression are two common mental-health problems for college students. Knowing what your resources are and asking for help can be critical for managing these conditions.

- You can use self-care to give yourself an emotional or physical boost. Try yoga, journaling, deep breathing, or a mindfulness activity and evaluate how it makes you feel.

- Sexual health is another key aspect of personal health. If you're sexually active, understanding and protecting yourself against sexually transmitted infections (STIs) through safe sexual practices, and practicing effective birth control if you're not planning to start a family yet, are critical.

- Managing your finances effectively can also help you mitigate stress and reach your goals. Creating a budget, and then refining it as needed, can help you manage your money effectively.

- Tactics for reducing spending include distinguishing between your needs and wants and, if need be, sacrificing your wants in order to get your spending under control.

- Tactics for increasing income include finding a job and getting financial aid.

- Understanding your credit card interest rate and paying down balances are keys to managing credit.

- The same behaviors that nurture your health in school can help you maximize your productivity and job satisfaction at work.

CHAPTER ACTIVITIES

Journal Entry

MAKING TIME FOR SELF-CARE

Self-care is any activity we engage in to take care of our mental, emotional, and physical health. It could be a simple activity such as saying "no" to one more commitment, burning a scented candle, scrolling through iFunny, or taking a nap. It could also be a more involved activity such as joining a running group, reading a good book, having coffee with a friend, or listening to live music. Self-care can improve our mood, decrease stress, and recharge our batteries. When we take time out of our busy lives to focus on our own needs, we can then return to work, school, and relationships with more energy, focus, and motivation.

For this journal entry, reflect on the following questions:

- What does self-care mean to you?
- What do you do for self-care now, if anything? What would you like to do for self-care that you don't currently do now?
- What are the barriers to engaging in self-care? How could you overcome these barriers to ensure you have time for these activities?
- Identify three things you'll do next week for self-care.

Adopting a Success Attitude

COPING WITH STRESS USING HUMOR

The phrase "laughter is the best medicine" is especially true when it comes to relieving stress. Laughing relaxes tense muscles; reduces blood pressure and heart rate; exercises the muscles in your face, diaphragm, and abdomen; boosts your immune system; and triggers your body to release pain-fighting hormones. In fact, after you've had a big laugh, you could be free of muscle tension for as long as 45 minutes. Plus, laughter boosts your mental health by distracting you from stress.

With these advantages in mind, do the following:

1. Find a funny cartoon, joke, quotation, or picture, and put it somewhere you can easily see it when you need a good chuckle.

2. Describe the item, where you placed it, and how often you glanced at it.

3. Explain what kinds of events made you want a laugh break. Then describe what impact, if any, these laugh breaks had on your stress levels.

4. Consider finding additional funny items and sharing them with others, or even creating a scrapbook or Pinterest board of things that make you laugh.

Applying Your Skills

USING YOUR FINANCIAL RESOURCES

As you read earlier in this chapter, many types of scholarships are available to help you pay for college. Take the following steps to learn about your scholarship options:

1. Choose two of the following sources of information and use them to search for scholarships you could apply for if you meet the qualifications.

    _____ Meet with a financial aid adviser or career counselor at your college.

    _____ Search your college's financial aid Web site.

    _____ Use the U.S. Department of Labor's free online scholarship search tool. Visit CareerOneStop.org and search for "Scholarship Finder."

    _____ Contact your employer to see if they offer any financial assistance.

    _____ Go to the library and search for books on college scholarships.

    _____ Identify state-specific scholarships. Go to your state's Web site (for example, **www.texas.gov**) and search for "college scholarships."

    _____ Inquire about scholarships through your membership in local religious, cultural, or community organizations.

    _____ Contact professional associations related to your field of interest and investigate any scholarship opportunities.

    _____ Learn more about Reserve Officers' Training Corps (ROTC) scholarships through the Army, Air Force, Navy, or Marines.

2. Review the scholarship opportunities that you found. Choose one scholarship that you'd like to apply for.

3. Write down the title of the scholarship, the application criteria, and the application instructions. Then apply!

College Success = Career Success

MANAGING STRESS AT WORK

Managing stress at work is similar to managing stress in college. In fact, if you practice these strategies now, they'll be easier to perform in a work environment.

Describe a situation that's causing you stress. Then examine the chart below, which presents four ways to deal with a stressful situation. Two ways involve changing the situation, and two ways involve changing your reaction to the situation.

Read through each box and select "yes," "no," or "unsure" as you determine if this is a strategy you can use to deal with your stressful situation. After completing the chart, write down what you think is the most useful strategy in this situation. Then implement it. What challenges, if any, did you encounter as you implemented this strategy? How did you manage those challenges? What results did you get by implementing this strategy? On a job interview, if you were asked to describe how you handle stressful situations, what would you say?

Change the situation		Change your reaction to the situation	
Strategy 1: Avoid the stress	**Strategy 2: Alter the stressor**	**Strategy 3: Adapt to the stressor**	**Strategy 4: Accept the stressor**
Can you say "no"? Yes　No　Unsure	Can you ask for help? Yes　No　Unsure	Can you think more positively about the situation (find a silver lining)? Yes　No　Unsure	Can you give yourself an incentive to complete the task? Yes　No　Unsure
Can you alter your behavior to avoid the stress? Yes　No　Unsure	Can you schedule your time differently to reduce the stress? Yes　No　Unsure	Can you adjust your standards and not seek perfection? Yes　No　Unsure	Can you accept that some things are beyond your control? Yes　No　Unsure
Can you pare down your to-do list? Yes　No　Unsure	Can you delegate some tasks to others? Yes　No　Unsure	Can you recognize and reduce self-defeating thoughts you're having ("should," "must")? Yes　No　Unsure	Can you see how you would do things differently next time? Yes　No　Unsure
Can you avoid or limit your time with the person causing the stress? Yes　No　Unsure	Can you communicate your feelings and concerns to the person causing the stress? Yes　No　Unsure	Can you understand the perspective of the person causing the stress? Yes　No　Unsure	Can you let go of anger and resentment toward the person causing the stress, and move on? Yes　No　Unsure

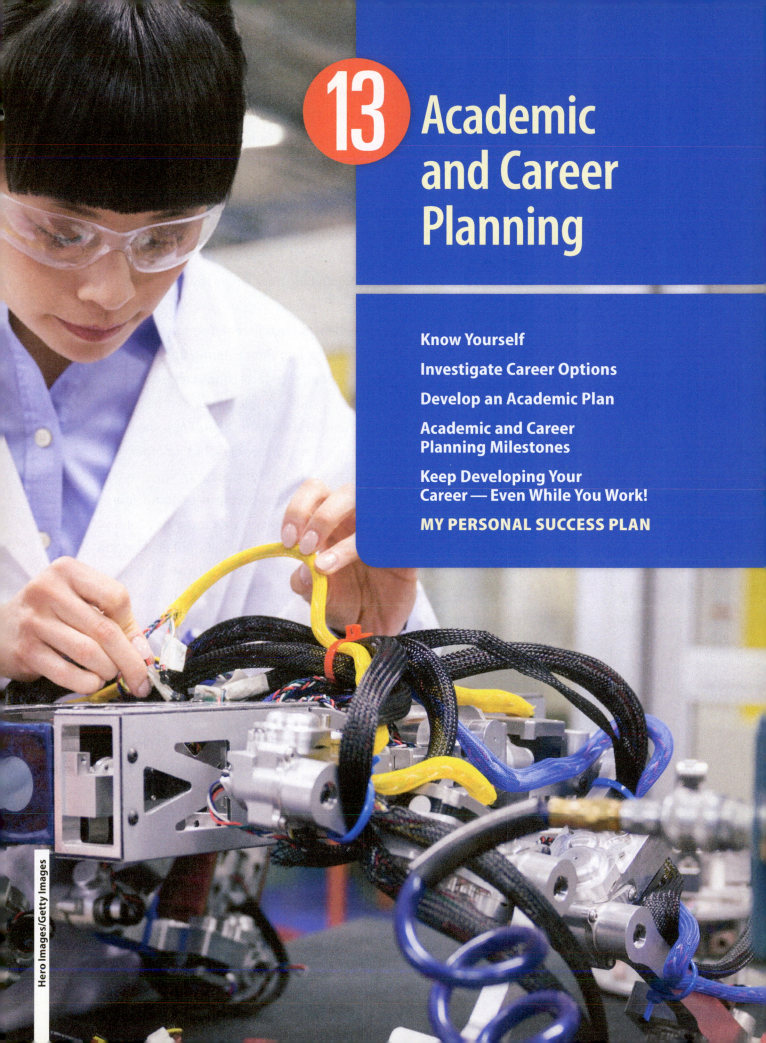

13 Academic and Career Planning

Know Yourself

Investigate Career Options

Develop an Academic Plan

Academic and Career Planning Milestones

Keep Developing Your Career — Even While You Work!

MY PERSONAL SUCCESS PLAN

Think of people you know who have completed college and have entered the work world. If you asked them to describe their academic and career experiences, you'd probably hear a variety of responses. One person might say, "I always wanted to go into teaching, so it was easy to decide on my degree, major, and classes." Someone else might say, "I thought I wanted be an anthropologist, but when I took some chemistry courses and loved them, I changed my mind." Another person may say, "I studied to get a job as an accountant, but after working in that field for a while, I wanted to try something new. I'm on my third career!"

As these responses suggest, everyone's academic and career experiences are different. You can think of going through college and then entering the work world as a *general* path: You start school, choose an area of academic study, complete your degree or certificate, graduate, and then find a job. For some people, this process is straightforward, but for others there are twists and turns along the way. Why? As you travel this path, you constantly learn about yourself — your dreams, your values, your interests — and you continually build new skills. You explore and experiment with ideas about what careers and areas of study might interest you. Along the way, you grow and change. Consequently, your plans may change. In the end, your academic and career paths will be unique to you.

This chapter helps you start your journey by providing the information you need to think critically about your options and make decisions that are right for you. First, we take a closer look at how your interests, values, and skills can inform your plans for the future. Then, we explore how to identify career paths that interest you, as well as how to establish a working academic plan by selecting a degree program, a major, and classes. Finally, we wrap up the chapter with a look at important milestones in academic and career development, and introduce tips you can use to keep developing your career, even after you've entered the work world.

ACES Reflection:
Academic and Career Planning

Take a moment to reflect on your Academic and Career Planning score on ACES. Find your score and add it in the box to the right.

This score measures your beliefs about how familiar you are with academic and career planning and how confident you are that you can create good plans. Do you think it's an accurate snapshot of your understanding? Why or why not?

■ **IF YOU SCORED IN THE HIGH RANGE** and you believe this score is accurate, you may be very knowledgeable about your academic and career options. However, plans can change, and strengthening your planning skills can help you feel confident that you're continuing to make the best decisions for you. As you read this chapter, use the new information you learn to solidify your goals for the future.

■ **IF YOU SCORED IN THE MODERATE OR LOW RANGE**, don't be discouraged. Many students are anxious and unsure about choosing a career and settling on a major. In this class, you'll have plenty of chances to strengthen your planning skills, learn about your options, and use insights about yourself to make these important decisions.

My ACES Score ....
- ☐ High
- ☐ Moderate
- ☐ Low

To find your **Academic and Career Planning score,** go to the LaunchPad for *Connections*, Second Edition.

ACES + ACTION

ACES paired with action is what leads to positive change. Now that you've reflected on your ACES results, how will you *use* what you learned about yourself to strengthen your academic and career planning skills? Try these concrete suggestions, or get inspired and create your own!

▶ **Schedule a meeting.** Arrange a meeting with an academic adviser or a career counselor to get a head start on planning for the future. Ask this professional to give feedback on your résumé, suggest online career exploration sites, and help you fine-tune your academic plan.

▶ **Focus on favorites.** You already know some of the things you're interested in (and *not* interested in). Use this information! Make a list of your favorite academic subjects from high school or college so far, then write down five job titles that relate to those academic subjects. Explore each of these options.

▶ **Weigh the pros and cons.** Think about a career path you're considering. Write down which aspects of that career attract you most, as well as aspects you're less excited about. Do the positives outweigh the negatives? Discuss your list with a career counselor or adviser.

Know Yourself

Your career choices and academic pathways will be as individual as you are, so the best way to start planning for these two important aspects of your life is to know yourself. And that means thinking critically as you gather and interpret information about your own interests, values, and skills—and then use the resulting insights about yourself to start building future plans.

Explore Your Interests

As we discuss in the chapter on building a foundation for success, your interests are your personal preferences—for example, what you like to do in your free time, what course subjects you enjoy, how you like to work, and with whom. These preferences can shed light on the types of careers and coursework you might find most satisfying. If you don't have a clear idea of your interests, or you want to learn even more about yourself, the strategies in this section can help.

Take an Interest Inventory.　One way to investigate your interests is to take an *interest inventory*, which is a survey of your preferences. A useful and free inventory is the O*NET Interest Profiler, which you can access at **www.mynextmove.org/ explore/ip** or by searching online using the phrase "my next move interest profiler." Completing this inventory may take 10–15 minutes but it's worth it—your results will help you think about jobs or professions that may appeal to you. Plus, the inventory can help you with academic planning by giving you insight into what kinds of courses and majors you'd find most intriguing. Complete this inventory now, and then we'll discuss how to interpret your results.

Understand Holland's Interest Types.　Once you have the results of your interest inventory, the next step is to look at what they mean. The inventory is based on the work of John Holland, a renowned career psychologist who developed a system that describes people and work environments using six categories: Realistic, Investigative, Artistic, Social, Enterprising, and Conventional.[1]

- **Realistic (R).** People with Realistic interests enjoy working with their hands, working outside, using tools, installing and repairing things, or working with animals, and they enjoy academic courses that give them these opportunities. They're drawn to occupations in such fields as construction, veterinary and earth sciences, landscaping, and other work that's done primarily outdoors or in physically rewarding environments.

- **Investigative (I).** People with Investigative interests like analyzing and solving problems and enjoy science, technical, or medicine-oriented courses. They find satisfaction in almost all areas of science and may work as college professors, doctors, and engineers or do research and development work in most industries.

- **Artistic (A).** People with Artistic interests are creative, intuitive, sensitive, and expressive. They prefer working with ideas and expressing their ideas through writing, sculpting, dancing, painting, acting, or musical performance. Some gravitate toward art-related studies and work as art instructors, as dance therapists, or as graphic or fashion designers. Others write for newspapers or magazines or work as freelance writers.

- **Social (S).** People with strong Social interests enjoy helping, coaching, teaching, or counseling others. They may be drawn to courses and careers related to teaching, child and elder care, or community leadership and social justice. They may become psychologists, physical therapists, social workers, or occupational therapists.

- **Enterprising (E).** People with strong Enterprising interests like to influence, lead, persuade, and manage others. They may enjoy business studies and may work as supervisors or managers in just about any industry, as fund-raisers or human resource workers, or as members of the legal profession.

- **Conventional (C).** People with Conventional interests usually prefer structure in their school and work environments. They tend to be detail-oriented,

CONNECT TO MY EXPERIENCE

Think about a job, an extracurricular activity, or a volunteer experience you had in the past. What Holland interest area best describes that experience? Write down which aspects of that experience you enjoyed the most and the least, and explain why. Use these insights to brainstorm the kinds of jobs you want to pursue (or avoid) in the future.

enjoy working with numbers or data, and are precise in their work. They frequently find satisfaction in the banking and finance industries, the computer sciences, or organizational departments such as payroll and purchasing.

As you consider the results of your inventory, keep in mind that it's perfectly normal to have interests in more than one of these areas. If your interests span two or three categories, the key is to consider which studies and occupations would let you combine your varied interest types. For example, in school, choosing a second major or a minor might let you explore several academic interests, such as business and recreation. In the work world, being an art gallery director might let you express both your Artistic and Enterprising interests, and working as an outdoor adventure counselor might satisfy your Social and Realistic interests. Later in this chapter, we'll look more closely at how to use knowledge of your interests to explore possible careers.

Explore Your Values

Your values are what you consider important—really important. (See the chapter on building a foundation for success.) They stem from your experiences with your family, your community, or your faith. Because you're in college, your academic values probably include getting a good education; if you're the first in your family to go to college, they may also include making your family proud.

In addition to academic values, you also have **work values**. These are the aspects of your work or your work environment that you consider important. To learn more about your work values, examine the items on the list below and ask yourself: How important are each of these values to me?[2]

- **Achievement:** using your abilities and gaining a feeling of accomplishment.
- **Independence:** trying out your own ideas, making your own decisions, and working without supervision.
- **Recognition:** having opportunities to advance in your career, direct the work of others, and be recognized for your accomplishments.
- **Relationships:** getting along with coworkers, doing things for other people, and not having to do things that violate your ideals.
- **Support:** receiving helpful supervision, being treated fairly by your organization, and getting appropriate training.
- **Working conditions:** being busy all the time, receiving appropriate pay, feeling secure in your job, and constantly doing different activities.

Understanding your work values—and their relative strength—can help you identify careers, and academic programs related to those careers, you might find satisfying. It can also help you make trade-offs. For example, if you become an elementary school teacher, you may have relatively little opportunity for

Realistic Interest in Action?
These women are working at a rehabilitation center for chimpanzees in Guinea. Their interests likely fall under Holland's Realistic type, which is characterized by a desire to work with one's hands, work outside, use tools, or work with animals. This interest may also have influenced their academic choices, including their degrees, majors, and classes.
Dan Kitwood/Getty Images News

work values: The aspects of your work or your work environment that you consider important.

Artistic Expression. This artist is working to create a colorful mural. What work values do you think he holds dear: Recognition? Independence? Achievement? If you're not sure, imagine yourself as an artist. If you're artistic already, what work values would *you* most like to express in your career? What kinds of jobs would best enable you to express those values? Stephen Simpson Inc/Getty Images

advancement, and you probably won't get rich. But you'll go to work each day knowing you're helping others learn. Depending on your work values, this trade-off might be worthwhile—or it might not.

Also note that some careers reinforce certain values and not others, depending on the setting or specialty. In the health services profession, for instance, nurses typically work directly with patients, whereas medical records specialists tend to work behind the scenes making sure billing is accurate and up to date. If you're interested in the health services industry and don't need to have direct contact with patients, you might aim for a career in medical records or accounting.

As you consider your work values, keep two things in mind: First, if you don't have much work experience, you may not have a clear picture of your work values just yet. That's okay: Your values will come into sharper focus as you get experience. Second, work values can change. For instance, someone who's raising a family may consider job security a critical work value. Once his children are grown, however, job security may not be as important, and perhaps he'll place more value on work that lets him feel that he's contributing to society. The upshot? Understanding your work values is an ongoing process, not a one-time event.

Explore Your Skills

As a college student, you probably excel at, and enjoy using, certain academic skills more than other skills. For instance, maybe you take accurate notes and ace most tests, but you find it more challenging (and terrifying) to make class presentations. The same is true with skills in the work world: You'll likely prefer some over others. By understanding which skills you enjoy and excel at most, you can find a job that emphasizes what you love to do.

Take Janelle, a computer programmer. Her work involves writing computer code, reading project specifications, using logic and reasoning to solve problems, understanding her clients' needs, and managing her time so her projects stay on schedule. She loves writing code, but she dreads meeting with clients. By understanding her skill set and preferences, she can look for a programming job that emphasizes what she's good at and what she enjoys—a position that focuses more on writing code than on tending to client relations.

When it comes to work skills, here's another important point: Some skills are specific and are needed in only a few careers, such as writing computer code. Others are transferable and are used in many different careers, such as solving problems with logic and reasoning, listening to others, and managing your time. Your transferable skills let you cast your "career net" more widely, which opens up a wider range of occupations that you could succeed in.

Also keep in mind that you don't have to limit your options to work experiences that call for *only* your best skills. You can also seek out experiences that will let you develop new skills or strengthen your current skills. For instance, suppose you'd like to enhance your leadership skills. You could identify volunteer opportunities, leadership positions in campus clubs, and training opportunities with your employer (if you're working now) that would help you become a more confident leader. You might even establish a goal to develop this skill over the next few months, which you can document in your Personal Success Plan.

As you've seen in this section, your interests, values, and skills play a key role in helping you identify a fulfilling academic and career path. But there's another factor that can help give you clarity about the future: becoming an active part of your campus community.

In one study, researchers measured the levels of campus engagement in a group of undergraduates — for example, they looked at whether students participated in active or collaborative learning opportunities and whether they interacted with their instructors. The researchers also measured *vocational identity*, which is a person's understanding of his or her career goals, interests, and strengths. In addition, they recorded each student participant's GPA at the end of the term.

When they reviewed the data they'd collected, the researchers discovered that students who were more engaged (meaning they interacted with instructors more frequently and participated in active and collaborative learning opportunities more often) had higher overall GPAs *and* had stronger vocational identities than students who weren't engaged on campus.

Understand Yourself through Campus Engagement

THE BOTTOM LINE

Now is a great time to become an active learner on campus. Interact with your instructors. Join campus clubs or organizations. Get to know your classmates. Doing so could help improve your GPA and teach you more about your interests, values, and skills — all things that will help you succeed in college and in your future career.

Being engaged on campus promotes positive academic and career outcomes.

Information from H. J. Yoon et. al., "The Effects of Hope on Student Engagement, Academic Performance, and Vocational Identity," *Canadian Journal of Career Development* 14, no. 1 (2015): 34–45. Images: garagestock/Shutterstock

Investigate Career Options

So far you've learned about yourself by exploring your interests, work values, and skills. What's next? You can use these insights to investigate possible career options that will be meaningful for you. To do this, conduct online research, talk with experts, and get direct experience that will help you discover more about careers of interest (see Figure 13.1). During this process, you can use your critical-thinking skills to gather, evaluate, and apply this information in a way that makes the most sense for you.

As you learn about your options, try not to put too much pressure on yourself to pick the "right" career. For some students, making an initial career decision is a paralyzing process, because it feels like this one choice could dictate the rest of their lives. In reality, career decisions are more flexible: You make the choice, evaluate how it feels for you, and if you don't like it, you change it! In fact, many people change careers several times during the course of their lives. For that reason, you can view the information-gathering experience as just one step toward finding a satisfying career.

FIGURE 13.1
Investigating Career Options

occupational projection: The predicted rise or fall in the number of new jobs in a particular field.

Get to Know the O*NET

One of the best places to start researching different occupations is the O*NET (Occupational Network), an occupational database maintained by the U.S. Department of Labor. (Go to **www.onetonline.org**, or search using the phrase "O*NET OnLine.") The site is overflowing with helpful job-related facts, including how certain occupations match people's interests, work values, and skills. Drawing on your self-knowledge, you can search for jobs that meet the criteria you consider most important. You can also use the O*NET to research what level of education and experience is required for a particular occupation (a category called the Job Zone), how much the occupation pays, and its **occupational projection** for the next ten years, which predicts how many of those jobs may be available when you graduate. You can also search for occupations by keyword, such as the name of your college major.

For a more detailed look at the O*NET, see Figure 13.2, which shows how to search for occupations using the results of the Holland interest inventory. An activity at the end of the chapter also gives you a chance to explore the O*NET firsthand.

Talk with Experts

As a college student, you have access to a wide range of experts who can help you with career planning, including career counselors on campus and people in the work world who can give you the "inside scoop" on particular types of jobs, employers, and careers.

FIGURE 13.2

Example O*NET Occupational Search Based on Interests

These O*NET screenshots show an advanced search for occupations by Holland interest type, a list of occupations sorted by Job Zone, and a summary report for a particular occupation. You can also search the O*NET by work values or skills.

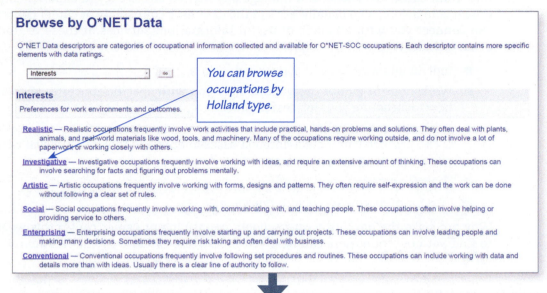

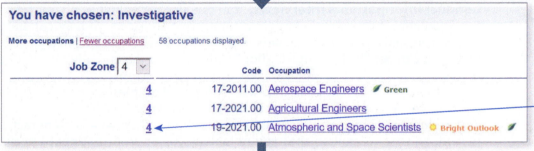

career counselor: A specially trained professional who uses career assessments and other resources to help students explore career options and make career decisions.

Meet with a Career Counselor. Some students have a hard time defining a career path or feeling confident about the path they've chosen. Fortunately, many campuses employ **career counselors**, specially trained professionals who use career assessments and other resources to help students explore career options, make important career decisions, and manage any related stress they're experiencing. Career counselors, who usually work in the campus's counseling or career center, can connect you with all kinds of useful information. Services at these centers often include:

- Individual meetings with career counselors.
- Workshops or groups designed to help you with specific concerns, such as how to structure your job search process.
- Subscriptions to online career information resources (often based on the O*NET), which can include interest assessments and video interviews with people working in various occupations.
- Tools for creating your résumé.
- Tips for preparing for job interviews.

Why not seize the day? Visit your school's counseling or career center this week to find out how counselors can help you investigate career options that are right for you.

Conduct Informational Interviews. You can also get valuable job information from someone currently working in a career that interests you. By conducting an *informational interview*, or conversation, with a person working in a particular field, you can get "insider information" about what a job is really like from day to day.

How can you find someone who works in a field of interest to you? Your best bet is to get referrals from friends and family, ask your instructors, and review alumni mentor lists at your school's career center. When you first contact this person, be sure to explain that you're looking for an informational interview, either face-to-face or by phone, to give them some context for your conversation. This is a fact-finding investigation—your purpose is not to job hunt but rather to find out what the work entails, what this person likes most and least about the job, and what benefits and opportunities for advancement this line of work offers. Table 13.1 shows questions you might ask during informational interviews.

TABLE 13.1

Questions to Ask at an Informational Interview

What kinds of tasks do you perform in a typical week?
How does this career affect your lifestyle?
What are some of the more difficult or frustrating parts of this career?
What are the best parts of your job?
Is this career changing? How?
Do you usually work independently or as part of a team?
Do you have any advice regarding how someone interested in this career should prepare?
What types of advancement opportunities are available for an entry-level worker in this career?
What is the average starting salary for someone in this career?

Get Experience

Even while you're in college, you can gain experience that helps you learn more about careers of interest and build the skills you'll need to succeed in those jobs. To get started obtaining professional experience, consider one or more of these ideas:

- **Service learning.** Most colleges and universities offer *service learning* opportunities that pair meaningful community service with personal reflection and instruction as a way to enrich the learning experience and give back to the community. For example, if Rhonda is interested in architecture and business, she might sign up for a service learning class with Habitat for Humanity, a group that builds houses for families with low incomes. Through this experience, she'd learn the intricacies of construction—something she'll need to understand as an architect—as well as the "business model" of a not-for-profit group that relies on donations to operate.

- **Internships.** Internships, which are formal programs that provide practical experience for beginners in an occupation or a profession, are another worthwhile option. In fact, recent research suggests that students who graduate with internship experiences receive more job offers and higher starting salaries than those without these experiences.[3] Internships are often available during the summer, though some come up during the academic year. Check with a career counselor at your school to find out which nearby organizations offer internship opportunities.

- **Co-ops.** College co-op programs offer alternating periods of academic study and periods of work experience in fields such as business, industry, government, and social services. These programs are a great way to learn about specific careers while also making a little money. In addition, during your work experiences you may forge helpful connections with people who can help you later—for example, when you're seeking job opportunities or when you need letters of recommendation for a potential employer.

- **Working.** Working while you're in college allows you to investigate career options as you build your skills and knowledge. The key is not to take on so many hours that you have difficulty juggling your coursework and your job.

Building Skills. By getting experience in an area that interests you, you can build the skills that you'll need to enter a particular profession. For example, if you're considering construction management and you're taking coursework in engineering, math, and computer-aided design, you could apply your learning firsthand through an internship or a co-op position at a job site.
Christian Science Monitor/Getty Images

Develop an Academic Plan

academic plan: A tool used by students and their advisers to plan and track a student's progress toward obtaining a degree or certificate.

In college it's never too early to create an **academic plan**, which documents the steps you'll take to complete your degree or certificate. Recognizing your interests, values, and skills can help you create this plan, as can having a rough idea of the type of career you might want to pursue and the goals you'd like to achieve. For example, if you're attending a two-year college and you want to earn a four-year degree, it's crucial to determine which of your current classes will transfer to your next institution. And if you're attending school and want to get a job right after graduation, you'll want to focus on courses needed to obtain your degree and prepare for the job market.

To build your academic plan effectively, you'll also need a solid understanding of your school's requirements — for instance, when you have to declare a major and the grade point average you need to be accepted into your chosen program. You'll also want to know if your school is participating in *guided pathways*, which some colleges and universities are implementing as a way to assist students in staying in college and graduating on time. A guided pathway is like a road map from the start of college to graduation. Once you've selected a major or even a general area of concentration — for example, health sciences, arts and humanities, or business — your course sequences and learning objectives are mapped out so you know you're taking the right course at the right time in the right term. In addition, many guided pathways incorporate assessment and feedback designed to alert you if you're at risk of falling behind. You can check with your instructor or an adviser to see if your school follows this approach.

Making academic planning decisions can sometimes be overwhelming for students, but trust that your critical-thinking skills can help you gather, evaluate, and use the information to make good choices, and that many people at your school will be there to lend a hand. Your plan may change in the future, but developing a road map early gives you initial clarity and helps you stay motivated to achieve your goals. To get started on your plan, learn the basics: information about degree and certificate options, picking a major, and selecting courses, as well as the benefits of seeking support from an adviser (see Figure 13.3).

FIGURE 13.3
Components of Academic Planning

Choose a Degree or Certificate

To choose a degree or certificate you have to know your options — and there are many! Schools across the country offer a wide range of degrees and certificates; Table 13.2 shows common examples. Generally, two-year colleges offer different types of degrees than do four-year colleges, though not always. For instance, some colleges that traditionally offered only two-year degrees now offer four-year bachelor's degrees in high-demand fields. And some four-year schools offer select two-year degrees.

As you research the options at your school, pay attention to terminology. For example, your school may use different terms to describe associate's degrees that prepare you to transfer to a four-year college and associate's degrees that prepare you to enter the workforce directly.

In addition, remember that everyone's life circumstances are unique. Not all students graduate in exactly two or four years, even if they attend what's considered a two- or four-year school. For example, your time line may be different if you're going to school part-time (as do nearly 38 percent of U.S. students[4]) or if you take foundational courses before you begin earning college credit. You can work with a professional adviser at your school to decide on a time frame and a degree or certificate program that make sense for you.

TABLE 13.2

Overview of Common Degrees and Certificates

Degree	Time required*	Schools offering degree	General purpose	Sample academic programs
Certificates	1–2 years	Two-year colleges, some four-year institutions, and specialty institutions	Prepare students with specialized skills for work	Computer coding, construction technology, practical nursing, medical assisting
Associate of arts, associate of science, associate of applied science	2 years	Two-year colleges and some four-year institutions	Prepare students for work or for transfer to four-year colleges	Fire science, emergency medical technology, sports and fitness management, early childhood education, visual and performing arts, science, computer science
Bachelor of arts, bachelor of science	4 years	Four-year institutions and some two-year colleges	Prepare students for work or postgraduate education	Physics, psychology, literature, engineering, nursing, history, mathematics, dance, business, foreign languages
Master's degree	1–3 years (depending on degree type)	Four-year institutions and some specialty institutions	Prepare students for entry into fields requiring advanced training	Social work, counseling, accounting, business administration, geology, nursing and teaching specialties
Doctoral degree	3–6 years (depending on degree type)	Universities and some specialty institutions	Prepare students for entry into fields requiring a doctoral degree for teaching, research, or practice	School or university administration, psychology, science, pharmacy, physical therapy
Professional degree	3–5 years (depending on degree type)	Universities and some specialty institutions	Prepare students for entry into fields requiring advanced training for practice	Medicine (all specialties), law, chiropractic, audiology, veterinary, podiatry, optometry

*Note: Times listed to complete degrees are minimum times. Some students take longer, depending on their life circumstances.

Choose a Major

college major: A collection of courses organized around an academic theme.

A **college major** is a collection of courses organized around an academic theme. A major enables you to understand one area of scholarship or practice in depth. To select a major, you need to consider your own career goals and what's important to you and to understand some logistics—for example, by when your college expects you to make this decision.

Consider Your Career Goals and What's Important to You. If you have a particular career in mind, investigate what type of degree is generally required and whether that career requires a specific major. To enter some fields such as nursing, engineering, education, and accounting, graduating with a pre-professional major is critical. And many academic programs in two-year colleges prepare you for immediate entry into a specific career, such as electrical technician, diesel mechanic, dental hygienist, and certified nursing assistant.

But other majors—such as sociology, English, psychology, and history—prepare you for a variety of careers by helping you build transferable skills valued by many employers. If your career of choice doesn't require a specific major, you can select a major based on other factors—for example, because of a class you enjoyed, because of your interests, or because you're skilled in a particular area (such as music or math).

As you weigh your options, it's also worth considering whether the career you have in mind calls for advanced schooling. Some careers (e.g., doctor, lawyer, or school counselor) require a graduate or professional degree, so if you're planning to enter one of these fields, investigate whether related graduate programs recommend or require specific undergraduate majors. An instructor in the field you're considering is an excellent source for this information. Also, if you're at a two-year school and plan to transfer to a four-year school, selecting certain majors may increase your chance of transferring, especially if you want to enter a specific program. To find out, consulting an academic adviser is your best option.

A Passion for Science.
Students select courses for different reasons. For example, you might take this course because you want a job involving scientific research, which requires you to pursue a specific degree and major. Or, you might register for this course because you've always been interested in science and want to learn more. Noel Hendrickson/Getty Images

Consider Time Frame and Qualifications. Many first-year students are undecided about which major to pursue, and that's okay—most schools have resources that can help students explore different academic and career pathways. However, you'll want to find out *by when* your school requires that decision to be made, so you can prepare yourself ahead of time.

In addition, you need to know your school's requirements for being admitted into a particular major so that you can plan how to meet those requirements. Take Nicolai, a first-year student attending a local two-year college. Nicolai wants to go into business and plans to transfer to a four-year college to complete his business degree. He knows that most business programs require a GPA of at least 3.3 to be admitted, but his current GPA is only 3.1. So he talks with his adviser about how he can improve his GPA (he might go for tutoring) and discusses other options to pursue if he's unsuccessful in doing so.

Choose Your Courses

Depending on your school and program, you'll need a certain number of credits to graduate, and those credits usually come from two areas: courses required for your major and general-education (or *core*) course requirements.

To complete your major, certain courses will be required. For instance, if you major in economics, you may have to take courses in the history of economic thought, microeconomic and macroeconomic theory, and economic analysis or statistics. Most majors also allow you to take electives—courses you choose to take based on your interests or career goals. If you're majoring in social work, for example, you may decide to take electives in psychology and sociology to understand how different disciplines view the human condition.

General-education courses, which are common at both two- and four-year colleges, give students a broad liberal education in the natural and social sciences, humanities, arts, and mathematics. These courses are important because they help you develop critical-thinking skills, use and evaluate data and numbers, and communicate through writing and speaking—all transferable skills. General-education courses also introduce you to a wide range of ideas and topics. Exposure to new knowledge can help you gain insight into your interests and values, which in turn can help you pick a major. In fact, you might find that you enjoy a course in your general-education curriculum so much that you end up selecting that area as a major.

Conveniently, sometimes you can satisfy general-education course requirements by taking courses related to your major (such as a social work major who takes a psychology course). An adviser can strategize with you about which general-education courses will help prepare you for a particular career.

Get Help from an Academic Adviser or Counselor

As you can see, academic planning involves working with a lot of information. To make sure you're aware of everything you need to know, you'll want to meet with an **academic adviser** or, in some states, a **counselor**—a highly trained professional who can help you make effective academic decisions and refer you to valuable campus resources. Although ultimately you're responsible for your own academic plan, an adviser can provide the support and information you need to think critically about your options. He or she can also help you stay informed about your school's course, transfer, and degree requirements.

**⌕ CONNECT
TO MY CLASSES**

Consider the courses you're taking this term. Write down which courses satisfy your college's general-education requirements and which, if any, you're taking in your major.

general-education courses: A set of course requirements that gives all students a broad liberal education in the natural and social sciences, humanities, arts, and mathematics.

academic adviser/ counselor: A highly trained professional who can help you make effective academic decisions and refer you to valuable campus resources.

CONNECT
TO MY RESOURCES
Write down four questions you'd like to ask an adviser when you meet. If you've already met, write down three things you learned during that visit about creating an academic plan.

There are many types of advisers, and schools organize their advising programs in different ways. For example, some schools have a central academic advising office that specializes in working with first-year students, while at other schools this work is done in counseling centers. And in some cases, academic departments have advisers (some of whom are faculty members) who specialize in working with students who have declared a major.

Given the variety in how academic advising is structured, investigate your school's approach and find out which advisers are responsible for helping you right now. Schedule an appointment with an adviser at least once each term (including this term, if you haven't done so already) to assess your progress toward your academic goals, to get ideas for overcoming any challenges you encounter, and to refine your academic plan as needed.

Academic and Career Planning Milestones

Now that you've learned about a variety of strategies you can use to investigate career options and create an academic plan, let's look at key milestones that come up in academic and career planning. Understanding these milestones can help you sketch out approximate times for completing them, which adds structure to your college experience and helps you stay motivated to meet your goals.

- **Find your path.** Are you currently at a two-year college? If so, Table 13.3 offers two sets of suggested milestones: one for those who want to enter the workforce directly after graduating and another for those who plan to transfer to a four-year college. Are you currently at a four-year school? Table 13.4 offers suggested milestones for you to follow. Feel free to modify these models to suit your educational time line; if you'll be in school for more or less time than the models show, make adjustments to fit your specific circumstances. In addition, exactly what you do for each milestone (and when you do it) may vary depending on your school's requirements. So talk with an adviser or a career counselor to see whether there are campus-specific recommendations to keep in mind as you make your plans.

- **Get started.** As you look at the suggested milestones, consider which primary tasks you need to address right now, such as maintaining a strong GPA or planning a course of study with an adviser. Many of these tasks will be familiar, as they're discussed in previous sections in this chapter as well as in other chapters.

- **Consider what comes next.** Can you get a jump on upcoming tasks right now? If so, how? Take a particularly close look at the final year in the model plans. Except for students who are going on to further schooling, this is a time when most students begin searching for a job in their chosen field. This is a vital stage of your career development and it requires serious attention. Research suggests that students who take an active role in their job search are much better off than those who don't.[5]

- **Make connections.** Even if you're not looking for a job just yet, it's a good idea to start building relationships with counselors in the career center *now*. When the time comes, they can help you prepare for job interviews, review and critique your résumé, show you how to gather information about employers you'll be interviewing with, and give you tips on negotiating pay and other employment terms with an organization once you receive a job offer. (This book's Appendix also provides valuable tips on preparing for and conducting a job search.)

> "I've tried to find elective courses that will not only fulfill requirements but also be useful in my career or daily life.

SELECTING A MAJOR AND CHOOSING CLASSES

NAME
Tony Kao

SCHOOL
University of Kentucky

MAJOR
Mechanical Engineering

CAREER GOAL
Mechanical Design

I'm a first-generation college student. My parents immigrated to the United States so I could get a better education. It was always assumed that I would go to college, and my parents and advisers have supported me throughout the process. I want to find a career path that I'll enjoy, but also one that will make them proud.

The people who know me can tell you that I'm a very logical and analytical kind of person. I always like to figure out how things work and how each component of a product contributes to the overall design, regardless of what it is. I thought that since I enjoy learning about how things work, why not make a career of it? I could continue to learn, put my own knowledge to the test, *and* get paid for doing something I love and enjoy.

Because of this passion and because of my aptitude in math and science, I chose mechanical engineering as my major. This degree will allow me to be creative but also develop my technical skills and knowledge. For example, I recently completed an internship in an automobile assembly plant, which taught me the importance of product reliability, construction, and installation.

My university also has general-education requirements. I've tried to find elective courses that will not only fulfill requirements but also be useful in my career or daily life. I chose Technical Writing and Personal Finance. I think these courses will apply no matter what job I get after graduating. I also wanted to take a course that was fun, so I enrolled in a tennis class. I really enjoy this class, and it gives me a break between my engineering classes.

I hope to find a job that will provide me with financial stability, the potential for growth, and fulfillment. I want a sense of pride from the work that I do.

> **YOUR TURN** Have you chosen a major? If so, how does the process you used to select your major compare with the one that Tony used to select his? If your school offers electives, do any appeal to you? If so, which ones — and why?

- **Revise as needed.** Finally, always remember: Academic and career planning is an ongoing process. As you go through college, you'll revisit your plans periodically and refine them as needed to reflect your most recent thoughts about your education and work life. By doing some reflecting and readjusting, you can be sure you're pursuing a path that's meaningful for you.

Courtesy of Tony Kao

TABLE 13.3
Two-Year College Planning Milestones

Year 1: Transitioning, Exploring, and Planning

All

- Develop and practice the success skills discussed in this book.
- Focus on establishing a strong GPA.
- Begin to identify your career-related interests, skills, and values.
- Get involved in campus activities.
- Develop a preliminary résumé.
- Explore work or volunteer activities that will strengthen your résumé.

Transfer Option

- Plan your course of study with an academic adviser to maximize transfer credits.
- Discuss colleges and universities that you are considering transferring to.
- If possible, meet with an academic adviser at the schools to which you may apply.
- Identify the application deadlines for schools to which you may apply.

Work Option

- Document how the success skills you're using at school translate to future careers.
- Discuss with a career counselor what career opportunities are available for graduates with your degree.
- Conduct informational interviews with people in your community who are employed in areas that interest you.

Year 2: Completing Your Program and Preparing for Another Transition

Transfer Option

- Prepare and submit applications for admission to four-year colleges.
- Gather information about the majors available at the schools to which you are applying.
- Meet with your adviser, or advisers at your target schools, to talk about declaring a major when you arrive.
- If possible, work with an adviser on your campus or an adviser at your target school to create a first-year course plan so that you can hit the ground running.
- Update your résumé annually.
- Continue to acquire practical experience through clubs and organizations, volunteering, and work.

Work Option

- Continue to develop the transferable skills that employers desire most.
- Meet with one or more instructors to discuss career options.
- Meet with a counselor at the career center to discuss the job search services the center provides.
- If available, register for on-campus interviews, or identify where employment opportunities are posted on your campus.
- Have a counselor at the career center critique your résumé.
- Conduct mock interviews with friends, colleagues, or a counselor at the career center.
- Continue to acquire practical experience through clubs and organizations, volunteering, and work.
- Consider leadership opportunities in clubs and organizations.

TABLE 13.4

Four-Year College Planning Milestones

Year 1: Transitioning and Exploring
• Develop and practice the success skills discussed in this book. • Focus on establishing a strong GPA. • Begin to identify your career-related interests, skills, and values. • Reflect on which topics covered in your first-year courses you find interesting. • Talk with an academic adviser about the majors you're considering. • Talk with career counselors about the relationship between various majors and the careers you're considering. • Get involved in campus activities. • Develop a preliminary résumé. • Explore work or volunteer activities that will strengthen your résumé. • Conduct one or more informational interviews.
Year 2: Finding Your Direction
• Declare an academic major. • Join a club or professional organization related to your academic major. • Develop relationships with instructors who can later support your job search with letters of recommendation. • Document how the success skills you're using at school translate to future careers. • Consider volunteer or employment opportunities related to your academic major. • Discuss with a career counselor what career opportunities are available for graduates with your major. • Update your résumé annually. • Research how to prepare for the careers that interest you. • Conduct an informational interview with a recent graduate in your major. (Try visiting the alumni center.)
Year 3: Confirming Your Path and Gaining Experience
• Evaluate your satisfaction with the direction you have chosen. If you're not satisfied, meet with an academic adviser or career counselor to assist you in changing direction. • Continue acquiring practical experience related to your major through clubs and organizations, volunteering, and work. • Continue to develop the transferable skills that employers desire most. • Consider whether you want to start working after getting your degree or enter a graduate or professional training program. • If appropriate, determine graduate school testing and application deadlines. • Begin researching graduate programs or employers related to the careers you are considering. • Review syllabi in the courses in your academic major to identify possible career and graduate school specialty options. • Update your résumé annually. • Meet with instructors in your academic major to discuss career and graduate school options. • Meet with a counselor in the career center to discuss available job search services.
Year 4: Preparing for Another Transition
• If you plan to continue your education, fill out graduate or professional school applications. • If you are seeking employment, register for on-campus interviews. • Meet with a counselor in the career center to polish your résumé. • Research employers with whom you will interview. • Conduct mock interviews with friends, colleagues, or a counselor at the career center. • Continue to acquire practical experience through clubs and organizations, volunteering, and work. • Find out what services the career center offers to students after graduation.

Keep Developing Your Career — Even While You Work!

The interesting thing about career planning is that it doesn't end once you find a job—it's just called *career development* from that point on. You can (and should) continue to develop your career even while you work by seizing opportunities to master new skills, advance in your chosen profession, or even try a different career if your work values, interests, skills, or other life circumstances change. In fact, if you make a change, you'll be in good company: According to the U.S. Bureau of Labor Statistics, people change their jobs an average of eleven times before they approach retirement age.[6] Below, we'll look at two case studies that show how continuous career development, even after graduation, can lead to new and exciting opportunities.

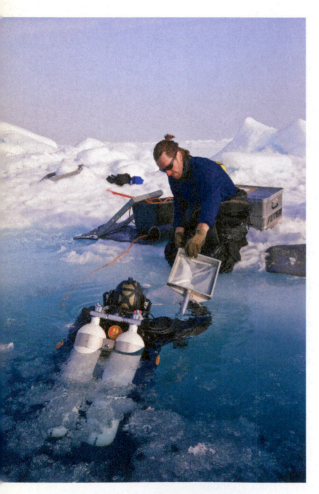

Work Values: Fluid — Not Frozen. As you gain work experience, your work values may shift, possibly prompting career changes. For instance, maybe you originally valued the structure and comfort that came with a desk job but later realized you needed more physical challenge and fresh air in your work environment. If so, a job studying melting ice in the Arctic might be perfect for you! Jenny E. Ross/Getty Images

Advance in Your Chosen Career

As you refine your professional goals, you may find that making a career plan helps you rise in the ranks at your company or organization. Consider Sam, who had been working for two years as a case manager at a local nonprofit social services agency. One day, Sam learned that her coworker, Elaine, was promoted to site manager at one of the organization's halfway homes. Sam wanted to get a similar promotion, so she did some career planning: She set out to learn what kinds of training and experience would best prepare her to take this next step in her professional life. Her plan included conducting informational interviews with her supervisor, Tomas, and with Elaine.

As it turned out, they were both delighted to hear of her interest in advancement, and took steps to help her reach her goal. Tomas asked her to lend a hand when he prepared budgets and updated client tracking data, and Elaine recommended an online course that she had used to prepare for her promotion. In this way, Sam's careful plan, and her willingness to take concrete steps to advance, helped her move her career forward.

Explore New Opportunities

For a different example of on-the-job career development, consider Seth's experience. As a gaming supervisor for a large casino in Las Vegas, Seth discovered that he liked working with people but wasn't happy with the job's unpredictable hours and stressful working conditions, which included constant noise, flashing lights, and dealing with disruptive customers. He thought about changing jobs but worried that he wouldn't make as much money in a new job without receiving considerable retraining. His work values had shifted: He had started a family, so financial security was important to him. And because being a parent was exhausting, he valued workplace settings that were quiet and relatively stress-free—a value that his current job didn't uphold.

> By creating and following a plan, I have a good handle on where my career will be in the next few years.

ON-THE-JOB CAREER PLANNING

I started figuring out my career plan back when I was in college. I had taken a few courses in computer security, and when I realized how much I liked them, I made that my focus and found ways to get experience. I participated in computer security–related events at school to network with information security professionals. One of my teachers, who also worked in the IT department, recognized my enthusiasm for the subject matter and recommended me for a Network Security Internship on campus.

I've since graduated and have a job in computer security, where I work on making credit card transactions more secure. While I'm off to a good start, in order to make sure my career develops the way I'd like it to, I picked up where I left off in college and went back to work on a career plan. I'm currently in year one of a three-year plan that I created. During this first year, I took some classes outside of college, picked up an extra certification, and started my first job. I also did some research and talked with colleagues in the information security field. I'm going to spend the second year of my plan gaining knowledge and expertise in the area of health care information security. I'll spend the third year building my skills and expertise around standards in the field. By creating and following a plan, I have a good handle on where my career will be in the next few years.

> **YOUR TURN** If you're currently working, where do you see your work life headed? Do you want to advance in your career? If so, could you build a multiyear plan for doing so, as Bilal did? What action steps would you include in your plan?

So Seth logged onto the O*NET and researched occupations that would let him work with people but that had more predictable hours, less stressful working conditions, and acceptable pay. After reviewing the search results, he zeroed in on one option he found particularly interesting: dental hygienist. Then he did additional research to find out what training he'd need to move into this job.

Whether you want to advance in your chosen occupation or change careers entirely, you can use the skills you're developing this term to make smart work-related decisions in the future. What kinds of career decisions do you see yourself making in the next ten years? Do you feel better prepared to make those decisions now than you did at the start of the term? Why or why not?

my personal success plan

Based on your ACES results and what you learned in this chapter, are you inspired to set a new goal related to academic or career planning? If so, the Personal Success Plan can walk you through the goal-setting process. Read the advice and examples; then sketch out your ideas in the space provided.

To access the Personal Success Plan online, go to the LaunchPad for *Connections*, Second Edition.

1 IDENTIFY A GOAL

Choose an academic- or career-planning goal to work toward this term. Here are some general ideas you might draw from; you can also create a goal of your own.

- ▶ Complete the online interest inventory and use the results to explore occupations.
- ▶ Conduct an informational interview.
- ▶ Explore service-learning options available on campus.
- ▶ Research possible majors.
- ▶ Meet with an adviser to discuss my academic plan.

2 MAKE YOUR GOAL SMART

Rewrite your specific goal so that it's SMART, and make sure to use the SMART goal checklist.

SAMPLE: I'll complete the online interest inventory this weekend and spend an hour researching two suggested careers by the end of next week.

3 CREATE AN ACTION PLAN

Outline the specific steps you'll take to achieve your SMART goal, and note when you'll complete each step.

SAMPLE: I'll log onto the O*NET Sunday afternoon, complete the interest inventory, and print out my results.

4 LIST BARRIERS AND SOLUTIONS

Think about possible barriers to your action steps; then brainstorm solutions for overcoming them.

SAMPLE: This week's busy schedule may prevent me from researching careers when I get home at night, so I'll print out the career summary information and bring it to work to review on my breaks.

5 ACT AND EVALUATE OUTCOMES

Now that your plan is in place, take action. Record each action step as you take it. Then evaluate whether you achieved your SMART goal, and make any adjustments needed to get better results in the future.

SAMPLE: I completed the interest inventory and got strong Social and Artistic interest results. I've printed out two related career summaries and feel good about my ability to review them this week.

6 CONNECT TO CAREER

List the skills you're building as you progress toward your SMART goal. How will you use these skills to land a job and succeed at work?

SAMPLE: Now that I know how to access information about career salaries and advancement opportunities on the O*NET, I can look up any job that interests me in the future.

my personal success plan

1 my general goal

2 my SMART goal

☐ Specific ☐ Measurable ☐ Achievable ☐ Relevant ☐ Time-limited

3 my action plan

4 my barriers/ solutions

5 my actions/ outcomes

6 my career connection

CHAPTER SUMMARY

In this chapter you learned about the building blocks of academic and career planning, including the importance of refining your plans as you continue to gain experience and insights about yourself. Review the following key ideas and consider how you might use them to develop sound but adaptable plans for success as you go through college and take steps along a career path.

- Understanding yourself—your interests, values, and skills—helps you identify lines of work and areas of study that you may find rewarding.

- Taking an interest inventory can help you clarify your interests. Gaining experience in different jobs and work environments can help you define your work values, which can change over time. In assessing your skills, it's helpful to distinguish between specialized skills and transferable skills.

- To investigate potential careers, gather information about the available options and how they match up with your interests, work values, and skills. You can gather information using the O*NET; talk with experts such as career counselors and people currently working in jobs that interest you; and gain experience through service learning, co-op, and internship programs and employment.

- An academic plan is a tool that shows the steps you'll take to complete a degree or certificate. Most academic plans involve declaring a major and completing both college major and general-education requirements. An academic adviser (and others on campus) can review your plan and help you refine it as needed and ensure that you meet critical deadlines, such as the deadline for declaring a major.

- Career planning doesn't end when you graduate and start working. As your interests, values, skills, and goals change, you may change your plans several times to continue building a rewarding professional and personal life.

CHAPTER ACTIVITIES

Journal Entry

MAKING A GOOD CAREER DECISION

A good career decision draws on your insights about yourself and your evaluation of information about the world of work. Write a journal entry about an occupation that interests you, using the following questions to guide you.

- What interests you about this occupation?

- In what ways would this occupation align with your work values? In what ways wouldn't it align?

- What skills do you have that would help you succeed in this occupation?

- What skills would you need to develop to succeed in this occupation?

- What information would make you more confident that this occupation is right for you? How will you gain this information?

Adopting a Success Attitude

PLANNING FOR THE UNEXPECTED

Academic planning is a great way to keep yourself on track to graduate or transfer. By planning out your coursework you can save time, money, and a lot of stress! For example, what if you're late to register for courses and a class you need is already full? What if that course is only offered once a year? What if that course is a prerequisite for other courses? Academic planning helps you avoid issues like these, and this two-part activity will get you started.

Part One: One way to plan for the unexpected is to review your school's academic calendar prior to the start of each term. The academic calendar lists important dates and deadlines such as when registration opens and closes, the last day you can add or drop classes, when classes begin and end, and the holidays during that term (days you won't have class). For the first part of this activity, print off your school's academic calendar for next term.

Part Two: For the second part of this activity, you'll create an academic plan. Begin by listing the courses you're required to take each term of your program. Include the course prefix and number, the title of each course, the number of credits you'll earn, and the day/time the course is offered (if you know it). The academic advising office may have a handout of the required courses for your program that you can consult or a worksheet you can use, or you can create a plan using the sample below as a model:

First Year, Spring Quarter			
Course Number	**Title**	**Credits**	**Schedule**
Math 070	Pre-Algebra	5	9-10:30 M–TH
English 100	Introductory Composition	5	11-12:30 M–TH
DT 100	Introduction to CADD/CAM	7	3-5 M–F

Once you've recorded which classes you'll need, create another table for each term in your program and enter three pieces of information:

1. Something you can do to ensure your academic success that term.
2. Something you can do to develop a skill you know you'll need.
3. Something you can do to make yourself more competitive in the career field you hope to enter.

For ideas, see Tables 13.3 and 13.4 in the chapter, or see the example below.

First Year, Spring Quarter		
Academic Success	**Skill Development**	**Competitiveness in Field**
• Meet with an academic adviser to go over my program of study. • Schedule weekly meetings with the math tutor to ensure I get a good grade in Pre-Algebra.	• Research opportunities on campus for leadership development. • Consider volunteer or employment opportunities related to my program of study.	• Join a club or professional organization related to my academic program. • Research and read magazines, journals, Web sites, and blogs that address my field of study.

Applying Your Skills

USING THE O*NET TO GATHER CAREER INFORMATION

This chapter introduced you to the O*NET, a comprehensive source of occupational information. For this activity, choose one occupation you'd like to learn more about. You may want to select something based on your interests, work values, and skills. Then follow these steps:

1. Type "O*NET OnLine" into your Web browser or go to **www.onetonline.org**.
2. Under the "Occupation Search" box, type the name of the occupation you want to investigate.
3. You will be given a list of occupations. Click on the appropriate occupational title.
4. You will see a "Summary Report" for your selected occupation.
5. Of the tasks listed for this occupation, which do you find most appealing? Least appealing?
6. Scroll from "Tasks" down to "Skills." Which skills in the list do you already possess? How did you acquire them? Which skills would you still need to develop to succeed in this occupation?
7. Scroll down to "Interests." How does your Holland interest type (from your interest inventory) match the interest type or code for this occupation?
8. Scroll down to "Work Values." How do your work values match those shown for this occupation?
9. Scroll down to "Wages." What is the median annual wage (the middle number in a list of annual wages sorted from lowest to highest) for this occupation?
10. Select your state, and compare the national median annual wage for this occupation with the median annual wage for your state. Note which is higher.
11. Determine what, if any, additional information you'd like to gather about this occupation and how you will find it.
12. Analyze the information you've gathered, and use your critical-thinking skills to determine whether this occupation would be a good match for you.

College Success = Career Success

CONDUCTING AN INFORMATIONAL INTERVIEW

Follow the advice for conducting an informational interview outlined in this chapter. Contact a person you'd like to speak with, and tell him or her that you'd like to spend 20 to 30 minutes asking questions to learn more about the person's career. Review the interview questions in Table 13.1 and bring them to the interview. To aid your memory, take notes on the person's responses to your questions. During your interview, pay close attention to the time, and don't go over. At the end, thank the interviewee for his or her time, and send a follow-up thank-you note or e-mail.

Then, after the interview, write down your responses to the following questions:

1. Whom did you interview?
2. What did you learn from this person?
3. How did what you learned affect your feelings about pursuing this career?

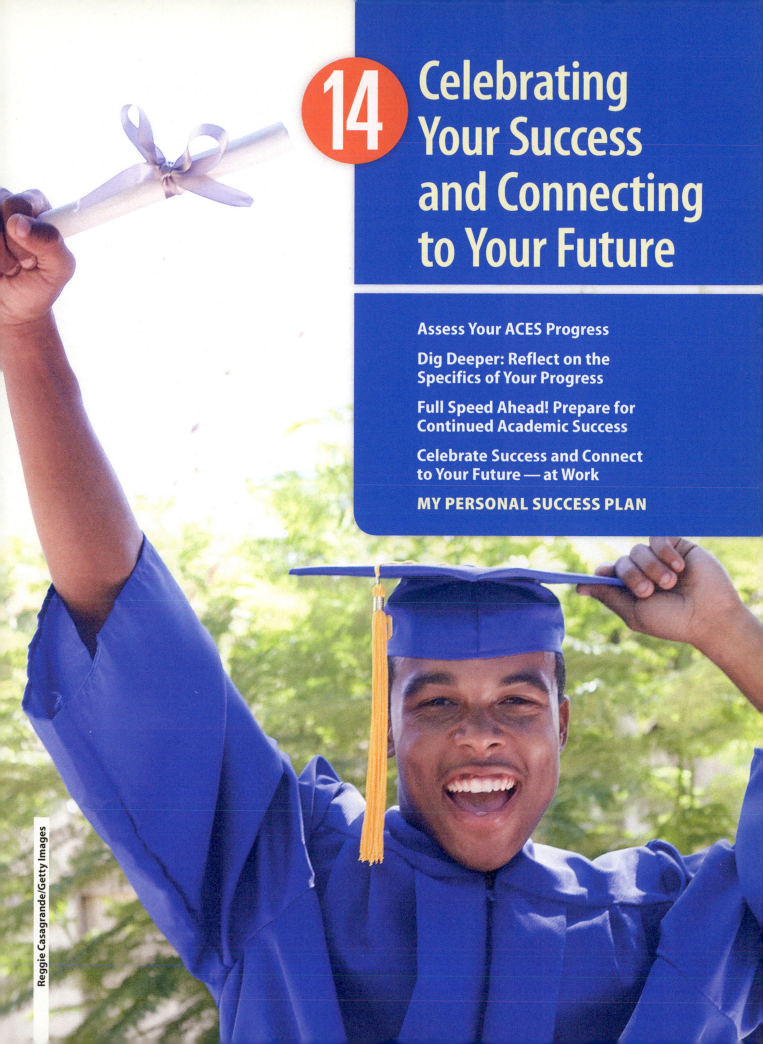

14 Celebrating Your Success and Connecting to Your Future

Assess Your ACES Progress

Dig Deeper: Reflect on the Specifics of Your Progress

Full Speed Ahead! Prepare for Continued Academic Success

Celebrate Success and Connect to Your Future — at Work

MY PERSONAL SUCCESS PLAN

f you're reading this chapter, that means you're almost finished with the term. Congratulations! This is a good time to reflect on how much you've learned and to take pride in your successes. Think of all the goals you've set for yourself and achieved. Consider how well prepared you are for your remaining terms in college. Imagine what a great impression you'll make when you interview for an exciting new job. You have a lot to celebrate!

This is also a good time to think about your future. What challenges lie ahead for you, both in college and in your work life? Are you more excited about some courses than about others? Are there work experiences you'd like to gain before graduating?

In this class you've had the opportunity to spend time each week learning about yourself and developing the skills and attitudes critical to your success at school and at work. Chances are, you'll probably never take a course like this again. So how will you sustain the good habits you've developed?

The fact is, what you've learned in this class transfers over to other classes you take and to the jobs you pursue. If you keep practicing the skills and mindsets you developed this term, you'll continue achieving successes. As a result, your confidence will keep growing. It won't always be easy, but the solid foundation you've built will carry you through even the toughest times. The key is to make connections between what you've learned in this class and the academic and career choices you'll make in the future.

This chapter helps you make those connections. First, we revisit many of the concepts we explored over the term, and you'll think metacognitively about your accomplishments and experiences. Then we turn to the challenges and choices that lie ahead of you — academically and professionally — and look at strategies for sustaining your success in the years to come. In fact, the structure of this chapter matches the structure you'll use to stay successful in life: Reflect on and learn from the past, then use the resulting insights to prepare for the future.

Reggie Casagrande/Getty Images

Assess Your ACES Progress

At the beginning of the term, you completed ACES, and in each chapter of this book you've had a chance to reflect on your scores and use them to target areas where you want to develop your skills. Now that you've reached the end of the term, it's time to complete a concluding activity: taking ACES again to receive your Progress Report. Completing ACES a second time will give you an updated report on the strengths and growth areas you evaluated at the beginning of the term; the questions will be familiar, but this time you'll respond based on how you're feeling now, as the course concludes.

To take ACES again and obtain your Progress Report, log into LaunchPad for *Connections*, Second Edition. As you respond to the items, think critically about where your skills lie right now, and take care to be honest in your responses—your results will be more useful that way!

Compare and Contrast: Initial Report Versus Progress Report

Once you've completed ACES for the second time, the next step is to compare and contrast your latest results (your Progress Report) with your scores from the beginning of the term (your Initial Report). By comparing your earlier results with your most recent scores, you can reflect on the progress you've made and target areas for future growth. Fill out Table 14.1 by entering your original ACES scores in the middle column and your most recent ACES scores in the right-hand column. (You can also complete this activity directly in LaunchPad.) Once the chart is complete, you'll have a handy snapshot of your overall change in skills and confidence over the term, and you can use this information to analyze your results more fully.

Scale	Score on Initial Report	Score on Progress Report
Critical Thinking/Goal Setting		
Motivation/Decision Making/ Personal Responsibility		
Learning Preferences		
Organization/Time Management		
Reading		
Note Taking		
Memory/Studying		
Test Taking		
Information Literacy/ Communication		
Connecting with Others		
Personal and Financial Health		
Academic and Career Planning		

TABLE 14.1
ACES Comparison Chart

End-of-Term ACES Analysis: Four Factors that Influence Results

How did your ACES scores change from the beginning of the term to the end? Did any of your scores improve? Did some remain largely the same? Which scores are lower now relative to when you started this class? There are many reasons why your scores might have changed—for better or worse. Let's take a look at four possible reasons now.

College Rigor. Many students arrive at college with high expectations for their own performance, only to be shocked by how hard college actually is. College is *rigorous*, which means that it's very challenging academically, and sometimes that catches students off guard. If your scores are lower now, it could be that you adjusted your expectations appropriately and conducted a more realistic assessment of your skills and attitudes at the end of the term, once you had a better grasp of college's significant demands.

For example, let's say that your original Organization and Time Management score on ACES was very high. At the beginning of the term, you were convinced that you were a time-management pro, but as the weeks progressed, you began to miss appointments and fall behind in your projects. As it turned out, managing your time was a lot more challenging than you had anticipated. Now that you've reached the end of the term, your score on the Organization and Time Management scale is lower because you're able to be more realistic about where you struggle.

Was your first term of college more or less difficult than your previous school experience? In reviewing your scores and observing how they changed, do you see any outcomes that might be the result of a college reality check?

Focus. Instructors don't always cover every chapter of the textbook in class—after all, different courses emphasize different concepts, and shorter courses can't cover everything that longer courses can. Because course structure varies, when you analyze your progress on a particular scale, it's worth considering whether you addressed that topic in your course. For example, if you didn't cover the personal and financial health chapter, that might explain why your scores didn't change during the term. But if your course really focused on the personal and financial health chapter—you completed assignments on this topic, you visited the financial aid office together as a class, and so on—that may positively impact your results.

Consider how much you focused on the various topics in this book, either by yourself through your own experience of being a college student or as a class. Does this level of focus help explain why your scores went up, went down, or stayed the same?

Effort and Engagement. As you've seen throughout the book, succeeding in college requires you to be an active participant in the learning process, not just a passive observer. The amount of effort you put into your coursework—how hard you tried to master the concepts, how engaged you were in class discussions, whether you completed the reading assignments—has a huge impact on the skills you build and the progress you make.

Reflect on how much effort you put into learning the different topics covered in this book. Can you identify any patterns in your scores that reflect your effort? For example, maybe you used the PSP to set and achieve a goal related to career development, or you worked hard to master the steps in the active-reading process; that type of increased effort could explain score increases on the Academic and Career Planning scale or the Reading scale. Of course, the opposite might also be true, and that's equally important to consider: If you didn't work hard on assignments, you came in late, and you avoided group projects and discussions, that could help to explain why your results went down.

Ask yourself: How engaged were you in this class this term? How much effort did you put into growing your skills and becoming an active participant in your own learning?

Life Complexity. Have you ever heard the saying, "The best laid plans of mice and men often go awry"? It captures the notion that even with careful planning, things don't always go as we anticipate. The first year of college can be challenging at the best of times; if you're also burdened by other challenges that you hadn't predicted, like an illness, a family emergency, or financial issues, you may have found it difficult to take full advantage of the learning opportunities available to you this term. As a result, your scores may not have improved as much as you would have liked.

Consider how your scores changed in light of your own personal experiences this term—including experiences that might be unrelated to your studies. Does this help to explain any of the outcomes you've observed?

Effort Has Impact! The time you spent studying in the library, researching sources for a paper, completing your reading, and working on projects can pay off at the end of the term—and beyond. With effort and engagement, you'll grow your skills and become even more confident in your ability to achieve your goals.
eclipse_images/Getty Images

Where Do You Go From Here?

Now that you've had a chance to review your ACES scores from the beginning of the term and from the end, take your analysis one step further by trying these tips:

- **Consider overall patterns in your results.** For example, are the scales on which you made the most progress related to one another? What about the ones on which you made the least progress? Now that you've read about the four factors listed above, can you think of explanations for why your scores moved in the direction they did?

- **Celebrate the major improvements you've made.** You've worked hard, and you deserve to reward yourself. As you take more difficult courses and make tougher academic and career decisions in upcoming terms, you can stay motivated by keeping your greatest successes in mind. And you can use the skills you've built to tackle each new challenge and make smart decisions.

- **Adopt a continual-learning mindset.** For skills in which you've made less progress than you'd hoped, remind yourself that it's hard to develop many different skills at the same time. As you progress through college and have more work experiences, you can keep striving to build certain skills. By taking this course, you've armed yourself with the tools you need to learn and improve in whatever areas you target. If you use these tools during the rest of your college journey, you'll continue to "move the needle" in a positive direction.

Dig Deeper: Reflect on the Specifics of Your Progress

Filling out Table 14.1 gave you an overview of changes that occurred during the term. Now you'll have a chance to reflect on your *specific* accomplishments in this class and what you've learned about yourself in the process. We'll revisit the key elements of college and career success, consider the impact they've made in your life, and celebrate everything you've learned during this term. Why? Because focusing on what you've accomplished strengthens your self-confidence and helps you stay motivated—and it just plain feels good!

What Did You Discover about Yourself?

In this class you've had many opportunities to strengthen your self-awareness—for example, by clarifying your interests, values, and skills. Self-awareness empowers you to take advantage of your strengths and address weaknesses. It's also a cornerstone of critical thinking, personal responsibility, and goal setting.

To prompt your thinking about self-awareness and the specifics of what you learned this term, let's begin with a quick exercise: In Table 14.2, identify the three most important insights you've gained about yourself in this class. Then write down why you consider each insight valuable and how you'll use it in your future classes and your future career. For example, perhaps you discovered how much you enjoy working with others in small groups. Now you can look for courses and volunteer opportunities that involve working with others, and you can investigate careers that involve collaboration. Concrete reflection like this gives you a way to process all that you've experienced over this busy term.

This reflection is a great first step, but remember that gaining self-knowledge is an ongoing process. You'll continue to learn more about yourself as you progress through college—and through life. In the coming terms, for example, you'll gain more insight into your academic and career interests as you take different courses or try out different jobs. You'll get better at interacting with various types of people as you work on group assignments for class or participate in school organizations. If you're working while going to school, you'll learn about yourself as a professional and a coworker. And once you've graduated, you'll continue building your self-knowledge as you face new opportunities and challenges in your professional and personal life. This course is only the beginning!

TABLE 14.2
Personal Reflection

What I learned about myself in this class	Why this knowledge is valuable	How I'll use this information in the future
1.		
2.		
3.		

Keep Flying. This term, your career as a college student took off. You learned about yourself, started achieving important goals, wrestled with some tough challenges, and grew as a person. During the rest of your academic career, the skills you've built in this class will help you keep flying — reaching new heights while heading toward the bright horizon that's waiting for you.
blackred/Getty Images

What Goals Did You Establish — and Achieve?

By now you've used the Personal Success Plan (PSP) multiple times to define goals and create action plans for achieving them. What did you think about this activity when you first tried it? Did simply setting a goal seem like a lot of work, or did it seem easy? How do you feel about the PSP process now? Do the steps come more easily to you, or less so?

As the next step in your reflection, take a few moments now to review the PSPs you created and to consider the progress you've made toward your goals. Then, in Table 14.3, record three goals you're most proud of achieving, how achieving each goal helped you, and why you're proud of achieving it. For example, perhaps you became skilled at taking notes using an outline, which helped you stay organized when it was time to study for a test. And perhaps you're proud of achieving this goal because you practiced over and over before getting it right—which showed you the power of persistence and how good it feels to improve at a skill through hard work.

TABLE 14.3

Revisiting Your Goals

Goal I achieved	How achieving this goal helped me	Why I'm proud of achieving this goal
1.		
2.		
3.		

What Kept You Motivated and Positive?

Motivation and positivity are key ingredients in success. Motivation keeps you moving forward—striving to reach your next goal, live your next dream, and build your next skill. Of course, motivation fluctuates depending on the goals involved, the rewards you expect to reap, and your academic and career priorities. It can also ebb and flow with the passage of time.

Now that you have some college experience, think about your motivation over the term. In which classes did you feel most motivated to work toward your goals? Why? Were they related to your major? Did they appeal to your interests? Did you believe those courses would best prepare you for your chosen career? Also think about times when you felt decidedly unmotivated, and consider how you handled the situation. Overall, do you think you're better at staying motivated, regardless of the task, than you used to be?

In Table 14.4, list three strategies that helped you maintain your motivation this term. Then describe why those strategies work so well for you and how you'll use them in future courses. For example, perhaps you stayed motivated by connecting your short-term goals to a long-term goal, such as landing a rewarding job. Each time you achieved a short-term goal and celebrated your progress toward the larger goal, it kept you energized. Now, if you're ever unmotivated to work on an assignment, you'll know that connecting it to a meaningful long-term goal will spur you on.

As you consider what motivates you, don't forget just how powerful a positive attitude can be, and how much it can drive you to succeed. To consider how positivity impacted you this term, think back over the last few months: Did you experience a setback during that time, such as performing poorly on a test or handing in an assignment late? How did you respond to the setback? Did you turn it into an opportunity for improvement, and if so, how? Now think of a time this term when you had a success. Maybe you achieved a PSP goal or received praise from an instructor about a project. How did you respond to this success? Did you gain confidence in your skills? Did your motivation grow? Consider what your responses to these questions suggest about how you'll handle setbacks in the future—and how you can use positivity to your best advantage.

TABLE 14.4

Reflecting on Motivation

Strategy for maintaining motivation	Why this strategy works for me	How I'll use this strategy in future courses
1.		
2.		
3.		

> I plan to maintain my success by taking what I know about myself and what I love and turning it into a successful career.

THE POWER OF UNDERSTANDING YOURSELF

NAME
Jennifer Field

SCHOOL
Dixie Applied Technical College

MAJOR
Drafting Technology Certificate

CAREER GOAL
Residential Construction Consulting

High school was challenging for me, and I chose not to go to college right after I graduated. I tried going to college a few times over the years, but I always approached those attempts with a fear of failure and ended up leaving. Deep down, though, I knew that I really wanted to get my education. I wanted to show my family that I had what it takes to graduate from college. I also wanted to show our boys how important school really is. That's exactly what I did. I focused on what really mattered. I put my fears aside and I did it: I went back to school.

I'm so glad I did! Even though college is difficult for me now that I'm in my thirties and have a family to consider, I've found a school and a program that fit my style of learning and my career goals. I love the open learning and communication environment in the Drafting Technology Program. I'm able to interact daily with other students and instructors and to work at my own pace. The work is challenging at times and a breeze at other times. Being in this type of environment allows for hands-on and applied learning. We're encouraged to collaborate with other students on just about every project, and I think that's excellent training for my career field, where projects are almost always collaborative.

Knowing that I value collaborative work environments has helped me establish some longer-term goals related to my career. I know I want to be on the front line, work with people, and feel like I'm making a difference in people's lives.

Now that I've experienced success in school, I plan to maintain my success by taking what I know about myself and what I love and turning it into a successful career.

> **YOUR TURN** How has learning about yourself this term impacted your goals and your decisions? Like Jennifer, do you have a better sense of what you want to do for a career and why you want to do it? If so, what gave you this clarity?

What Skills Did You Build?

Knowing yourself, establishing and achieving goals, and staying motivated and positive are all vital elements of success—but in themselves they're not enough. You also need to develop additional skills that will help you excel in college and beyond. The good news? During this term, you've done just that.

- You've developed critical-thinking, decision-making, and metacognitive skills. All of these helped you reflect on your own motivations, values, and interests, master course content, understand how you learn, *and* figure out which strategies are most effective in which learning situations.

- You've developed specific academic and life skills: managing your time, reading, taking notes, studying, taking exams, working with information, interacting effectively with others, and maintaining your personal and financial health.

- You've developed valuable *transferable skills*. You may already be using skills you've developed in this class to excel in your other classes, and you can apply those same skills to a job you have now and to your future career. (See the Appendix for tips on crafting résumés and cover letters that spotlight your key skills.)

Of all the many skills you've developed this term, list the three *most* important ones in Table 14.5. (For ideas, revisit Table 14.1 or the Connect to Career skills you recorded in each PSP.) Describe how you developed each skill and why it's important to your success. For example, maybe you strengthened your public-speaking skills by volunteering to deliver a group-project presentation in your world cultures class. You prepared your presentation in advance, rehearsed it until you knew it by heart, and then practiced delivering it to a family member to get feedback. The next time you have to present—either in future classes or at work—you'll be confident that you know what to do.

TABLE 14.5
Most Important Skills

Skill I developed this term	How I developed this skill	Why this skill is important to my success
1.		
2.		
3.		

Who Supported You?

Everyone needs help at times, and as you've learned in this class, getting help is a major component of success. Think back to all the campus resources you explored during this term, including tutoring programs, academic advising, counseling and career centers, and the financial aid office. Which of these resources did you find most useful? Why?

In addition to campus programs, consider especially helpful individuals who supported you during the term. For instance, think about your instructors. Who was your biggest supporter? Why? How did you secure his or her support? And think about family members and friends who helped you this term. How did their encouragement differ from the help provided by your instructors or campus resources?

In Table 14.6, create your own Supporter Hall of Fame. List three people who provided you with the most support this term, describe the support they provided, and explain how you benefited from their support.

For example, Tito doesn't make friends easily, but he knew when he met Stephen at the campus gym that they'd get along. An excellent student, Stephen freely shared tips on how he kept his life organized, managed his time, and handled stress—tips that Tito used to stay successful all term long. By being positive and encouraging, Stephen snagged the top spot in Tito's Supporter Hall of Fame. Who gets the top spot on your list?

TABLE 14.6
Supporter Hall of Fame

Name of supporter	Support he or she provided	How I benefited from his or her support
1.		
2.		
3.		

Full Speed Ahead! Prepare for Continued Academic Success

You've learned a lot this term, scoring successes and facing challenges that gave you valuable new insights. But as a first-year college student, you've still got a long academic future ahead of you. As you take more courses, you'll continue strengthening the transferable skills and attitudes essential for success. This class has helped you lay a foundation that you can build on as you continue on your academic journey. But how, exactly, can you build on that foundation? Keep achieving goals. Adapt to new challenges. And stay connected with your supports.

Keep Achieving Goals

Goal setting is an ongoing process. You don't just set goals for one term, achieve them, congratulate yourself, and call it a day. Rather, as you go through college, you constantly define new goals, review your progress toward those goals, and revise them as needed. The following tips can help you remain a goal-setting pro, long after this class concludes.

- **Remember that *you're* in charge.** This term we've suggested setting goals related to the book's chapter topics, but as you move forward in your academic career, the goal-setting process won't be so structured. You'll be responsible for defining your own goals and tracking your own progress. If this sounds a little scary, remember: You have the resources, skills, and self-knowledge you need to define your own path. For example, you can use the PSP to guide you all the way to graduation—and beyond.

- **Connect your short- and long-term goals.** Step back occasionally from the day-to-day grind of college, and ask yourself what short-term goals you can accomplish now to keep working toward your long-term goals. Doing this is a great way to stay motivated and invested in your progress.

  Luis is a case in point. During the first term, his PSP goals included maintaining a high GPA, developing a strong support network of peers and faculty mentors, and gaining experiences that would prepare him to work in counseling. In the second term, Luis set a goal to practice the study skills he developed in his first term so that he could continue maintaining a high GPA. To support his goal of broadening his network, he set new goals to interview his psychology instructors about their research interests and attend student council meetings. And to support his long-term goal of working in counseling, he set a new goal to volunteer with his community's crisis hotline.

- **Reframe setbacks.** Did you have a perfect term, accomplishing all the goals you set for yourself? If so, you can skip to the next section! If not, remind yourself that most people experience a few setbacks as they work toward their goals. As you've seen throughout this book, instead of viewing setbacks as failures, you can reframe them as opportunities for future success by analyzing what caused you to fall short, and identifying changes you can make to get the results you want.

In Table 14.7, list two goals that you were unable to achieve this term. For each goal, note something positive you learned about yourself as you tried to achieve the goal. And if you still want to achieve the goal, write down what you'll do differently next term to accomplish it.

TABLE 14.7
Identifying Ways to Improve

A goal I didn't achieve this term	Something positive I learned as I tried to achieve this goal	What I'll do differently to achieve this goal next term
1.		
2.		

The Power of Optimism

As we note in the chapter on personal and financial health, stress is a normal part of college life (as well as work life). Psychologists have long searched for insights on how to manage stress, and a recent study suggests that *optimism* — having hope and confidence about your future — can help. Researchers asked more than three hundred undergraduate students from a midwestern university to complete measures of optimism, stress, and coping. Here's what they found:

▶ Students with low levels of optimism were more likely to report being stressed in school than those with higher levels of optimism. Students who were more optimistic were more likely to report low levels of stress.

▶ The more optimistic students felt better equipped and more confident in their ability to manage — or cope with — their stress.

THE BOTTOM LINE

When you're optimistic about your future, you may feel *less* stressed overall and *more* confident in handling stress when it does occur.

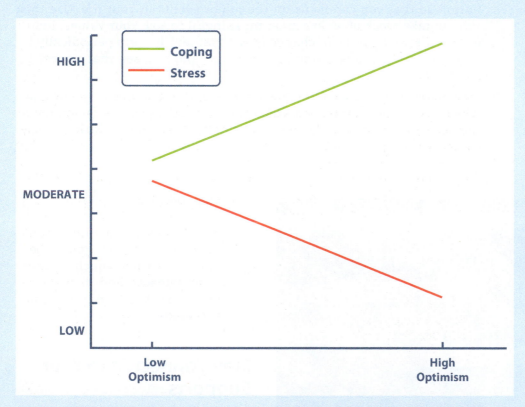

Being optimistic about your future is associated with developing and using effective coping strategies which, in turn, help you manage stress.

Information from M. N. Krypel and D. Henderson-King, "Stress, Coping Styles, and Optimism: Are They Related to Meaning of Education in Students' Lives?," *Social Psychology of Education* 13 (2010): 409–24.

Adapt to New Challenges

Now that you've spent time celebrating your successes and reflecting on the insights you gained from tackling challenges, it's time to consider how you'll keep learning and growing during the remainder of your college career. As you progress in school, you'll face new kinds of challenges: For one thing, your classes may not have the formal structure that this class had, so it may be harder to know how to prioritize your learning. What's more, as you take higher-level courses, your instructors will assign longer papers, and your tests and reading assignments will become more difficult.

Fortunately, during this term you've built foundational skills that you can use to adapt to the challenges you'll encounter during the rest of your academic career. Here are some tips.

- **Hit the "pause" button.** Research suggests that reflection is an important component of learning,[1] so schedule time throughout each term to reflect on your "big ticket" items: the demands you're facing, your goals and action plans, the barriers you're working to overcome, and the progress you're making. Think of these sessions as hitting the "pause" button so that you can focus on the major events in your life. Use this time to take stock of what's most meaningful to *you*. Your values, interests, skills, and goals can change over time; revisit them periodically to be certain that you're pursuing the major and courses that appeal to you most.

- **Take motivation time-outs.** Once a week, stop for a moment to consider which tasks motivate you and which ones don't. Connect the nonmotivating tasks to a long-range goal—for example, "If I read this boring article carefully enough, I'll be better equipped to pass the test. If I pass enough tests, I'll pass the course, which I need for my major." Once you've completed those nonmotivating tasks, reward yourself.

- **Stay positive.** Celebrate your successes and look for positive life lessons when things don't go as you'd hoped. Remember: You can learn as much or more from setbacks and disappointments as you can from your successes.

Stay Connected to Your Supports

Success is a team sport, and you've started building your all-star support team this term, including your instructors, an academic adviser, family, and friends. You'll continue building your team in college as you gain new experiences and as your needs change. For example, if you take a difficult math class next term, you might add a math tutor to

Climb toward Your Goals. As you advance along your academic path, you'll encounter new challenges, including tougher courses and more demanding assignments. But if you start to feel overwhelmed, remember: You've built a strong foundation of vital skills this term. And by deploying these skills, you can keep climbing toward your goals, one step at a time. Philip & Karen Smith/Ascent Xmedia/Getty

your roster of connections. Or if you need help with a challenging term paper, you can visit the writing center. To keep building your support team, try these strategies:

- **Stay connected.** At the start of each term, list the resources you may need to help you manage your course schedule as well as the personal and professional priorities you're juggling. Each term, check in with an adviser to make sure you're on track to graduate.

- **Connect early.** Seek out help as soon as you recognize a need. For example, if you need more financial aid but you're not sure what's available and when the application has to be submitted, meet with someone in the financial aid office right away. Otherwise, you risk missing the deadline.

- **Find a mentor.** A mentor can provide you with the information, advice, guidance, and feedback you need to help you grow. If you're struggling with important academic decisions, such as what major to declare, a mentor can be a great sounding board. A good mentor might be someone who has already taken one of the classes you're in now (an advanced student), a person who knows the subject matter (an instructor), someone who graduated from your college (such as an older sibling or a neighbor), or an adviser. For more on how to find a mentor, see the activity at the end of the chapter.

- **Network.** Take every opportunity to *network*—to meet and get to know new people. They can share valuable insights on such topics as schools you might want to transfer to, interesting job opportunities, and contacts with whom you can discuss careers that interest you. To stay in touch with people in your network, enter them into your phone's contacts list or connect with them on platforms like LinkedIn. And remember, networking goes both ways: Your contacts try to help you, and you try to help them. If you have any leads that they might benefit from, be reciprocal and pass them along.

Nurture Your Network. The support network you started building this term will be crucial to you in later terms, so keep cultivating it. Maintain connections with your supports — mentors, advisers, career counselors, and others who have helped you. Forge connections with new people, too, and include them in your network if they can offer you additional forms of help. Monkey Business Images/Shutterstock

Celebrate Success and Connect to Your Future — at Work

Celebrating your successes and connecting to your future are good ways to keep learning and growing while you're in school, but these strategies will be equally valuable in your work life. Just as your values, interests, skills, and goals can change during college, they can shift in your professional life as well. Ongoing personal reflection, the ability to adapt as you encounter challenges, and a willingness to network will help you build a satisfying, successful career.

Keep Reflecting

When you celebrate your successes at work, you take stock of the new skills that you've acquired or talents you've strengthened, and these insights can help when you're seeking a promotion, supervising others, and refining your career path. Likewise, when you experience setbacks at work, you can take personal responsibility for analyzing what caused them and identifying the changes you'll make to get a better outcome in the future. Employers appreciate people who take initiative, turn setbacks into learning opportunities, and keep honing their skills. Ongoing personal reflection helps you do just that.

The One Constant? It's Change. Change will be a constant not only in your academic career but also in your professional life. The organizations you work for will face major shifts in their environment, including technology advances that you'll need to adapt to. Take mobile phones — they've changed a lot already. Imagine what they'll look like in five or ten years! Malcolm Haines/Alamy

Adapt to Change

In the world of work, one thing's for certain: You can expect constant change. Over time, the job market for various careers can grow or shrink. Some careers emerge (like Internet-related jobs that didn't exist thirty years ago), while other careers disappear. (When was the last time you spoke to a telephone operator?) Moreover, skills that employers value today may differ from skills they'll want five years from now. The most pressing challenges and the most exciting opportunities that organizations face will also keep changing, thanks to new technologies, changes in consumers' preferences or needs, and radical moves by competitors.

By staying up-to-date on developments in your field, you can better anticipate what changes may be lurking on the horizon, and adapt as needed to take advantage of emerging opportunities or tackle fresh challenges. For instance, Paolo has just learned that his employer is installing new accounting software that requires some basic coding skills in SQL, a computer language for accessing and manipulating data. Proficiency in SQL would advance his career in any company, so Paolo purchases a book on SQL programming and creates a study schedule so he's prepared for the transition. By doing so, he is building valuable skills that will open up new doors for him.

Continue Networking

Networking is just as important in your professional life as in your academic life: According to data from LinkedIn, in 2016, 70 percent of people surveyed got a job at an organization where they had a personal connection of some kind.[2] So take just as much care to build and maintain your professional network as you do your academic network.[3]

NAME
Michael Garcia

PROFESSION
Admission Counselor

SCHOOL
Santa Clara University

DEGREE
Bachelor of Science

MAJORS
Anthropology and Political Science

THE VALUE OF CONTINUOUS PERSONAL REFLECTION

I've been employed for six years since college, and when I reflect back on how I thought about work when I first graduated versus how I think about it now, I'm amazed at how much I've grown and all I've learned. I had to find out through trial and error how to thrive as a professional, and I've learned a number of important lessons along the way. For example, I've learned that it's important to stay positive and to always be on the lookout for professional development opportunities. I've also learned that I'm not an expert at everything. I have my strengths and my weaknesses. When I'm reflecting on my work I try to leverage my strengths and look for ways to improve in areas where I'm not as strong.

I've also relied heavily on mentors since starting my first job. My mentors have been excellent sounding boards and have supported my development at work. Some of my best mentors are people in my own organization who know the ins and outs of my work and how to be successful here. My mentors also helped me understand my need for structure and organization. My job can be pretty chaotic and I've learned that I have to impose some semblance of structure on my day. Every morning I start with a daily reflection, asking myself "What did I accomplish this week?" and "What are my remaining goals for the week and how will I accomplish them?" I reflect again at the end of the day, but I focus on my personal life instead — on my relationship with family and friends and my own self-care. This helps me keep a balance between my work life and my personal life and gives me the time I need to celebrate my successes and identify work that remains to be done.

It hasn't always been easy to find the time for reflecting but I've made it a priority for myself. Understanding my strengths, using them, sharpening them, and taking advantage of every opportunity to improve has helped me succeed.

> **YOUR TURN** If you're currently employed, do you continuously reflect on your performance and progress, as Michael does? Do you take time to celebrate your successes? Why or why not? If not, or if you're not yet employed, what strategies might you use to prompt self-reflection and appreciation in the future? How might these strategies benefit you as an employee?

To network on the job, find out whether your company has a mentor program. A mentor can help you define career goals, connect you with people who know about job opportunities within the organization, and advise you on how to navigate the organization's political landscape. And remember that you can make connections outside the office as well: Contact your local chamber of commerce to find out more about networking events in your community.

my personal success plan

This is your final Personal Success Plan for this class! So far, each PSP you've completed has been related to the specific chapter content. This time, you're in charge of defining your own goal for *next* term on any topic you choose. Read the advice and examples; then sketch out your ideas in the space provided.

To access the Personal Success Plan online, go to the LaunchPad for *Connections,* Second Edition.

---

1 IDENTIFY A GOAL

Think about a goal that you would like to accomplish next term. Here are some general ideas you might draw from; you can also create a goal of your own.

- ▶ Make a plan to identify and connect with a mentor.
- ▶ Identify a strength I'd like to develop further.
- ▶ Pick an area where I've struggled that I'd like to improve.
- ▶ Revisit a goal I didn't achieve this term that I'd like another crack at.
- ▶ Consider possible career opportunities that I'd like to investigate.

2 MAKE YOUR GOAL SMART

Rewrite your specific goal so that it's SMART and make sure to use the SMART goal checklist.

SAMPLE: I'll secure a mentor during the first month of class.

3 CREATE AN ACTION PLAN

Outline the specific steps you'll take to achieve your SMART goal, and note when you'll complete each step.

SAMPLE: During the first week of the term, I'll visit the Career Center to inquire about the campus mentor program.

4 LIST BARRIERS AND SOLUTIONS

Think about possible barriers to your action steps; then brainstorm solutions for overcoming them.

SAMPLE: If no one is available through the campus mentor program, I'll meet with an adviser in my major and ask if she can recommend a mentor in my field.

5 ACT AND EVALUATE OUTCOMES

Because you're setting a goal for next term, you can't record your action steps and evaluate whether you have achieved your goal just yet. But you can make a commitment to pursue this goal. In fact, you can set a reminder in your calendar this very minute so that you'll follow up next term and implement your action steps.

6 CONNECT TO CAREER

List the skills you'll build as you progress toward your SMART goal. How will you use these skills to land a job and succeed at work?

SAMPLE: Having a mentor will provide me with valuable insights into my future career. I'll also get great experience building my network, which I'll want to do as a professional as well.

my personal success plan

1 my general goal

2 my SMART goal

☐ SPECIFIC ☐ MEASURABLE ☐ ACHIEVABLE ☐ RELEVANT ☐ TIME-LIMITED

3 my action plan

4 my barriers/ solutions

5 my actions/ outcomes

6 my career connection

CHAPTER SUMMARY

You've worked hard this term to build skills, score successes, and prepare for your future, regardless of what career you choose. Review the following list, celebrate your achievements in each area, and ask yourself what work still lies ahead.

- You've learned about your own motivations, interests, and values.
- You've become skilled at critical thinking.
- You've learned an effective strategy for setting and achieving goals.
- You've become a responsible and active learner.
- You've learned how to practice metacognition.
- You've discovered how you learn.
- You've developed and strengthened academic skills.
- You've connected with others and explored the benefits of personal and financial health.
- You've launched academic and career plans.
- You've considered how you can strengthen and sustain all of this learning as you progress through your academic and work life.

CHAPTER ACTIVITIES

Journal Entry

CELEBRATING YOUR SUCCESSES

In this chapter you reflected on what you've accomplished this term and celebrated your successes. For your journal entry, describe one thing you're proud of accomplishing this term in each of the following areas: (1) school, (2) career, and (3) your personal life. In your description of each accomplishment, answer the following questions:

1. What did you do during the term to achieve this success?
2. What challenges did you encounter along the way? How did you overcome them?
3. What campus resources or personal supports helped you achieve this success?
4. How does this accomplishment make you feel? How will you celebrate it?

Adopting a Success Attitude

LOOKING TOWARD THE FUTURE WITH OPTIMISM

As you learned in this chapter, optimism means having hope and confidence about your future. Maintaining this success attitude will help you deal with stress and cope with challenges and will provide motivation when the going gets tough. Think optimistically by creating a list of your hopes for next term, using the following questions to brainstorm ideas.

- What do you hope to learn in each of your classes?
- What skills do you plan to build?
- How will you get involved in the campus community or meet new people?
- Do you plan to join any campus clubs or activities?
- Do you plan to use any campus resources?
- What faculty members, advisers, and counselors do you hope to connect with?
- How will you prepare for your future career?

These hopes for your future are more likely to become reality if you take personal responsibility for making them happen. Choose one of your hopes for the future, and describe in detail the steps you'll take to meet your goal.

Applying Your Skills

DESCRIBING YOUR SKILLS

During this term you've developed a wide range of skills, and you'll want to remember what these skills are, how you developed them, and what they helped you accomplish. Why? Describing your skills on a résumé, on a job application, on a scholarship application, or during an interview can help you stand out from the crowd. For practice describing your skills, both verbally and in writing, follow the steps below:

1. Begin by writing down three of your top skills. If you need ideas about which skills to spotlight, review Table 14.1, Table 14.5, the Connect to Career skills you've recorded on your Personal Success Plans, or this book's table of contents.

2. For each skill you've listed, describe in detail how you demonstrate that skill. For example, if you select "working with others" as one of your top skills, write down what you do at school or work to show that you have this skill. Maybe you approach group work with an open mind, use conflict-management strategies to work through disagreements, and listen to the ideas of others.

3. Reflect on what each of the skills you've chosen to highlight has helped you accomplish. Continuing the example of "working with others," you might say, "This skill helped me successfully lead a project team that delivered high-quality work on time and earned the team members a glowing letter of recommendation."

4. In order to become more comfortable describing your skills and accomplishments out loud, ask a friend or family member to help you practice talking about your top skills.

College Success = Career Success

FINDING A MENTOR

Throughout this book we've talked about the importance of finding and using personal supports, and in this chapter we explored the value of having a mentor (both in college and at work) who can provide information, advice, guidance, and feedback to help you grow. In some cases these relationships can last a lifetime and become extremely meaningful to both the mentor and his or her protégé. This activity will walk you through the steps you can take to connect with an academic or a professional mentor.

1. To begin, reflect on what you're looking for in a mentoring relationship by answering these questions:
   - What would you like to learn from your mentor? What type of guidance or support could he or she offer you? Are these forms of support valuable to you? If so, why?
   - How would you communicate with your mentor, including how often and where?
   - Do you have anyone specific in mind as a mentor? If so, how might you establish a mentoring relationship with this person? If not, how could you find someone who might make a good mentor?

2. Once you've identified someone you respect and admire, do your homework: Read your potential mentor's *vita*, which describes this person's accomplishments and experience, as well as any articles he or she has written or blogs he or she maintains.

3. Request an initial meeting — something informal — where you get to know this person better. You can suggest meeting at his or her office or even for coffee. When you set up the meeting, provide details — how you learned about this person, what you know about him or her, what you respect and admire about him or her, and the fact that you're seeking advice and guidance.

4. Keep your meeting to less than an hour. During that time, be prepared to talk in more depth about the details you provided when setting up the meeting.

5. At the end of the meeting, if you feel this person would be a good mentor for you, ask him or her to serve that role. Be sure to define what you think a mentor is and does and describe how you see this person fitting into that role. In addition, describe your time commitments and ask about your potential mentor's availability, keeping in mind that a little negotiation may need to take place. If this person doesn't have time to mentor you, thank him or her for agreeing to meet and ask if there is someone else who you could speak to. If this person agrees to mentor you, be sure to outline your expectations and ask about your mentor's expectations as well.

6. Finally, take care to follow through and sustain the mentoring relationship by making good use of your mentor's support and expressing how much you appreciate the help. When the mentoring relationship ends, be sure to provide a more formal thank you such as a card or e-mail letting your mentor know how he or she impacted your development and your career path.

Are you in the process of searching for a new job right now, while you're in school? Are you anticipating how you'll enter the job market once you finish your academic program? Whatever your situation, we've designed this appendix to walk you through the steps of writing a résumé, locating a job, and presenting yourself in a cover letter and interview. Although this information comes at the end of the book, its importance shouldn't be minimized. The job market is competitive. You may be applying for jobs alongside 10, 100, or even 1,000 other people. Thus, we don't just want to help you prepare for the job search, we want to help you stand out and successfully sell employers on your skills and abilities.

Before digging into the details, let's begin with a few general suggestions, several of which you'll recognize as messages emphasized throughout this book. First, adopt a positive mindset. Recognize that you may not get offered the first, the second, or even the tenth job you apply for. The job search is a process, meaning it takes time and effort. Second, if you begin to feel frustrated or anxious, use your resources. Rely on your connections — reach out to friends, family members, or those in your professional network to gain support, feedback, or advice. Third, take personal responsibility. The job search is an exciting opportunity for *you* to change the course of your future! Spend time reflecting on what type of job you're looking for based on your interests, skills, and values. Fourth, be proactive. Find job openings through multiple sources, including your professional networks. And fifth, remember that you're selling yourself in the résumé, cover letter, and interview. What do you bring to the company? Be sure to highlight the skills and experiences that make you a good fit for the job.

Write a Résumé

At the most basic level, your **résumé** is a summary of your education, work experience, and extracurricular activities. It gives potential employers a sense of your prior experience and qualifications for the position you're targeting. Recruiters will often skim a candidate's résumé for this basic information before deciding whether to read more closely, so it's important that these basics stand out in the visual layout of your document.

résumé: A document that lists your education, work experience, and extracurricular activities.

At a deeper level, your résumé is an opportunity to detail your responsibilities, highlight accomplishments, and spell out transferable skills. It can be challenging to place all pertinent information on a page without it looking cluttered, but the key is to briefly list only the most critical information. The goal of the résumé is to get an interview—you can provide detail about your experiences during the interview. Although most people prefer a one-page résumé, you may need to use two pages if you have a significant amount of work experience and accomplishments. Ultimately, your goal is to show how your qualifications align with the requirements of the job in a clear, professional way.

Résumé Basics

As you can see in Figure A.1, your name and contact information should appear prominently at the top of your résumé. You might also include a link to your LinkedIn profile, Twitter feed, or another element of your online presence if appropriate. And remember that your e-mail address should be professional—you may want to obtain a new one for the job search process.

Many job applicants choose to open their résumé with a summary section. Think of this as a place to tell employers what kind of professional you are. This description should highlight the characteristics and skills that you would bring to a job, while citing previous accomplishments as support for these points. Note that each statement in this section of Figure A.1 begins with a skill or quality that the student has chosen to emphasize. This puts the most important information in a prominent place and makes this section easy for a reader to digest, even if he or she is reading quickly.

Next, add your educational history. This should consist of all the institutions where you've completed undergraduate coursework, as well as any technical certifications you hold. On the first line of each entry, list the name of each institution, its location, and your dates of attendance. Underneath this, consider including your grade point average if it is 3.0 or above, as well as your area of study. You might also wish to include your high school name, location, and year of graduation, plus any study abroad experience, scholarships, or even Honor Society membership. If you can fit them in, these kinds of details make your résumé more informative and help to spark conversation with an interviewer.

Chronological or Functional

chronological résumé: A résumé that lists work and extracurricular experiences in reverse chronological order, with the most recent appearing first.

functional résumé: A résumé that groups entries by skills and experiences.

After your education section, list your work and extracurricular experience in one of two styles: chronological or functional. On a **chronological résumé**, entries simply appear in reverse chronological order, with your current or most recent experience first. Figure A.1 shows a chronological résumé, a style commonly used by college students. This format is a great choice for students who have taken on increasingly complex responsibilities over time, as it demonstrates this growth in a linear fashion. A chronological résumé also makes sense for students whose experiences are all somewhat relevant to the positions for which they're applying.

In a **functional résumé**, entries are grouped based on the nature of the experience they reflect rather than the order in which they occurred. This style of résumé can be helpful when only some of your past experiences are directly related to the position you're seeking. For example, a student applying for a research assistant position may wish to highlight a summer research position from several years ago more prominently than her current part-time job in food service. To do so, she might develop a "Related Experience" section that includes work experience involving data collection and analysis, and then an "Other Experience" section that includes the rest of her work history. Functional résumés can also be useful for applicants

Maria A. Student

2525 Market Street, #459
Springfield, WA 90546
403.555.1245

maria.student@email.com
linkedin.com/mariastudent
@mariaontwitter

Qualifications Summary

Dedicated, hard-working professional with strong communication, leadership, and critical-thinking skills. Demonstrated ability to organize and lead teams in workplace and education settings. Strong interest in and extensive experience with computer hardware, software, and social media applications. History of excellent customer service. Commitment to bringing demonstrable value to and delivering measurable outcomes for the organization.

- Promoted to team lead within 4 months of hire
- Commitment to volunteering and community service
- Elected treasurer of Marketing Club
- Tripled Marketing Club's Twitter followers through collaborative efforts within 2 months at Mountain College

Education

2018–present	Mountain College—Springfield, WA GPA 3.75; major in Business Administration
2016–2018	Valley College—Hampton, OR GPA 3.0; coursework in Accounting, Information Technology, English
2016	River High School—Carlisle, OR

Relevant Experience

2018–present　　　*Team Lead*—All Things Tech

Promoted to Team Lead after 4 months of outstanding work and customer service. Supervise 3 technicians. Monitor and respond to customer feedback regarding repair services. Provide outstanding customer service to promote repeat business. Collaborate with store manager to increase social media presence for store.

2018　　　*Technician*—All Things Tech

Provided excellent customer service in repairing customer computers, mobile phones, and tablets. Applied extensive background and expertise with computer and phone hardware to efficiently complete assigned repairs.

2017–2018　　　*Facilitator and Mentor*—Girls in STEM

Planned and facilitated monthly meetings for 15 members of the Girls in STEM club at Green Valley Elementary. Researched and designed activities to engage and promote students' interest in science, technology, engineering, and math. Mentored three elementary school-age students in the club.

2015–2016　　　*Server & Cook*—Neugent's Burger Stand

Performed duties of server and cook. Demonstrated strong customer service in taking orders. Supported coworkers in responding to customer complaints. Quickly learned tasks of line cook. Performed well in fast-paced and stressful environment during lunch and dinner rush. Recognized as employee of the month 3 times, August and December 2015, July 2016.

applying for different types of positions. A student who is applying for both marketing and editing jobs, for example, might develop two different functional résumés: one for marketing positions in which the "Related Experience" section cites social media accomplishments, and another for editing positions in which the "Related Experience" section details his work in the college writing center and involvement with the school newspaper.

No matter which style you choose, you'll need to develop descriptions of your responsibilities and accomplishments in each position you've held. As you can see in Figure A.1, the style used for writing a résumé is quite different than the style used for written course assignments. Résumés use short phrases rather than complete sentences and begin each statement with an active verb. By describing what you accomplished in such vivid terms, you'll help employers visualize how your skills might apply to their open positions.

In addition to the sample résumé provided in this section, you can access résumé examples online through your career center or by doing your own online search (type "sample résumé" into a search engine). Your local library or bookstore may also have résumé-writing books with samples of both chronological and functional résumés.

Find Job Opportunities

Once your résumé is ready to go, what's the next step? Search for open positions that interest you. Just as the word *search* implies, this is an active process that often requires patience and persistence. The good news is that there are employers out there looking to hire students and recent graduates. In this section, we'll look at some of the places where employers advertise openings and interact with students who are interested in these opportunities.

Get Online

When employers have an open position to fill, they develop a description of the responsibilities and qualifications the job requires. While few employers make use of newspaper classifieds in this digital age, some do list opportunities on online job boards like **Monster.com**, **CareerBuilder**, or **Simply Hired**. Keep in mind that while there will be some part-time and entry-level positions on these sites, online job boards will also have jobs for more experienced professionals. So do pay close attention to the qualifications and requirements listed in these postings.

If there are specific companies you would like to work for—perhaps you admire their product or the way they run their organization—you might also look for job opportunities in the employment section of the organization's Web site. Keep in mind that these sites are updated as jobs become available, so if you don't see any openings the first time you look, don't lose hope! Instead, visit the site once or twice per week to look for new postings. You can also check out the target company's Twitter account or Facebook page, or look on LinkedIn. The federal government also advertises jobs online (**www.usajobs.gov**), as do some cities and states.

Use Campus and Community Resources

If your school has a career center, set up an appointment to get personalized guidance on your job search. Some college career counselors have vast networks of local and national hiring managers, and they may be able to steer you toward specific companies or industries that are hiring. Additionally, your college career center may host on-campus interviews and have an online job search engine, free seminars on job search strategies, or other resources to help you in your job search.

Job fairs hosted by your school or in the community are another great place to network and learn about many open positions at once. Even if you aren't actively looking for a job at the time the fair is happening, take advantage of this opportunity to learn about employers in your area and make connections with recruiters.

When attending a job fair, dress professionally. This signals to recruiters that you're taking this process seriously and you want to make a good impression. In addition, print copies of your résumé on high-quality paper so you can provide them to employers whose opportunities interest you. And finally, to make the most of your time at the fair, develop a brief summary of the kinds of job you're looking for and your relevant experiences and skills.

Join a Professional Association

Affiliation with a **professional association** is another good source of employment information. Professional associations are nonprofit organizations through which individuals who share a specific trade or job function can network, share best practices, and promote their profession and its interests. Student memberships in these organizations are generally quite affordable and provide access to job listings on members-only Web sites and listservs. More generally, professional associations allow you to learn about your chosen industry from insiders who may be hiring now or in the future. By attending professional association meetings or events, you can introduce yourself and ask for advice on how to gain entry-level employment.

One way to identify appropriate professional associations is to consult your library's copy of *National Trade and Professional Associations of the United States*. This comprehensive directory of professional organizations includes membership and contact information, as well as dates and locations of upcoming conferences. You might also look for LinkedIn groups of professionals in your field, as this is another popular place to find job listings. Professors are often members of these professional associations and can help you identify which associations are most appropriate for the career you are considering.

> **professional association:** An organization through which individuals who share a trade or job function can network and promote the interests of their profession.

Network

As we've mentioned throughout the book, networking is a great way to find a job opening. Networking is really just about talking to people—everyone from fellow members of professional associations to instructors, classmates, friends, family members, neighbors, or those affiliated with your faith community, volunteer work, or recreational pursuits. Once you've identified the people you already know in your network, start contacting them. Explain that you're looking for a job, and be specific about what type of job or career field. Then ask them if they have any job leads or know anyone who could give you some advice on following your chosen path. If they give you a name, follow up with that person immediately.

When you get in touch with a contact, your best strategy is to ask him or her for advice or insight—*not* for a job. Many people like to give advice, but if you ask for a job outright, you're putting them on the spot and they may feel ambushed. A better strategy is to meet with your contact and ask for insight into the field. If your contact does know of a job, he or she may tell you how to apply or give you an additional person to contact. Networking is about establishing relationships with people, so be sure to follow up any networking meeting with an electronic or handwritten thank-you note.

Write a Cover Letter

cover letter: A formal letter in which you introduce yourself, your interest in a job, and your appropriate skills and qualifications.

Once you've identified an open position that interests you, it's time to work on a **cover letter** to accompany your résumé. Whereas your résumé can be somewhat generic—you might have a few versions highlighting different sorts of experiences—your cover letter should be highly tailored to the organization and position for which you're applying. This document is the place where you explain exactly how your previous experiences have prepared you to excel in this next job. Successful cover letters address the specific job requirements and duties described in the job ad.

As you can see in Figure A.2, this document should be formatted like a formal business letter, with your name and contact information at the top, followed by the date and the address of the company to which you're sending your application. If there's a contact person associated with the job posting, address that person by name. If no contact information is provided, you can use "To Whom It May Concern." In the first sentence of your letter, identify the position that you're applying for, and comment on your excitement about the position. You might follow this with another sentence that elaborates on why you're interested in working for this organization and why you're a good fit for the role.

In the body of the document, zero in on specific aspects of the job description and draw connections to positions you've held in the past. This is the place to emphasize your transferable skills and demonstrate why they've prepared you to succeed in the post you're seeking. For example, April is applying for a pharmaceutical sales position that requires the employee to "develop strong relationships with customers through face-to-face interaction." In her cover letter, she might describe how she built close relationships with advertisers for her college's student newspaper. By emphasizing in-person visits to local businesses and the number of repeat orders she received from advertisers, she could make a convincing case that she's well prepared for the responsibilities of her target position.

In your conclusion, it's appropriate to thank the reader for his or her time and consideration. You might also summarize the reasons for your interest in the position, and express your interest in discussing the opportunity further during an interview.

One additional word of caution: It's important to spell check your cover letter at least twice—once using your computer's spell check function and another time by reading it over carefully. Typos can sneak past computer spell check programs, so it's best to give everything a second look yourself to avoid potentially embarrassing mistakes. If you're worried about your own proofreading skills, ask a friend or family member to review your letter.

Interview Effectively

After you get an employer's attention with your résumé and cover letter, the next step is an interview. Interviews may be conducted in person, over the phone, or via video chat. Some firms conduct several rounds of interviews, while others speak with applicants just once before making an offer. No matter the process, the employer's goal in interviews is to learn more about you and your qualifications, assess your interpersonal skills, and evaluate your fit with the job and organization.

Maria A. Student
2525 Market Street, #459
Springfield, WA 90546
maria.student@email.com
403.555.1245

April 27, 2019

Madeline Iverson
Director of Human Resources
Techstar Inc.
45983 Ocean Drive
Springfield, WA 09546

Dear Ms. Iverson:

I am excited to apply for the Enterprise Solutions Account Manager position at Techstar Inc. I have admired the work of Techstar Inc. for the past few years, and I believe that I bring an optimal combination of experience, skills, and drive that will result in superb customer care and excellent sales within the division.

My past and current experiences are a strong match for the qualifications and skills you are seeking in your next Account Manager. As you can see from my résumé, I have a demonstrated history of meeting customers' needs, and I have placed customer service as my highest priority. I believe that when clients are satisfied, they are more likely to return, and they are our strongest advertisers to generate referrals and sales. I also possess the technical skills to excel in this position, as evidenced by my experience in repair and the fact that I currently serve as the leader of a team of repair technicians. Further, I have a demonstrated history of exceeding expectations.

- Completed 78% of customer repairs on or under time, highest rate in the branch
- Tripled number of followers on Marketing Club Twitter account
- 3-time employee of the month

Thank you for taking time to consider my application. I am very excited about implementing my current skill set at Techstar Inc. and believe that as I complete my Bachelor's degree at Mountain College, I will have even more to offer. If I can provide any additional information, please do not hesitate to contact me. I look forward to discussing this position further.

Sincerely,

Maria A. Student

Prepare for an Interview

To prepare for your interview, review the job description for the position you applied for, and do some research on the larger company itself. Does the organization have prominent competitors or established partnerships with other firms that you should know about? Are there trends and recent news related to that industry that you should be aware of? This level of research prepares you to speak from an informed position and signals to the employer that you're serious about joining their team. Interviewers may even ask directly what you know about their organization, in which case you'll be glad you did background research.

It's also helpful to prepare responses for commonly asked interview questions. Be ready to walk the interviewer through your résumé and to tackle open-ended questions like "What can you tell me about yourself?" You should also reflect on your personal strengths and areas for growth as an employee. (We've discussed the value of self-awareness throughout the text—here's another application!) You may also be asked to explain why you're interested in the position, why you believe you're a good fit for the job, and how this position fits into your larger career goals.

As you prepare, you'll want to develop a sense of what you plan to say without memorizing responses that make you sound too rehearsed. Try practicing with a friend or arranging a mock interview if offered by your college career services office.

Be Ready for Behavioral Interview Questions

behavioral interview questions: Specific interview questions designed to reveal information about how you act and react in certain situations.

In addition to standard interview questions, you may also be asked behavioral questions. **Behavioral interview questions** are designed to reveal information about how you act and react in certain types of situations. These questions usually begin with a phrase like "tell me about a time when . . ." and the interviewer will then ask you to focus on the details of a past experience. For example, you might be asked to discuss a time you tackled a large, open-ended project, or to describe how you handled a conflict with a classmate or coworker. The logic behind this type of interview question is that past behavior is the best predictor of future behavior. In learning how you've handled challenging situations in the past, the interviewer will draw conclusions about how you'd conduct yourself as an employee in his or her organization.

For this reason, you'll want to choose your examples carefully. Behavioral interview questions are often more difficult to anticipate and prepare for than the more standard interview questions, so it's wise to take a few seconds to think about potential responses and consider which will show you in the best light. Employers know that behavioral questions can require a bit of thought, and the interviewer will likely appreciate that you're taking the process seriously.

Once you've identified the example you'd like to share, it's important to tell the story in a clear way. The STAR *approach*—Situation, Task, Action, Result—is a great structure to use when answering behavioral questions.[1] After sharing the who, what, when, and where of the story (the situation), summarize the objective that you were aiming to accomplish (the task). Then provide a step-by-step description of how you proceeded (the action), and comment on the outcome (the result). The interviewer may ask follow-up questions during or after your story in order to thoroughly understand your thought process and actions.

Master Interview Etiquette

As important as your responses to interview questions will be, employers will also consider how you present yourself and draw conclusions about your interpersonal skills and level of professionalism. Be mindful of your dress and grooming, and err on the side of formality if you're unsure about the organization's dress code. On the day of the interview, aim to arrive a bit early and be sure to behave courteously toward the support staff and other people you meet in the building. Hiring managers sometimes seek input from reception staff as they evaluate candidates, and may even test job applicants by asking employees to pose as fellow job seekers in the waiting area.

After the interview, it's customary to send thank-you notes to your interviewers. Handwritten notes are a nice touch, but e-mail is also an acceptable—and more timely—medium. In your note, thank the interviewer for his or her time, summarize what you learned during the interview about the organization and how you might fit in there, and reiterate your excitement about the position. Aim to send your thank-you note within 24 hours of your interview.

Typically, interviewers will let you know what their time line is for making decisions. If the interviewer says she will make a decision in two weeks, for example, expect to hear from her then and don't take further action after you send your thank-you note. But delays can happen, so if you haven't heard from the interviewer within the time specified, it's appropriate to reach out and ask about the status of your application. Not only does this provide you with peace of mind, it also signals your ongoing interest in the opportunity.

Know Your References

At some point in the hiring process (possibly during the interview) you'll be asked to provide the contact information for two or three references: people who are familiar with your skills and work ethic who will vouch for you. No matter how great an impression you make, employers will want to speak with people who can weigh in on your character and abilities before they make a job offer. This is just one reason why it's valuable to cultivate strong relationships with your instructors and to stay on good terms with past employers. The stronger an impression you make, the more enthusiastically these contacts will recommend you to prospective employers! Note that while most professors and supervisors will readily agree to serve as references, be sure to ask permission before passing their contact information along to potential employers.

Once you receive permission from two or three references, print out their name, title, company name, company address, work phone number, work fax number, and e-mail address on a piece of paper that you could hand to an interviewer. Be sure to place your name, centered, at the top of the page and a title such as "List of References." That way, if the interviewer asks for a list of references, you'll have your document ready to go.

After your interview, contact your references and let them know what position you interviewed for and what company you interviewed with. This gives your references a heads-up to expect a call, and gives them time to gather their thoughts about what a strong employee you would make.

In this appendix, we've worked to provide you with guidance in your career search, but always keep in mind that many other resources exist—both within and outside your school—to help you with these tasks. We encourage you to seek out these resources and use your personal and professional networks to support you in your transition from school to work.

Although the job search can be stressful, this course and this book have helped you develop the knowledge, attitudes, and skills you need to successfully navigate this process. Remember to reflect on what you've learned this term about your interests, values, and skills and how you'd like to use them in a career. And take responsibility for your future by looking for a job proactively.

Good luck to you in the job search process. We wish you all the best in making your dreams a reality!

glossary

academic adviser/counselor: A highly trained professional who can help you make effective academic decisions and refer you to valuable campus resources.

academic plan: A tool used by students and their advisers to plan and track a student's progress toward obtaining a degree or certificate.

accountable: Responsible for completing tasks and meeting obligations.

action plan: A list of steps you'll take to accomplish a goal and the order in which you'll take them.

active reading: A reading strategy that involves engaging with the material before, during, and after reading.

attribution theory: Theory about how people use information to explain the events that occur in their lives.

barrier: A personal characteristic or something in your environment that prevents you from making progress toward a goal.

behavioral interview questions: Specific interview questions designed to reveal information about how you act and react in certain situations.

budget: A plan that documents income and expenses for a specific period of time.

career counselor: A specially trained professional who uses career assessments and other resources to help students explore career options and make career decisions.

chronological résumé: A résumé that lists work and extracurricular experiences in reverse chronological order, with the most recent appearing first.

cite: To give another author credit when you include his or her ideas in your paper or project.

cloud: A place on the Internet where you can store your files.

college major: A collection of courses organized around an academic theme.

Cornell system: Method of note taking that organizes each page of content into sections: initial notes on the right, key points in a cue column on the left, and a summary section at the bottom of the page.

cover letter: A formal letter in which you introduce yourself, your interest in a job, and your appropriate skills and qualifications.

creative thinking: The ability to consider information or problems from a fresh perspective using processes like imagination, innovation, playfulness, and curiosity.

critical thinking: The ability to consider information in a thoughtful way, adopt logical and rational thinking skills, and apply these skills in your classes and your life.

culture: Shared concepts, ideas, values, norms, and rules of behavior of a specific group of people.

cumulative exams: Exams that cover everything you've learned in the course up to that point in the term.

discrimination: Treating people less favorably because of their membership in a particular group.

diversity: Characteristics or attributes that make us different from one another and that can be the basis for membership in a group.

elaborative rehearsal: The process of making connections between new ideas and other information already stored in your memory.

emotional intelligence: The ability to recognize, understand, and manage your own and others' emotions.

empathy: The ability to understand another person's emotions.

encoding: Taking in information and changing it into signals in our brain.

extrinsic motivation: Motivation that derives from forces external to you, such as an expected reward or a negative outcome that you want to avoid.

fixed mindset: The belief that one cannot improve one's talents, skills, and abilities.

functional résumé: A résumé that groups entries by skills and experiences.

general-education courses: A set of course requirements that gives all students a broad liberal education in the natural and social sciences, humanities, arts, and mathematics.

goal: An outcome you hope to achieve that guides and sustains your effort over time.

growth mindset: The belief that one can further develop or improve one's talents, skills, and abilities.

information literacy: Finding information, evaluating its quality, and effectively communicating it to others.

integrity: Being honest and displaying behavior that is consistent with one's values.

interpersonal communication: An active exchange of information between two or more people.

intrinsic motivation: Motivation that stems from your inner desire to achieve a specific outcome.

long-term memory: Memory that stores a potentially limitless amount of information for a long period of time.

metacognition: Thinking about how you think and learn.

mnemonic: A learning strategy that helps you memorize specific material.

multimodal learner: Someone who uses multiple learning strategies and methods to learn.

occupational projection: The predicted rise or fall in the number of new jobs in a particular field.

paralinguistics: Changes in the voice (such as volume or pitch) that convey emotion.

paraphrase: To restate information in your own words.

Personal Success Plan (PSP): A tool that helps you establish SMART goals, build action plans, evaluate your outcomes, and revise your plans as needed.

plagiarism: When one person presents another person's words or ideas as his or her own.

positive psychology: A branch of psychology that focuses on people's strengths rather than on their weaknesses and that views weaknesses as growth opportunities.

prioritize: To give an activity or a goal a higher value relative to another activity or goal.

procrastinate: To delay or put off an action that needs to be completed.

professional association: An organization through which individuals who share a trade or job function can network and promote the interests of their profession.

purposeful reading questions: Specific questions you want to be able to answer when you've finished reading.

resilience: The ability to cope with stress and setbacks.

résumé: A document that lists your education, work experience, and extracurricular activities.

rote rehearsal: Memorization of specific information or facts by studying the information repeatedly.

self-efficacy: Your belief in your ability to carry out the actions needed to reach a particular goal.

sensory memory: Process that uses information from the senses to begin creating memories.

service learning: Classes that combine classroom instruction with volunteer experience in the community.

sexually transmitted infections (STIs): Illnesses, some treatable and some incurable, that are spread through the exchange of bodily fluids during sexual activity.

short-term memory: Memory that stores a small number of items for a short period of time.

SMART goal: A goal that is specific, measurable, achievable, relevant to you personally, and time-limited.

Supplemental Instruction: A student-led study program for especially difficult classes.

test anxiety: Nervousness or worry about performance on an exam.

thesis: The main idea or argument of a paper or an essay.

transferable skills: Skills that can be applied in many different settings, such as work, home, and school.

work values: The aspects of your work or your work environment that you consider important.

working memory: The part of short-term memory that actively processes memories and information.

endnotes

Chapter 1

[1] See, for example, Betsy O. Barefoot, Carrie L. Warnock, Michael P. Dickinson, Sharon E. Richardson, and Melissa R. Roberts, eds., *Exploring the Evidence: Reporting Outcomes of First-Year Seminars: The First-Year Experience*, vol. 2, Monograph Series, no. 25 (1998), http://eric.ed.gov/?id=ED433742.

[2] "Educational Attainment," United States Census Bureau, accessed October 15, 2017, https://www.census.gov/topics/education/educational-attainment.html.

[3] "Educational Attainment in the United States: 2016," United States Census Bureau, accessed October 15, 2017, https://www.census.gov/data/tables/2016/demo/education-attainment/cps-detailed-tables.html.

[4] J. Ma, M. Pender, and M. Welch, "Education Pays 2016: The Benefits of Higher Education for Individuals and Society," CollegeBoard (2016), https://trends.collegeboard.org/sites/default/files/education-pays-2016-full-report.pdf.

[5] A. P. Carnevale, N. Smith, and J. Strohl, "Recovery: Job Growth and Education Requirements through 2020," Georgetown University, accessed October 15, 2017, http://cew.georgetown.edu/recovery2020.

[6] For a list of these and other reasons, see M. K. Eagan, E. B. Stolzenberg, H. B. Zimmerman, M. C. Aragon, H. Whang Sayson, and C. Rios-Aguilar, "The American Freshman: National Norms Fall 2016," Higher Education Research Institute at UCLA (2017): 43, https://www.heri.ucla.edu/monographs/TheAmericanFreshman2016.pdf.

[7] For more on positive psychology, see C. R. Snyder and Shane J. Lopez, eds., *Oxford Handbook of Positive Psychology*, 2nd ed. (New York: Oxford University Press, 2009); C. R. Snyder, Shane J. Lopez, and Jennifer Teramoto Pedrotti, *Positive Psychology: The Scientific and Practical Explorations of Human Strengths*, 3rd ed. (Thousand Oaks, CA: Sage, 2015).

[8] For more on resilience, see Jacqueline Aundree Baxter, "Who Am I and What Keeps Me Going? Profiling the Distance Learning Student in Higher Education," *International Review of Research in Open and Distance Learning* 13, no. 4 (2012): 107–29, http://www.irrodl.org/index.php/irrodl/article/view/1283; Robert Holloway, "From School to University: A Senior College Model," *Independence* 39, no. 1 (2014): 10–12; Steven M. Southwick and Dennis S. Charney, *Resilience: The Science of Mastering Life's Greatest Challenges* (Cambridge: Cambridge University Press, 2012); John W. Reich, Alex Zautra, and John Stuart Hall, eds., *Handbook of Adult Resilience* (New York: Guilford Press, 2010).

[9] C. R. Snyder, K. L. Rand, and D. R. Sigmon, "Hope Theory: A Member of the Positive Psychology Family," in *Handbook of Positive Psychology*, eds. C. R. Snyder and S. J. Lopez (New York: Oxford University Press, 2002), pp. 257–76.

[10] A. M. Wood, P. A. Linley, J. Maltby, T. B. Kashdan, and R. Hurling, "Using Personal and Psychological Strengths Leads to Increases in Well-Being over Time: A Longitudinal Study and the Development of the Strengths Use Questionnaire," *Personality and Individual Differences* 50 (2011): 15–19; D. T. Kong and V. T. Ho, "A Self-Determination Perspective of Strengths Use at Work: Examining Its Determinant and Performance Implications," *Journal of Positive Psychology* 11 (2016): 15–25.

[11] S. A. Karabenick and R. S. Newman, *Help-Seeking in Academic Settings: Goals, Groups, and Contexts* (Mahwah, NJ: Erlbaum, 2006).

[12] "Top Ten Things Employers Look for in New College Graduates," Association of American Colleges & Universities, accessed October 16, 2017, http://www.aacu.org/leap/students/employers-top-ten;

[13] A. Willard, "Top Ten Skills Employers Seek," YouTube, accessed October 16, 2017, http://www.youtube.com/watch?v=ItL01G3Kovs.

[13] For example, "Employers: Verbal Communication Most Important Candidate Skill," National Association of Colleges and Employers (February 24, 2016) https://www.naceweb.org/career-readiness/competencies/employers-verbal-communication-most-important-candidate-skill/.

Chapter 2

[1] Bureau of Labor Statistics, U.S. Department of Labor, *Occupational Outlook Handbook, 2016–17 Edition*, Forensic Science Technicians, accessed August 17, 2017, https://www.bls.gov/ooh/life-physical-and-social-science/forensic-science-technicians.htm.

[2] Edward M. Glaser, *An Experiment in the Development of Critical Thinking* (New York: Teachers College, Columbia University, 1941).

[3] "Key Facts About Seasonal Flu Vaccine," Centers for Disease Control and Prevention, accessed August 30, 2017, http://www.cdc.gov/flu/protect/keyfacts.htm. See the Vaccine Benefits section.

[4] For example, K.C. Tsai, "Being a Critical and Creative Thinker: A Balanced Thinking Mode," *Asian Journal of Humanities and Social Sciences* 1, no. 2 (2013), http://ajhss.org/archives/Vol1Issue2.htm.

[5] For more on cognitive development in an educational setting, see Julie Dockrell, Leslie Smith, and Peter Tomlinson, eds., *Piaget, Vygotsky, and Beyond: Central Issues in Developmental Psychology and Education* (London: Taylor & Francis, 1997).

[6] For example, B. S. Bloom, M. D. Engelhart, E. J. Furst, W. H. Hill, and D. R. Krathwohl, *Taxonomy of Educational Objectives: The Classification of Educational Goals. Handbook I: Cognitive Domain* (New York: David McKay, 1956); B. S. Bloom, "Reflections on the Development and Use of the Taxonomy," in "Bloom's Taxonomy: A Forty-Year Retrospective," ed. Kenneth J. Rehage, Lorin W. Anderson, and Lauren A. Sosniak, *Yearbook of the National Society for the Study of Education* (Chicago: National Society for the Study of Education) 93 (2); L. W. Anderson and D. R. Krathwohl, eds., *A Taxonomy for Learning, Teaching, and Assessing: A Revision of Bloom's Taxonomy of Educational Objectives* (Boston: Allyn & Bacon, 2001).

[7] "Study Focuses on Strategies for Achieving Goals, Resolutions," Dominican University of California, accessed August 30, 2017, http://www.dominican.edu/dominicannews/study-highlights-strategies-for-achieving-goals.

Chapter 3

[1] See Albert Bandura, *Self-Efficacy: The Exercise of Control* (New York: W. H. Freeman, 1997), p. 382.

[2] S. G. Rogelberg et al., "The Executive Mind: Leader Self-Talk, Effectiveness, and Strain," *Journal of Managerial Psychology* 28 (2013): 183–201; Christopher A. Wolters, "Self-Regulated Learning and College Students' Regulation of Motivation," *Journal of Educational Psychology* 90, no. 2 (1998): 224–35; and D. Creswell, J. M. Dutcher, W. M. P. Klein, P. R. Harris, and J. M. Levine, "Self-Affirmation Improves Problem-Solving under Stress," *PLoS ONE* 8, no. 5 (2013), http://journals.plos.org/plosone/article?id=10.1371/journal.pone.0062593.

[3] E. Kross, E. Bruehlman-Senecal, J. Park, A. Burson, A. Dougherty, H. Shablack, R. Bremner, J. Moser, and O. Ayduk, "Self-Talk as a Regulatory Mechanism: How You Do It Matters," *Journal of Personality and Social Psychology* 106, no. 5 (2014): 304–24.

[4]N. A. Vasquez and R. Buehler, "Seeing Future Success: Does Imagery Perspective Influence Achievement Motivation?," *Personality and Social Psychology Bulletin* 33, no. 10 (2007): 1392–405.

[5]C. S. Dweck, *Mindset: The New Psychology of Success* (New York: Random House, 2006).

[6]H. S. Waters and W. Schneider, *Metacognition, Strategy Use, and Instruction* (New York: Guilford Press, 2010).

[7]A. Duckworth, *Grit: The Power of Passion and Perseverance* (New York: Scribner, 2016).

[8]For example, see Marylène Gagné, ed., *The Oxford Handbook of Work Engagement, Motivation, and Self-Determination Theory* (Oxford: Oxford University Press, 2014).

[9]Douglas J. Swanson, Ed.D., "Narratives of Job Satisfaction Offered by the '100 Best Companies to Work for in America,'" Annual Meeting of the Western Social Science Association, Denver, CO, April 2013, http://works.bepress.com/dswanson/69.

[10]M. Gottschalk, "How to Harness Career Power," LinkedIn (March 15, 2013), http://www.linkedin.com/today/post/article/20130315141647-128811924-harnessing-career-power-the-beauty-of-personal-responsibility.

Chapter 4

[1]A. C. McCormick, "It's about Time: What to Make of Reported Declines in How Much College Students Study," *Liberal Education* 97 (2011): 30–39.

[2]N. J. Cepeda, N. Coburn, D. Rohrer, J. T. Wixted, M. C. Mozer, and H. Pashler, "Optimizing Distributed Practice: Theoretical Analysis and Practical Implications," *Experimental Psychology* 56 (2009): 236–46.

[3]Tony Schwartz, *The Way We're Working Isn't Working* (New York: Free Press, 2010).

Chapter 5

[1]For more about the research behind the techniques spotlighted in this section, see a recent comprehensive review of learning research published by psychologist John Dunlosky and his colleagues: J. Dunlosky, K. A. Rawson, E. J. Marsh, M. J. Nathan, and D. T. Willingham, "Improving Students' Learning with Effective Learning Techniques: Promising Directions from Cognitive and Educational Psychology," *Psychological Science in the Public Interest* 14 (January 2013): 4–58. There is also an informative article based on this review: J. Dunlosky, K. A. Rawson, E. J. Marsh, M. J. Nathan, and D. T. Willingham, "What Works, What Doesn't," *Scientific American Mind* 24, no. 4 (September/October 2013): 47–53.

    For more on research-based learning strategies, including self-testing and interleaving, see P. C. Brown, H. L. Roediger III, and M. A. McDaniel, *Make It Stick: The Science of Successful Learning* (Cambridge: Harvard University Press, 2014). For more on these and other strategies (including dual coding and using concrete examples), see M. Smith and Y. Weinstein, "Six Strategies for Effective Learning," The Learning Scientists, accessed May 9, 2017, http://www.learningscientists.org/blog/2016/8/18-1; and "Learn to Study . . ." posters from The Learning Scientists, accessed May 9, 2017, http://www.learningscientists.org/posters.

[2]J. D. Bransford, A. L. Brown, and R. R. Cocking, eds., *How People Learn: Brain, Mind, Experience, and School*, exp. ed., (Washington, DC: National Academy Press, 2000), pp. 114–27, http://www.nap.edu/read/9853/chapter/8#116.

[3]The Royal Society, "Brain Waves Module 2: Neuroscience: Implications for Education and Lifelong Learning," (February 2011), https://royalsociety.org/~/media/Royal_Society_Content/policy/publications/2011/4294975733.pdf. See also "Neuroplasticity: The Potential for Lifelong Brain Development," SharpBrains, accessed May 9, 2017, http://sharpbrains.com/resources/1-brain-fitness-fundamentals/neuroplasticity-the-potential-for-lifelong-brain-development/.

[4]R. Sylwester, "How Emotions Affect Learning," *Educational Leadership* 52, no. 2 (October 1994): 60–65, http://www.ascd.org/publications/educational-leadership/oct94/vol52/num02/How-Emotions-Affect-Learning.aspx.

[5]V. Camos and S. Portrat, "The Impact of Cognitive Load on Delayed Recall," *Psychonomic Bulletin & Review* 22, no. 4 (August 2015): 1029. See also J. Sweller, "Cognitive Load Theory, Learning Difficulty, and Instructional Design," *Learning and Instruction* 4, no. 4 (1994): 295–312.

[6]A. S. Benjamin and J. Tullis, "What Makes Distributed Practice Effective?," *Cognitive Psychology* 61, no. 3 (2010): 228–47.

[7]Steven Pan recently described why this technique might be so effective: S. C. Pan, "The Interleaving Effect: Mixing It Up Boosts Learning," *Scientific American Mind* (August 4, 2015), http://www.scientificamerican.com/article/the-interleaving-effect-mixing-it-up-boosts-learning/.

[8]"Interleaving" definition, Dictionary.com, accessed May 9, 2017, http://www.dictionary.com/browse/interleaving.

[9]D. J. Menke and M. Pressley, "Elaborative Interrogation: Using 'Why' Questions to Enhance the Learning from Text," *Journal of Reading* 37, no. 8 (1994): 642–45.

[10]R. Azevado and V. Aleven, *International Handbook of Metacognition and Learning Technologies* 28 (2013): 1–16.

[11]A. Paivio, *Imagery and Verbal Processes* (New York: Holt, Rinehart, and Winston, 1971).

[12]H. Pashler, M. McDaniel, D. Rohrer, and R. Bjork, "Learning Styles: Concepts and Evidence," *Psychological Science in the Public Interest* 9, no. 3 (December 2008): 105–19.

[13]For more about the dimensions identified in the MBTI, see Isabel Briggs Myers and Peter B. Myers, *Gifts Differing: Understanding Personality Type* (Mountain View: CPP, 1995).

[14]N. D. Fleming and C. Mills, "Not Another Inventory, Rather a Catalyst for Reflection," *To Improve the Academy* 11, no. 1 (1992): 137–55.

[15]National Survey of Student Engagement Report, *Engaged Learning: Fostering Success for All Students*, Annual Report (Bloomington: Center for Postsecondary Research, School of Education, Indiana University Bloomington, 2006).

[16]Job Outlook 2015, "Employers Seek Teamwork, Problem-Solving Skills on Resumes," National Association of Colleges and Employers, February 16, 2017, http://www.naceweb.org/about-us/press/2017/employers-seek-teamwork-problem-solving-skills-on-resumes/.

Chapter 6

[1]R. Emanuel et al., "How College Students Spend Their Time Communicating," *International Journal of Listening* 22 (2008): 13–28.

[2]N. K. Duke and P. D. Pearson, "Effective Practices for Developing Reading Comprehension," in A. E. Farstrup and S. J. Samuels (Eds.), *What Research Has to Say about Reading Instruction*, 3rd ed. (Newark, DE: International Reading Association, 2002), pp. 205–42.

[3]V. S. Gier, D. Herring, J. Hudnell, J. Montoya, and D. S. Kreiner, "Active Reading Procedures for Moderating the Effects of Poor Highlighting," *Reading Psychology* 31 (2010): 69–81.

[4]Act, Inc., *Workplace Essential Skills: Resources Related to the SCANS Competencies and Foundational Skills* (Iowa City, IA: Act, 2000).

Chapter 7

[1]N. D. Rahim and H. Meon, "Relationship between Study Skills and Academic Performance," *AIP Conference Proceedings* 1522 (2013): 1176–78.

[2]V. Slotte and K. Lonka, "Review and Process Effects of Spontaneous Note-Taking on Text Comprehension," *Contemporary Educational Psychology* 24 (1999): 1–20.

[3]D. Cohen, E. Kim, J. Tan, and M. Winkelmes, "A Note Re-structuring Intervention Increases Students' Exam Scores," *College Teaching* 61 (2013): 95–99.

[4]B. Christe, "The Importance of Faculty-Student Connections in STEM Disciplines: A Literature Review," *Journal of STEM Education: Innovations and Research* 14 (2013): 22–26.

Chapter 8

[1]R. C. Atkinson and R. M. Shiffrin, "Human Memory: A Proposed System and Its Control Processes," in *The Psychology of Learning and Motivation: Advances in Research and Theory*, vol. 2, eds. Kenneth W. Spence and Janet Taylor Spence (Waltham, MA: Academic Press, 1968), pp. 89–195.

[2]I. Winkler and N. Cowan, "From Sensory to Long-Term Memory: Evidence from Auditory Memory Reactivation Studies," *Experimental Psychology* 52 (2005): 3–20.

[3]N. Cowan, "The Magical Number 4 in Short-Term Memory: A Reconsideration of Mental Storage Capacity," *Behavioral and Brain Sciences* 24 (2000): 87–105; Y. Kareev, "Seven (Indeed, Plus or Minus Two) and the Detection of Correlations," *Psychological Review* 107 (2000): 397–402.

[4]Y. Hu, K. A. Ericsson, D. Yang, and C. Lu, "Superior Self-Paced Memorization of Digits in Spite of a Normal Digit Span: The Structure of a Memorist's Skill," *Journal of Experimental Psychology* 35 (2009): 1426–42.

[5]W. Klimesch, *The Structure of Long-Term Memory: A Connectivity Model of Semantic Processing* (Hoboken: Taylor and Francis, 2013).

[6]S. D. Gronlund and D. R. Kimball, "Remembering and Forgetting: From the Laboratory Looking Out," in *Individual and Team Skill Decay: The Science and Implications for Practice*, eds. Winfred Arthur Jr., Eric A. Day, Winston Bennett Jr., and Antoinette M. Portrey (New York: Routledge/Taylor and Francis, 2013), pp. 14–52.

[7]N. J. Cepeda, N. Coburn, D. Rohrer, J. T. Wixted, M. C. Mozer, and H. Pashler, "Optimizing Distributed Practice: Theoretical Analysis and Practical Implications," *Experimental Psychology* 56 (2009): 236–46.

[8]C. Gillen-O'Neel, V. W. Huynh, and A. J. Fuligni, "To Study or to Sleep? The Academic Costs of Extra Studying at the Expense of Sleep," *Child Development* 84 (2013): 133–42.

[9]M. S. Birnbaum, N. Knornell, E. L. Bjork, and R. A. Bjork, "Why Interleaving Enhances Inductive Learning: The Roles of Discrimination and Retrieval," *Memory and Cognition* 41 (2013): 392–402.

[10]L. E. Levine, B. M. Waite, and L. L. Bowman, "Electronic Media Use, Reading, and Academic Distractibility in College Youth," *CyberPsychology and Behavior* 10 (2007): 560–66.

[11]G. D. Hendry, S. J. Hyde, and P. Davy, "Independent Student Study Groups," *Medical Education* 39 (2005): 672–79; Donita J. Shaw, "Promoting Professional Student Learning through Study Groups: A Case Study," *College Teaching* 59, no. 2 (2011): 85–92.

Chapter 9

[1]K. A. Rawson, J. Dunlosky, and S. M. Sciartelli, "The Power of Successive Relearning: Improving Performance on Course Exams and Long-Term Retention," *Educational Psychology Review* 25 (2013), 523–548.

[2]P. Baghaei and J. Cassady, "Validation of the Persian Translation of the Cognitive Test Anxiety Scale," *Sage Open* 4 (2014): 1–11.

[3]J. C. Cassady, "The Influence of Cognitive Test Anxiety across the Learning-Testing Cycle," *Learning and Instruction* 14 (2004): 569–92.

[4]M. Mavilidi, V. Hoogerheide, and F. Paas, "A Quick and Easy Strategy to Reduce Test Anxiety and Enhance Test Performance," *Applied Cognitive Psychology* 28, no. 5 (2014), 720–6.

Chapter 10

[1]"Michael Gorman vs. Web 2.0," *Chronicle of Higher Education* 53 (2007): B4.

[2]"Wikipedia: Wikipedia Is a Volunteer Service," Wikipedia, accessed January 19, 2018, https://en.wikipedia.org/wiki/Wikipedia:Wikipedia_is_a_volunteer_service.

[3]B. Burnsed, "Wikipedia Gradually Accepted in College Classrooms," *U.S. News* (June 20, 2011), http://www.usnews.com/education/best-colleges/articles/2011/06/20/wikipedia-gradually-accepted-in-college-classrooms.

[4]See, for example, T. Cronan, J. Mullins, and D. Douglas, "Further Understanding Factors that Explain Freshman Business Students' Academic Integrity Intention and Behavior: Plagiarism and Sharing Homework," *Journal of Business Ethics* 147 (2018): 197–220; and S. Tolman, "Academic Dishonesty in Online Courses: Considerations for Graduate Preparatory Programs in Higher Education," *College Student Journal* 51 (2017): 579–86.

[5]National Association of Colleges and Employers, "The Key Attributes Employers Seek on New College Graduates' Resumes" (November 30, 2017), http://www.naceweb.org/about-us/press/2017/the-key-attributes-employers-seek-on-students-resumes/.

[6]C. B. Pull, "Current Status of Knowledge on Public-Speaking Anxiety," *Current Opinion in Psychiatry* 25 (2012): 32–38.

[7]Hart Research Associates, "It Takes More Than a Major: Employer Priorities for College Learning and Student Success," *Liberal Education* 99 (2013): 22–29.

Chapter 11

[1]"Build Better Listening Skills," National Education Association, last modified 2015, http://www.nea.org/tools/build-better-listening-skills.html.

[2]Emotional intelligence has been defined in various ways by different people. Our definition and model of emotional intelligence is a synthesis of the following works by Mayer and Salovey: J. D. Mayer and P. Salovey, "Emotional Intelligence: New Ability or Eclectic Traits?," *American Psychologist* 63, no. 6 (2008): 503–17; and J. D. Mayer and P. Salovey, "What Is Emotional Intelligence?," in *Emotional Development and Emotional Intelligence: Educational Implications*, eds. P. Salovey and D. Sluyter (New York: Basic Books, 1997), pp. 3–31.

[3]Mayer and Salovey, "Emotional Intelligence," 503–17.

[4]M. Bayrami, "Effect of Assertiveness Training on General Health in the First Year of Students of Tabriz University," *Psychological Research* 14, no. 1 (2011): 47–64.

[5]J. Darrington and N. Brower, "Effective Communication Skills: 'I' Messages and Beyond," *Families and Communities* (April 2012), Utah State University Cooperative Extension.

[6]S. Miller and P. A. Miller, *Core Communication: Skills and Processes* (Evergreen, CO: Interpersonal Communication Programs, 1997).

[7]A. W. Astin, *Achieving Educational Excellence: A Critical Assessment of Priorities and Practices in Higher Education* (San Francisco: Jossey-Bass, 1985).

[8]Ibid.

[9]S. Uusiautti and K. Maatta, "I Am No Longer Alone — How Do University Students Perceive the Possibilities of Social Media?," *International Journal of Adolescence and Youth* 19, no. 3 (2014): 293–305.

[10]P. M. Hudelson, "Culture and Quality: An Anthropological Perspective," *International Journal of Quality in Health Care*, 16 (2004): 345–6, https://academic.oup.com/intqhc/article/16/5/345/1822533.

[11]S. R. Ennis, M. Rios-Vargas, and N. G. Albert, "The Hispanic Population: 2010," *2010 Census Briefs*, U.S. Census Bureau (May 2011), http://www.census.gov/prod/cen2010/briefs/c2010br-04.pdf.

[12]"Gender," World Health Organization (2017), http://www.who.int/gender-equity-rights/understanding/gender-definition/en/.

[13]"Guidelines for Psychological Practice with Lesbian, Gay, and Bisexual Clients," *American Psychologist* 67 (January 2012): 10–42.

[14]Ibid.

[15]American Psychological Association, Task Force on Socioeconomic Status, *Report of the APA Task Force on Socioeconomic Status* (Washington, DC: American Psychological Association, 2007).

[16]M. E. Kite, "Multicultural Competence: Engaging in Difficult Dialogues that Are Inherent in Teaching about Diversity," American Psychological Association (February 2015), http://www.apa.org/ed/precollege/ptn/2015/02/multicultural-competence.aspx.

[17]M. Adams, L. Bell, and P. Griffin, *Teaching for Diversity and Social Justice: A Sourcebook* (New York, NY: Routledge, 1997).

Chapter 12

[1]Mayo Clinic Staff, "Chronic Stress Puts Your Health at Risk," last modified April 21, 2016, http://www.mayoclinic.org/healthy-living/stress-management/in-depth/stress/art-20046037.

[2]Ibid.

[3]American College Health Association, "American College Health Association–National College Health Assessment II: Reference Group Undergraduate Executive Summary Spring 2017" (Hanover, MD: American College Health Association, 2017), p. 12, http://www.acha-ncha.org/docs/NCHA-II_SPRING_2017_UNDERGRADUATE_REFERENCE_GROUP_EXECUTIVE_SUMMARY.pdf.

[4]F. J. He, C. A. Nowson, M. Lucas, and G. A. MacGregor, "Increased Consumption of Fruit and Vegetables Is Related to a Reduced Risk of Coronary Heart Disease: Meta-analysis of Cohort Studies," *Journal of Human Hypertension* 21 (2007): 717–28.

[5]ChooseMyPlate.gov, "MyPlate Tip Sheets," United States Department of Agriculture, last updated November 16, 2016, http://www.choosemyplate.gov/ten-tips.

[6]"Eating Disorder Statistics," National Association of Anorexia Nervosa and Associated Disorders, accessed January 29, 2018, http://www.anad.org/get-information/about-eating-disorders/eating-disorders-statistics/.

[7]H. W. Bland, B. F. Melton, L. E. Bigham, and P. D. Welle, "Quantifying the Impact of Physical Activity on Stress Tolerance in College Students," *College Student Journal* 48 (2014): 559–68.

[8]World Health Organization, *Global Recommendations on Physical Activity for Health* (Geneva: WHO Press, 2010).

[9]D. C. Lee, R. R. Pate, C. J. Lavie, X. Sui, T. S. Church, and S. N. Blair, "Leisure-Time Running Reduces All-Cause and Cardiovascular Mortality Risk," *Journal of the American College of Cardiology* 64 (2014): 472–81.

[10]O. Pikovsky, M. Oron, A. Shiyovich, Z. Perry, and L. Nesher, "The Impact of Sleep Deprivation on Sleepiness, Risk Factors, and Professional Performance in Medical Residents," *Israel Medical Association Journal* 15 (2013): 739–44.

[11]National Alliance on Mental Illness, *College Students Speak: A Survey Report on Mental Health* (Arlington, VA: National Alliance on Mental Illness, 2012); also D. Eisenberg, S. Goldrick-Rab, S. K. Lipson, and K. Broton, *Too Distressed to Learn? Mental Health Among Community College Students* (Madison, WI: Wisconsin Hope Lab, 2016), http://wihopelab.com/publications/Wisconsin_HOPE_Lab-Too_Distressed_To_Learn.pdf.

[12]"The Core Alcohol and Drug Survey," Core Institute, Southern Illinois University, accessed January 29, 2018, http://core.siu.edu/results.

[13]Centers for Disease Control and Prevention, "CDC Fact Sheets," accessed February 22, 2018, http://www.cdc.gov/std/healthcomm/fact_sheets.htm; Centers for Disease Control and Prevention, "CDC Fact Sheet: HIV Incidence: Estimated Annual Infections in the U.S., 2008–2014 Overall and by Transmission Route," February 2017, https://www.cdc.gov/nchhstp/newsroom/docs/factsheets/hiv-incidence-fact-sheet_508.pdf; Centers for Disease Control and Prevention, "2016 Sexually Transmitted Diseases Surveillance," accessed February 22, 2018, https://www.cdc.gov/std/stats16/toc.htm.

[14]"Contraception," Centers for Disease Control and Prevention, updated February 9, 2017, http://www.cdc.gov/reproductivehealth/unintendedpregnancy/contraception.htm.

[15]American Psychological Association, *Stress in America: Paying with Our Health* (Washington, DC: American Psychological Association, 2014).

[16]"2014 National Student Financial Wellness Study: Key Findings Report," Ohio State University, Office of Student Life, Center for the Study of Student Life, http://cssl.osu.edu/posts/documents/nsfws-key-findings-report.pdf.

[17]"College Student Employment," National Center for Education Statistics, last updated May 2017, https://nces.ed.gov/programs/coe/indicator_ssa.asp.

[18]National Center for Education Statistics, *Undergraduates Who Work While Enrolled in Postsecondary Education, 1989–1990* (Washington, DC: National Center for Education Statistics, 1994).

[19]"Fast Facts: Financial Aid," National Center for Education Statistics, accessed May 9, 2017, http://nces.ed.gov/fastfacts/display.asp?id=31.

[20]R. Crawford, "Financial Stress Impacts Work Productivity," *Employee Benefits* (2014): 3, http://www.employeebenefits.co.uk/.

Chapter 13

[1]J. L. Holland, *Making Vocational Choices: A Theory of Vocational Personalities and Work*, 3rd ed. (Odessa, FL: Psychological Assessment Resources, 1997).

[2]Based on O*NET Work Values: "Browse by O*Net Data," O*Net OnLine, updated December 5, 2017, http://www.onetonline.org/find/descriptor/browse/Work_Values/.

[3]J. Gault, E. Leach, and M. Dewey, "Effects of Business Internships on Job Marketability: An Employer's Perspective," *Education + Training* 52, no. 1 (2010): 76–88.

[4]U.S. Department of Education, National Center for Education Statistics, *Digest of Education Statistics*, Table 105.20, "Enrollment In Elementary, Secondary, and Degree-Granting Postsecondary Institutions, by Level and Control of Institution, Enrollment Level, and Attendance Status and Sex of Student: Selected Years, Fall 1990 through Fall 2026," accessed January 26, 2018, https://nces.ed.gov/programs/digest/d16/tables/dt16_105.20.asp?current=yes.

[5]Alan M. Saks, "Multiple Predictors and Criteria of Job Search Success," *Journal of Vocational Behavior* 68 (2005): 400–12.

[6]U.S. Department of Labor, Bureau of Labor Statistics, "National Longitudinal Surveys: Frequently Asked Questions," last modified November 13, 2017, http://www.bls.gov/nls/nlsfaqs.htm#anch41.

Chapter 14

[1]M. Shircore, K. Galloway, N. Corbett-Jarvis, and R. Daniel, "From the First Year to the Final Year Experience: Embedding Reflection for Work Integrated Learning in a Holistic Curriculum Framework—A Practice Report," *International Journal of the First Year in Higher Education* 4, no. 1 (2013): 125–33; S. Qinton and T. Smallbone, "Feeding Forward: Using Feedback to Promote Reflection and Learning—A Teaching Model," *Innovations in Education and Teaching International* 47, no. 1 (2010): 125–35.

[2]LinkedIn Corporate Communications Team, "Eighty-Percent of Professionals Consider Networking Important to Career Success," LinkedIn (June 22, 2017), https://news.linkedin.com/2017/6/eighty-percent-of-professionals-consider-networking-important-to-career-success.

[3]For more information on the importance of networking and how to do it effectively, see Ivan Misner and Michelle R. Donovan, *The 29% Solution: 52 Weekly Networking Success Strategies* (Austin, TX: Greenleaf Book Group Press, 2008).

Appendix

[1]For more information on the STAR approach to behavioral interviewing, see M. Barbeau, "Be a 'STAR' Interviewer," iGrad (August 4, 2010), http://www.igrad.com/articles/behavioral-interviewing-and-the-star-approach; and "Refining Your Sales Pitch — Practice," Virginia Education Wizard, https://www.vawizard.org/wiz-pdf/STAR_Method_Interviews.pdf, accessed March 5, 2018.

index